THE SECRET WAR
ON THE UNITED STATES
IN 1915

A TALE OF SABOTAGE, LABOR UNREST, AND BORDER TROUBLES

by

HERIBERT VON FEILITZSCH

First Edition

Every effort has been made to locate and contact all holders of copyright to material reproduced in this book. For information about permission to reproduce selections from this book, write to Henselstone Verlag LLC, P.O. Box 201, Amissville, VA 20106.

Library of Congress Control Number

2014912991

Keyword Data

von Feilitzsch, Heribert, 1965-
The Secret War on the United States in 1915 / Heribert von Feilitzsch.
p. cm
Includes biographical references and index.
ISBN 978-098-503-17-7-0

1.   United States – History – World War I – 1914 to 1917
2.   Germany – History – World War I – 1914 to 1917
3.   Mexico – History – Revolution, 1910-1920 – Diplomatic History
4.   United States – Foreign Relations – Mexico
5.   United States – Foreign Relations - Germany
6.   Mexico – Foreign Relations – United States
7.   Mexico – Foreign Relations - Germany
8.   Germany – Foreign Relations – Mexico
9.   Germany – Foreign Relations – United States
I.   von Feilitzsch, Heribert. Title.

www.secretwarcouncil.com

Printed in the United States of America

"... the entire German people with one voice are execrating the American people and the American Government for the continued delivery of munitions to England and its allies. Is it for a moment conceivable that Germany would, under these circumstances, permit the delivery of a few dollars [sic] worth of munitions at any price or under any circumstances to go to Mexico[?]"

American businessman Andrew D. Meloy to U.S. Ambassador to Great Britain Walter Hines Page, August 23rd, 1915

For Philip

CONTENTS

LIST OF ILLUSTRATIONS

ACKNOWLEDGMENTS

THIS CURRENT MONOGRAPH IS ONE of three books whose completion was possible through the continued support and encouragement of fellow scholars, friends, family, and others whose intellectual curiosity made me dig deeper. Originally drafted as a single comprehensive analysis of the German secret service in the U.S. during World War I, the manuscript grew into three distinct pieces: *The Secret War Council* (to be published later in 2015), which describes the establishment of German clandestine operations in the U.S., as well as, the efforts to combat Entente interests on U.S. soil in 1914. *Felix A. Sommerfeld and the Mexican Front in the Great War* (2015) explores in detail the German efforts to use the Mexican Revolution against the U.S. *The Secret War on the U.S. in 1915* (2015) analyzes the German clandestine war in the United States in 1915. One chapter in this book, *Junta X*, also appears in the book on the Mexican Front. It was clear after extensive consideration that this chapter in its entirety is indispensable to the storyline of both books. I apologize for the repetition if you have read both books, but I hope it will provide a new perspective within this context.

This third book on the topic of the German secret service emerged from the help and understanding of my family, colleagues and friends. The late Michael C. Meyer of my Alma Mater, the University of Arizona, set me on the course of this research. Reinhard R. Doerries, the preeminent scholar on the topic of German secret agents and Ambassador Johann Heinrich Count von Bernstorff, gave me his time and kind feedback. Justus D. Doenecke dedicated his time and consideration to my project. He read my seemingly endless early manuscript and gave me lots of valuable suggestions. Thank you both! Charles H. Harris III and Louis R. Sadler, the masters of thorough research, objectivity, and artful storytelling, have helped me through my first, second, and now third book. They shared with me their most recent research and manuscripts. I am humbled and grateful for their friendship and support.

I have continued to explore behavioral science, and especially personality preference models, to better understand motivation, reaction, and behavioral patterns of the characters in my stories. Marc Cugnon and Alaina Love's *The Passion Profiler*™ opened my mind to a thorough understanding of how personalities unveil themselves. Thank you! My friend and artist, Otto Conner, tirelessly listened to my theories about what really happened and helped me edit the manuscript. Many thanks for your patience! I enjoy bouncing ideas and concepts off my friend Charles Karelis, as well. Thank you for sharing your incredible knowledge and analytical mind with me. Rosa King, a novelist, Spanish teacher, fabulous editor, and genius when it comes to layout, typesetting, and design, once more worked her magic on this manuscript. Thank you so much! Celebrated author, historian, translator, intellectual powerhouse, and friend, C. M. Mayo, has been an incredible inspiration not only for her storytelling ability, research, and intellectual curiosity, but also for her creative and innovative genius in dealing in an ever-changing and complicated publishing world. Thank you!

I have met many scholars on my journeys across the U.S. to attend history conferences and present most of the main ideas in this book over the last years. The encouragement, constructive criticism, and appreciation for my work made me a better scholar and gave me the energy necessary to continue my research. I especially would like to mention Nicholas Steneck, Jesse Hingson, Tim Thibodeau, Helena Waddy, Mark Benbow, Tim and Brandy Miller, and Roberto Cantu for their kindness, interest, and feedback.

The support and expertise I found in the National Archives in Washington, D.C., where I met several of the most dedicated, motivated, and knowledgeable archivists in the world, is beyond words. I owe immeasurable gratitude to Richard Peuser and his staff. They assisted me not only in finding the documents I requested, but also in recommending archival materials I was not aware existed. Thank you! In the Politisches Archiv des Auswärtigen Amtes in Berlin and in the Bundesarchiv für Militärgeschichte in Freiburg I spent valuable time and discovered important documents. I would like to especially thank Achim Koch, Andrea Meier, and Jan Warssischek who assisted me with great knowledge and dedication. I am eternally grateful for their courtesy towards an unknown researcher who barged in from overseas with little time and an insatiable appetite for obscure files. Michael Hieronymus, Curator of Special Collections in the Benson Library of the University of Texas at Austin, and David Kessler in the Bancroft Library of the University of California at Berkeley have shown incredible dedication and kindness toward my requests to see ever more boxes of materials. Thank you!

There are many more: Fred Opitz, Tom Pingle, Juan Carlos Garling, Pat Egan, Mary Prevo, Ralph Getsinger, and Cheryl Mayer. Last, but not least, is my wonderful family who continues to support me on the quixotic quest to unveil the secrets of clandestine operations in our past. My wife Berkley remains my most devoted gatekeeper and supporter. Thank you! I salute the thousands who read, comment, and like my weekly blogs. Also, I am grateful to the many of you who have proven the pessimists in the publishing industry dead wrong. Thank you for reading my books. You keep reminding me why I do this. For the many others who helped me along the way that I may have inadvertently failed to mention by name: Thank you.

CAST OF CHARACTERS

Albert, Heinrich Friedrich German lawyer and Commercial agent for the German government in New York during World War I. German Commercial Attaché 1915 to 1917. Head of the Secret War Council, the German clandestine organization in New York in charge of propaganda, economic war, sabotage, and finance during World War I. German Treasury Secretary and Secretary of Reconstruction 1923.

Bernstorff, Count Johann Heinrich German ambassador to the United States from 1908 to 1917 and to Turkey from 1917 to 1918. After World War I, co-founder of the Democratic Party in Germany (Deutsche Demokratische Partei). Member of the Reichstag 1921 to 1928. Went into exile during Nazi regime.

Bielaski, Alexander Bruce American lawyer and Chief of the Bureau of Investigations, 1912 to 1919.

Boy-Ed, Karl German Naval Attaché in New York from 1913 to 1915. Then head of the *Nachrichtenabteilung* N in Berlin 1915 to 1918 (Naval Intelligence).

Bryan, William Jennings American lawyer and Democratic politician. Ran as a candidate for the U.S. presidency three times. Served as Secretary of State under Wilson between 1913 and 1915. Resigned in 1915, campaigned on behalf of the American peace movement, and pursued law practice.

Buchanan, Frank American politician and union leader. Congressman for Democratic Party 1913-1914. Member of David Lamar's Anti-Trust League. Member of Rintelen's Labor's National Peace Council.

Canova, Joseph Leon Businessman from Florida. Became special envoy to Mexico. Expelled by Pancho Villa in 1915. Headed the Mexican desk in the State Department from 1915 to 1918.

Carranza, Venustiano Mexican politician from Coahuila. Led the Mexican opposition against Victoriano Huerta. Mexican President from 1915 to 1917.

Cobb, Zach Lamar Democratic politician and U.S. customs collector in Texas. Also served the intelligence organization of the State Department. Arranged for the arrest of Victoriano Huerta in 1915. Warned his superiors of the approaching Villistas before the raid on Columbus, New Mexico in March 1916.

Dernburg, Bernhard Imperial Secretary of Colonial Affairs 1907 to 1910. Head of German propaganda in the United States 1914 to 1915. German Finance Minister and Vice Chancellor in 1919. Member of the German parliament 1920 to 1930.

Díaz, Félix	Mexican politician and soldier. Nephew of Porfirio Díaz. Conspirator in the overthrow of Francisco Madero. Aligned with Victoriano Huerta in quest to regain power in Mexico in 1915.
Dilger, Anton	Medical doctor and German intelligence agent born and raised in the U.S. Tasked with weaponizing anthrax and glanders. Worked out of a secret laboratory in Maryland.
Fay, Robert	German sabotage agent sent to the U.S. to build rudder bombs against Allied ships. The project was discovered. Fay briefly escaped from prison but gave himself up in Spain a few months later.
Garrison, Lindley Miller	Lawyer and Democratic politician. Served as Secretary of War under Woodrow Wilson between 1913 and 1916.
Goltz, Horst von der	German agent with the real name Franz Wachendorf. Worked for Sommerfeld in Mexico before the war. Sent to sabotage the Welland Canal in 1914. Mission was aborted. Goltz ended in British detention and testified against German agents in the U.S. in 1917.
Gompers, Samuel	Founder and leader of the American Federation of Labor 1886 to 1894 and 1895 to 1924. Opposed Rintelen's Labor's National Peace Council.

Hale, William Bayard   American journalist and author. Supported and became friends with Woodrow Wilson in 1912. Went on missions for the president to Mexico where he also met and became closely acquainted with Sommerfeld. Joined the German propaganda team in 1914 as an editor. Largely discredited for his support of Germany in the war, he moved to Europe for the remainder of his life.

Heynen, Carl   Wealthy German-Mexican businessman with companies in Mexico City, Veracruz, and Tampico who represented HAPAG and North German Lloyd in Mexico before the war. Came to the U.S. on orders of the German naval intelligence and worked for Heinrich Albert as his treasurer and logistics expert. Headed the management of the Bridgeport Projectile Company.

Hilken, Paul Jr.   German-American businessman. Headed the offices of the North German Lloyd in Baltimore. Worked for German naval intelligence in the U.S. during World War I. Provided agents and resources for clandestine missions in the U.S. and Canada. Responsible for firebombing, germ warfare, and sabotage. Worked with Hinsch on the logistics of the German merchant submarine *Deutschland* and the explosion of Black Tom Island in 1916.

Hinsch, Friedrich Karl — German navy captain. Reported to Karl Boy-Ed at the outbreak of the war. Handled various intelligence missions, firebombing, biological warfare, and sabotage. Organized the logistics for the German merchant submarine *Deutschland* in 1916. One of the key agents responsible for the explosion of the Black Tom loading terminals in New Jersey in 1916.

Hoadley, George W. — American businessman who served as the figurehead in Germany's acquisition and operation of the Bridgeport Projectile Company between 1915 and 1917.

Horn, Werner — German agent sent to blow up a bridge between the U.S. and Canada. Project was discovered.

Huerta, Victoriano — Mexican general and usurper of the presidency in 1913. Held responsible for the murder of Francisco Madero. Went into exile in 1914. Attempted a return to power in 1915 but was arrested in Texas.

Kleist, Charles von — German merchant marine captain. Descendent of an old and well-known German noble family. Worked for Water Scheele in New Jersey. Convicted and sentenced to penitentiary in 1916. Died in prison.

Koenig, Paul   German secret service agent (not to be confused with the submarine captain of the same name). Headed the HAPAG corporate security office in the Americas before World War I. Under military attachés Franz von Papen and Wolf von Igel, Koenig and his many agents in harbor cities on the East Coast collected intelligence, bribed various officials, hired and fired agents, and provided security for the offices of von Papen, Boy-Ed, and Albert from 1914 to 1918.

Krumm-Heller, Arnold   German doctor and occultist. Became Francisco Madero's personal physician and spiritual adviser in 1911. Worked for Felix Sommerfeld in the Mexican secret service 1912 to 1913. Joined Carranza faction while serving the German naval intelligence. Became Obregón's chief of artillery. Supported the implementation of the *Plan de San Diego* in 1915 and 1916. Went to Germany in 1916 and served as Mexican military attaché in Berlin until the end of World War I.

Lamar, David   American Wall Street operator. Known as the "Wolf of Wall Street" he engaged in schemes against Rockefeller and Morgan. Joined Franz Rintelen in creating the Labor's National Peace Council, a labor organization financed with German money in 1915. Arrested and imprisoned multiple times.

Martin, Henry B.   American politician and union leader. Secretary of David Lamar's Anti-Trust League. Member of Rintelen's Labor's National Peace Council.

Meloy, Andrew D.   American businessman with financial interest in Mexican railways. Conspired with Franz Rintelen, Felix Sommerfeld and others to end the Mexican Revolution. Arrested with Rintelen in England in 1915 but released.

Mondragón, Manuel   Mexican general. Secretary of War under Mexican Dictator Porfirio Díaz. Part of the putsch against Francisco Madero. Aligned with Victoriano Huerta in his quest to regain control of Mexico in 1915.

Nadolny, Rudolf   Chief of the political section of the German General Staff, Section IIIB, from 1914 to 1916. Issued the sabotage order against American and Mexican targets in 1915. Dispatched German agents with biological weapons to the U.S. Had a long diplomatic career starting in 1916 with ambassadorships to Persia, Turkey, and the Soviet Union. Opposed Hitler and became president of the German Red Cross after World War II.

Orozco, Pascual   Mexican businessman and revolutionary chieftain. Led uprising against Francisco Madero in 1912. Joined Victoriano Huerta in 1915. Killed while fleeing from U.S. authorities in 1915.

Papen, Franz von   German Military Attaché in New York from 1914 to 1915. After World War I German politician and member of the Prussian parliament. German Chancellor in 1932.

Plochmann, George   Austrian banker with the Transatlantic Trust Company in New York. Maintained the accounts of Franz Rintelen.

Rintelen, Franz German naval intelligence agent. Came to the United States in 1915 to incite labor unrest and oversee sabotage operations. Was discovered and arrested in England in the summer of 1915. Convicted and sentenced to penitentiary in 1917, he spent the rest of the war in prison. Wrote two books about his time in the United States. Settled in England in the late 1920s and during Nazi regime.

Rumely, Edward A. American physician and businessman from Indiana. Served the German war effort as the figurehead of the German-owned *New York Evening Mail*. He went to trial for "trading with the enemy" in 1918.

Scheele, Walter T. German scientist and secret agent. In World War I Scheele invented the firebombs used against Entente shipping, as well as American production and logistics installations. Fled to Cuba in 1916. Switched sides in 1917 and worked for the U.S. military.

Schmidt, Hugo German banker who headed the Deutsche Bank in the United States in World War I. As a secret agent for the German government he was a specialist in circumventing the British financial system when moving German government funds from Germany to the U.S. Interned in 1918 and released after one year.

Schweitzer, Hugo German chemist, secret agent, and businessman. Managing Director of Bayer Corporation in the United States. Supported German clandestine operations in the U.S. Became Heinrich Albert's successor in 1917 but died that same year.

Scott, Hugh Lenox   American general. Commander of Fort Bliss, then Army Chief of Staff under Woodrow Wilson 1914 to 1917. Considered a friend by both Felix Sommerfeld and Pancho Villa.

Sommerfeld, Felix A.   German naval intelligence agent under the command first of Minister to Mexico Paul von Hintze then German Naval Attaché in New York, Karl Boy-Ed. Chief of Staff for President Madero, chief of the Mexican secret service, 1912 to 1913. Chief weapons and munitions buyer for Pancho Villa 1914 to 1915. Pancho Villa's diplomatic envoy to the U.S. 1914 to 1915.

Stallforth, Frederico   Mexican-German businessman from Hidalgo del Parral, Mexico. Became a German secret agent in 1913. Worked closely with Felix Sommerfeld, Franz Rintelen, Heinrich Albert, and Andrew Meloy. Had financial responsibilities in the German sabotage campaign in the U.S. between 1915 and 1917. Arrested several times during the World War. After 1919 he became prominent financier in the United States and Germany. Joined the OSS in 1942.

Tauscher, Hans   German agent and representative of Krupp Arms and several other German arms manufacturers in the United States. Married to the famous soprano Madame Johanna Gadski. Worked for Franz von Papen during World War I.

Tirpitz, Alfred von　German Grand Admiral and Secretary of State of the Imperial Naval Office. Headed the buildup of the German navy before World War I. Despite being distinctly pro-submarine warfare in the German cabinet, his prioritization for ship building budgets neglected the submarine. He fell out of favor with the German emperor during 1915 and resigned in March 1916.

Tumulty, Joseph Patrick　American lawyer and politician. 1911 to 1921 he was the personal secretary (Chief of Staff) of Woodrow Wilson.

Viereck, George Sylvester　American poet, intellectual, and journalist. Published the German propaganda paper *The Fatherland* during World War I.

Villa, Francisco "Pancho"　Mexican general and revolutionary chieftain. Raised the largest army of the Mexican Revolution. Attacked the United States in 1916. Assassinated in 1923.

Wilhelm II of Prussia　German Emperor 1888 to 1918. Presided over the outbreak of World War I. Resigned in 1918 and went into exile to Holland.

Wilson, Thomas Woodrow　Democratic politician, educator, and intellectual. President of Princeton University. Governor of New Jersey, 1910 to 1913. U.S. President 1913 to 1921.

PROLOGUE

DESPITE PRESIDENT WILSON'S DECLARATION OF neutrality at the onset of the Great War, the United States became the main supplier of arms, munitions, military and civilian goods for the enemies of Germany and her allies in early 1915. The lure of profits from munitions sales on a grand scale trumped any efforts by the German Empire to resume non-contraband trade with the United States. Germany's representatives in New York and Washington D.C. deserve blame for this development. From the onset of the war, they missed ample opportunities to counter British propaganda and use the anger of American business leaders, farmers, and merchants over the British sea blockade to exert political pressure. Their ineffective use of American surrogates to oppose the tightening English blockade, and the inability to coalesce American support into promoting trade in cotton, dyes, food, and fertilizer, all helped push American foreign policy away from true neutrality. The biggest fear of the German government, namely unleashing the unbridled power of the American economy in support of the enemy, thus became a painful reality in 1915.

The frustration in Germany with this development, disregarding the fact that German officials had a lot to do with it, brought a group of hardliners from within the German military and civilian government to the fore. The belief was that a determined war effort against the United States and England would bring the war to a quicker conclusion. Based on intelligence that German military attaché in New York, Franz von Papen, his predecessor Hans-Wolfgang Herwarth von Bittenfeld, and other German intelligence assets had gathered in 1913 and 1914, the hardliners firmly believed that the American military would never play any significant role in the European conflict. Viewed from a military standpoint, they deemed an armed conflict with the U.S. inconsequential. Rather, an American declaration of war might be helpful in bringing moderate 'politicians' to support an uncompromising war effort. The flow of supplies and materiel from the U.S. to European battlefields in support of the Entente had a devastating effect on Germany's war effort. An accommodating diplomatic approach, which the Foreign Office preferred, in their estimation, did not have the power to disturb these Entente supply lines.

This group of hardliners consisted of influential members of the navy chain of command starting with Grand Admiral Alfred von Tirpitz at the very top and reaching to submarine force commander Hermann Bauer and the German naval attaché in the United States, Karl Boy-Ed.[1] The German General Staff including its secret service, Political Section IIIB under Rudolph Nadolny, also supported a hardline strategy. HAPAG Director Albert Ballin, who longed for a quick end to the conflict to get his massive merchant marine fleet back afloat, supported a tougher approach towards the United States, as well. Interior Secretary Clemens von Delbrück, who worked and agreed with Ballin, joined the group. Delbrück was the direct superior of Germany's commercial agent in the U.S., Heinrich F. Albert.

Albert had come to the United States as a German purchasing agent without diplomatic status in August 1914. He not only coordinated the German efforts of blockade running and trade, but also commanded the entire financial structure of the German empire in the United States. Albert was in charge of a secret organization in New York City. Publicly, this Secret War Council managed German propaganda, supported the German-American community, sold German war bonds, and engaged in legal trade. However, the darker mission of this council consisted of organizing clandestine activities in the U.S. during the neutrality period of 1914 to 1917.[2] Albert approved and financed the German intelligence cells across the U.S. The leading members of the Secret War Council included the German officials in New York, Franz von Papen (military attaché), Karl Boy-Ed (naval attaché), Bernhard Dernburg (propaganda chief), Karl Alexander Fuehr (propaganda), and Heinrich Albert as chief (commercial agent and financial controller).

Acting consul general in New York Erich Hossenfelder was not a member of this group of hardliners.[3] Hossenfelder belonged to the more accommodating faction that did not condone the U.S. supply of Germany's enemies, but feared dire consequences of a U.S. entry into the conflict. German Chancellor Theobald von Bethmann Hollweg headed this faction, which included most officials in the Imperial Foreign Office, in particular the ambassador to the U.S., Johann Heinrich Count von Bernstorff. This moderate group supported a military strategy subordinate to diplomacy and political considerations, and sought to keep the United States out of the European war.

German war strategy shifted significantly in the spring of 1915 and, consequently, reinforced hardliner attitudes. Britain had destroyed the German naval battle group of Admiral Spee in the Falklands in November 1914. Except for small excursions, the German High Seas Fleet remained moored in German ports. Germany's naval raiders had either been destroyed or saved themselves by agreeing to internment in neutral harbors. The German navy, for all intent and purpose, had been neutralized in the Atlantic and Pacific oceans. The army also reeled from its failure to swiftly take France. The German forces dug in on the western front and consolidated the gains made in Belgium and eastern France. The momentum now shifted to the east and the Russian front. The German army made important gains in the spring of 1915, as it collapsed the Russian lines and steam-rolled into the strategically important south. The static war on the western front, where material and supply would determine the eventual outcome of the war, moved the United States into strategic focus.

Albert, Dernburg, Boy-Ed, and von Papen's efforts from August up to the end of 1914 had had virtually no impact on the German war effort. The German team organized attacks on transportation installations in Canada, supplied remnants of the German Navy from U.S. ports, bought arms and munitions, which they sent to neutral countries or in support of separatist and nationalist movements in India, Ireland, and China. Except for Naval Attaché Karl Boy-Ed, the German team in the U.S. lacked sufficient funds, and added to the amateurish impression of German operations and propaganda in the U.S.

Other than a lack of funding, the main reason for the ineffectiveness of the German team was that the Secret War Council lacked a strategic plan underlying the various efforts. All of that changed in the beginning of 1915. The recognition, albeit late in the game, that the American theatre of war indeed impacted the European fronts, triggered the formulation of a new strategy towards the United States. The German officials in New York had worked hard on achieving this kind of recognition as a prerequisite for realistic financing of their efforts. Since the beginning of the war, the Secret War Council in New York had peppered Berlin with a barrage of facts, demands, ideas, requests, and suggestions in the hope of funding for its mission.

The German clandestine war against industrial and government targets in the United States in 1915 has spawned countless books in the years since. While the World War still raged in Europe, journalists, retired investigators, and other real or imagined eyewitnesses told the story of outrageous German acts of war against a neutral United States. Sensationalist tales of virtually unlimited funding, armies of German conspirators, and devastating damages to American factories, ships and logistics installations intermingled with a few fact-based reports. Several examples were accounts of Captain Thomas J. Tunney, the chief of the New York Bomb Squad, as well as John Price Jones and Paul Merrick Hollister, two of the most notable investigative journalists in New York. After the war, several of the actors in this tragic tale of asymmetric warfare, all with their own agendas to build or correct a lasting legacy, put to paper their memories of a story that has yet to find definitive treatment.[4]

The historiography of the German sabotage campaign of 1915 in the United States is wrought with inaccuracies, half-truths, and remnants of misinformation the Allies has disseminated as part of their wartime propaganda campaign in the U.S. Standard works, such as Barbara Tuchman's *The Zimmermann Telegram,* written in the 1960s, could not yet take advantage of the various archives available to researchers today and consequently missed crucial sources. Subsequent events in the German war on America, such as the explosions of the Black Tom Island in the New York harbor in July of 1916, and of the Canadian Car and Foundry factory in Kingsland, New Jersey, in January 1917, have led scholars to make assumptions about earlier, less documented German acts of war. Even recent studies and journalistic accounts contain serious errors because their authors allowed flawed assumptions, the uncritical use of misleading personal accounts, and superficially researched facts to co-mingle with British war propaganda and hearsay. This book has the purpose of setting the record straight using diplomatic, military, financial, and investigative files from German and American archival sources. The German secret war against the United States in 1915, and its discovery and publication, combined with the disastrous sinking of the *Lusitania* in May of that year, prepared the American public to finally accept joining the Entente powers against Germany in 1917. German war planners, members of the Admiralty, the General Staff, and political hardliners in the German government underestimated or purposely ignored the risks and cost of a large-scale clandestine campaign in the United States. In hindsight, the decision to execute a secret war in the nominally neutral United States in 1915 was a colossal blunder. This is the story of a group of German agents in the United States who executed this mission.

CHAPTER 1: SABOTAGE ORDER

O N JANUARY 6TH 1915, THE Imperial German Admiralty requested that the military and naval attachés in Washington, Franz von Papen and Karl Boy-Ed respectively, initiate sabotage in the United States and Canada.[5] This request only surfaced as a memorandum in the Imperial Foreign Office.[6] Initially, the Admiralty envisioned Irish nationalists conducting sabotage operations in the U.S. This understanding resulted from an agreement between Sir Roger Casement and the German government. Berlin had agreed to support an Irish uprising against England with funding, arms, and ammunition. In addition, Germany had agreed to recognize an Irish state after the war. Casement, in return, committed to support German efforts of stopping munitions production and shipments in the United States.[7] The Foreign Office subsequently received a formal sabotage order from the Chief of the Political Section of the Imperial General Staff, Section IIIB, Rudolf Nadolny, for transmission to the United States on January 23rd.[8] These fateful instructions clearly linked the German government to attacks on the then neutral United States.

This order specified three members of the Irish resistance movement in the United States as resources for contracting sabotage agents. The document reached Franz von Papen, the German military attaché in the United States, on January 24th. When it surfaced after the war, the sabotage order would have grave consequences for Germany. In a mixed claims commission that Germany and the United States set up after the war to settle losses of blood and treasure resulting from Germany's actions between 1914 and 1919, German lawyers desperately denied the existence of a clandestine war before the American entry into the conflict. Nadolny, himself a lawyer and reserve officer who became German ambassador to Persia later in the war, would join his superiors and Franz von Papen for decades in the categorical denial that this directive dated January 24th 1915 was binding or had had any impact.

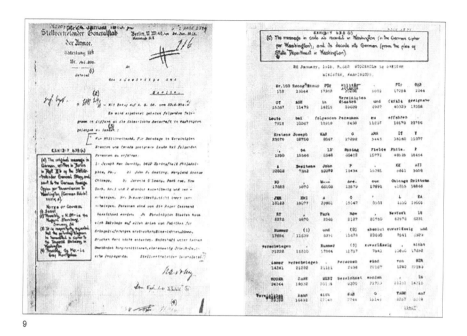

9

From the Acting General Staff of the Army, Section IIIB   Berlin, January 24, 1915

– Secret

To the Foreign Office, Berlin.

It is humbly requested that the following telegram is transmitted in code to the Imperial Embassy in Washington:

'For military attaché. To find suitable personnel for sabotage in the United States and Canada inquire with the following persons:

1) Joseph Mac Garrity [sic], 5412 Springfield Philadelphia, Pa.,
2) John P. Keating, Maryland Avenue Chicago,
3) Jeremia [sic] O'Leary, Park row [sic], New York.

No. 1 and 2 completely reliable and discreet, No. 3 reliable, not always discreet. Persons have been named by Sir Roger Casement.

In the United States sabotage can cover all kinds of factories for military supplies; railroads, dams, bridges there cannot be touched. Embassy can under no circumstances be compromised, neither can Irish-German propaganda.

Assistant chief of the General Staff

Nadolny[10]

If there were any doubts as to the authenticity and meaning of the directive, these can quickly be dispelled with periodic reports from von Papen back to Nadolny. Bearing Nadolny's signature as the recipient the military attaché provided updates to his efforts. On March 17th 1915, von Papen wrote in a secret telegram, "Sabotage against factories over here is making little progress, since all factories are guarded by hundreds of secret agents and all German-American and Irish workers have been fired... Steamer *Touraine* has regrettably arrived with munitions and 335 machine guns. Signed Papen"[11] The head of the American section of the Imperial Foreign Office, Adolf Count Montgelas, scribbled on the telegram document numbers of three other related reports.[12] Heinrich Albert, the chief of the Secret War Council in New York, transmitted a cable to Secretary of the Interior Clemens von Delbrück on April 20th 1915, in which he clearly referred to the implementation of the sabotage order:

As your Excellency knows, I have supported the military attaché, Mr. von Papen, in the handling of munitions questions. Upon submitting our last proposal via telegraph (cable No. 479) we received the order to proceed with respect to preventing or restricting of the exportation of munitions from the United States. The order said: 'Fully agree with your proposal' and has been interpreted by us [the Secret War Council], that we are not only to tie up production through contracts in a specific sense, but also take <u>all other</u> [emphasis by author] necessary measures to reach the envisioned goal. With respect to the latter I have undertaken a series of steps under the guidance of *Exzellenz* [Excellency] Dernburg, which for understandable reasons I cannot put into writing.[13]

Thus, the sabotage order was neither a loose directive nor anything that the officials in New York simply ignored, as Nadolny and von Papen's testimony before the Mixed Claims Commission wanted to spin it in later years.[14] At least three departments, War (where the order originated), Interior (where it was funded in the United States), and the Foreign Office (as Count Montgelas' signature documents) had knowledge of the order. By extension, Chancellor von Bethmann Hollweg and the Kaiser must have known about it, even if they did not specifically approve it. Ringing the bell for a new round of relations between the United States and Germany, the order was immediately implemented, funded, and acted upon. Different from orders to injure Canada from U.S. soil or to supply the German fleet from U.S. harbors under false manifests, the sabotage order of January 24th constituted, by all international standards, the authorization of deliberate acts of war against the United States.

CHAPTER 2: MONEY AND PERSONNEL

DESPITE ALBERT'S COMPLAINTS ABOUT THE disappointing results of German war bond sales and despite him showing the disbursements of the "Perez" money (propaganda) from funds raised by these bonds, there is an indication that Albert simply created a smokescreen for investigators. One-and-a-half months before war bonds hit the market and three weeks before the Foreign Office approved the project, the Deutsche Bank deposited $210,000 ($4.4 Million in today's value) with G. Amsinck and Co. on February 19th 1915.[15] One week later, another $790,000 ($16.6 Million in today's value) appeared as a deposit for the Deutsche Bank.[16] The director of the Deutsche Bank in the United States was Hugo Schmidt. He proved to be an expert in finding ways around the tight control of financial transactions through Britain. Virtually all international financial transactions passed through London in one way or another. British authorities made sure that German transactions did not make it any further. Through dummy accounts, fake bank connections, straw men from neutral countries, especially those in Latin America, Schmidt became the essential lifeline to the German officials in the United States.[17] An assistant, Frederico Stallforth, who had many international connections and plenty of financial savvy worked at his side. Stallforth's work for Hugo Schmidt and Felix Sommerfeld allowed him to purchase a new home in Westchester County, New York in September 1915, barely a year since his virtual bankruptcy.[18] Stallforth was so effective that in April 1916 Albert decided to finance a new company called Stallforth Inc., which the German commercial attaché would use as a cover for large currency exchanges, as well as financing of clandestine operations.

The one million dollars that Albert received in February 1915 were not coded in his ledgers as credits for shipping supplies to Germany as part of the blockade-running operation. Another entry in the same month from the Deutsche Bank shows "Deposit by Deutsche Bank, *SS Wilhelmina* from Guaranty Trust Company."[19] These million dollars came from the Imperial War Department with the express purpose of financing the sabotage order that the New York team had received on January 24th. Proceeds from the sale of war bonds further filled the coffers in April 1915. Within weeks of receiving the revenue from the war bonds, Albert and Count Bernstorff opened dozens of new accounts all over the country, ostensibly to have funds where the bonds would eventually be redeemed after nine months. Rather than cashing the coupons, these regionally distributed bond proceeds actually funded clandestine operations. Within days of the arrival of the sabotage order, meetings with Irish nationalist Jeremiah O'Leary and others ensued. Albert entered the cryptic notation in his diary on February 6th, "O'Leary (31, 50) advert. Personal 30.III."[20] Regrettably, the original German diary entry has been lost, making it hard to discern any translation errors. However, an entry on January 23rd, "O'Leary ./. men." in conjunction with the later entry, seems to reference 'personnel' and a date, March 20th 1915.[21] The German word *Personal* means personnel. The English word, personal, would be *persöhnlich*.

Journalists and historians have portrayed Naval Commander Karl Boy-Ed as the alter ego of Franz von Papen – arrogant, militaristic, ruthless, unintelligent, and dishonest. Certainly, his work in the United States put the naval attaché into situations in which, by definition of his duties as chief of naval intelligence for the Western Hemisphere, he violated American laws and the diplomatic code of conduct. He followed orders of the Admiralty without regard to personal consequences for himself or his agents. His memoirs about the time in Washington indignantly titled *Verschwörer?* (*Conspirator?*) do not reveal an inkling of regret over his activities in the war or feeling for the victims of his schemes.[22] Scores of his co-conspirators and supporters lost their reputations, livelihoods, and freedom. Boy-Ed simply moved on under the cloak of diplomatic immunity. However, to judge him solely through the eyes of the eventual victors would not do justice to this otherwise complex and sophisticated man, who grew up in a uniquely intellectual family, who liked to read and write, and who could not compensate the stresses of his wartime assignment.

Karl Boy-Ed saw the first light of day on September 14th 1872 in Lübeck, on the German Baltic seacoast, as the oldest of three children.

Karl's father, Karl Johann Boy, was a merchant in town. Ida Ed, Karl's mother was the daughter of the German parliamentarian, publisher, and newspaper editor Christoph Marquard Ed. Carl Johann Boy and his wife Ida Ed separated in 1878, and Ida subsequently moved to Berlin with her son. There she worked as a journalist and began writing novels. Ida's estranged husband forced her and Karl to move back to Lübeck in 1880. She continued her career as a writer and published an amazing volume of seventy novels and essays. She supported the early career of Thomas Mann and corresponded regularly with his brother Heinrich, also a well-known literary figure. A major influence in the art and music scene in Lübeck, Ida supported the early careers of conductors Wilhelm Furtwängler and Hermann Abendroth. As a little boy, the future naval officer met and interacted with the frequent literary and musical visitors in the Boy-Ed household.

Karl joined the German navy at the age of nineteen. Rising through the ranks to become lieutenant commander, he served on dozens of naval assignments. He witnessed the American occupation of the Philippines in 1898. Shortly before the Boxer war, Kaiser Wilhelm's brother, Prince Heinrich von Preussen, sent the navy lieutenant on a secret mission to assess the "value of the Chinese navy." Boy-Ed considered his report a major accomplishment as a writer. In view of the hostilities that broke out with China a year later, Boy-Ed's "research" certainly was timely. Boy-Ed served on the staff of Grand Admiral Alfred von Tirpitz between 1906 and 1909 and took over the *Nachrichtenabteilung N* (office of naval intelligence) from Paul von Hintze during this period. After three years in Berlin, Boy-Ed served as first officer on the *SMS Deutschland* and commander of the naval tender, *Hela*. By then promoted to lieutenant commander, he sailed on the *SMS Preussen* in 1911, the flagship of the second squadron.

His navy career took Boy-Ed to the United States as naval attaché responsible for the United States and Mexico in the beginning of 1912. He traveled to Jamaica, the Panama Canal Zone, and Mexico before he took over his assigned post in Washington D.C. in 1913. Well-read and intellectual, yet funny, smart, and cosmopolitan, he enjoyed a great deal of popularity and respect among American naval officials before the war.

Ida Boy-Ed and son Karl, ca. 1873 [23]

Karl Boy-Ed [24]

The single Boy-Ed began dating the daughter of an Episcopal Bishop from Pennsylvania, Virginia Mackay Smith in 1914. The couple married in Germany in 1921.

Despite appearances, not all was well with the German navy officer. Boy-Ed suffered from phagomania, a constant desire to eat. The disorder required tremendous self-discipline in social circumstances.

Another, more severe disorder he suffered was insomnia. Boy-Ed could not get a good night's sleep. On the one hand the handicap increased his productivity dramatically, but on the other it wore on his health. The stresses of his New York assignment and, possibly, an unexpressed sense of regret for the consequences of his actions, took a heavy toll on him physically and mentally. He admitted in an autobiographic sketch that, as a result of his wartime assignment, his nerves suffered a permanent "crack."

Naval Attaché Boy-Ed started clandestine operations immediately at the outbreak of the war. The same was true for Franz von Papen, his army counterpart and another key player in the Secret War Council. Von Papen returned from Mexico on August 7th 1914. The Prussian Junker cut quite a different figure from Karl Boy-Ed. Tall, handsome, and thin, the dashing officer made a splash in New York's social scene. Von Papen's wife remained in Germany, which he compensated with a full social schedule in New York's high society.

Karl Boy-Ed has largely disappeared from the pages of world history. In contrast, Franz von Papen remains a highly controversial figure to this day, despised by some as a ruthless war criminal, considered a man of limited intelligence by others, and a statesman by few. The son of Friedrich von Papen zu Koeningen and Anna Laura von Steffens grew up on a large estate in Werl in the province of Westphalia. Keeping with tradition among noble families, the first son inherited the estate, the second joined the military. At the tender age of twelve, the Papens sent their son to several boarding military academies. After graduation from *Gymnasium*, the young aristocrat joined the Düsseldorf Cavalry School as a lieutenant in the elite 5th Uhlan Regiment. An expert horseman, the cavalry sent him to the Hanover Cavalry Riding School in 1902, through which he represented the German army in international competitions. Von Papen acquired a good knowledge of the English language during this time period, since he spent considerable time competing in Great Britain. He married Martha von Boch-Gelbau in 1905 with whom he fathered five children. Professionally, the ambitious young cavalry officer advanced his career when the army admitted him to the General Staff School in Berlin in 1908. The now thirty-four year-old Papen completed his training in March of 1913, and briefly joined the Great General Staff of the Army as a captain. The army assigned the staff officer to the embassies of Mexico and Washington as military attaché in December of that year. He arrived in the United States in the spring of 1914. Subsequently, he spent several months in Mexico and witnessed the American occupation of Veracruz in April 1914. World War I broke out while von Papen was still in Mexico. In order to take charge of his wartime assignment he rushed back to Washington in the beginning of August.

A progress report dated March 17th 1915 proves that von Papen did become active immediately after the sabotage order arrived in the United States. As noted earlier, all clandestine operations overseas, other than intelligence gathering, traditionally fell under the responsibility of the Imperial Department of the Navy. In the case of North America this responsibility rested with Karl Boy-Ed. Historians have assumed that Boy-Ed did not have control of the sabotage organization, since all the captured documents pointed to von Papen. However, Boy-Ed's financial accounts contain numerous disbursements to "secret agents,"[25] "Boy-Ed travel expenses,"[26] and "special advances" in the time period after the sabotage order.[27] Boy-Ed also used codenames for agents that received a salary.[28]

While he was busy organizing the supply for the German fleet in the Atlantic and Pacific oceans in the fall of 1914, the naval attaché ceded a portion of his authority to von Papen. Thus, it was von Papen who organized attacks against Canada and supported the Indian resistance movement against England. The military attaché also controlled the office of the former HAPAG police chief in North America, Paul Koenig, including his small army of secret agents in New York. The division of responsibilities between the two attachés was a murky mess that was functional only because of Boy-Ed's willingness to cede authority to his ambitious colleague, and Albert's firm financial control over the entire organization in the United States. Dr. Walter T. Scheele, a chemist, bomb maker, and German sabotage agent, recounted after the war, "The reports to Albert [concerning expenditures for the bomb plots] came through Boy-Ed and not through von Papen."[29]

Franz von Papen in New York in 1915

The New York offices of von Papen pooled and analyzed intelligence, then sent it to the naval and general staff authorities in Germany on a regular basis. Important data came through Karl Boy-Ed, Bernhard Dernburg, Heinrich Albert, as well as the embassy in Washington D.C., the regional German consulates, and a host of pro-German citizens and organizations. Not many of these intelligence assessments automatically found their way to the Foreign Office or the Department of the Interior. This allowed the responsible officials such as Arthur Zimmermann (Foreign Office) and Count Johann Heinrich von Bernstorff (Foreign Office), Clemens von Delbrück (Interior), Karl Helfferich (Treasury) and others plausible deniability of illegal activities. Count Bernstorff's claims of ignorance, in particular, belie the fact that almost all communications between Germany and the United States passed through the embassy in Washington. Most of the important dispatches certainly crossed the ambassador's desk.

The collection and dissemination of intelligence, as well as the dispatch and payment of secret agents, occurred at the War Intelligence Office at 60 Wall Street, the office of Franz von Papen and his assistant, Wolf von Igel, in New York. The financial control of the intelligence operation rested with Heinrich Albert's office around the corner in the Hamburg-America building on 45 Broadway. Any sum over $10,000 had to be approved by Albert.[30] The German agent Walter Scheele told investigators in March 1918, "In all matters of policy, it is stated that Dr. Albert ranked Bernstorff, Von Papen [sic] and Boy-Ed by many points. They all had to go to him. There was no plot or scheme which was unknown to him. As a result, literally nothing of import went on without Albert's approval or at least his knowledge."[31]

Heinrich F. Albert, the designated head of the Secret War Council, and the person officially assigned to purchase essential supplies in America, arrived from Copenhagen on August 26th 1914. The neutral Scandinavia-America Line steamer SS Oskar II tied up at its New York pier two days after Count Bernstorff and Dernburg had set foot on North American soil.[32]

Born on February 12th 1874 in Magdeburg, Germany, Heinrich Friedrich Albert came from a well-to-do household. His father Friedrich owned a private bank. Albert studied law after graduating high school with a baccalaureate.[33] He passed his bar exam with the grade "good" in 1901.[34] His career took him through various jobs as a legal assistant in the Department of Interior. He rose through the ranks as an administrator specialized on economic questions, especially the role of cartels in the German economy. He married his wife, Ida, in 1905 and fathered three children. Although often called "Dr." Albert, he probably never pursued any PhD studies.[35]

Albert received the rank and title of *Geheimer Oberregierungs-rat* (Privy Chancellor) in 1911.[36] Albert's responsibilities reflected his pre-occupation with details, his understanding of bureaucratic process, and also managerial qualities. His talent for details, combined with relative fluency in English, secured him a managerial role in setting up Germany's exhibitions in the St. Louis and Brussels world fairs in 1904 and 1910, respectively. His responsibilities for the German exhibits brought the young lawyer in contact with officials from many realms of the Prussian economic and political power structure. Most notably, Albert worked directly under Clemens von Delbrück, who became Secretary of the Interior and Imperial Vice-Chancellor in 1909.[37] Their working relationship was close enough that the Secretary actually expressed to Albert's wife in 1915 that he "missed him [Albert]."[38] Albert Ballin, the managing director of HAPAG, also noticed Heinrich Albert and took a liking to this uncomplicated, meticulous, hardworking, yet decisive, and results-oriented manager. Ballin invited Albert on a relaxing cruise through the Mediterranean in 1911, fully paid for by HAPAG.

The courtship worked. Albert joined HAPAG on April 1st 1914. For a pitiful annual salary of six thousand German Marks (approximately $30,140 in today's value before the war and with deteriorating value thereafter), HAPAG executive Arndt von Holtzendorff appointed the German lawyer to become the private assistant to Dr. Otto Ecker.[39] Ecker was slated to join HAPAG directors Albert Polis and Dr. Karl Buenz in New York that year as part of the senior management team in North America for the duration of the war.[40] The contract ran for two years with the option of being extended.[41] Albert had become a protégé of HAPAG director Ballin. No "smoking gun" records have survived illuminating the author's assumption that between 1904 and 1914 Albert also worked undercover as a spy for Germany. However, it is very likely that especially members of the team assembling the St. Louis exhibits in 1904 had been German agents entrusted with gathering and reporting intelligence. Albert seemed to transition seamlessly from a successful government career, in which he rose to privy counselor, to the private sector with HAPAG, and then back to working for the German government for his wartime assignment in the United States. Despite the lacking archival evidence (which is not unusual with respect to intelligence officers), Albert's career indicates that his true occupation was indeed in the intelligence sector. The various "career" moves were nothing but cover jobs for various intelligence missions. Certainly, one of the main responsibilities of his war assignment in New York was to establish command and control over secret service activities. Despite British propaganda ridiculing German agents' skills in the U.S. during the war, which several scholars picked up unchallenged, it is unlikely that the German government would have entrusted this important function in New York to an amateur without any previous experience.[42]

When the war broke out, Emperor Wilhelm II tasked Ballin with creating and managing the Central Purchasing Agency for the German Empire through Albert's former boss, Secretary of the Interior Clemens von Delbrück. Ballin decided to put Heinrich Albert in charge of the critically important New York office. The war was just taking shape when Albert arrived on August 26th 1914 with his boss Dr. Otto Ecker and Director Albert Polis in tow.[43] Albert's wife and children remained in Berlin. The newly created *Zentrale Einkaufsgenossenschaft* (Central Purchasing Agency) reported to Albert Ballin but was officially a department of the Interior Ministry.[44] HAPAG's resources, human and otherwise, were entirely at Albert's disposal because of the re-organization of the German economy for the war effort. Ballin and his managers opened their network of German-American merchants to the German lawyer, as well as business and banking connections. By the time the United States entered the war on the side of the Entente powers in 1917, Albert's New York office had disbursed over thirty-four million dollars ($714 Million in today's value), a staggering amount that even baffled senior U.S. investigators at the time.[45]

Heinrich Albert in his office in April, 1916.[46]

Six months after Albert's arrival in New York, the Secret War Council's activities were in full swing. Every day, German sympathizers and agents sent reports to von Papen's War Intelligence Office. This raw intelligence detailed factories involved in producing supplies for the Allies, named sympathizers who could be approached inside those businesses, as well as all kinds of plans, from inventions to bomb designs, to arson, to sabotaging manufacturing facilities. The acting German Military Attaché, Wolf von Igel, and other officials had destroyed many of these telegrams and letters as American investigators tried to search the premises of the German operation in New York between 1915 and 1917. However, some examples have been preserved that show the amount of intelligence von Papen had at his disposal to decide what to attack, how, and when. For example, he filed one of his bi-weekly intelligence reports copied to his superiors in Berlin, as well as those of Boy-Ed and Albert on February 11th 1915. The New York team was then still planning to corner the munitions market in the U.S. However, in view of the earlier sabotage order, which may or may not have arrived in the U.S. by the second week of February, von Papen seems to allude to potential sabotage targets using words like "there come into consideration..."

... Bethlehem Steel Works are shipping on the steamer *Transylvania* 2 heavy naval guns, 16" caliber, which are said to represent a part of a large order... The entire order is estimated at 200 guns. The Savage Arms Co. delivers weekly about 50 Lewis machine guns... Westinghouse Electric Co. ... got contracts for 125,000 shrapnel, the J.W. Bill Co. Projectile Works (shrapnel), the Western Cartridge Co., Alton, Ill. (cartridge shells) and the Bridgeport Brass Co. (cartridge shells). Machines for making shrapnel are furnished... by Gisholt Machine Co. and the Steinle Turret Co... For infantry ammunition there come into consideration [underline by author], besides those already reported, the Western Cartridge Co., Alton, Ill (caliber 30-20 and 7m.m. cartridge shells) and the Bridgeport Brass Co. (cartridges, shells and 50 million copper bullets for French machine guns [ ]). The Curtis Flying Machine Co. is supplying 400 flying machines to England... These machines are equipped... with the only recently invented gyroscope of the Sperry Gyroscope Co... The well-known parts are produced by the Union Twist Drill Co. and the Union Twist Reel Co... It is rumored that the allies are ready to take as many as 1,000,000 daily.

The shipments of horses and war automobiles continue in increased degree. The Ford Mfg. Co. has received an order for 40,000 vehicles... the factory can produce about 1,000 a day.

The Locomobile Co. of America makes heavy freight automobiles and even sends its trained chauffeurs along to France with the autos... 35 heavy guns were sent by the Bethlehem Co. to Vancouver, to be shipped from there on the steamer *Tambov* of the Russian volunteer fleet to Vladivostok... The same factory furnished also the ammunition for this gun, and a report is before me that one train took 15 car loads of this. The steamer *Tambov* is said also to be taking powder from the DuPont Powder Co., also dynamite...

The Baldwin Locomotive Works shipped on the steamer *Indradeo* twenty-five locomotives to Vladivostoc.

Automobiles are shipped on every steamer leaving Vancouver for Vladivostok, and the Case Automobile Co. is specially to be mentioned here... Signed Papen[47]

Von Papen's reports represented a collection of roughly assessed raw intelligence to be further evaluated in Germany, which then might or might not trigger tangible actions. This was the image the German government tried to convey in the decades-long post-war Mixed Claims Commission proceedings that sought to settle damages to U.S. property and persons that Germany had caused in the war.

However, this report, as well as others, shows a remarkable level of detail on factories, products, and shipping dates. Many of the businesses on von Papen's lists would suffer mysterious fires and explosions in the following two years. To be fair, only a few of these incidents had their origin at 60 Wall Street. Many fires and perceived acts of sabotage resulted from accidents. Factories, many of which handled explosives and complicated metal work production, had sprung up starting in the spring of 1915. Fires and explosions that the press and embarrassed managers laid on the "Huns" resulted to a certain extent from shabby production processes, untrained laborers, in a few cases discontented workers, and in even fewer cases, German or German-American saboteurs. Still, in an ideal environment where the expanding factories competed for laborers and indiscriminately hired almost anyone, the German sabotage agents easily slipped through.

CHAPTER 3: FERTILIZER AND PILLS

THE FIRST MAJOR PROJECT DESIGNED to stop or severely slow down allied shipments from the United States had its origins in the fall of 1914. Through Dr. Hugo Schweitzer, a German secret agent and chief executive of Bayer Corporation in the U.S., von Papen and Albert met a brilliant chemist with a small laboratory in Hoboken, New Jersey. Walter Theodor Scheele, born in Cologne, Germany in March of 1865, had satisfied his mandatory military service requirement in an artillery unit after graduating from high school. Discharged with the rank of first lieutenant of the reserves, he studied chemistry at the universities of Bonn and Freiburg. As a member of a student fraternity he received the telltale "Schmiss" across his right cheek from fencing without protection.[48] Scheele earned a doctorate in chemistry from the University of Freiburg around 1884. The young chemist remained active as a reserve officer and earned the rank of captain before deciding to come to the United States in 1890.[49] The German army retained the scientist as an intelligence officer for $1,500 per year.

Scheele settled first in Albany, New York, and then moved to Long Island.[50] He married Marie Magdalene Jensen, a Danish-American from New York, ten years his junior, in 1895. After living and working in Rahway, New Jersey for several years, the Scheele family moved to Catonsville near Baltimore, Maryland in 1900. While in Baltimore, he filed his most important patents indicating that he worked as a research scientist in organic chemistry.[51] He settled in New York in 1910. There, he listed his profession as "druggist" with his "own shop."[52] An American secret service agent described the chemist as "a quiet, reserved man, who is constantly in deep thought, and very preoccupied. He is an intensive smoker... The tone and demeanor of Mrs. Scheele is rather domineering, and it is apparent that she is 'boss' in their home."[53] Maybe this observation explained Scheele's heavy drinking and smoking habits, even carrying a "pearl handle" side arm on his belt in public.[54] Scheele worked on projects for the Bayer Chemical Company with Dr. Hugo Schweitzer as chief executive between 1912 and 1914.[55] The Bureau of Investigations agents that debriefed Scheele in 1918 alleged that between 1910 and 1914 he also worked on the creation of high-powered explosives for the German military.[56]

The British sea blockade posed a huge supply problem for Germany at the beginning of the war. The definitions of unconditional and conditional contraband not only included arms and ammunition, but vital raw materials such as rubber, cotton, and oils. Scheele had developed a process by which oils and lubricants could be solidified, packaged, and shipped, manifested falsely as "artificial fertilizer."[57] The crafty doctor had also invented methods to produce artificial rubber and conceal it much the same way. "Ordinary Para rubber [is reduced] to a brown powder... The... rubber reduced to powder was exported as fertilizer... to continue with the reduction of rubber to powder, Dr. Scheele dissolves the rubber in benzene and then mixes [it] in a rotary drum with magnesium carbonate. To reconstitute the brown powder, the 'fertilizer' is treated with sulphuric [sic] acid, which forms magnesium sulphate [sic] 'epsum salts' [sic] and the rubber comes to the surface in a conglomerate mass... the process for reducing lubricating oil to a powder is similar..."[58]

Through Dr. Schweitzer, Scheele offered these inventions to Heinrich Albert in the fall of 1914. Probably because of the shortages of funds or because of other priorities, the German purchasing agent decided not to finance the construction of a fertilizer plant at that time. Albert re-examined the proposals as the blockade tightened in November of 1914, and again in March 1915. Also interesting to the German government was a process for the dehydration of vegetables. Scheele held a patent on it since 1906.[59] The British mischievously held Germany-bound cargoes of fresh vegetables in harbor "for search procedures" until the food spoilt or the shippers volunteered to sell rather than lose their profits. Without the existence of refrigeration, Scheele's invention proved to be a game-changer to the dynamics of the blockade. The doctor's work was nothing short of chemical sleight of hand.

Dr. Walter T. Scheele on a ship back to the U.S. after being captured in Cuba in 1918.[60]

One of the projects most memorable for its guile illustrates the creativity of this scientist. Not only did Scheele help food-stuffs, oil, and rubber to reach the homeland, he also managed to inflict damage on the Entente food shipments. He developed a heterocyclic aromatic chemical compound compressed into little grains the size of wheat kernels. German agents secretly bribed dock hands in East and Gulf Coast harbors to do little favors. As they loaded grain on ships destined for the Entente powers, a few hundred of these kernels ended up, once in a while, in the bags undetected. The grain then crossed the ocean, went into storage facilities, and finally moved to the mills for processing. So far, the grain displayed nothing strange or noticeable. After milling, workers packed the flour into portioned bags and sent them to bakeries. The odorless, dark green kernels had now been ground to dust and mixed into the regular grain. They remained invisible until the baker added water. The water unlocked what really was methylene dye. The dough suddenly turned "a bright blue."[61] If the baker did not notice it then, the problem appeared clearly in the product coming out of the ovens. Of course, not knowing what caused the blue discoloration, the bakery goods ended up in the trash. Scheele, who was still snickering about his feat when he described it to American investigators in 1918, testified that the dye was not poisonous. He caused, therefore, maximum damage to the food supply of the Entente powers without hurting anyone. Scheele claimed to have produced 10,000 such tablets. Nineteen railroad carloads of wheat thus treated shipped from New Orleans between March 1915 and 1916.[62] No record exists whether the blue dough conspiracy was ever uncovered and how much damage it caused the Allies.[63]

The Hoboken laboratory churned out more than blockade circumvention products. Scheele had amassed an astonishing repertoire of formulations for explosives, explosive incendiary chemicals, and artillery missiles propelled by compressed air.[64] Among other things, he had experimented with rapid accelerants and timed incendiary devices that could be used on a tactical level.

American investigators and subsequent historians defined Dr. Scheele's participation in the German sabotage campaign with the founding of a "fertilizer company," the New Jersey Agricultural and Chemical Company of Bogota [New Jersey] in March of 1915. The truth was that this eminent German chemist and spy devoted all his time and resources to the Fatherland as soon as the war began. The money for his ventures came from three sources: Hugo Schweitzer used resources that the Bayer Chemical Company had overseas and which the War Department refunded in Germany. The commercial funds for rubber and fertilizer first came to Scheele from Heinrich Albert via one of his confidential agents, Theodore R. Lemke. Lemke, who operated the radio station in Tuckerton, New Jersey for the German government, purchased $124,000 worth of rubber ($2.6 Million in today's value) in the spring of 1915 in Brazil, which Scheele's factory "converted" into fertilizer.[65] Under codenames such as "Otto," Lemke organized the transfer of Scheele's products to Germany via several of Albert's dummy corporations.[66] Later in 1915, Naval Attaché Boy-Ed forwarded $125,000 ($2.6 Million in today's value) to Oelrichs and Co., the freight forwarder of the North German Lloyd that handled Scheele's shipments as well as those containing other contraband.[67] Boy-Ed's payment is significant since it connected the naval attaché with the contraband smuggling operation. Scheele was under contract with Albert and had to share his profits, which according to Albert amounted to $130,000 ($2.7 Million in today's value) for the rubber and oil smuggling alone.[68] How many of these proceeds Albert diverted for the sabotage campaign is unknown, since the New York officials destroyed a large part of their documentation in 1916 on the order of German authorities.[69]

B.No. 5731   New York, den 3. November 1915.

Vertraulich!

An den

Herrn Generalbevollmaechtigten

der Hamburg-Amerika Linie

New York, City

HAMBURG-AMERICAN LINE,
OFFICE OF THE
GENERAL REPRESENTATIVE.
Rec'd NOV 4 1915

Bitte ergebenst moeglichst noch heute aus meinem
Guthaben 125000 $ (hundertfuenfundzwanzig tausend Dollar)
an die Firma Oelrichs & Co. zu Gunsten des Norddeutschen
Lloyd New York zu zahlen.

In vorzueglicher Hochachtung

Kapitaen zur See

MEMORANDUM. 0024

New York, 191

From

G. AMSINCK & CO.,

P. O. Box 242.

Gentlemen:

In accordance with instructions from
Mr. Boy. Ed; we hand you herewith our check
for $1200 000 - for his account. Kindly sign the
accompanying receipt.

Yours Very truly

G. AMSINCK & CO.

Boy-Ed's instruction to pay $125,000 for the fertilizer
and the $1.2 Million Amsinck Check. [70]

CHAPTER 4: FIRST FIREBOMBS

WITH THE SABOTAGE ORDER OF January 24th, the Secret War Council in New York proceeded in earnest to stop the production and shipment of war materials to the Entente powers. Von Papen, Albert, and Schweitzer decided to ask Scheele for a proposal of ways to firebomb factories and sink allied ships. Sinking a ship with a bomb was an especially difficult undertaking. The explosives had to be close enough to the exterior hull and below the waterline to cause any significant damage. In order to create a leak sufficiently large to sink a ship, the bomb had to be physically large, the size of a suitcase or bigger. German sabotage agent Werner Horn's explosives that only caused minor damage to the Vanceboro Bridge in 1914 consisted of sixty vials of nitro glycerin. Assuming that a bomb of that size or larger would make it into the hold of a ship undetected, which in itself was a difficult proposition given the tight security on the piers, a complicated timing mechanism had to be devised to set it off. Time-bombs typically worked with clocks, making a telltale sound. Traditional time-bombs also were notoriously unreliable. In this context, Dr. Scheele's invention of a new type of time-bomb was nothing short of ingenious. The Czech spymaster in New York, Emmanuel Voska, one of von Papen's biggest nemeses in the secret war, described Scheele's design in his memoirs,

> The device was so simple that one cannot even call it ingenious. The literature of the First World War has named these infernal machines indifferently 'pencil bombs' and 'cigar bombs.' They looked externally like a cross between the two. Inside a copper disk bisected the bomb vertically. A chemical which has a rapid corrosive effect on copper filled the upper compartment. When it had eaten through the disk it came into contact with the chemical in the lower compartment.

The combination produced instantly a flame as hot as
a tiny fragment of the sun. The acid did not begin to
work on the copper until one broke off a little knob at
the upper end. Then it became a time-bomb, the time
– from two days to a week – being regulated by the
thickness or thinness of the copper disk.[71]

Scheele had solved the issue of size, and changed the target from a
hard-to-destroy steel hull of a freighter to setting its cargo on fire.
Thus, he relegated the complicated timing and firing mechanisms of
yesteryear to the heap of outdated bomb-building technology. The
little bombs burnt so hot that their lead hulls melted completely. Even
the use of lead screws made sure that the incendiary devices left virtually no trace. Workers could easily hide the three-inch 'cigars' in their
clothes and casually drop them within the cargo they were stacking.[72]
The firebombs worked especially well with cargoes of sugar, which,
when ignited, developed such intense heat that it became very difficult to extinguish the resulting fire.

Scheele seemed to have started working on the development
of the 'cigar' bombs in the middle of January 1915, if purchases of the
tell-tale lead pipes are an indication.[73] A firm order to proceed with
the production came from Franz von Papen within weeks of the sabotage order against ships and factories in the U.S. Von Papen "sent
for Walter Scheele..." on February 10th 1915, ostensibly to familiarize
himself with the chemist's bomb designs.[74] The doctor obliged, and
on February 19th 1915, a grateful von Papen wrote: "I have received
the various samples (four boxes) and thank you for the same. In conclusion with the importance of the matter, I have cabled your offer
to the Minister of War and have written them... Since the telegram
and connections are slow, some time will elapse before I will receive
an answer which on receipt I will immediately forward to you. I again
thank you for your offer and the motive of your action."[75] Obviously,
the answer came faster than anticipated, on or around March 1st. Von
Papen sent a letter via "special delivery" to the doctor on March 5th:

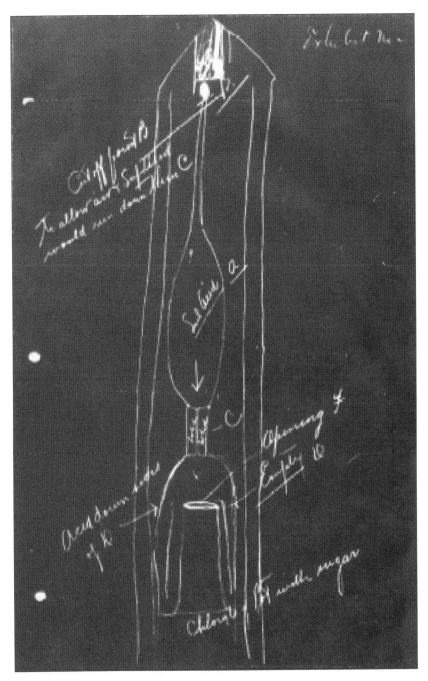

Drawing of a "cigar" bomb by sabotage agent Frederick L. Herrmann[76]

I have diligently looked for you for the last five days at my office #6 Hanover St., room 25 [von Papen's apartment in the German Club], and would ask that you call tomorrow Saturday at 12 o'clock noon.

With best regards.

Respectfully yours,

Von Papen.[77]

Four days later, on March 9th 1915, Heinrich Albert paid Scheele $10,000 ($210,000 in today's value) to cloak his laboratory behind a "fertilizer" company.[78] Other payments from Albert coded as "artificial fertilizer" and listed in the accounts of von Papen amounted to $20,067.64.[79] Historians have misinterpreted these funds as being designated to buy oil and fertilizer. However, as previously described, that money came through Theodor Lemke and later directly from Karl Boy-Ed. The payments from von Papen and Boy-Ed for incendiary bombs are not listed in Scheele's bank accounts. Lemke and Oelrichs clearly handled the purchasing and shipping of contraband for the chemist.[80]

Two weeks after Albert's $10,000 seed money, on March 17th, von Papen reported in code to his superiors in Germany, "Regrettably steamer [SS La] Touraine has arrived unharmed with ammunition and 335 machine guns."[81] Von Papen was being facetious. She had indeed sailed on February 27th from New York to Le Havre, France, and caught on fire five hundred miles off the coast of Ireland on March 6th.[82] The New York Times reported the next day, "only the barest facts of the disaster on the Touraine are known, and there is no hint of the cause of the fire on board the vessel... A message from Queenstown said that the fire on the Touraine was 'fierce.'"[83] The fire had broken out in two separate cargo areas. French authorities immediately suspected foul play. After a thorough investigation, authorities identified a suspect who, as it turned out, had not caused the fire.[84] Either way, von Papen's superiors now had evidence that the sabotage campaign they had ordered was in full swing. If it had been Scheele's work, the bomb maker had scored a first, documented success. None of the eighty-four passengers were hurt. However, the cargo was ruined.

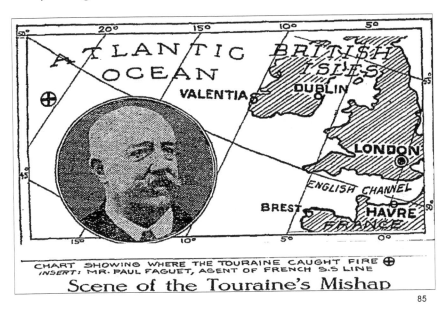

CHART SHOWING WHERE THE TOURAINE CAUGHT FIRE ⊕
INSERT: MR. PAUL FAGUET, AGENT OF FRENCH S.S LINE
Scene of the Touraine's Mishap
85

Nonetheless, the first batch of Scheele's bombs did not seem to have worked entirely as designed. The difficulty in the construction had to do with the material and thickness of the separating metal plate. The initial separating material that had to corrode and set off the bomb consisted of paraffin that proved to be unreliable as a timer. Rather than firing in the set timeframe, when the ships had cleared the United States and entered international waters, they did not fire at all or were discovered in the cargo before any damage could occur. An associate of Dr. Scheele recalled: "One day I heard that there was a row going on upstairs in Dr. Scheele's laboratory between him and Captain Steinberg... I went upstairs and inquired: 'What is all this noise about?' Steinberg then said: 'The G— D— pills should work in 5 days, and they don't work in 5 months. Scheele is a faker!'"[86] It is unknown when exactly this heated exchange took place. However, the plot had come to full fruition in July and August 1915, when Albert's stolen briefcase and the discovery of sabotage agent Franz Rintelen (whose involvement appears in subsequent chapters) ravaged the ranks of the conspirators. The five-month timeframe places the order to produce firebombs into the date range of von Papen's first inquiries a few weeks after he received the sabotage order, maybe even before. A mysterious letter among Dr. Scheele's possessions, dated February 5th 1915, refers to the quality issues with his bomb design. "This letter refers to pills [code name for 'cigar' bombs] taken by a woman [von Steinmetz], mother of four children [people placing the bombs on ships] who is in a precarious condition [time pressure]. She thanks him for the pills, but as yet they have proven of no value."[87]

Captain Thomas J. Tunney, who recounted his experiences in the war as head of New York's bomb squad, detailed several mysterious fires on ships in January and February 1915. According to Tunney, three ships, the SS Orton, SS Hennington Court, and SS Carlton, caught fire without an apparent reason in those first two months of the year. None of these three ships made it into the papers and, therefore, could not be verified as the beginning of the bomb plot.[88] However, other ship blazes entered the news: On February 7th, the British freighter SS Grindon Hall caught on fire in Norfolk harbor.[89] On February 16th, the Italian steamer Regina d'Italia, loaded with oil, kerosene, and cotton burst into flames at Pier B in Jersey City, New Jersey. The steamer's destination was Naples, Italy. The fire destroyed the entire cargo. No reason could be determined other than that the conflagration started among the cotton bales in the forward hold. Dockworkers found a 'cigar' bomb hidden in a bag while loading sugar onto the English freighter SS Knutsford in New York harbor on February 29th.[90] The Italian steamer SS San Guglielmo sailed from Galveston, Texas, "by way of New York" with six thousand bales of cotton on March 16th. The ship made it to Naples but mysteriously caught fire as it docked at the destination on April 11th. The entire cargo burned, causing $200,000 in damages ($4.2 Million in today's value).[91] These ship fires were not the only ones.

There are indications that the Foreign Office memorandum from January 6th 1915, that mentioned the Admiralty's request to initiate sabotage in the United States, yielded other immediate results. One week before the formal sabotage order but five days after Dr. Scheele received his first lead pipe delivery, a large steel mill of the John A. Roebling's Sons Company in Trenton, New Jersey, mysteriously caught fire and burnt to the ground on January 18th 1915.[92] The factory was located approximately sixty miles from Scheele's lab.

Roebling specialized in steel wires and produced anti-submarine netting and artillery chains for the Entente. Insurance companies estimated the extensive damage (without any loss of life) to be a staggering $1,500,000 ($315 Million in today's value).[93] According to the owners, there were no combustibles in the plant.[94]

A second fire at Roebling in November 1915 destroyed another twenty-nine factory buildings on the grounds. Again, the cause was mysterious. The fire had started in a pile of jute rope. Most likely soaked in some type of accelerant, the fire spread quickly and was out of control. When workers tried to use the factory fire alarm they realized that it had been disabled.[95] The *Metal Industry Magazine* reported in April 1915, "...the recent $1,000,000 fire at the plant of the John A. Roebling's Sons Company was caused by some one [sic] not in sympathy with the concern manufacturing trace chains for the Allies. Previous to the fire an attempt was made to blow up the big plant."[96] Whether or not the fire started as a result of Dr. Scheele's early versions of the 'cigar' bomb has never been established. The fact that investigators found no trace of what caused the fire supports the theory that Scheele's incendiary bombs were the culprits, since they were much smaller than traditional explosives and melted completely after ignition. These early fires typically do not figure into accounts of Dr. Scheele's activities because they happened before the "official" start of the firebomb plot as described in sabotage agent Franz Rintelen's wartime memoir, *The Dark Invader*. However, the fires bear a striking similarity to the admitted sabotage acts that started in the end of April.

There are two reasons why the two German officials involved in the sabotage campaign did not want to tell the truth. Franz von Papen, who became German Chancellor in 1932, wanted as little as possible to do with the sabotage campaign. He denied ever working with Dr. Scheele on bomb plots. Rintelen, desperate for attention, an acknowledgment of his service by the German government, and in order to boost his book sales, tried to take all the credit for the sabotage campaign. Since he only arrived on April 3rd, there could not have been earlier firebombs to fit his story.

The German chemist produced the first bombs in his laboratory on 1133 Clinton Street, in Hoboken, New Jersey. The place did not appear to be as sophisticated as one might expect:

There are three doors to be passed before entering
the works, and an electric contact bell rings when the
doors are being opened. On the ground floor are a
number of bags, which are said to contain manure. In
the rear [,] are two large hogsheads, one of which is
empty, and the other, apparently, full, said to contain
a chemical which is used for the manufacture of artificial rubber. There are six barrels of naphtha and smoking is prohibited. There were about four live chickens
in the yard. On the upper floor (one flight up) Kleist
has a small live alligator in a small aquarium. On the
upper floor, which is divided into three compartments
are located what appear to be laboratories... These
compartments are extremely hot... [97]

As a manager of the plant, Scheele had hired Charles von Kleist. The
black sheep of a very renowned, old noble family in Germany, Ewald
Wilhelm Hermann Carl von Kleist decided to join the merchant marine
rather than follow in the prescribed footsteps of his forefathers, military men, university professors, poets, and clergy.[98] "Before the war,
von Kleist was in the command of the freighter *Haulloway*, owned by
Church Bros. of Tiffany, R. I."[99] Von Kleist had retired at age 66, at
the outbreak of the war, to a small house in Hoboken, New Jersey,
with his wife Mary, a former opera singer and diva. Possibly out of
boredom and feeling a call to duty, the retired merchant marine captain decided to support the Kaiser and Fatherland. He took a job as
superintendent of Walter Scheele's 'fertilizer' plant. Captain Thomas
Tunney described him as a "funny little man who looked like a cartoon
of the late Prussian eagle."[100] Indeed, the five-foot, seven-inch tall,
proud Germanic-looking veteran of the Franco-Prussian war of 1870
to 1871, with a well-kempt chin beard, spectacles and bowler hat, did
not quite blend into the New York crowds as one would expect from
a secret agent.

The plot was still in its infancy in March 1915. Von Papen and
Boy-Ed assigned two project managers that were to organize the
bomb deliveries in the New York harbor. The agents responsible for
placing the bombs onto ships were two pier superintendents that

worked for HAPAG.[101] Captain Otto Wolpert, a forty-two year-old naturalized U.S. citizen, was married with three children and lived in Jersey City.[102] The retired merchant marine captain had responsibility for the crews of the interned ships of the Atlas Steamship line, a subsidiary of HAPAG.[103] At six feet, two inches tall and 260 pounds, he commanded respect among the sailors in his charge.[104] The piers were located on 23rd Street in Manhattan, across the harbor from Scheele's bomb shop. Captain Enno Bode, forty-eight years old and a twenty-year veteran of the German navy, had the same job up the waterfront in Hoboken where he worked for HAPAG. Also in Hoboken, tied up at the HAPAG piers, lay the North German Lloyd flagship SS *Kaiser Friedrich der Grosse*. As an active navy asset, Bode remained on Boy-Ed's payroll throughout the war, tasked with more than just the firebomb mission.[105] Boy-Ed remained his direct superior.

Initially, Bode and another naval intelligence agent, Erich von Steinmetz, carried the bombs from Scheele's laboratory to the loading docks. [106] Von Steinmetz had come to the United States in March 1915 "through Roumania [sic], Russian [sic], via Vladivostok, and into this country, disguised as a woman."[107] Besides helping with the fire bombings, von Steinmetz had been sent to the U.S. with tubes of glanders cultures, tetanus, and a powder believed to be Anthrax to infect horses destined for the Allies. The bacteria were highly contagious, causing coughing, fever, a large discharge of mucus, and vomit that was infectious. Horses died within days of inoculation. Dr. Scheele reportedly descended into a violent rage when von Steinmetz brought the germs into his laboratory, "and after a violent altercation, [Scheele] struck Steinmetz in the face and knocked him down, and put him out of the office with his germs."[108] Steinmetz escaped in July 1915, when the firebomb plot came into the open.[109] He was never arrested, tried, or even properly identified. Scheele later claimed that the biological agents Steinmetz had carried with him were worthless. Supposedly, the germs were dead on arrival. However, a few months later, whether caused by new supplies of germs or because German agents reconstituted and grew Steinmetz' biological agents, large numbers of horses all along the East Coast and Gulf Coast died as a result of poisoning.[110]

After Steinmetz and Bode had accosted Scheele for the malfunctioning 'cigars,' Scheele refused to let them set foot in his laboratory. Especially after Scheele and Steinmetz had come to blows, "neither Captain Bode, Wolpert or [sic] Steinmetz were ever allowed up-stairs in his private laboratory."[111] He considered them both inferiors in rank, as well as, at the same time dangerous and extremely disagreeable associates. The chemist particularly despised Steinmetz who he considered to be "a scoundrel of the lowest order, capable of doing anything and states that it was the sending of men of the type of Steinmetz and Bode to work with him, which caused his first feelings of bitterness and resentment against his own German Government."[112] Captain von Kleist and sailors from interned German ships now had the task of being the bagmen for the bombs.

In line with the order to utilize Irish activists, an Irish-American from New Orleans named Norton O'Leary suddenly appeared on the scene.[113] Captain Thomas J. Tunney, the head of the New York bomb squad, asked von Kleist after his arrest, whether or not he had ever seen anybody take away packages from the factory.

Captain Charles von Kleist in court in 1916.[114]

Captain Charles von Kleist leaving court in 1916.[115]

Yes, once; - a day or two before this row [between Dr. Scheele and Captain Steinberg] I came out of my office, the door to the laboratory was open, and I observed a tall young man packing shells in a grip. He afterwards introduced himself to me as 'Mr. O'Leary, from New Orleans.' I left the factory with him and walked along the street for quite some distance, noticing that he was changing his grip from one hand to the other. It appeared to be heavy. I asked him: 'What have you got in that satchel?' and he remarked: 'Oh, about thirty 'pills'. I am going to New Orleans.[116]

As a matter of fact, O'Leary had introduced E. J. Reilly (or O'Riley) and Maurice D. Conners to the bomb makers in Hoboken. Steinmetz joined the two Irish-Americans around the 4th of April, and took the 'cigars', as well as glanders and tetanus cultures to New Orleans.[117]

While von Papen, Boy-Ed, Albert, Schweitzer, and Scheele worked hard on implementing the sabotage order, the pace was too slow for their anxious superiors in Germany. The war had turned into one of attrition and American supplies started to leave their deadly imprint on the battlefields. Von Papen kept sending reports containing intelligence, but other than the failed and embarrassing Horn mission of the fall of 1914, he had no tangible successes to report. The archival evidence is unclear as to the disposition of the General Staff towards the American team. Clearly, German military leaders placed urgency on the goal of stopping American munitions from reaching their enemies. Von Papen's updates, like the one on March 17th, show that the Secret War Council was clearly on the defensive in February and March 1915. Albert's negotiations with DuPont to secure the U.S.'s entire annual production of smokeless powder from Aetna also dragged into the month of March. The Bridgeport Projectile Company project came together slowly and was hampered by the need to put together contracts that secretly protected the German investment.[118]

In hindsight, the work of the Secret War Council to inhibit the shipments of war supplies to the Allies in the spring of 1915 was on track to score big on several levels. John A. Roebling's Sons Company in Trenton, New Jersey burned to the ground in February, causing hundreds of millions of dollars (in today's value) in damages. Well-funded sabotage teams had formed on the West Coast under the command of German Consul General Franz Bopp and his Vice-Consul, Wilhelm von Brincken. Agents under their auspices would blow up a dynamite laden ship in the Seattle harbor in May, causing large damages to shipping bound for the Russian front. In Detroit, Consul Curt von Reiswitz supported Albert Kaltschmidt's group in attacking targets in Canada and the industrial areas of the Great Lakes region. In New Orleans, a German cell under the leadership of O'Leary successfully planted firebombs on Allied ships starting in March of 1915. The Haskell, New Jersey, gun cotton drying plant of DuPont blew up on March 5th 1915, killing five and wrecking four buildings.[119] The Equitable Powder Plant in Alton, Illinois suffered a large explosion on April 1st. Three days later, the New Jersey Freight Depot at Pompton Lakes, New Jersey, went up, destroying train loads of percussion caps for artillery shells.[120] It is not clear if these explosions all resulted from sabotage by individuals, from attacks organized by the German government, or from simple work accidents. However, all incidents suspiciously supported the push to slow munitions production and shipment to Germany's enemies.

The New York team, and von Papen in particular, did not and would not take credit for these explosions for fear of messages being intercepted, thus also leaving their superiors in the dark regarding unfolding events. We know today that their caution had been justified, since starting in the spring of 1915 all the New York offices of the Secret War Council had been bugged, the phones tapped, and the employees shadowed.[121] In addition to the suspicious explosions, Heinrich Albert managed to tie up a year's worth of American smokeless powder production on April 1st 1915, locked down the hydraulic press market a few weeks later, and were pursuing the cornering the Phenol market, all within a few months of having the necessary funds for these projects. Given the phlegmatic response of the German General Staff and Admiralty to suggestions of the Secret War Council, and given the fact that funding only became available in February 1915, the hardliner's impatience with the American team appears unjustified only a month later. Yet, impatient they grew, and especially with Franz von Papen who had set afoot disastrous sabotage missions twice: Horst von der Goltz at Welland, and Werner Horn in Vanceboro. The impression of the Imperial General Staff was that von Papen did not recruit the right people, did not manage his projects, and took too much time. Given the barrage of suggestions over the previous three months, his superiors thought that he had oversubscribed his commitments. The Admiralty dispatched an agent with the task of "cleaning up" the mess in New York on the 20th of March. He would be the "Dark Invader."[122]

CHAPTER 5: TERROR ON THE HIGH SEAS

BRITISH AUTHORITIES SEIZED THE SS *Wilhelmina*, owned and operated by the Secret War Council to take foodstuffs to Germany, in January 1915. The British action triggered a significant shift in the attitude of German officials towards the United States.[123] Albert had purchased the freighter in October through a dummy firm to ship foodstuffs and cotton. For the German officials in New York, her seizure underscored the fact that the U.S. was unwilling to support the shipment of non-contraband and humanitarian freight to Germany. During the winter, and without U.S. protest, the British government had added foodstuffs to their contraband lists, which became the legal foundation for seizing the freighter. All German attempts to respect U.S. neutrality and expend huge efforts in organizing and financing export operations so that U.S. laws would not be violated did not result in any tangible appreciation or acceptance by the U.S. government.

As it turned out, the United States was categorically unwilling to permit German efforts against the Entente from U.S. soil. Von Papen's fraudulent passport scheme, the attack on Canadian installations, and the supply of German cruisers from the U.S. were all, without question, illegal activities.[124] However, German officials thought these operations to have been peccadilloes that, at worst, would trigger a slap on the wrist from the American government. However, the severe reactions of the American public, pushed by the increasingly effective English propaganda, forced the U.S. government to sanction the German operations later in 1915 with severe sentences for former German minister to Mexico and HAPAG director in New York, Karl Buenz, and a whole host of his employees. Even before the landmark trials in the fall of 1915, the United States had become noticeably more partial in the European conflict. The lure of profits from munitions sales on a grand scale trumped any efforts by the German Empire to resume non-contraband trade with the United States. Germany's representatives in the United States missed opportunities in the very beginning of the war to counter British propaganda. Their ineffective use of American surrogates to oppose the tightening English blockade, the inability to coalesce American support into promoting trade in cotton, dyes, food, and fertilizer, and the unchallenged increase in arms and munitions exports, all helped push American foreign policy away from true neutrality.

The frustration in Germany with this development, disregarding the fact that German officials had a lot to do with it, brought a group of hardliners from within the German military and civilian government to the fore. The belief was that a determined war strategy against the United States and England would bring the war to a quick conclusion. Based on the intelligence, which von Papen and others had sent in 1913 and 1914, the hardliners firmly believed that the American military would never play any significant role in the European conflict. They deemed an armed conflict with the U.S. inconsequential from a strictly military standpoint, while potentially helpful in bringing the 'politicians' in Germany to support an uncompromising war effort.

Simultaneously, and probably driving the resolve of hardliner attitudes, the German war strategy shifted significantly in the spring of 1915. Britain had destroyed the battle group of Admiral Spee in the Falklands in November 1914. Except for small excursions, the German High Seas Fleet remained moored in German ports. The last of Germany's cruisers had either been destroyed or saved themselves by agreeing to internment in neutral harbors. Effectively, the German navy had been neutralized. The army also reeled from its failure to take France swiftly. The German forces dug in on the western front and consolidated the gains made in Belgium and eastern France. The momentum now shifted to the Russian front. There was a lot of action in the east in 1915 where the German army made important headway, collapsing the Russian lines and steam rolling into the strategically important south. The static war on the western front, where material and supply would determine the eventual outcome, moved the United States into the strategic focus.

Albert, Dernburg, Boy-Ed, and von Papen's efforts up to the end of 1914 had had virtually no impact on the war effort. Certainly, Berlin appreciated the Secret War Council's efforts to send reservists to Europe with false passports, scare the Canadians in the attempts to sabotage logistics installations, and supply the remnants of Germany's navy. However, there was no strategic plan underlying these disconnected efforts. All that changed in the beginning of 1915. The recognition, albeit very late in the game, that the American theatre of war indeed impacted the European fronts, triggered the formulation of a new strategy towards the United States. The German officials in New York had worked hard on achieving this kind of recognition.

The efforts finally bore fruit through a coordinated effort in which the Foreign Office, Interior Ministry, the German General Staff of the Army, and the Admiralty initiated a military campaign directed at the United States of America. The strategic goal was the elimination of munitions exports by any means. Richard Meyer of the Imperial Foreign Office issued the following memorandum on January 6th 1915: "The Admiralty Staff requests to instigate the Irish in America... to far-reaching sabotage in the United States and Canada. For the purpose of naming the tasks, the Admiralty requests to instruct them to get in touch with the Naval Attaché [Captain Karl Boy-Ed] or the Military Attaché [Franz von Papen] in Washington."[125] Orders to the effect went to the German officials in New York on January 24th, authorizing sabotage against factories and ships.[126] On February 4th, Germany announced unrestricted submarine warfare against commercial shipping. The arrival of proper funding of clandestine and public operations in the U.S. and of teams of sabotage agents came in March and April.[127] The Imperial Foreign Office had the thankless task of maintaining a diplomatic effort to keep the United States neutral as long as possible. This balancing act of mounting operations against the United States and retreating slightly, only to push the limits of American patience again, took into consideration the calculated risk of an eventual entry of the United States into the war on the side of the Entente. The challenge of American resolve never was a question of chance or trial and error. Heinrich Albert wrote on May 10th 1915 to his superior, Interior Secretary Clemens von Delbrück,

> Imagine the extreme case that the United States would resort to rigorous measures, such as either declaring war on their own initiative or force us to declare war because of their extreme actions such as

impounding all our ships in these harbors, what would be the result? First, a huge relief, because the government would use all its power to fill up stocks of munitions here, would therefore make the exportation of weapons and ammunition impossible because it would need the total domestic production or at least a majority of it. I certainly do not have to point out that militarily or from a naval perspective the United States would have any impact. The situation would be one of standing at attention, which we can calmly sit out, because everything the United States can do against Germany, it is practically already doing: Financing our enemies, arms and ammunition transports, compliance in all matters concerning England...[128]

When the United States finally entered the war on the side of the Entente, the German government, including all her military and most of her political leaders, had decided that American neutrality had outlived its usefulness. Historians have long stressed the apparent resistance of Chancellor von Bethmann Hollweg and Ambassador Count Bernstorff to posture aggressively against the United States. However, all archival sources in the decision-making process on the German actions against the United States clearly showed not only knowledge of, but an integral participation of the Foreign Office in the planning, financing, and execution of German operations in the U.S. The friction within the German government and the military leadership focused on how far to tension the bow. The definitions of risk and reward remained the undefined and hotly debated issues. War planners and politicians, hardliners and accommodators disagreed upon the point that an American entry into the war had little or no impact on the German execution of its war strategy.

Germany fired the first shot in the new battle against America on February 4th 1915, when she announced a "blockade" against England to begin on February 18th.

The waters around Great Britain and Ireland, including the English Channel, are hereby proclaimed a war region. On and after February 18th every enemy merchant vessel found in this region will be destroyed, without its always being possible to warn the crews or passengers of the dangers threatening. Neutral ships will also incur danger in the war region, where, in view of the misuse of neutral flags ordered by the British Government, and incidents inevitable in sea warfare, attacks intended for hostile ships may affect neutral ships also. The sea passage to the north of the Shetland Islands, and the eastern region of the North Sea in a zone of at least 30 miles along the Netherlands coast, are not menaced by any danger.

(Signed) Berlin, February 4th,
VON POHL,
Chief of Marine Staff[129]

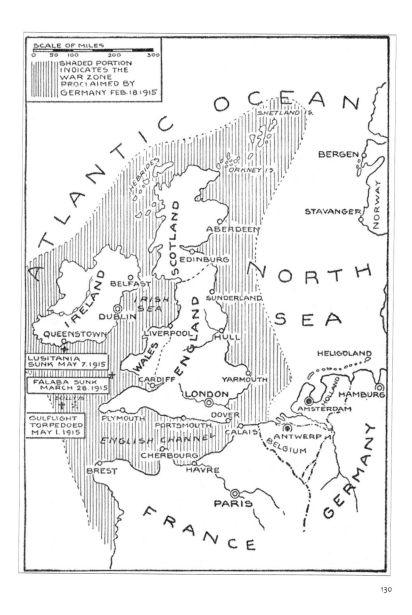

130

The German response to the English blockade, which had begun in August 1914 and was officially announced in November, consisted of declaring a war zone around the British Isles. Any ship operating in these waters did so at its own risk and was liable for destruction. Declaring a commercial war on the high seas against combatant and neutral shipping clearly aimed at American trade. The initial hope of the German war planners was that neutrals would refrain from trading with England as a result of the risks of destruction.

President Wilson protested vehemently on February 10th, insisting on the right of neutrals to operate in international waters and to travel on any ship, even if it flew a combatant's flag. Wilson held the German government to a standard of "strict accountability."[131] Wilson's interpretation of the law did not stand up to international law. Undoubtedly, by international legal standards any person traveling on a combatant ship automatically became a combatant.[132] England rejoiced at the American attitude towards the rights of neutrals. Effectively, the United States offered its citizens as human shields anytime they traveled on an English ship. Cunard and other British shipping lines blatantly violated rules of contraband, carrying small arms ammunition and other items on the same ships that carried American passengers. Paul Koenig's detectives meticulously documented the infractions to the German officials in New York. However, true to the German tactics of applying and releasing pressure before causing too much damage, the German government offered several accommodations to the Wilson administration on February 16th. The German government promised not to attack neutral ships without prior warning, and to observe 'cruiser rules' in the case of neutrals. However, the tactics Germany chose to enforce the blockade virtually insured that Americans would sooner or later be injured either materially, physically, or both. The execution of the German blockade came through a new weapon: the submarine.

The noose around Germany's supply channels started to show effect in the spring of 1915 as the British blockade tightened with continuously expanding lists of absolute and conditional contraband. Great Britain imported an ever-increasing amount of supplies across the Atlantic from the United States. Close to five thousand ships with "more than 300 tons net [gross registered tons]" arrived and departed from British harbors between August 1914 and March 10th 1915.[133] On November 2nd 1914, the British government had declared the entire North Sea a war zone, and laid mine fields in the narrows between the continent and the British Isles. Any possible approach to the neutral countries of Norway, Denmark, and Holland was mined. Despite international law to the contrary, the British navy did not search ships on the high seas and take contraband as prizes into English ports. All ships had to come into English ports to be searched. Neutral shippers that carried no contraband and had to be cleared to continue their voyages faced huge losses triggered by the time-consuming detention in British ports. English officials regularly purchased non-contraband items such as cotton and food, rather than letting the commercial steamers continue to their destinations. The detained freighters more often than not willingly cashed in on their loads to reduce the costly detention time. Heinrich Albert purposely tested the British blockade and meticulously documented the practice of detention and confiscation of non-contraband supplies. In fact, the appropriation of his shipments by England became a sizable source of funding in New York.[134] The weapon of choice to change this modus operandi and fight English supremacy on the high seas was the U-boat.

The *Unterseeboot* (submarine or U-boat) had undergone tremendous technical improvements since the 1860s. The most notable engineer in U-boat technology was an Irish-American entrepreneur in New Jersey, John Philip Holland. Holland invented dozens of features of the modern submarine, such as the pressure chamber technology that allowed submarines to submerge and raise using compressed air. His patents and ideas created the technology on which modern submarines are based. While both sides in the war used Holland's patents, German submersibles differed significantly from the English ships, although neither Britain nor Germany had a good idea for the tactical use of the weapon. Originally envisioned to operate in support of battle groups centered around the large naval dreadnoughts, Britain constructed longer and heavier versions of the submarine, with 2,500 tons of displacement and powered by gas engines. The German navy constructed its submarines much smaller, between 500 and 850 tons of displacement while submerged.[135] Initially, these German vessels were powered by gas engines. However, beginning in 1910, the German spec called for diesel engines while surfaced and battery powered propulsion while submerged. Because of the smaller size, German subs could remain submerged for longer periods, could dive quicker and deeper, and, most importantly, did not show the telltale exhaust smoke while cruising on the surface when recharging their batteries.

Germany had a fleet of twenty-eight U-boats in August 1914.[136] Immediately at the onset of hostilities the German navy sent their fourteen ocean-going diesel subs into the North Sea to raid the British navy. Vice Admiral Scheer, the commander of the second squadron of the High Seas Fleet, wrote in 1920: "The first proof of the submarine to remain at sea for a long time had been given [in the raid of early August]... so that the submarine, from being merely a coastal defence [sic] machine, as was originally planned, became the most effective long-range weapon."[137] The effort became a resounding success. On September 5th 1914, the German U-boat *U-21* sank the British cruiser *HMS Pathfinder* off St. Abbs Head, Berwickshire, Scotland.[138] On September 22nd 1914, the German submarine *U-9* came upon three English armored cruisers, the *HMS Aboukir*, *HMS Hogue*, and the *HMS Cressy* in the North Sea. Never surfacing, the U-boat commander, Kapitän-leutnant Otto Weddingen, fired all six torpedoes on board, reloading while submerged. Winston Churchill described what happened:

> At 6.30 a.m., shortly after daylight, the *Aboukir* was struck by a torpedo. In twenty-five minutes this old vessel capsized. Some of her boats were smashed by the explosion, and hundreds of men were swimming in the water or clinging to wreckage. Both her consorts had hurried with chivalrous simplicity to the aid of the sinking ship. Both came to a dead standstill within a few hundred yards of her and lowered all their boats to rescue the survivors. In this posture they in their turn were both sunk, first the *Hogue* and then the *Cressy*, by the same submarine. Out of over 2,200 men on board these three ships, only 800 were saved, and more than 1,400 perished.[139]

German Postcard from 1914, public domain

The result was a huge victory for the "unwanted stepchild of the von Tirpitz era," the submarine forces.[140] While the High Seas Fleet had scrambled into German harbors in late August and preferred mooring to fighting, this 500-ton submersible, considered a naval toy by the German admiralty, had members of the British navy gasping for air. The German commander of the submarine fleet, Lieutenant Commander Hermann Bauer, rejoiced in his memoirs: "A U-boat of 500 tons and 28 men had annihilated 3 armored cruisers, each of which had 12,000 tons displacement, heavy armor and crews of 750 men. The type of weapon the U-boat represented, the potential of which if used properly surpassed any other naval weapon, was highlighted here for the first time and on a most impressive scale... "[141] Although British Intelligence knew the exact numbers of the tiny German submarine fleet, the thought of a German push for an expanded submersible fighting force raised a well-founded fear of starvation by blockade.[142] The U-9 sank another British warship in October. The British government announced the entire North Sea to be a war zone on November 2nd as a result of several successful German submarine raids. All commercial ships had to come into Falmouth to be inspected. The fear of a superior submarine force decimating the British fleet precipitated a new phase in the British blockade. Luckily for Britain, Grand Admiral Alfred von Tirpitz, in charge of the German Navy, did not yet believe the U-boat to be a viable weapon.[143]

Von Tirpitz had directed the construction of Germany's fleet of dreadnoughts that now was pinned down in the harbors of northern Germany. To the old-timers in the German admiralty, submarine warfare was a complicated and untested development. Under international cruiser rules, any man-of-war including submarines had the right to stop an enemy ship for search and seizure procedures. The warship usually sent a shot across the bow of the vessel to be stopped. Once the enemy ship agreed to stop, the crew had to be taken into safety (usually the warship took the crews to the next port) before the commercial steamer was sunk. Submarines such as the U-9 were small, slow vessels with only limited maneuverability. The cruising speed of a U-boat was 14.2 knots surfaced, while submersed it could travel at a speed of eight knots. The *Lusitania* cruised at twenty-five knots, by comparison. Submarines also had no space to accommodate additional crew or prisoners of war. Visibility and the ability to properly identify targets were limited with the periscope protruding only feet over the surface of the rough Atlantic sea. Moreover, hidden guns on the stopped ship made the U-boat vulnerable to attack when surfaced. The advantage of the submarine consisted of its stealth, the ability to approach another ship unseen, and launch a deadly torpedo into its hull. Once surfaced, this strength evaporated.

British instructions to naval officers were to either steam away as fast as possible or to ram a surfaced submarine. Already in the first days of the naval war, a German U-boat, the *U-15*, sank after the British cruiser *HMS Birmingham* rammed it.[144] Ramming, in particular, posed a deadly threat to the U-boat with its thin and vulnerable hull. Therefore, submariners could not employ traditional cruiser rules in a naval confrontation. Though sinking enemy ships under disregard of cruiser rules was legal, the main problem became the just treatment of neutral shipping of countries such as the United States. Thus, Grand Admiral von Tirpitz, a traditional naval leader, initially did not believe that the submarine was a viable weapon to break the English blockade. It remains one of the great blunders of the imperial war effort that German naval expenditures continued to flow into surface ships rather than to rapidly expand the U-boat fleet.[145]

To be fair, even when the submarine commanders had orders to obey 'cruiser rules,' Britain sabotaged the effort. Conscientious submarine captains, such as Lieutenant Hans Rose of the *U-53*, actually towed crews of sunken merchantmen to the next harbor, risking detection and destruction by enemy ships.[146] This procedure was not practicable on a larger scale and as a matter of procedure. The German government argued that the violation of 'cruiser rules' by submarines had to become an internationally recognized fact dictated by technological advancement. However, England had no interest in either letting the German navy obey international law or in changing it. Friction between Germany and neutral countries stood to benefit Britain as a matter of course. After losing the first merchant vessels to submarine attack, the British admiralty began flying neutral flags on their steamers and even ocean liners.[147] By then, British skippers were also instructed to run down submarines and sink them through ramming. Several U-boats were thus dispatched in collisions or fell victim to sudden attack by nearby cruisers while surfaced. The German admiralty ordered stealth torpedo attacks without warning in response. This is exactly what Britain had intended.

Even before the German blockade was fully in place, German submarines scored a "formidable" hit. *U-24* sank the British armored cruiser *HMS Formidable* off the coast of Portland Bill on January 1st 1915. Five hundred forty-seven sailors perished in the attack. It was the second large armored battleship that the British navy had lost. The *HMS Audacious* sank after it struck a mine in the first days of the war. The German High Seas Fleet sortied into the middle of the North Sea on January 23rd to challenge the British fleet in an area called Dogger Bank. The engagement resulted in the loss of a German dreadnought and the near loss of a second. The British warships had proven to be better armed, better coordinated, and faster than the German squadron. The loss of the *SMS Bluecher* caused Wilhelm II to dismiss Admiral Ingenohl and appoint Admiral von Pohl to take command of the High Seas Fleet. While von Pohl ordered periodic sorties from Kiel, the German admiralty refused to risk a direct confrontation with the numerically superior British Grand Fleet. Thus, the blockade of England, which the admiralty estimated would take 220 submarines to enforce,[148] was taken up by twenty-five U-boats, only five or six of which patrolled the ocean at any given time.[149] The German blockade was illegal by the standard of the Declaration of London, as was the English counterpart.

Two days before the German Empire announced its war on

commerce, Colonel Edward House, President Wilson's friend and con-fidante, left New York on the *Lusitania* for Britain on January 30ᵗʰ 1915. The president had sent him on a diplomatic mission to the warring nations of Europe hoping to get both sides to accept a mediation offer from the United States. As the ship neared the Irish Coast, the captain of the large passenger liner gave orders to hoist the American flag. Colonel House, who witnessed the ruse, was furious. He filed a report to the State Department and denounced the abuse of neutral flags on British ships. The affair caused a raucous in the House of Repre-sentatives and in the American press, yet without any tangible con-sequences for Britain.[150] The German claim that Britain had ordered her merchant marine to use neutral flags in the war zone had become fact, certified by one of the highest officials of the U.S. government.

The first submarine to patrol the newly declared war zone left Ems on February 11ᵗʰ 1915. *U-30* under Lieutenant Commander von Rosenberg-Gruszczynski crossed the Channel at Dover and reached the patrol area on the 17ᵗʰ. Another gas-powered sub, the *U-16* under Captain Claus Hansen, had taken position in the Channel on February 1ˢᵗ. On the February 16ᵗʰ *U-16* torpedoed the British Collier *Dulwich* off the coast of France, giving the crew time to launch lifeboats.[151] Han-sen blew up the small French steamer, *Ville de Lille*, a day later. The German commander meticulously followed search and seizure pro-cedures as mandated by international law, even towing the lifeboats with the crew to the coast.[152] Another French steamer, the *Dinorah*, suffered damages from a torpedo on the 18ᵗʰ. This time, in accordance with the new orders, the *U-16* attacked without warning.

The first potentially serious mistake occurred on the follow-ing day, when Captain Hansen failed to properly identify his target and torpedoed the 9,000-ton Norwegian steamer *Belridge*. The Stan-dard Oil Corporation tanker transported oil from the United States to the Netherlands.[153] Luckily for Germany, no one was injured in the attack and the steamer beached itself before it could sink. However, the impracticality of the German admiralty's orders not to harm neu-tral ships now showed the first result. Germany quickly admitted to the mistake and committed to paying for the damages to the ship in order to quell public attention.[154] A mistake it was! According to the files of Heinrich Albert, the *Belridge* served as a blockade-runner for his office since the fall of 1914 and carried benzene (gas) for the

German government.[155] *U-30* also scored hits on February 20th, sinking two English freighters without warning.[156] *U-8*, under Lieutenant Commander Stoss, which left on February 16th, destroyed five steamers in the shipping lanes between Dover and Calais. It sank on that voyage after hitting a mine. *U-6*, another gas-powered boat returned home after it suffered damage from a ramming by a freighter it had attacked.[157] Despite the bad winter weather, which forced *U-30*, in particular, to abandon targets and submerge for the rough sea to pass, the four submarines scored one sinking per day since the campaign began.

The German submarine fleet, consisting of fourteen boats, entered the theater of war full force in the month of March.[158] *U-12* sank after the British cruiser *HMS Ariel* rammed it. *U-17* suffered mechanical damage from a wave and had to return to port. *U-37* disappeared without a trace after damaging one steamer and sinking two others. *U-29* sank on March 26th without survivors after the British armored cruiser *HMS Dreadnought* rammed it. The British media noted with enthusiasm that justice had been done, since the commander of the *U -29* was Otto Weddingen, who had sunk the three British cruisers in the beginning of the war. *U-33* barely escaped a ramming attempt after it stopped a British freighter under observance of 'cruiser rules.' *U-28* sank the British cargo-passenger steamer SS *Falaba* on March 28th, causing the first American submarine casualty of the war, the thirty-one year-old mining engineer of Massachusetts, Leon Thrasher. One hundred-four of the 242 passengers, including Thrasher, drowned. According to the German government, the *U-28* had signaled the *Falaba* to stop. The steamer, however, attempted to flee and signaled nearby British warships for help. The *U-28* then torpedoed the ship.[159] The cargo contained munitions, an absolute contraband. Whether or not the German version of events was true, the sinking took place well within the confines of international law. The presence of enemy warships likely caused the U-boat captain to abandon plans for time-consuming rescue operations. One of the surviving passengers shot a host of photographs documenting the tragic end of the ship. The pictures wound their way onto the front pages of American dailies, bringing home the brutality of Germany's naval war, an ever-growing public relations fiasco.[160] The U-boat fleet sank thirty-six ships in that month alone, amounting to 79,000 GRT with six ships damaged, amounting to 22,000 GRT.[161] The use of neutral flags by British and French shipping, the losses, especially of the valuable diesel-powered *U-29* and *U-37*, and the ramming attempt from a stopped freighter all contributed to snuffing out the last remaining efforts to respect cruiser rules.

The submarine which sank the *Falaba*

The campaign proceeded full steam in April 1915. Thirty-seven ships – seventeen British, three French, three Russian, and eight neutrals (no American) – with absolute or conditional contraband sank after U-boat attacks. Two freighters, one French and one British, suffered damages but could be hauled into safety. One British and three neutral freighters were captured and hauled into German harbors for prize court proceedings, in which a panel of judges decided on the distribution of the captured ships and property. The submarine campaign thus destroyed 62,000 GRT and damaged 11,000 GRT in April, using fifteen submarines, of which thirteen were equipped with ocean-going diesel engines and tanks.[162] The rapid increase of diesel-powered boats particularly alarmed the British war planners. Despite the raw number showing less than one percent of shipping vessels in and out of England being physically attacked, the psychological effects on seamen and neutral shippers began to show. A growing number of ocean carriers refused to take on freight destined for the war zone. Seamen, as well, rather switched to shipping lines not involved European trade.

The First Sealord of the Admiralty, Winston S. Churchill, proposed to arm the merchant marine to defend against submarine attacks in response to the German aggression. This proposal further sealed the decision of the German admiralty that traditional search and seizure procedures could not be followed in the case of a submarine. Once surfaced, these vessels had little chance of defending their vulnerable hulls against ramming, machine gun, or cannon fire. The German 'hardliners' in the submarine debate, especially the commander of the submarine fleet, Hermann Bauer, demanded that restrictions on targeting, such as excluding neutral vessels, would be dropped. He cited the British policies of ramming, false flagging, and now arming of merchant vessels as the justification.

The opposite happened. After accidentally sinking a Dutch steamer, *Katwyk*, in the declared war zone in April, the German government acknowledged the mistake and committed to paying for the damages. A new order went to the submarine command: "For political reasons it will be necessary for the time being to try to spare neutrals in the submarine war. Special care should be taken with respect to Dutch ships, since the Dutch public is very irritated as a result of the sinking of the *Katwyk*. Please, give orders to the submarines in accordance."[163] Bauer refused to forward the order to his fleet. Political wrangling followed, even an attempt to fire the commander. However, in the end, he survived his insubordination to the civilian leadership of the empire.[164]

This episode illustrates the increasing divergence between the military war planners and the civilian government of Germany, and particularly the growing power of the hardliner group. Any watering down of the rules of engagement, to them, meant a weakening of the already scarce resources available for the submarine war. This faction within the German leadership resented the order to spare neutral ships.[165] Bauer's insubordination, in this case, illustrates that as early as the spring of 1915, the German navy pursued her own strategy in the commerce war, one that did not fear an entry of the United States into the war, but one that eventually caused exactly that. Bauer was not fired precisely because the highest echelons of the navy leadership agreed with his action.

The struggle for a unified war strategy within the German leadership may have found its most inhumane expression on May 7th 1915. The British government had tightened the sea blockade of Germany in response to the German commerce war, and instituted very effective measures against submarines. British harbors and narrows received steel nets and other submarine warning systems. Mine fields limited access to wide approaches into British shipping lanes. The use of false flagging, the order for merchant marine skippers to ram submarines, the arming of merchant ships, and the introduction of decoy ships all forced the German submariners to abandon any search and seizure proceedings according to cruiser rules. Remaining submerged, U-boat commanders had much more difficulty in properly identifying their targets, which led to either abandoning attacks or committing mistakes such as attacking the *Belridge* and *Katwyk*. The German submarine, *U-30*, torpedoed the American tanker *Gulflight* on May 1st 1915, causing the death of two crew members and, indirectly, that of the captain who died of a heart attack. Two British patrol boats had escorted the *Gulflight*. As a result, even the British admiralty had to conclude that this fact made the freighter a legitimate target under international law. The German government apologized to the United States for the attack but did not agree to pay for damages. The incident added to the bad press in the United States.

British propaganda cunningly extolled German barbarian submarine commanders sinking commercial ships without warning in the American press. Images of helpless civilians drowning in the cold depths of the Atlantic Ocean combined with statistics claiming that the German campaign had no real effect on the war. Much of this propaganda found its way as fact into history books up to the present day. Defiantly, the English passenger lines such as White Star and Cunard advertised "safe" transatlantic travel on board of their fast ocean liners that could "easily escape any U-boat" attack. Indeed, a fast-traveling ocean liner of the time topping twenty-five knots and using the evading tactic of zigzagging would be nearly impervious to a submarine attack. The British press and propaganda in the United States flaunted the *Lusitania* and the uninterrupted transatlantic service to England and thereby dared Germany to do anything about it. The British propaganda cited the *Lusitania* as a formidable example of why the German submarine campaign was so ineffective. German officials in New York could literally see the liner arrive and depart on schedule from their lower Manhattan offices while the HAPAG flag-ship *Vaterland* and a dozen other German super liners rusted at their piers. Much like Islamic extremists viewed the World Trade Center as a symbol of American power, Germans in New York perceived the great British ship as a symbol of the British supremacy of the sea and thus a target of great psychological importance.

German agents had carefully observed the comings and goings of British passenger liners from New York since the onset of the war. German secret agent Paul Koenig issued regular lists provided by informants in the New York customs department, among others, of contraband freight loaded on passenger ships. Heinrich Albert noted in his diary in February, "Shurz ./. Lusit. Armed – Malone."[166] It is unknown whether the cryptic notation meant that Albert had received information as to armaments on the *Lusitania* from Dudley Field Malone, the Collector of the Port of New York whom Albert con-sidered pro-German, or whether he intended to approach him with that information to take action against the ocean liner. The second possibility seems more likely since Malone later testified that there were no gun emplacements on the ship. However, as the *RMS Lusita-nia* readied herself for a return voyage to the United States, German agents might have suspected that she would be converted to an aux-iliary cruiser while in port in Britain.

The importance of this notation is the fact that the day before the official start of the German submarine campaign, Albert and his agents eyed the *RMS Lusitania*, the largest and one of five four-fun-neled British ocean liners in service at the time, with more than casual interest.[167] Just a week prior, American newspapers had reported the false flagging incident witnessed by Edward House. A British liner hav-ing carried contraband on many of her recent voyages, and listed in British naval registers as a potential auxiliary cruiser, she was a target for the German navy. Indeed, she represented a prize of highest sig-nificance, one that would show the world that the German submarine fleet had the means and resolve to stop traffic to the British Isles. The May 12th 1915 issue of the *Fatherland* voiced the German desire to see the large passenger liner sunk. "Before long, a large passenger ship like the *Lusitania*, carrying implements of murder to Great Britain, will meet with a similar fate [as the *Gulflight*]…"[168] When the paper went on sale in the newsstands, the dire forecast had already become reality.

Already in March 1915, the voyage after the highly publicized flag ruse with Colonel House on board, the submarine *U-27* lay in wait in the transatlantic shipping lane off Liverpool. Captain Wegener of the *U-27* logged in his war diary: "The *Lusitania* was expected to arrive in English waters on 4 March and in my present position I believed I had a good chance of attacking her."[169] The specter of losing one of the large ocean liners to submarine attack did not go unnoticed in the press. The *New York Times* reported as early as February 21st, "... the sinking of the British steamer *Cambank* was not in itself a serious matter, but the presence of a German submarine near the route which the Atlantic liners take on their way to and from Liverpool, and along which many steamers pass daily, is bound to cause uneasiness..."[170] The Cunarder was as appealing to German hardliners in the spring of 1915 as the World Trade Center in New York was to Al Qaeda in the decade leading up to its destruction.

On May 1st, the same day *U-30* torpedoed the American tanker *Gulflight*, the Cunard passenger liner, *RMS Lusitania*, readied herself in New York for the 202nd transatlantic crossing. She was the largest and fastest ship on the transatlantic circuit at the time, crossing the great divide between the United States and Europe in slightly less than five days.[171] Ostensibly believing that the "American Government... still underestimated the dangers of the situation, and failed to take any measure of precaution," Ambassador Count Bernstorff is credited with issuing a stern warning to potential passengers traveling on British ocean liners, which appeared in the *New York Times* on May 1st.[172]

Confronted with the warning, the Cunard Line press agent, Charles Sumner, tried his best to dispel the fear. "No passenger is permitted aboard them [Cunard Line ships] unless he can identify himself... Every passenger must identify his baggage before it is placed aboard. There are no German cruisers in the Atlantic, and the 'danger zone' does not begin until we reach the British Channel and the Irish Sea. Then one may say there is a general system of convoying British ships. The British Navy is responsible for all British ships, and especially for Cunarders." The journalist then asked: "Your speed, too, is a safeguard, is it not?"... "Yes [Sumner answered]; as for submarines, I have no fear of them whatever."[173] The *Lusitania* would neither travel at her full speed of twenty-five knots nor would she receive a British naval escort in the danger zone. She cleared pier 54 in New York on May 1st around noon with 1,257 passengers and 702 crew members on board. Only a handful of passengers had opted out of the voyage as a result of the published warning and sailed with slower and less luxurious neutral passenger ships.[174] The *Lusitania* carried over 4,200 cases of small arms munitions, 1,000 rounds each, and 1,250 cases of empty shrapnel casings in her hold, considered absolute contraband by all warring parties.[175]

The New York Times, May 1, 1915

Walter Schwieger who commanded the U-20 in May 1915. He died in September 1917
after having sunk 190,000 GRT of Allied shipping.[176]

Whether to save money (Cunard's explanation) or because the naval war caused a shortage of willing trimmers and firemen (Boy-Ed's explanation), the *Lusitania* only fired three of her four boilers. The German submarine *U-20* under the command of the thirty year-old Walter Schwieger cruised near the Old Head of Kinsale on May 6th heading to a station off Liverpool with orders to "sink troop trans-porters."[177] He sank the British steamers, *Centurion* and *Candidate*, two cargo ships, without warning. Two other submarines, the *U-30* and the *U-27* had orders to the same effect with stations hundreds of miles away off Dartmouth and the Bristol Channel, respectively.[178] Despite specific warnings sent to the *Lusitania* after the *U-20* attacks on May 6th to watch for submarines off the Old Head of Kinsale, her Captain, Bill Turner, steered the Cunarder straight into the channel at reduced speed. He did not follow his orders for evasive measures, such as zig-zagging and using speed as the most effective means to lose a stalking submarine traveling at fifteen knots. Additionally, the thick fog on the morning of May 7th caused the *Lusitania* to sound her fog horns "once every minute," broadcasting her approach for miles.[179]

A chain of unfortunate events unfolded that, in combination, brought the *Lusitania* into the fateful contact with Schwieger's *U-20*. Around 1:40 pm on May 7th, Schwieger launched a torpedo from 700 meters (2,100 feet) distance at the ocean liner. The impact under the bridge on starboard created an explosion, followed by another even more massive than the first. The forward movement of the ship caused an almost immediate list and submersion. Captain Schwieger described the scene in his war diary:

> Clear bow shot at 700 [meters]... Shot struck starboard side close behind the bridge. An extraordinarily heavy detonation followed, with a very large cloud of smoke (far above the front funnel). A second explosion must have followed that of the torpedo (boiler or coal or powder?)... The ship stopped immediately and quickly listed sharply to starboard, sinking deeper by the head at the same time. It appeared as if it would capsize in a short time. Great confusion arose on the ship; some of the boats were swung clear and lowered into the water... Many people must have lost their heads; several boats loaded with people rushed downward, struck the water bow or stern first and filled at once... The ship blew off steam; at the bow the name *Lusitania* in golden letters was visible. The funnels were painted black; stern flag not in place. It was running 20 nautical miles. Since it seemed as if the steamer could only remain above water for a short time, went to 24

m. [meters] and ran toward the Sea. Nor could I have fired a second torpedo into this swarm of people who were trying to save themselves.[180]

The mortally wounded super liner disappeared below the waves of the Atlantic Ocean after only eighteen minutes. Of the 1,959 passengers and crew on board, 1,198 perished in the ice-cold Irish Sea. One hundred twenty-eight of the victims were Americans. The international outrage over the senseless killing of civilians, many of them women and children, overshadowed any previous disagreements with the German conduct of the war. Spontaneous demonstrations against Germany broke out in New York and other large cities. The newspapers, filled with pictures of scores of caskets and eyewitness accounts, decried the barbarity of the German action. The large secondary explosion that hastened the demise of the ocean liner remains one of the hotly debated topics of the sinking. German propaganda immediately alleged that munitions and explosives aboard the ship caused the explosion. British propaganda alleged that multiple torpedoes were fired while passengers were trying to save themselves. Neither allegation was true.

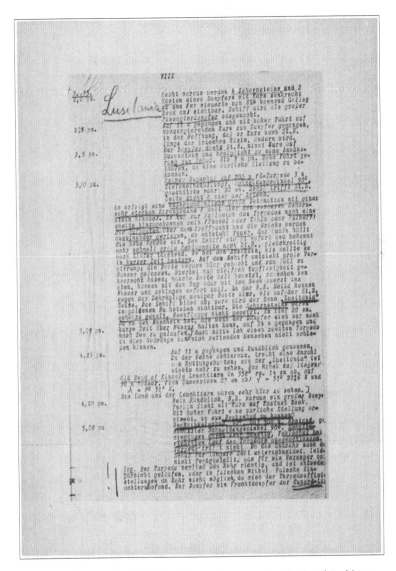

Excerpt from Walter Schwieger's war diary, courtesy National Archives, Naval Records Collection of the Office of Naval Records and Library.[181]

Courtesy of the Library of Congress, Prints and Photographs Division, Washington, D.C.

Scientists have inspected the wreckage in recent years and documented that a large boiler explosion or the combustion of coal dust in a forward compartment completed the destruction of the ship.

Karl Boy-Ed wrote in retrospect in 1920, "... the psychological impression of the *Lusitania* sinking on the seafaring English population was minimal... Despite the 5,400 cases of ammunition it would have undoubtedly been better for the German cause, if the chance meeting of the *U-20* with the *Lusitania* had not occurred, or if fate would have let the torpedo pass by her."[182] Boy-Ed's post war analysis cannot cover up his support of the naval strategy in 1915 and 1916. His role in New York places him at the center of the theory that the sinking of the British liner was a premeditated attack. There is some evidence of a concerted naval conspiracy leading up to the sinking of the ship. Since the beginning of the commerce war in February the German navy planned and actively pursued the sinking of the *Lusitania*. The publication in the *New York Times* of the warning on the day when the *Lusitania* sailed for Europe has confounded conspiracy theorists for nearly a hundred years. One of the most important unanswered questions to support or unhinge the charge of premeditation is whether the embassy warning on May 1st 1915 originated in the naval chain of command or in the Foreign Office. If it originated anywhere but in the

Foreign Office, the military authorities in Germany who were planning the attack on the *Lusitania* likely ordered its publication.

Heinrich Albert referenced his authorship of the note in a letter to the German Interior Secretary Delbrück three days after the sinking. "I am mentioning the warning also for personal reasons since I proposed it and worked out all the details."[183] Albert reported to several authorities. He filed regular reports to Rudolph Nadolny, the chief of the intelligence division of the German General Staff, *Abteilung IIIB*. Albert's relationship with the German naval intelligence, *Nachrichten-abteilung N* is less defined other than he was a conduit on some financial matters concerning naval missions. There are no sources explaining who ordered Albert (or approved his suggestion) to draft the warning. Neither Heinrich Albert's diary nor any statement attributed to Bernhard Dernburg, Franz von Papen, or Karl Boy-Ed allows a conclusion. Ambassador Count Bernstorff's recollection, being the one that officially 'initiated' the publication of the warning, clearly attributes the origin of the idea to Dernburg, not Albert. "In the middle of April I held a meeting in New York, with the representatives of the other German administrative departments, and in view of the great responsibility incumbent on us, we resolved on the motion of Dr. Dernburg to issue a warning to the Press..."[184]

However, the meeting likely never took place. Albert and Alexander Fuehr's diaries that meticulously recorded meetings with Ambassador Count Bernstorff did not contain references to such a meeting anytime in April.[185] An important fact that will be discussed later is even more ominous: Dernburg was in personal contact with Admiral Henning von Holtzendorff around this time on the matter of causing an incident along the Mexican-American border.[186] He was a staunch supporter of unrestricted submarine warfare, and publicly welcomed the sinking of the *Lusitania*. The highest ranking German official in New York, he was head of propaganda, and a clear supporter of a hardline strategy against the U.S. Dernburg was the man who would have known about the planned attack and who would have proposed or supported a proposal to issue a warning to keep Americans off the liner.

Boy-Ed's categorical denial to have had any knowledge of the existence of the warning until April 23rd is also suspicious.[187] As a matter of fact, Boy-Ed was a member of the Secret War Council, and as naval attaché he would have had to sign off on the publication of the note. It was dated April 22nd and transmitted to New York on that date.[188] Albert's diaries show that he had almost daily meetings with Boy-Ed around that time, even joined him on April 16th for a lecture on submarines.[189] Count Bernstorff provides an explanation why the warning originated with him and not the Consulate General, which would have been the agency for issuing such a publication. Keeping in mind the hostile relationship between Boy-Ed, Dernburg, and Albert with Consul Hossenfelder, it appears that Boy-Ed went straight to the ambassador with a suspicious sense of urgency.

The circumstantial evidence supporting a concerted navy effort to sink the *Lusitania* on her 202nd voyage is overwhelming: The *Lusitania* represented a target that German officials publicly talked about. *U-27* actively tried to sink the liner a month earlier. *U-20* was sent into the shipping lane of the *Lusitania* in the week she was to cross with orders to sink "troop transporters," which included large liners. The Dernburg office in New York, filled with supporters of the unrestricted submarine campaign, not the German embassy, initiated the publication of a warning to appear only on May 1st 1915, the departure day of the *Lusitania*, and only in New York papers.[190] The American press also interpreted the warning as being directed specifically to *Lusitania* passengers. The *Washington Times* wrote prophetically on May 1st: "*Lusitania's* Passengers Warned of Ship's Doom."[191]

The counter argument, namely that the sinking occurred as the result of a host of circumstances that could not have been planned, is weak. Any such project requires luck. It is reasonable to assume, however, that the tremendous loss of life caused by the rapid sinking of the ship had not been intended. Sabotage agent Franz Rintelen told a B.I. agent in New York what many German officials likely believed, "… it was never intended that those on board the *Lusitania* should have been drowned as they believed under any conditions that the *Lusitania* would stay afloat for four or five hours at the least, and that all of these people would be rescued."[192]

Defining the German strategy as one designed to decimate the cargo capacity of the world's merchant marine through destruction, the German campaign showed disappointing results. With only one U-boat on average patrolling per day, eleven ships with a total of 22,184 GRT (Gross Register Tons) were sunk in the last ten days of February 1915.[193] A total of 2,855 freighters had arrived or sailed from British ports in the time period between February 18th and the 28th, more than 6,000 in the month of March.[194] The record improved somewhat through the remainder of 1915 with 715,997 GRT sunk in the Atlantic theatre.[195] However, even this significant number had yet to show a perceptible impact on the volume of British sea trade.[196] Interestingly, only thirty-six percent of the destroyed ships had been torpedoed without warning.[197] The German submarine forces sank on average 3,100 GRT per day with an average of 3.5 boats on patrol in 1915. The estimated global merchant marine registered about 35 Million GRT, of which two percent fell victim to the U-boat.[198] Also, the number of casualties as a result of submarine torpedoes paled in comparison with that of a single day of battle on the western front.

Still, it would be presumptuous for a historian to conclude that the German naval leaders had thus presided over a disastrous and ineffective strategy. Clearly, the German admiralty knew that they had only a handful of U-boats in service, which they rather would have saved from likely destruction instead of trying to destroy the global merchant marine.[199] In his memoirs, the commander of the submarine forces, Hermann Bauer, quoted his top-secret plan for a sea blockade of England dated December 27th 1914. The plan listed the strategic goals of Germany's commerce war using four U-boats on patrol on average per day: "... Deterrence and as a result reduction [of the merchant traffic to and from England] and... increased cost through forcing uneconomical routes and high insurance premiums."[200]

The effects of the German campaign in the spring and summer of 1915 supported Bauer's claims, showing immediate and resounding results. Insurance premiums for neutral shippers skyrocketed. Shipping lines stopped service or re-directed business to less risky markets such as Africa, Asia, and South America. According to Hermann Bauer,

> 130 ships lay moored in English harbors [in March 1915] with the crews refusing to report to work. 19 British steamlines [sic] ceased operation completely, 42 other companies offered only limited service. The traffic of the Nordic empires [i.e. Scandinavia] to the east coast of England stopped altogether. Also some Dutch shipping lines had interrupted their voyages for the time being... Although initially there was no talk of scarcity

the prices of wheat, flower and sugar rose between 43 to 75 percent... [201]

While Bauer's numbers could be inflated, several studies of retail price development in Britain show a significant jump of twenty to thirty nine percent between 1914 and 1915.[202] Much of this effect must be credited to the submarine campaign of 1915. Historian Koerver, although decidedly convinced that the unrestricted submarine war of the German empire was a failure, characterized the true strength of the U-boat weapon as follows:

> The danger of the merchant war was less founded in the general reduction of the world tonnage... It was more dangerous because it tried to squeeze in a short period and in a determined place the economic Aorta of Britain... And it was costly to defend one's Achilles' heel. The Germans themselves were the first to experience it. A handful of British submarines were operating in the Baltic [Sea] in 1915 and 1916... More than 200 drifters, armed trawlers and old torpedoboats [sic], manned by 5,000 men, were needed in defence [sic] against 5-7 British submarines... [203]

Whether the German submarine campaign was a failure is not an easy question to answer. While statistically destroying a minute fraction of ocean traffic, the campaign triggered costly and time-consuming security checks in all U.S. harbors, increased insurance rates, and slowed down loading of freighters. Freight cost, passage fares, and other logistics costs rose dramatically. Available charter capacity declined sharply, while the freight rates increased. The economic impact of the attacks proved to be significant, yet difficult to clearly delineate. The lack of clear delineation provides the opportunities for analysts to find arguments supporting both sides of the question of effectiveness.

The German supporters of unrestricted submarine warfare certainly took into account the possibility of losing the battle for public sympathy in the United States. They did not care. Frederico Stallforth explained the general feeling of Germany's public opinion about the sinking of the *Lusitania*: "...the German Admiralty thought that the greatest demonstration of the efficiency of the U-boat as a weapon of war could be the sinking of the *Lusitania*, but the English claimed it could not be sunk by a submarine due to its speed, and that Captain Turner of the *Lusitania* had boasted before he left New York that his boat could not be destroyed in that way. There were warnings sent out from some source ... it was likely that the boat was going to be sunk... the truth was that the U-boats were looking out for it [the *Lusitania*].[204] A service clerk who worked in the Hotel Astor at the time testified, "Summerfeld [sic] appeared very elated and expressed the hope that Germany would win..."[205] Heinrich Albert wrote to his direct superior, Secretary of the Interior Clemens von Delbrück, on May 10th 1915: "...the *Lusitania* case is from a military- naval perspective one of the most significant victories we have achieved. Despite the hostile atmosphere I can currently conduct my work with a lightened heart."[206] A potential entry of the United States into the war as a result of the submarine campaign not only factored into the calculation but was considered desirable and purposefully provoked. Bauer wrote in his top-secret plan for a blockade under the heading "Amerika," "An unbearable economic crisis which our U-boat blockade will cause with certainty could drive America into an intervention against us. This intervention.... would... be without deciding military influence on the war."[207] Albert seconded his opinion in the previously quoted letter to Secretary of the Interior Delbrück:

> Under no circumstances should we go any further than express our purely humanitarian regret over the loss of life of non-combatants and of Americans... we have to avoid under all circumstances... any excuse for the issue [of unrestricted submarine warfare]... and leave no doubt about the fact that we feel completely justified to conduct submarine warfare and will continue pursuing it. The submarine war is the <u>only</u> [original underline] possibility to defeat England.[208]

Bauer and the naval chain of command above him, as well as the American team of Albert, Dernburg, von Papen, and Boy-Ed, strongly believed that an unmerciful submarine campaign could fulfill what was the worst nightmare for the British war planners. They believed that stopping supplies from the United States to England was crucial to a successful turnaround for Germany on the battlefields of Europe. Despite huge efforts in the spring of 1915, supplying intelligence, begging for funding, and emphasizing the scant successes of their efforts, the hardliners in the German government could not convince the decision makers, most notably Emperor Wilhelm II and Chancellor von Bethmann Hollweg to follow their recommendations. It is with this background that the sinking of the *Lusitania* took on such importance.

Only a cataclysmic event such as this and a *fait accompli* such as a U.S. declaration of war could force a clear decision on whether to pursue a hardline war strategy or whether to waffle and bend to public pressures. An entry of the United States into the war, therefore, did not deter the military authorities in Germany from pursuing an aggressive strategy. On the contrary, they tried to clear the deck for an all-or-nothing military war strategy. The German General Staff had authorized sabotage acts against U.S. munitions plants and shipments of contraband in the end of January.[209] The submarine war against merchant shipping started in February. Large sums of money suddenly appeared at the doorstep of the Albert organization in March. Several teams of sabotage agents, most notably Franz Rintelen, landed on the shores of the United States armed with germs, explosives, and money in April. Despite the international outcry, despite the diplomatic wrangling that followed the sinking of the *Lusitania* in May, and despite the attempts of the moderate forces of the German government to stop it, the war against the United States was already in full swing.

CHAPTER 6: "THE DARK INVADER" ARRIVES

THE SS *CHRISTIANIAFORD* DISCHARGED THE self-styled "dark invader" on April 3rd 1915. He was Lieutenant Commander of the Reserves and German naval intelligence officer Franz Rintelen.[210] Five feet, eight inches, 155 pounds, "smooth, oblong face, high forehead, light hair, light blue eyes, light erect carriage, quick actions, speaks with decided German accent, dapper appearance," he entered the U.S. with a false Swiss passport issued to Emile Victor Gasché.[211] The name came from his younger sister Emilia Fischer Gasché, who lived in Berlin and was married to Navy Lieutenant Robert Fischer.[212] Rintelen's mission was to take over the foundering sabotage projects of Franz von Papen and prevent the shipment of munitions "by all [legal] means available."[213] The trained banker was neither a nobleman, as he and subsequent historians portrayed him, nor did he have much experience in intelligence matters. He was highly ambitious, spoke English fluently, albeit with a German accent, and had a host of connections within banking circles in the United States and Latin America. The German admiralty considered him a go-getter, and that seemed to be what they needed in the war against the United States.

Franz Dagobert Johannes Rintelen was born on August 19th 1878 in Frankfurt on the Oder. His influential father, Councilor Friedrich Ferdinand Rintelen, greatly influenced Franz' character development, career, and later life.[214] A well-respected judge, parliamentarian, and director of the Deutsche Bank, Friedrich Rintelen fathered nine children: seven boys and two girls, with his only wife, Adelheid. Franz, one of the younger siblings, grew up in a cultured and wealthy home. Not much is known about the relationship between him and his parents. An ambitious and respected Prussian administrator, Friedrich Rintelen was a towering figure of authority in Franz' youth. His mother was twenty-six, when he was born, while Friedrich Rintelen was in his forties.

Franz Rintelen's passport photo in 1915. He grew the mustache just for the picture.[215]

After finishing high school with a baccalaureate in 1897, Franz joined the Imperial Navy as an officer. It is unclear whether he participated in the expedition to put down the Boxer Rebellion in China in 1900 or not. Rintelen resided in the United States as a naval reserve officer from October 1904 to June 1905.[216] He indicated on the immigration documents that he was a merchant. Money did not seem to be in short supply for the twenty-six year old. He traveled first cabin and stayed in New York's Waldorf Astoria before he went on to Philadelphia.[217] There he stayed in the household of James Francis Sullivan, the president of Philadelphia's Market Street National Bank, an influential industrialist and friend of the Rintelen family.[218] The young banker courted Sullivan's daughter, Lita (one of four siblings), "but was rejected."[219] Rintelen maintained a close friendship with her brother R. Livingston Sullivan, despite the rejection of the latter's younger sibling. Rintelen, probably through Sullivan's sponsorship, became a member of the prestigious New York Yacht Club in 1906.[220]

Upon his return to Germany, Rintelen joined the Deutsche Bank in Berlin, where his father was a director. Through the Deutsche Bank, Rintelen returned to the United States sometime in the winter of 1905 or in the spring of 1906 and stayed in New York until May.[221] His friend and banking colleague, George Plochmann, testified that Rintelen worked for the commercial bank Kuhn, Loeb and Co. in Manhattan on that visit.[222] Under the chairmanship of Hans Jacob Schiff, Kuhn, Loeb and Company had become one of the most powerful investment banks in the United States. It had financed the expansion of railroads and establishment of some of the most powerful American companies. As Kuhn, Loeb and Company was the largest competitor of J. P. Morgan and Co., Schiff and his son-in-law, Max Warburg, supported the commercial efforts of the German empire. Morgan became the financier of Entente purchases in the U.S. during the war.

According to Sullivan, Rintelen was charged with opening a branch of the Diskonto Gesellschaft in New York, but failed.[223] The Diskonto Gesellschaft Berlin was a large commercial bank with far-reaching international connections and business, in addition to being a fierce competitor of the Deutsche Bank. Whether he worked at Kuhn, Loeb and Co. while he tried to establish representation for this bank, or before he failed to do so, is not clear. After he returned to Germany, he joined the home office of the Diskonto Gesellschaft where he climbed the corporate ladder.[224] Rintelen appears as the Prokurist of the bank in 1909, equivalent to the controller in a modern corporation.[225] This position represented a highly successful banking career for a thirty year-old. The ambitious banker made his next career move in 1912 and joined the Board of Directors of a smaller, yet rapidly growing commercial bank, the Nationalbank für Deutschland.[226] He remained a member on the board of directors until 1920. He was disappointed, however, when the board dropped him a year before he returned to Germany from incarceration in the U.S. because of his wartime activities. The Admiralty listed him "missing" in 1915. One of his most hurtful experiences when he returned in 1921 was that he seemed to have been all but forgotten.[227]

While he pursued his career in banking and international finance, the fanatically nationalistic Rintelen also worked for the Deutscher Flottenverein (German Navy League) in charge of publicity.[228] This organization was a political arm of the navy designed to garner support for the large fleet expansion under Emperor Wilhelm II and his Secretary of the Navy, Grand Admiral Alfred von Tirpitz. Rintelen became acquainted with all the major players in the future war through this function, especially Secretary of the Navy, Grand Admiral von Tirpitz, Ambassador and later Foreign Secretary, Paul von Hintze, and the Naval Attaché in the United States, Karl Boy-Ed. Rintelen moved up in the naval ranks and, by the beginning of the war, had advanced to Lieutenant Commander of the Reserves. He spoke French and English as he wined and dined with the crème de la crème of Berlin society. His father's fortune, which likely had to be divided among the siblings, seemed to have been a nice foundation for his financial well-being. He built upon his inheritance with the high salary he earned as bank director. The worldly, thirty year-old banker married the daughter of a Jewish-German university professor, Emilie "Milly" von Kaufmann in 1909.[229] The couple had their only child, a daughter, the following year. Marie-Louise was Rintelen's pride and joy, later a source of the greatest pain in his coming incarceration.

At the outbreak of the war, Rintelen immediately joined the Imperial Admiralty as a financial expert. "On August 18, 1914 I was ordered to organize the supply of money for New York based on earlier agreements [with Kuhn, Loeb and Company to provide a loan for 100 Million]..."[230] He headed Department BT2 within the General Staff of the *Reichsmarineamt* (Admiralty) and reported directly to Grand Admiral von Tirpitz. His responsibilities not only extended to financing operations of the navy in the United States, but anywhere in the world. However, the naval attaché in the United States, Karl Boy-Ed, had the largest responsibility, namely supplying Germany's remaining fleet in the Atlantic and Pacific. Rintelen worked closely with Boy-Ed and his financial contacts in North and South America from the Admiralty headquarters in Berlin. Virtually all the funds Albert, Boy-Ed, and von Papen received in 1914 came from Rintelen in Berlin.[231] The most important contact for Rintelen became his former colleague in the Deutsche Bank and fellow intelligence agent, Hugo Schmidt. On orders of the Admiralty Schmidt had transferred significant funds all over the world as early as July 31st 1914, the day before Germany's declaration of war against Russia. In a top secret memorandum to Grand Admiral von Tirpitz Schmidt detailed, "we are honored to confirm to you that we... opened the following credits yesterday: ...1,000,000 Marks Rio de Janeiro... 1,000,000 Marks Buenos Aires... 500,000 Dutch ... Batavia... $250,000 via New York to Manila..."[232] On September 19th 1914, Rintelen informed his boss von Tirpitz, "... we have opened a credit of Mark 2,000,000 ... in Valparaiso [Chile]... "[233]

The Admiralty dispatched Schmidt to the United States in October 1914. His mission was to insure that subsequent money transfers, now organized by Rintelen, actually arrived at their destinations in New York, Mexico City, Caracas, Buenos Aires, and the Philippines. Schmidt quickly established a network of important financiers and businessmen, all engaged in knitting together a masterful web of international finance for blockade-running, propaganda, and sabotage projects. Dr. Hugo Schweitzer, who met Rintelen in August 1914 in Berlin, as he prepared to return to the U.S., not only carried instructions to the Secret War Council but also transferred $300,000 within the multiple Bayer Chemical Company's subsidiaries in North and South America to Karl Boy-Ed in New York.[234] Rintelen reimbursed the funds to Bayer from the Imperial War Department's treasury.[235] Using funds of his former employer, the Diskonto Gesellschaft, Rintelen transferred $250,000 to G. Amsinck and Company on August 22nd and September 1st 1914 via the National City Bank in New York.[236] All transfers had to be confirmed with Secretary of the Navy, Grand Admiral von Tirpitz, thus documenting the important position Rintelen held within the German military leadership. Schmidt transferred another $500,000 to G. Amsinck and Company in New York on August 24th 1914 per Rintelen's instructions. Schmidt wrote, "Your Excellency [von Tirpitz], we are honored to tell you that we transferred the amount of U.S. $500,000 to the firm Amsinck and Co. [sic], New York via telegraph based on the verbal instructions of lieutenant commander Rintelen."[237] These were the initial funds with which Heinrich Albert established the Secret War Council. Rintelen sent $1,000,000 directly to Karl Boy-Ed from the German Reichsbank via the New York banking house of J. and W. Seligman and Co. on September 12th 1914, thus funding the supply operation of the German naval assets in the Atlantic and Pacific.[238]

Gustav B. Kuhlenkampf, the U.S. manager of a commodity brokerage firm based in Bremen, also transferred funds to New York for Rintelen.[239] Some of the funds came through Kuhlenkampf to Speyer and Company, where the German embassy kept accounts.[240] The German broker was best friends with Frederico Stallforth. Through this connection, Stallforth met Hugo Schmidt, who hired him as a financial advisor in the fall of 1914. George Plochmann, another banking contact Rintelen had in the United States, worked as treasurer for the Transatlantic Trust Company, an Austrian investment bank. Both Plochmann and Rintelen claimed that they knew each other from times past, which is possible but not documented. According to the banker, they "worked together in a London bank."[241] They met again in New York in 1905, when Rintelen "worked in the office of Kuhn, Loeb and Co. learning the banking business. He remained in New York ... until about 1907..."[242] There is no independent archival evidence supporting any of Plochmann's claims. They certainly could have met in 1905 or 1906, when Rintelen was in the U.S. Rintelen definitely worked with Plochmann when he transferred money to North and South America in the summer and fall of 1914. This seems to be the obvious connection between the two. Once in New York, Rintelen sublet offices first with George Plochmann at the Transatlantic Trust Company and then, starting in June 1915, with Frederico Stallforth.

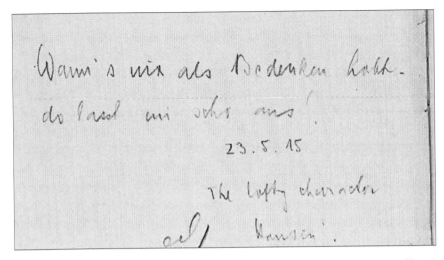

"[in Bavarian dialect] If you all have nothing but worries, then you will achieve nothing."
Diary of Frederico Stallforth, entry signed "The lofty character Hansen [Rintelen]."
(Picture courtesy Prevo Collection) [243]

While Rintelen played a pivotal role in the financial dealings of the Department of the Navy, there are indications that the position he held caused him to overestimate his power. After all, he had the rank of *Korvettenkapitän* (Lieutenant Commander), a few stripes in a forest of the highest navy brass of the country. Most notable are tensions between Max Warburg, Albert Ballin, and Rintelen. A large loan was at issue, which former Colonial Secretary and member of the Secret War Council, Bernhard Dernburg, negotiated in August 1914 with Warburg and his corresponding bank in New York, Kuhn, Loeb and Co. Through the transfer of funds within HAPAG, Dernburg only received a mere $400,000 at a very unfavorable interest rate of six percent, for which he had to commit treasuries worth twenty-five million German marks as security. This negotiation, which Albert characterized a disaster (in addition to the exorbitant interest rates and securities he could only access half of this expensive credit line), took place not only between Dernburg, Ballin, and Warburg, but was also conducted by Rintelen as the representative of the Admiralty. Probably with the applause of Dernburg and Albert, Rintelen accused Max Warburg's bank and Albert Ballin's HAPAG of ripping off the German government. He sent scathing messages to both financial tycoons personally, alleging unrealistic service charges, inflated exchange rates, and the like.[244] The "memo war" came to a head because Rintelen copied Secretary von Tirpitz on the letters. Grand Admiral von Tirpitz, watching budgets like a hawk, initially supported Rintelen's efforts. Warburg refused to cut his commissions after some back and forth, and Albert Ballin wrote an indignant rebuttal to von Tirpitz. Not surprisingly, the *Korvettenkapitän* lost the uneven match, causing a huge embarrassment for the Grand Admiral.[245]

Rintelen's activities at the Imperial navy headquarters bring other important facts to light. Undoubtedly, he was well acquainted with all the members of the Secret War Council in New York from the onset of the war. He was familiar with the tasks, finances, challenges, and personalities of the New York team. Karl Boy-Ed had been working closely with Rintelen right from the start of the war, maybe even before.[246] Rintelen fought Bernhard Dernburg's battles from his office in the navy headquarters. Heinrich Albert definitely knew of Rintelen and worked with him on the daunting task of *Geldbeschaffung* (fund-raising). Most likely, the two had met before Albert took his assignment in New York, based on Albert's instructions and Rintelen's position. The lieutenant commander reported directly to von Tirpitz. Despite boasts of knowing the Kaiser that sounded inflated to Americans in his social circle, he occupied a key position in the Admiralty. Through that he gained visibility into the highest echelons of the German government. Thus, it is no surprise that Rintelen, upon his arrival in the United States, activated the connections he had made in the earlier visits to the U.S., especially with the Sullivans. He had been a vital part of a financial network in Germany through his position at the Admiralty, which he now also leveraged in the U.S. to further his goals. It included Heinrich Albert, Karl Boy-Ed, Bernhard Dernburg, Hugo Schweitzer, George Plochmann, Frederico Stallforth, and Hugo Schmidt. The only person he did not seem to know, and who would become his nemesis in New York, as well as later in Germany, was Captain Franz von Papen, the German military attaché.

When he disembarked the SS *Christianiaford*, the thirty-six year-old agent was full of zest to "prevent or delay the exportation of materials of war, especially of munitions, by all means."[247] Excitedly, he related his interpretation of the instructions as "bomb, burn, and destroy" to anyone in the German community who wanted to listen.[248] The naval intelligence agent did not mention in his memoirs that his instructions also defined that he reported to the Secret War Council, specifically Karl Boy-Ed and Heinrich Albert. Rintelen also claimed that he carried with him a new edition of Germany's most secret code.[249] Along with many of the agent's claims, this one also belonged under the heading, 'probably not.' Rintelen was a high-ranking officer, known in political and military circles in Germany, who gave his residence in the ship manifest as "Berlin."[250] The risk of bringing Germany's most secret code to the U.S. via Rintelen would have been nothing short of reckless.

The 3rd of April, 1915 was the Saturday before Easter. According to Rintelen, nobody met him at the piers. Over a foot of snow had fallen that day, which might explain the lack of attention he received. The agent went straight to his friends, the Sullivans in Philadelphia, where he stayed over the Easter holidays until April 13th.[251] Rintelen met with German Ambassador Count Johann Heinrich von Bernstorff at the Ritz Carlton in New York on Wednesday, April 14th, "in mufti," since his suitcases had "gone astray."[252] Count Bernstorff denied knowledge of Rintelen's mission in his memoirs. The fact that the ambassador met with the agent immediately after his arrival proves the opposite, and attests to either an attempt by Count Bernstorff to influence Rintelen's mission or to show support. Count Bernstorff knew about Rintelen's arrival and his mission in either case. Rintelen also conferred with his superior, Naval Attaché Karl Boy-Ed, who invited him to dinner at the German Club in New York that same week.[253] The naval attaché had received instructions from Berlin on April 4th to "inform him [Rintelen] about Papen's proposals."[254] The German embassy in Washington received a similar wireless the next day, "Inform Boy-Ed as to Papen's proposals for transmission to Rintelen."[255] The two attachés in New York were obviously prepared for the arrival of the agent. Post-war investigators testified, "Boy-Ed then tells in some detail his relations with Rintelen who appeared at his office in New York 'at the beginning of April 1915'..."[256] He granted the agent access to $500,000, which came from money Rintelen had sent to the naval attaché in October 1914.[257] At that time, $1.2 Million had been reserved for the purchase of supplies for the remaining German fleet.[258]

Only a fraction of these funds were needed by December, since the majority of the German fleet had been obliterated in the Falklands. Rintelen also brought some money with him. He arrived with $8,485 ($178,000 in today's value) in cash from his superiors, which the agent deposited with Plochmann's Transatlantic Trust Company on April 7th.[259] Also during the first week of his arrival, he deposited $219,785 ($4.79 Million in today's value) in the Transatlantic Trust account "F. Rintelen" and $170,692 on the account of "E. V. Gibbons and Co."[260] Rintelen registered this dummy corporation as soon as he received the funds from Boy-Ed.[261] It is significant to note that Rintelen's funding came through the Admiralty and not the War Department. The German government tried to make the point in the latter 1920s that Rintelen's funds served purely commercial purposes, mainly to buy up munitions.[262] However, studying the funding of such projects, the Imperial Navy had not supplied any funds for market-cornering activities in the past. All market-cornering activities happened with money assigned by the War Department for such purposes, coded in Heinrich Albert's ledgers under the accounts von Papen I through von Papen V.[263] Rintelen's mission clearly was sensitive enough to completely stay out of Albert's bookkeeping. The German sabotage agent claimed to people like Frederico Stallforth, Felix Sommerfeld, and Dr. Walter Scheele that he had vastly larger funds at his disposal. Sommerfeld, for his part, was so impressed that he told investigators, "Hansen [alias Rintelen] had the powers of a chancellor and millions to spend if needed."[264] There is no indication that significantly larger funds were available. It is possible that Albert and Boy-Ed gave him the impression that the remainder of the $1.2 Million could be used if needed. However, considering the difficulties the Secret War Council faced in raising money for their projects, Rintelen's claims were simply self-aggrandizing exaggerations. He checked into the Great Northern Hotel on 57th Street, room 327, as Edward V. Gates on Monday, April 12th.[265] His mission had now begun in earnest.

A fuming military attaché, von Papen, dictated a scathing letter to the Chief of the General Staff Erich von Falkenhayn from his office in the Transatlantic Trust Building, a block down the street from Boy-Ed's office, probably after some frustrating sessions with an arrogant Rintelen.[266] The army captain vented his frustration quite directly after "thanking" the General for "at last" making a commitment to "curtail the supplies of war material for our enemies in every way possible [underline by author]:"[267] "As I gather from Mr. Rintelen's explanations that the army administration has sent him over here 'to bring order into the confused conditions and make positive proposals,' I beg to be allowed to submit very respectfully to your Excellency the following short exposition."[268] He continued listing all the proposals he and Albert had made to buy up munitions in the United States, and the lack of response from the General Staff. He accused the Army Chief of Staff of having procrastinated until the American economic recovery made buying up war materials too expensive.[269] Von Papen concluded the letter with a rejection of any innuendo against his performance. "I believe I should submit to your Excellency this short statement, because I most urgently wish to guard against (the imputation) [parentheses in original] that we did not see the situation here and recognize it in time. I also forced the contract involving some 8 ½ million dollars now concluded through [sic] only in face of great opposition from his Excellency Dernburg, who wanted to use the funds from the loan for other purposes."[270]

As a matter of fact, von Papen and Albert had made significant progress, but only after Rintelen had received his marching orders. The Secret War Council had officially founded the Bridgeport Projectile Company on April 1st, and concluded the contract with Aetna to buy up all available capacities of smokeless powder in the U.S. for a year. All this happened literally on the day before Rintelen's arrival. Rintelen had met the New York merchant and DuPont board member, Melvin Rice, on two social occasions in Germany, who had promised him some sway in concluding a large powder contract for the German government.[271] Rintelen's disappointment must have been great when he learned that the members of the Secret War Council in New York had beaten him to the punch. Rintelen wrote in his memoirs, "... within a few days I was satisfied that it would be quite impossible to buy up the vast quantities of explosives that were by now available in the American market."[272] Should his recollections be trusted, Rintelen determined in a few afternoon strolls in New York what the members of the Secret War Council and their vast network of informants and agents had been working on for the past six months.

Whether Rintelen's mission included finalizing the smokeless powder contract or not, he definitely did not receive funds from Boy-Ed and Albert to "procure supplies."[273] Indications are, however, that he operated under the commercial cover of a buyer of supplies to be exported to Scandinavia.[274] Melvin Rice joined the important network of commercial and financial contacts of which Rintelen made use during the coming months. The New York business executive apparently had enough sway to report directly to President Wilson on the "feeling of Germany towards the United States."[275]

One of Rice's business acquaintances was Andrew D. Meloy, a business promoter with a crowd of unhappy investors left in almost every project he ever undertook.[276] Meloy had organized a consortium to invest in the development of public works, mainly railroads, in Mexico in 1902. The project had gone sour even before the Mexican Revolution. One of the key customers for the Mexican Western Railroad, the company Meloy had organized, was a mining and smelting operation in Guanacevi, Durango, that the Stallforths owned. Stallforth's business closed down during the recession of 1908 and the ensuing Mexican Revolution, but not before the two businessmen had lured financiers from Boston, Chicago, and New York into investing both in Meloy's railroad and Stallforth's mining company. Stallforth eventually moved to New York in 1913 and became, at least financially, partners with Meloy. Born in 1867 in Carlyle, Pennsylvania of Irish immigrants, Meloy had made (for himself) and lost (for his business partners) fortunes. His reputation in East Coast investment circles was terribly stained, owing to the financial disasters the promoter had caused for his investors, and the various lawsuits he had faced as a result. An agent of the Bureau of Investigations described Meloy in a brief: "Meloy was another adventurer on the high seas of finance. He promoted things --- a hole in the ground in Mexico became a gold mine surrounded with engraved certificates of stock under his hand, and he exchanged these frail mementoes [sic] of experience for the public's more substantial gold. He had performed similar miracles with railroad rights of way drawn in convincing red streaks across a map of Mexico..."[277]

Now Meloy was looking for money to support any Mexican faction that could unseat or co-opt Pancho Villa, Venustiano Carranza, and Emiliano Zapata, in order to recover his investments in Mexico that had soured over the course of Mexico's unrest. The arrival of Rintelen, boasting of the fabled funds he supposedly had at his disposal, attracted Meloy and a host of other disreputable characters to the German agent like flies to a cadaver. Five feet, nine inches tall, high forehead, gray eyes, and brown hair, Meloy projected the image of a tough, even ruthless businessman. His only apparent weakness was his hearing, or lack thereof, which required him to converse in a booming voice with a large funnel held to the side of his head. He became a key contact for Rintelen's Mexican endeavors.

The market-cornering of strategic supplies was well on its way and in the hands of Schweitzer and Albert at the time of Rintelen's arrival. Instead, his funds came to serve large-scale sabotage activities and efforts to create labor unrest in munitions factories. Boy-Ed and von Papen expressly discussed these plans with the agent in the first days of his American mission. Within days of the meetings, and with Boy-Ed's transfer of funds, the sabotage agent took charge of Dr. Scheele and his firebomb project. According to von Papen's letter to General von Falkenhayn, the military attaché did not happily cede his projects. However, both he and Boy-Ed had received clear instructions and, much to von Papen's chagrin, Rintelen, with a big chip on his shoulder, likely pulled rank on the army captain.[278]

Rintelen took over the firebomb project within days of the contentious meetings with the military and naval attachés. Dr. Scheele, Captains Bode, and Wolpert, as well as Captain von Steinmetz, all now reported to Rintelen. Von Steinmetz had left for New Orleans in the beginning of April with the Irish conspirators to inoculate horses with his bacteria.[279] The mission failed. The cultures the agent had brought with him from Europe had somehow expired, leaving this first known biological attack on the United States in the failure columns of history's accounts. The descriptions of who met whom first vary among the different testimonies of people involved in the firebomb plot. Believing Dr. Scheele's assertion that responsibilities were assigned by rank, he probably was one of the first people Rintelen visited and integrated into his team. The supplies the German chemist purchased for the production of the bombs give an indication that, within ten days of Rintelen's arrival, movement came into the project. Scheele ordered a load of lead pipe on April 13th 1915, which the truckers delivered first to Scheele's laboratory but were told to transfer to the North German Lloyd pier the next day.[280] Scheele purchased more lead on April 20th, and again on April 28th.[281] All these purchases ended up at the North German Lloyd pier.

Indications are that the group around Scheele was in disarray when Rintelen took over. Von Steinmetz, Wolpert, and Bode were banned from the doctor's premises, the production of the bombs was slow and tedious, and many of them had not functioned as designed. After meetings involving Boy-Ed, who by rank and responsibility had to have given the nod to proceed, the sabotage team decided to move production of the lead hulls of the 'cigar' bombs to the interned North German Lloyd steamer, *Kaiser Friedrich der Grosse*. This decision came sometime between April 11th and April 13th. The steamer awaited the end of the war tied up in Hoboken at the HAPAG piers. Captain Enno Bode, an agent on the payroll of Karl Boy-Ed, supervised the crews of the German ships moored in that part of the harbor. Carl Schmidt, the chief engineer, and Ernst Becker, the chief electrician, were in charge of the new production in the workshops of the moored liner.[282] Becker was a watchmaker by profession, and seemed to be an obvious choice for precision manufacturing.[283] It is likely per the input of these two naval officers that the firebombs received zinc-tin instead of paraffin separators, which improved the reliability of the timer.[284] The workmanship of the 'cigar' garnered the admiration of people like New York Bomb Squad Captain Thomas Tunney. He investigated their origin later in 1915 and called the quality of the bombs "thorough."[285]

The production of the 'cigars' in the workshop of the *Kaiser Friedrich der Grosse* proceeded in earnest on April 13th 1915.[286] Becker had hired three additional sailors with the skills to produce a precision product. For an additional fourteen dollars in cash per day sailors Ernst Friedrich Garbade, Wilhelm Paradis, and Georg Preidel cut the lead pipes to size, soldered the corroding aluminum membrane, and cut the fill caps into the 'cigars.'[287] Von Kleist and Becker then carried the bomb casings to Dr. Scheele's laboratory, where the chemist inspected them, and filled them with the volatile chemicals.[288] Becker and von Kleist then took the filled bombs back to Bode and Wolpert, who arranged for them to be placed on ships.[289] The bomb factory produced between thirty-five and forty bombs per day.[290] Scheele put the total amount of bombs produced between April 1915 and April 1916 at five hundred.

Without a doubt, the *Kaiser Friedrich der Grosse* produced far more bombs than the arrested conspirators would admit. Scheele's generally accepted number seems far lower than conservative estimates would yield with the historical facts in mind. The bomb shop received three deliveries of lead pipe in April 1915, one per week for three weeks. If the weekly spacing represented the actual use of the lead, and considering the production volume of thirty-five per day, the shop worked for fifteen days, producing 525 bombs in April alone. Even with the assumption that Rintelen halted the production after bombs had been discovered on the *Kirk Oswald* in Marseille and were reported in U.S. papers in mid-June, over 1,400 bombs must have been manufactured in 1915, in addition to those Dr. Scheele made before April in his own shop. If the chief engineer of the *Kaiser Friedrich der Grosse* can be believed, ten bombs were placed on any ship selected for destruction.[291] It seems that only about one third of the targets could be identified in the end.

However, this is not all. Three more lead pipe purchases in January and February 1916 support the fact that another slew of fire-bombs hit U.S. installations in the first seven months of that year. Fifteen additional ships reportedly caught on fire, allowing for the suspicion that another fifty had been bombed. 'Cigar' bombs even set the Canadian parliament in Ottawa on fire in February 1916. Multiple factories exploded in May, June, and July 1916. The grand prize, the largest loading dock for Entente munitions on Black Tom Island in the New York harbor, exploded in the end of July, after German agents used incendiary devices to start the conflagration.

Other German agents were important to the operation, as well. Dr. Karl Max Schimmel, a German lawyer usually working on legal issues for the embassy, was accused later to have researched the sailings of the vessels that were to be targeted. Rintelen paid him $100 per week for services of some kind. If he worked on the target list at all, he was just one of the many spokes in the German intelligence wheel. The employees attached to Franz von Papen's office, Wolf von Igel, Paul Koenig and his detectives, and Carl Heynen all helped assemble the target list. Information poured in from all sorts of paid informants in banks, shipping offices, from harbor masters, even U.S. customs officials. The shipping lines published weekly lists of sailings, as did dailies such as *The New York Times*.[292] The propaganda team under Dernburg spent much of its time cutting out snippets of information from American and international papers that had to do with the Allies. They, as well, added to the volume of intelligence. Employees in Heinrich Albert's office, the German embassy, and the consulates all had the duty to forward any and all information about shipments bound for the Entente powers to von Papen's intelligence bureau.

Friedrich Henjes, a customs broker and North German Lloyd shipping agent, played a major role in arranging the delivery organization for the bombs. Henjes had a history of working directly for Karl Boy-Ed. In the fall of 1914, the customs broker was instrumental in falsifying manifests for colliers sent to supply the German fleet.[293] He helped Boy-Ed with customs documents in January 1915, when the latter tried to smuggle contraband from the "Submarine Signalling [sic] Company to Germany."[294] The customs broker and freight forwarder also handled Dr. Scheele's 'fertilizer' shipments.[295] He, Wolpert, and Bode hired the delivery crews that could place the 'cigars' into the cargo holds of the freighters. One would assume that these workers had to be inconspicuous and non-German, especially since British secret service agents tightly guarded the allied ships. Quite the opposite was the case! The sabotage team found six captains of German or Scandinavian origin in charge of river freighters (called lighters) that moved cargo from warehouses and manufacturers along the New York waterfront to the transatlantic ships for loading.[296] The German agents paid them a whopping $275 a week ($5,775 in today's value) for their and their crews' services.[297] Constantly on the move from the warehouses to the transatlantic steamers, the crews of these lighters had plenty of time to plant bombs in what were mostly sugar bags and cotton bales. These 'bomb delivery crews' remained inconspicuous until premature fires at the loading docks caused suspicion.[298]

The bombing operation extended to other parts of the country, as well. Von Steinmetz, Reilly, and Conners operated in the port of New Orleans, as mentioned earlier, albeit unsuccessfully. Dr. Scheele and Captain Bode went to New Orleans in the end of April to organize the cell for firebombing ships from that harbor.[299] The two agents received instructions to abandon the effort and come back after failed negotiations. Connors had demanded $50,000 ($1 Million in today's value) for his participation, which far exceeded what Boy-Ed and Rintelen were willing to pay.[300] Before he left, Scheele issued two checks amounting to $5,000 ($105,000 in today's value) in what seems to have been hush money.[301] Substantiating Scheele's account, there are no records of ships catching on fire that left from this gulf port anytime in 1915, although Bureau of Investigations agents referred to such fires in 1916.[302] Within weeks of Rintelen's arrival, he and Boy-Ed made contact with a sabotage cell in Baltimore under the direction of

Consul Karl von Lüderitz. The consul had already helped out Franz von Papen with the von der Goltz mission to bomb Canadian installations. Boy-Ed's expense ledger shows reimbursements for his personal travel expenses on April 8th and April 15th 1915. The travels in the beginning of April occurred suspiciously close to the arrival of Rintelen, who stayed in Philadelphia at the time. Another travel reimbursement is dated June 10th, which is the week the discovery of 'cigar' bombs in Marseille on the steamer *Kirk Oswald* graced the headlines of New York's dailies. These reports sent the German agents scurrying for cover. Boy-Ed would have been the person to arrange that.[303]

The Baltimore harbor was home to most of the moored North German Lloyd steamers. Rintelen connected with Paul G. L. Hilken through the customs broker, Friedrich Henjes, who wrote a letter of introduction.[304] Hilken would become the kingpin in the largest German sabotage project, the explosion of Black Tom Island in July 1916. The junior owner of Schumacher and Company, the freight forwarder for the North German Lloyd at Baltimore

> ...lived with his wife and young daughter in a big house in Roland Park, a posh, wooded and secluded section of Baltimore... Hilken was a boyish looking man in his midthirties [sic], with a mustache... He had much in common with Franz von [sic] Rintelen. Both had benefited from having powerful fathers, were well schooled and well-traveled, and showed off their pedigrees. Hilken's father was honorary German consul in Baltimore and the local head of the North German Lloyd... Hilken had been raised in the United States, studied engineering at Lehigh University, and settled near where he had grown up... In December 1913, Hilken moved to Germany to work in the German Lloyd's Bremen office... He was scheduled to move to New York in January 1915 to become the North German Lloyd's managing director... Internment put a halt to all of the German Lloyd's business. Ships were idle, gathering barnacles in Baltimore Harbor... Hilken was a captain with no command.[305]

He had just returned from a trip to South America when Rintelen made his introductory call, most likely with Boy-Ed or von Papen at his side. Hilken and Rintelen immediately saw eye-to-eye. The German naval commander liked the jovial manager who was itching to prove his worth to the German cause. Hilken's diary contains a conference with "H." and "L." on April 20th. Rintelen had meanwhile assumed the alias of Fred Hansen under which he conducted his business as a German merchant. "L." probably stood for Consul von Lüderitz, who also joined the meeting of the conspirators. The conversation centered on the firebombing project. The next day, Hilken joined Rintelen for a quick trip to New York, where the two had "various conf. [erences in] Hoboken [at Scheele's laboratories or Bode's HAPAG office].[306] The conspirators agreed to work on sabotage projects in the region.

Instrumental to the operation was the captain of the moored SS *Neckar*, Friedrich Karl Hinsch, another key member to the Black Tom plot in 1916. Born in May 1878 in Deichstücken, a city in the far northern state of Oldenbourg, Germany, the burly merchant mariner spent most of his adult life at sea. "A huge, ruddy man, with blue eyes and yellow hair, agile and energetic," Hinsch fit the mold of an old sea bear whose effectiveness stemmed from his "vicious and ruthless disposition."[307] The German navy listed him as a reserve officer starting in 1905.[308] It is fair to assume that the captain, who was not listed by rank, had been an agent of the German Naval Intelligence, the Nachrichtenabteilung N, since that time. He had scurried the SS *Neckar* into Baltimore harbor in September 1914, where she tied alongside her sister ship, the SS *Rhein*. The captain then immediately went to New York and offered his services to Karl Boy-Ed, who gladly accepted them. Hinsch hired captains of tenders and lighters, and leased some American steamers to undertake the supply shipments for the German fleet in the fall of 1914. "A fellow captain would describe Hinsch as being 'fearless… He knew how to handle the men on the docks and commanded their respect by his shrewd intelligence, his flow of seafaring language, and the ready use of his fists when necessary.'"[309]

The Sunday following Hilken's trip to Hoboken, April 25th 1915, Rintelen met with Hinsch in Baltimore.[310] It is unclear what role Franz von Papen had in these meetings with Hinsch. However, a mysterious telegram dated April 24th 1915 indicates that von Papen helped set up the meetings and personally participated. He wrote to his assistant von Igel, "Please inform him (Rintelen) to see me Sunday afternoon but do not sign my name. Von Paurin [sic]."[311] Rintelen met Hinsch in Baltimore that Sunday. Multiple meetings between "Hansen," Hilken, and Hinsch followed in May.[312] Although the Baltimore cell stood accused of sourcing firebombs from Scheele, *The New York Times* never mentioned a single ship leaving the Baltimore harbor that caught on fire in that year.[313] However, serious fires severely damaged the American warship USS *Oklahoma* in the Camden, New Jersey, shipyard. Two more U.S. navy ships mysteriously caught on fire in the Philadelphia navy shipyard a few weeks later. The government, obviously embarrassed about this string of "accidents," never admitted that sabotage was a probable cause. However, *The Philadelphia Evening Ledger* quoted government insiders in Washington as saying, "The fire on the *Oklahoma* strengthened the suspicion that the United States is being subjected to the hostile activities of partisans of the war in Europe."[314] The *Oklahoma* entered service with a year delay in 1916. She succumbed to flames and capsized in the Japanese attack on Pearl Harbor in 1941, taking 429 members of the crew down with her.

Authorities suspected seventeen major fires that occurred in Pennsylvania, New Jersey, and Maryland in 1915, in addition to the navy yard fires, as the handiwork of German agents. Most notable were the explosions in the facilities of major producers of war materials for the Allies, all to the south of New York. Several munitions plants of DuPont, the Aetna factory in Grove Run, New York, Bethlehem Steel in the eponymous Pennsylvania town, the Baldwin Locomotive Company in Eddystone, New Jersey, John A. Roebling's and Sons in Trenton for a second time, all blew up or caught on fire that year. The two consecutive fires that destroyed large portions of Bethlehem Steel's production facilities caused celebrations in German pubs with toasts to the destruction of this hated company. A fire that could have started as a result of firebombs in Baltimore harbor in June 1916 incinerated two steamers and caught the grain elevators on fire. Insurances estimated the damage to be over $2,000,000.[315] The prized jackpot of all targets blew up in the summer of 1916, which subsequent investigations traced to several German agents, including Hilken and Hinsch. The Lehigh Valley Railroad Company's loading terminal on Black Tom Island in New Jersey had enough explosives stacked in its warehouses and dock sheds that their combustion caused an explosion powerful enough to cause an earthquake registering 5.5 on the Richter scale. It could be felt as far south as Baltimore, where the conspirators toasted to the success of their mission.

Paul Hilken with Captains Friedrich Hinsch, and Paul Koenig (not to be confused with the New York secret agent of the same name) in 1916.[316]

CHAPTER 7: THE SUPPLY PYRAMID

WHILE RINTELEN, SCHEELE, AND VARIOUS other sabotage cells engaged in their violent plots, Albert, von Papen, and Boy-Ed conceived a more devastating, economic attack on the United States. German military authorities authorized one of the most daring and effective intelligence projects of the entire war in March 1915. Through meticulous intelligence-gathering efforts, the military and naval attachés in New York had long tried to establish a baseline for effective measures against the U.S. supply of the Entente armies. While the Hindu conspiracy was taking its course starting in October 1914, von Papen, as well as Boy-Ed and Albert remained hard at work to find more ways to prevent the Entente powers to provision themselves in the United States.

Weekly reports from Felix Sommerfeld, Theodore Otto, and others painted a dim picture of the developments in the industry. Munitions factories multiplied, capacities were booked twelve months out. The idea of buying up the entire industrial output became more and more elusive. Von Papen sent reports on October 31st, November 16th and December 9th with details of the Entente contracts.[317] The numbers had been meticulously assembled from intelligence reports from three sources: Hans Tauscher (and his informant, George W. Hoadley), Theodore Otto (doctor in Bethlehem, Pennsylvania), and Felix Sommerfeld. Some information also reached the military attaché from miscellaneous sources, such as German-American employees of banks and munitions concerns. However, Sommerfeld and Hoadley had the most important and complete intelligence for the German government. There is no trace of payments for these reports. Almost all of these reports had been destroyed in 1916 by order of the German government.

However, as evidenced from the dates and frequency of the handful that have survived, von Papen and Boy-Ed received bi-weekly intelligence summaries from their agents. Felix Sommerfeld submitted a report to Boy-Ed on the 11th of November with details on the main manufacturers and their orders:

> …Remington [underlined in original] Contracts for cartridges which will keep the factory busy until July next year. [Contracts] for cartridge shells for artillery munitions for over one year.
>
> Winchester approximately similar maybe one or two months longer.
>
> Colt Automatic are beginning to deliver
> to France 500 machine guns Cal. .303
> to England 200   "
> That means the factory up to March can deliver nothing further.
>
> France has purchased the following arms.
>
> 100,000   Remington rifles 7mm single load-ers (have been manufactured at Remington U.M.C. Co. [United Metal Cartridge Company in Bridgeport, CT]
>
> 3,000   [Remington] rifles (ready for delivery) 7mm.
>
> 1,300,000   Cartridges 7mm.
>
> 1,800   Rifles and carbines
>   Remington Lee Magazine 30/40
>
> 1,700,000   Cartridges 30/40.
>
> Earlier they bought
> 15,100 rifles and carbines 30/30
> 2,000 rifles Springfield 45/70.

> With that [order] they now bought 4 different calibers.
>
> Russia is trying to buy
> 5,000,000 cartridge shells or casings for artillery [illegible] munitions
>
> France 300,000
> England 2,000,000
>
> Remington U.M.C. Co has a contract with England and delivers 3,000 per week, which is the maximum capacity....[318]

Two weeks later, Sommerfeld submitted another intelligence report, the contents of which, save for the first page, have not been preserved. "Dear Captain. Enclosed I am sending you some data. Your servant, F. A. S."[319] Again three weeks later, on December 18th 1914, Sommerfeld, who was out of town dealing with the Naco affair, transmitted a message to Ambassador Count Bernstorff via Karl Boy-Ed. The message revealed a supposed German buying agent operating in Chicago working on behalf of the Italian government. Sommerfeld came upon him when the agent wanted to source 50,000 Mauser rifles through him.[320] The letter, like all of Sommerfeld's reports, was copied to Franz von Papen and Heinrich Albert. It is possible that this buyer did work for some branch of the German government or military. Whether he was a hostile agent using German credentials or whether he was authorized by some entity in Germany circumventing Albert's office, the attachés now had his number – literally, since Sommerfeld added the agent's New York address in the report.

Hans Tauscher added to Sommerfeld's intelligence complementary data from George Hoadley, the president of the British and American Manufacturing Company in Bridgeport, Connecticut on January 4th 1915. Hoadley reported on negotiations between the National City Bank and various manufacturers for seven million shrapnel artillery shells. The French, Russian, and English buyers now pressured the American Locomotive Company and the New York Airbrake Company to switch their manufacturing to war supplies because of the overburdened capacities of Remington and Winchester to which

Sommerfeld had attested. These initial negotiations for contracts amounting to $47 million ($1 Billion in today's value) failed. However, the looming profits indeed brought dozens of new manufacturers to the table.

According to Hoadley, the British government so far had only placed orders with Bethlehem Steel for "200 British Fieldpieces 3.03 inches on trucks with two munitions carriers each; 1,000,000 shrapnel with them, delivery starting in three months and ending after 12 months."[321] Von Papen's push in the War Department, Heinrich Albert's similar efforts in the Interior Department, and Count Bernstorff's reporting to the Foreign Office finally eroded the resistance in Berlin to buy up capacities in the U.S. The German team in New York not only reported the facts of Entente supply lines in the U.S., they also devised a brilliant strategy. The new approach satisfied the need to curb munitions exports, while staying within the laws of the United States, and at a much-reduced cost from their previous proposals. Noticeably absent from the brain-storming sessions in New York was Bernhard Dernburg. According to Franz von Papen, Dernburg opposed spending money on curbing the munitions trade. He would rather have seen any available funds flow into his propaganda efforts.[322] The main input seemed to have come from Tauscher's agent, George W. Hoadley. Hoadley not only had a good overview of the production data in Bridgeport, he also understood the second and third tier supply lines for the U.S. arms manufacturers. There were two types of suppliers to the arms manufacturers: raw materials needed for production, and equipment needed for expansion.

The New York team feverishly gathered intelligence on these types of supplies. They identified three products: Smokeless powder, presses to manufacture shells and casings, as well as the two base chemicals for high explosives, toluene and picric acid. All three product groups came from a handful of manufacturers. Almost all the powder came from Aetna Explosives Company, DuPont's subsidiary. About five U.S. manufacturers, chiefly the Hydraulic Press Manufacturing Company in Mount Gilead, Ohio, the Harrisburg Pipe Bending Company, and the Camden Iron Works had the technology and capacity to produce the hydraulic presses needed for making shell casings.[323] Bethlehem Steel had been the leading manufacturer of such presses. However, with its business now firmly in the munitions production, the company ratcheted down its tool production, since the tools would only create more competition for them. The toluene and picric acid market, as well, only consisted of three key manufacturers. The team needed two ingredients in order to make their plan work: A green light from Berlin, and money. Both prerequisites fell into place in the second week of February 1915. Von Papen sent the outline of a new strategy to the Imperial War Ministry on February 11th. He informed the Secretary of War that England and France were trying to conclude a contract for ten million artillery shells. Since there was no available production capacity in the United States, he proposed creating a new manufacturing facility, act as if it were producing shells for the Entente, tie up manufacturing equipment and powder in the process and, in the end, purposely fail to deliver on the contracts. The Entente would not get their munitions and no other production facility could be opened because the companies that produced the heavy presses to make shells would be tied up working on presses for the proposed new plant. Once production began in earnest, the shells could be sold off to neutral parties. Albert co-signed the cable.

> Russia and France are negotiating new contracts for an estimated 10 million artillery shells, for which new [production] companies are being set up. Preventing entry of these companies into munitions business, as well as preventing them from accepting this order can be achieved through tying up the total production of powder, antimony and machines until end of December [1915] by placing an order of only two million artillery shells. This would probably prevent companies already in the munitions business to accept any new orders after they have finished the current ones. Delivery of a part of the two million shells possible at a later date to the American government, smaller neutral states[,] and possibly Italy, which is in the market with orders. The rest will be warehoused until the General Staff decides what to do. Total cost about 12 million dollars. From that three million right away, the rest depending on delivery schedule.[324]

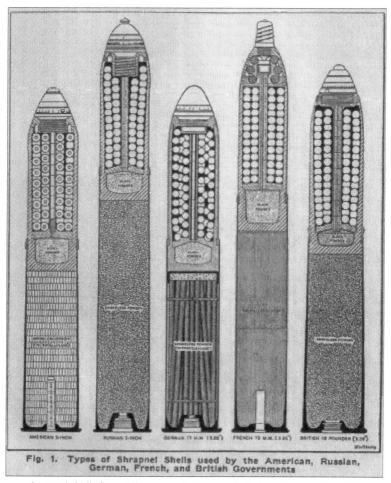

Shrapnel shells for artillery use. The tips exploded and inflicted horrible damage as the small lead and steel pieces flew in every direction.[325]

The plan was simple and brilliant, much cheaper than the first idea, and, if executed properly, almost undetectable. Key to the operation was George Hoadley. There would be no suspicion if he concluded new contracts for the American military, given his previous business connections with the U.S. government. Adding capacity to his existing plant in Bridgeport under a new corporate name would also appear completely legitimate. As a side benefit, the new company could hire away the trained workforce from the largest cartridge-manufacturing plant next door, which was just being finished, the U.M.C Remington plant.

The German government would have to bring in a top expert to control the venture. This manager had to have a strong business background, managerial experience, and ability to handle large sums of money. Money – the last and highest hurdle. The New York team waited anxiously for an answer. The Imperial Secretary of War finally replied in a secret telegram sent through the German embassy in Washington on the 20th of March 1915: "Secretary of War to Military Attaché: Relative to report 11. February # 386/15. Are looking immediately for more detailed suggestions about the steps to be taken to tie up artillery munitions companies and to report, how you are envisioning the delivering and controlling the produced munitions."[326] The group huddled and sent another, even more detailed report to Berlin ten days later.[327] They reported that Hoadley had started negotiations, meanwhile, with the Aetna Explosives Company. With Albert in the background, expertly coaching Hoadley through the talks, Aetna had agreed to sell a year's worth of production to Hoadley, 4,450,000 pounds of smokeless powder for $1 per pound.[328] However, they required a twenty-five percent down payment. Von Papen explained further, that George Hoadley would be the front man. He admitted that there was a certain risk in partnering with an American businessman in such a huge clandestine operation. The risk was mitigated by the fact that Hoadley would end up with a brand new factory financed by the German government. If successful, Hoadley would be set after the war. Von Papen also mentioned for the first time the person he proposed to manage the German interests in the new venture: Carl Heynen.[329]

Heynen had just arrived from Mexico and joined Albert's office in New York. The former head of Mexico's HAPAG office was the absolute expert in anything concerning international shipping. Born in February 1869 in Rheydt near Mönchengladbach, the heart of Germany's industrial Ruhr area, Heynen came to the United States for the first time in February 1888. The nineteen year-old listed his occupation as "clerk."[330] Two years later, he entered again, this time from London, which he listed as his city of residence.[331] Heynen wrote "merchant" as his current occupation. Five feet, nine inches tall, blond with blue eyes, Heynen had the features of a 'Teutonic' northern German. He had left Germany right after his baccalaureate and clerked with shipping companies in London and New York. His move to the United

States and England freed him from mandatory conscription in the German army. Heynen's occupation apparently not only took him to New York but also to Mexico City in the early 1890s, where he again gave his occupation as "clerk."[332]

His career quickly transitioned him to the booming port city of Tampico, Mexico in 1894. American and British entrepreneurs had found 'black gold' in the decade before Heynen's arrival. Tampico grew from a few thousand residents to over 100,000 within the decade. The harbor of Tampico was buzzing with oil tankers, supply ships, passenger liners and the like. It was the perfect place for a young and enterprising shipping expert to start his own business. In a statement in 1918, he wrote, "...I was established in the Maritime and Custom House Agency business, representing chiefly American Steamship Companies, American Importers and Exporters and American Oil Companies."[333] Indeed he was not established in, but had actually established a company of that name together with a young shipping agent from Hamburg, Richard Eversbusch in 1894. His other partners were Carl F. Ganahl, Charles Bishop, and the British shipping agent, Charles C. Pearl.[334] Eversbusch counted HAPAG and North German Lloyd among his clients, and already had an office in Veracruz. The German shipping lines' business had only recently been established and was comparatively small before the turn of the century. However, with the growth of HAPAG and the boom in the oil industry, the new shipping agency grew rapidly. Heynen, Eversbusch Y Cia. had become the largest customs broker on the gulf coast within a few years, and the two entrepreneurs grew very wealthy in the process. Heynen endeared himself to the foreign communities, and especially the American colony, in 1903, when he organized and financed the fight against a yellow fever outbreak in the city.[335]

By 1906, Heynen's operation included underwriting marine insurance, booking freight, customs brokering, freight forwarding, and ship leasing. Heynen became director of the Banco de Tamaulipas in 1908,[336] and founded the International Banking Company, which represented the Deutsche Diskonto Gesellschaft and the Deutsch-Südamerikanische Bank.[337] Flush with cash, the two entrepreneurs bought up shipping line representations for most of the large companies serving Mexico, with exclusive representations for HAPAG and North German Lloyd, in particular. The German government appointed

Heynen vice consul for the state of Tamaulipas in 1909.[338] He also represented Sweden and the Netherlands in the city. According to German diplomatic papers, Heynen's business now represented the largest German-owned enterprise on the East Coast of Mexico. By 1910 the business had offices in every major port in Mexico. Heynen moved to Mexico City that year to manage the headquarters of the agency in the capital. Eversbusch became German consul in Tampico after Heynen moved away from there. The consulate and Heynen, Eversbusch Y Cia. were all in the same building, staffed and managed by the same people.[339]

Heynen became one of the most popular leaders of the foreign community in Mexico City. He had joined the American Club early in 1903, as well as the *Deutscher Verein* (German Club).[340] Now a wealthy businessman, Heynen was in all the right country clubs and organizations. Americans who knew him then, although aware of his German background, considered him "one of us."[341] His personal friends in Mexico City read like a list of *Who is Who* of the American colony: Harold Walker (Standard Oil Company), George Clynes (Mexican Railways), William S. Layer (Sonora News Company), William N. Brown (National Railways), and George McCarthy (Mercantile Banking Co.).[342] According to those who knew him, Heynen stood at the fore when it came to charitable projects. He offered to import arms for the German colony in the capital in 1912. The Germans wanted to arm themselves as a defense against increasing Mexican violence.[343] Then he helped organize the transportation of American and German refugees from Mexico City to Veracruz in 1913. He did the same in the spring of 1914, when American marines landed in Veracruz.[344] The Brazilian ambassador appointed Heynen consul general for Brazil when the American Charge D'Affairs Nelson O'Shaughnessy left the capital during the U.S. intervention in Veracruz. This resulted in helping with consular work for the United States as part of his responsibilities. While never officially appointed as such, the German businessman briefly served as a de-facto American consul.[345] Heynen was well acquainted with Felix Sommerfeld. In his capacity as chief arms buyer for both Carranza and Pancho Villa, Sommerfeld came into frequent contact with the shipping agent.

Heynen came to New York and placed himself at the disposal of the German embassy on October 18th 1914.[346] "In consequence of the revolution and the discontinuance of the Hamburg American Line service with the outbreak of the European war, business became very dull…"[347] While his business certainly had suffered from the loss of German shipping, Tampico became one of the most important and busiest harbors on the American continent: Mexican oil fueled the British fleet to such an extent, that the German government ordered von Papen in January 1915 to blow up the wells.[348] It is not known which company provided loading, unloading, storage and other services for the British ships leaving from Tampico. The British did not consider the German businessman for the job for obvious reasons. Throughout the fall of 1914, Heynen and his partner Richard Eversbusch ran the supply mission for the German fleet in the Atlantic. However, orders had been given to the German cruisers to transfer into the Pacific. That, more than anything else, triggered Heynen's "boredom." There are no archival records documenting the time between his arrival in New York and him starting to work for Heinrich Albert in January 1914. Heynen testified that he worked in the New York offices of the HAPAG, "… after conclusion of my own business affairs and finding no opportunity to reach Germany, I placed my services, as a volunteer, at the disposal of my country through Mr. Ballin, the Director General of the Hamburg American Line at Hamburg, who after some time cabled me to report to Dr. H. F. Albert, the Commercial Attaché [sic] of the German Embassy at New York… This was in January 1915…"[349] Heynen's recollection seems to be reasonably true. However, rather than settling his "own business affairs," the German shipping specialist ran the supply ship operation for Karl Boy-Ed until the end of the year. Clearly, Heynen was the most experienced specialist for this operation available on the American continent.

The German business executive settled into the offices of Heinrich Albert at 45 Broadway in January 1915. While the German team in New York contemplated ways to prevent the shipment of munitions to the Allies, Heynen's first job had to do with another project of Albert's. Since the English blockade had tightened to such a degree that neutral shipping lines refused to risk losing ships to prize court proceedings, the German government had authorized Albert to acquire ships. That project became Heynen's job. Intimately familiar with the legal framework in which shipping companies operated, he devised a system of dummy firms that owned Albert's ships. A. Bruce

Bielaski, the chief of the American Bureau of Investigations, character-ized the worthy opponent he saw in the German agent in 1918: "He... came to New York, and soon became one of the right-hand men, if not the right-hand man, of Albert in his commercial enterprises. He was one of the most intelligent and most clever of the German agents..."[350]

Immediately after Heynen's arrival in New York, Albert's efforts shifted into a markedly higher gear. His accounts with G. Amsinck and Company, which represented Albert's main commercial activities, showed six transactions from August to October 17th, the day Heynen arrived in New York, then twenty-two commercial transactions from October 26th to December 31st. Albert began shipping food, cotton, and supplies in earnest. To be fair, organizing shipments, financing the purchases, and founding dummy corporations to establish 'neu-tral' appearance all took time. However, the timing of Heynen's arrival with the need to organize the logistics of Albert's purchases could not have been coincidence. Albert knew virtually nothing about ship-ping, war risk insurance, bonding, and manifesting, all integral parts of Heynen's Mexican business. His services became the more import-ant when neutral shippers refused to risk their vessels as the English blockade tightened and included ever stricter contraband rules. As German shipments made through K & E Neumond, Larsen Export Company (Petersen), Southern Products Company (John Simon), and Paul Tietgens reached Germany, Albert received millions in credits to finance his purchases.[351] Heynen, as the head of Albert's shipping oper-ation, began leasing and purchasing steamers. By the end of January, Albert's office had chartered seven steamers.[352]

Albert paid for the first of six commercial steamers, the SS *Wilhelmina* $175,000 ($3.7 million in today's value) on February 3rd 1915.[353] Albert actually had bought the steamer in December. British authorities had seized the *Wilhelmina* in England on her first run with a full load of foodstuffs by the time he made his payment in February. The ship and her cargo went into prize court. Albert did not mention Heynen by name as the person in charge; however, in his chapter on ships he wrote, "A portion of these charters was done through the company, Phelps Bros. & Co., that operated as agents of the Austro-Americans. The chartering was accomplished through confidential agents of the Office [Albert's office] in other cases."[354] Heynen was, in short, Albert's right-hand man in running the business of the Central

Purchasing Corporation. Given the commercial agent's (he became attaché only later in 1915) legal background, understanding of government processes, and fiscal savvy, Heynen brought years of experience in shipping and logistics, as well as, executive management to the table.

One other noteworthy addition to the New York team also arrived on October 14th 1914: One of the members of the board of directors of the Deutsche Bank and head of U.S. operations, Hugo Schmidt.[355] He settled into the German Club, where Consul Hossenfelder, Naval Attaché Boy-Ed, and Military Attaché von Papen lived. He rode on horseback in Central Park for exercise, where Felix Sommerfeld and Franz von Papen also conducted their equestrian morning exercises.[356] It had become clear by the time of Schmidt's arrival that Dernburg was unable to raise a large loan in the United States. James Speyer, Hans Jacob Schiff, Ladenburg, Thalmann and Company, as well as Max Warburg, had also not been able to finance the German undertakings in the U.S. as was originally expected. The lack of support from German and international banking was largely a function of the inherent risk of a German loss of the war, but also a purely logistical issue. Since virtually all German corporations used the London exchange for international commerce before the war, German banks were cut off from international markets. Lacking the willingness of American financiers to float a large loan for Germany, and without the possibility of simple money transfer, Director Schmidt had to devise schemes that allowed German money to flow into the United States. As a matter of fact, Hugo Schmidt had been sent to take over the responsibilities in which Dernburg had failed. His methods were brilliant and went undetected until the very end of the war. Liquidity of Albert's accounts showed a marked improvement after Schmidt's arrival. Through a complicated system of exchange, dummy corporations transferred the proceeds of Albert's shipments back from Germany through Latin American banks via London to the United States.

The schemes required trustworthy businessmen, such as Frederico Stallforth (Stallforth Y Hermano de Parral), Heynen (Banco Tamaulipas and his own International Banking Company), Adolph Pavenstedt, (G. Amsinck Company), Alberto Stein (Banco Nacional de México), and Elias A. De Lima (National Bank of New York). Under the direction of Hugo Schmidt, these men created a confusing web of international transactions and credit swaps that the British government and American investigators failed to unravel. The result was an incredible success for the German coffers in New York. While Albert barely had access to $2 million in all the months before November 1914, between November and February his accounts showed balances of over $2.5 million, $1.2 million of which came from the Deutsche Bank alone.[357] The German bank director organized further credits of $3.9 million from his bank in March, specifically for use in the scheme to build an arms manufacturing facility.

Frederico Stallforth, who owned the (bankrupt) Stallforth Y Hermano bank of Parral together with his brothers, Alberto and Alfredo, not only supported Schmidt's financial schemes. He joined Albert's team in New York in the fall of 1914. Schmidt and Stallforth's acquaintance went back as far as 1910 when the Deutsche Bank gave a loan of 600,000 German Marks to Stallforth and a credit of 200,000 German Marks.[358] Ostensibly working for Schmidt out of his office at 55 Liberty Street, Stallforth in actuality floated offers and quotations for chemicals, guns, munitions and other supplies throughout the country.

These quotations served two purposes. They provided Heynen and Albert with accurate data on market prices of these supplies, as well as the names of the Allied buyers who showed interest. Simultaneously, the members of the Secret War Council now had a constant flow of information about what was being offered, where it came from, who produced it, and how much it cost. Agents of the Bureau of Investigations briefly arrested Stallforth in 1917 and captured an obvious intelligence file with these quotes in his offices.[359] Dated August 10th 1915 under the heading "Buyers or Agents thereof to whom I have offered war supplies as noted herein below," it listed seven agents of the Entente.[360] American manufacturers authorized Stallforth to broker more than 12,000 tons of picric acid, 2.5 million Mauser rifles, 10 Million shrapnel 3-inch rounds, 5,500 military trucks, and one million aerial bombs.[361] Of course, the real purpose of these quotations was to test the purchasing power of the Entente buyers and to tie up manufacturing capacities of American factories. The manufacturers had no idea that they were dealing with German secret agents rather than Allied buyers.

Albert also floated the second German war loan, ten million dollars of war treasuries, on April 1st. The first issue had sold so badly that the German Reichsbank had to withdraw the notes. Albert had organized the new issue somewhat differently. Since he could not get one of the large investment banks in New York to take treasury bills, these German war notes were issued not by the German central bank, but by the German government itself. Albert contracted with the small New York investment bank of Chandler and Company for distribution. Chandler, in turn, sold the notes through the Central Trust Company of New York. "...They were printed by the American Bank Note Company, and signed by Mr. Von [sic] Haniel and by engraved signature of Count Von [sic] Bernstorff."[362]

One of the biggest promoters of the German war bonds was Frederico Stallforth. His efforts contributed to the relative success by a significant degree. Albert's office had placed $7.1 million worth of bonds by May 1915. Stallforth did not receive commissions through Albert's office, but through Chandler and Co.[363] However, evidence of his involvement with the sale of war bonds before 1916 appears in a letter addressed to one of Stallforth's customers from Heinrich Albert. Albert advised Mr. Cohn to ask for a receipt from Frederico Stallforth for a $1,000 war bond.[364] Stallforth's efforts in promoting the German war bonds and assisting in the market-cornering activities of the Secret War Council gained him such confidence with Heinrich Albert, that the latter put the German-Mexican banker in charge of selling the next issues of war bonds in 1916 and 1917.

With money in the bank, personnel in place, and an option to buy up a year's worth of powder, the German team in New York received the green light from Berlin on April 1st. The message from Berlin not only authorized the Bridgeport project, but the purchasing of munitions and explosives on the U.S. market on a grand scale. "...[your approval] was interpreted by us to the effect that not only contracts for the purpose of tying up [munitions] in the narrower sense were to be concluded but that all other measures necessary for the accomplishment of the purpose aimed at were to be taken..."[365] Secretary Delbrück did not correct Albert's impression of his approval. A new corporation came into existence, the Bridgeport Projectile Company, on April 5th 1915, the day after Easter Sunday. The new arms manufacturer showed a capitalization of $2,000,000. The board of directors consisted of three Americans, Walter H. Knight, Carl Foster, and George W. Hoadley, each receiving an obligatory ten shares in order to legally qualify them as board members.[366] Carl Heynen, the unofficial manager of the whole project became treasurer. Heynen reported to Franz von Papen under whose responsibility the project fell.

Heynen moved his offices to 60 Wall Street, one floor above von Papen's office, as a result. He received an annual salary of $12,000 ($250,000 in today's value). "...The other 19,970 shares was [sic] issued to me [Hoadley]. This stock was afterwards placed in trust with Hans Tauscher under the trust agreement... Mr. Tauscher was my trustee, and any dividends or returns from the stock at any time was to be delivered to me. The trusteeship was conditioned upon the completion of a contract..."[367] The contract represented the brilliance of the plan. Hoadley and Tauscher had the rights for the Erhard shell in the U.S., which enabled them to receive orders from the U.S. army, the first of which was for 105,750 three-inch artillery shells.[368] Through Director Schmidt's financial juggling, the Bridgeport project raised $3.3 million dollars through the use of several New York banks, mainly the Equitable Trust Company. Hoadley proceeded to build a new plant in Bridgeport, right next to the U.M.C. Remington factory under the eyes and, indeed, with the blessing of the U.S. government. The capacity of the plant was designed for two million shells per year. "... The truth of the matter is I got $2,200,000 from the Germans on the contract, built a beautiful plant, which the United States Government knew all about from its inception, and knew that the shells that were being built were built under the specifications of the United States Government, all the shells that were made were sold to the United States Government and that the only material product that was built in the plant was built for the Unites States Government."[369]

The ownership of the new company remained completely in the shadows. Hoadley with his co-director, Walter H. Knight, a former executive of the American Locomotive Company (that now made trucks for France), concluded a contract for five million pounds of smokeless powder with the Aetna Explosives Company, as promised to the German government. Knight delivered the down payment of $40,000 ($840,000 in today's value) and a bond issued by the Guarantee Trust Company (on behalf of the Deutsche Bank) to activate the order.[370] Effectively, one full year before the new factory would even be operational, the New York team had locked up the entire U.S. powder market for a pittance.

It did not stop there. A few weeks later, Hoadley ordered seventy-two hydraulic presses from the Hydraulic Press Manufacturing Company in Mount Gilead, Ohio. Even more presses came from the Camden Iron Works. This order consisted of

> ...100 sets of shrapnel presses at $6,100 each, of which total sum 27 ½ per cent. [sic], or $167,750, was to be paid down. The presses were to be delivered at the rate of five sets a week, the normal capacity of the Camden plant. It was provided expressly that the contract called for the total output of projectile presses up to Jan. 1 next, and that R. D. Wood & Co. were not to sell to any other firm in that period except to fill certain orders already under contract, nor were they to manufacture any other presses.[371]

The German government contracted with several other press manufacturers the same way.

> During the year [1915]...our New York Office was approached by parties representing themselves as representatives of the Bridgeport Projectile Company. We had no reason to doubt that it was an American Company [sic]. Our negotiations finally resulted in our agreeing to build for the Bridgeport Projectile Company, exclusively, shell forging and drawing Presses [sic], to the capacity of our shops.
>
> The contract provided that money should be deposited with the Guarantee Trust Company of New York, that we were to draw on this account for the agreed price for Presses [sic] manufactured by us, as rapidly as the machines were completed.[372]

The Bridgeport Projectile Company ordered 534 presses from various American manufacturers, including Bethlehem Steel by May 1915.[373] Only 132 were actually reserved for the production of artillery shells. Heynen, Hoadley, and Knight had inserted cancellation clauses in their contracts, which allowed them to cancel the remaining 392 presses, after those manufacturers had set up their facilities and refused orders from other customers. The disruption in the press man-ufacturers' businesses was worth $238,945 to the German government, which was the indemnity for contract cancellations and upholding the commitment of not producing for other customers.[374] Altogether, the team spent a total of $717,225 ($15 million in today's value):

> $417,550   for presses which had actually been produced
> $238,945 for indemnities on cancelled contracts still binding the manufacturers
> $ 60,730 indemnities still pending.[375]

As a result of German order cancellations, the Camden Iron Works became insolvent and went into receivership later in 1915. The fac-tory churned out other metal parts for the rest of the year rather than making presses for shells in order to regain a cash position. *The New York Times* sarcastically reported that Camden was "enjoying one of the greatest periods in its history."[376] It is hard to estimate the amount of hydraulic presses needed for manufacturing two million artillery shells per year since the exact specs and the plant design are not known. However, it is safe to say that Heynen and his busi-ness partners purchased a ten-fold amount of what the plant actually needed, then cancelled seventy-five percent, and used only a frac-tion of the remaining machinery. In addition, they purchased all kinds of presses, not just the ones needed for the manufacture of large shells. According to the Hydraulic Press Manufacturing Company in Mount Gilead, Ohio, the presses they delivered "…were being stored in Warehouses at Bridgeport, Connecticut, no use being made of same."[377] The Hydraulic Press Manufacturing Company had developed a process that made their machines the most efficient in the indus-try.[378] Amazingly, Heynen, Knight, and Hoadley ordered presses that were not installed in their new factory even after it started production in 1916. The German strategy of preventing munitions to reach their enemies naturally extended to the production of cartridges.

The suspicion looms that the presses the group ordered had not all been specified for artillery shell production, but included the forging and drawing presses needed for smaller caliber cartridges.

Carl Heynen wrote in an assessment of the success of the Bridgeport project, in September 1915, "In order to complete the success of our operations in this direction it has become necessary to place a further definite order for 20 presses with the manufacturers of the largest type of presses [Hydraulic Press Manufacturing Company in Mount Gilead, Ohio], manufactured for projectile forging, thereby binding such a factory to us until December 31st of this year... Thereby practically all the manufacturers of hydraulic presses for projectile forging are committed to us for the remainder of this year."[379] Clearly, Heynen was alluding to "all" types of presses for all types of projectiles. Curiously coincidental, only one factory that manufactured cartridges was built at the time when the German government had cornered the hydraulic press and smokeless powder market. That factory went up in East Alton, Illinois. Felix Sommerfeld's old friend and business partner, Franklin W. Olin, had made plans to build his new brass mill for the production of 7mm shell casings. Production started in May 1916, using the same type of hydraulic presses that the Bridgeport Projectile Company had bought and stored in warehouses around Bridgeport. Since Olin's biggest customer was Felix Sommerfeld, and he did not sell to the Entente buyers, the presses for his factory were likely a German grant.

Hoadley started hiring thousands of workers away from the U.M.C. Remington factory next door as the construction of the Bridgeport factory commenced in the summer of 1915. Remington not only desperately needed factory workers, but since their facility was being expanded at the same time, the loss of construction workers turned into an even larger problem. This started a virtual bidding war for workers, raising wages, delaying the completion of Remington's factory, and increasing the cost of munitions for the Entente at the same time. Heynen set the target for completion of the new facility for September 1st 1915 in a report to the New York team of Albert, von Papen, and Norvin Lindheim, the German embassy's legal counsel. Meanwhile, since Hoadley could only use a fraction of the powder from Aetna, Heynen tried his best to sell one million pounds of the smokeless to the Spanish government.

Count Bernstorff had negotiated an initial agreement with the Spanish ambassador, Juan Riaño, on May 28th 1915.[380] However, the negotiations dragged on until the summer of 1915 because the powder specification did not match the Spanish requirements.[381] Albert finally concluded the contract with Spain in July, and received a $256,250 down payment ($5.4 million in today's value). Heynen showed a $25,000 profit on the powder sale with another $5,000 interest earned in the final accounting.[382] The first deliveries of the smokeless powder from Aetna to Bridgeport started in December, four months behind schedule.[383] Additionally, all customers who came to Aetna to buy powder were referred to the Bridgeport Projectile Company. Initially, Heynen simply ignored these requests. However, as the Russian and English government actually made offers that included non-refundable down payments, Heynen's ears perked up. Without any interest whatsoever in selling powder to producers of shells for the Entente, Heynen conducted negotiations, "… even if they primarily had the purpose of delaying the actual placement of orders. The result of these negotiations is, that representatives of the Russian as well as the English government are making bona fide offers in the next days. As soon as this happens, we will have to conduct a 'war council meeting' with B. [Albert] to discuss, whether it is advisable to take these orders – although without telling that in the contract there will be a stipulation for a non-delivery penalty."[384] It seems that the Allies indeed gave Heynen the idea of promising deliveries that he had no intention of ever fulfilling, while at the same time raising cash.

Heynen and the rest of the team had reasons to celebrate. The Bridgeport factory turned out to be a tremendous success in virtually every aspect. The contracts Heynen and his partners had concluded in April and May of 1915 significantly disrupted the U.S. arms production. Heinrich Albert reported to the Imperial Secretary of the Interior on April 20th, "… The large Russian orders for many millions of shrapnel in the market here, in regard to which negotiations have now been going on for weeks, have not yet been placed, and for this very reason, because the factories concerned were compelled to learn the truth that it is not possible to get the necessary powder… if the orders are consummated the factories concerned will find that they cannot get the necessary special machines. Accordingly [,] no doubt exists that our timely intervention has, if not entirely prevented, yet delayed large orders of our enemies, by many months."[385]

The cornering of the American munitions market did not stop with the Bridgeport Projectile Company. One of the most important assets Germany had in the United States at the outbreak of the war was Dr. Hugo Schweitzer. Schweitzer had received his doctorate in chemistry from the University of Freiburg, Germany. In July 1889, the twenty-eight year-old scientist from Upper Silesia moved to New York. There he met the German-American Adele Hammerslough, twelve years his junior. The couple married in 1892 and had one son, Edward, a year later. The accomplished scientist found employment as a chemist with the Bayer Chemical Company in Englewood, New Jersey.[386] At Bayer he worked with the brilliant researcher and holder of multiple patents, Dr. Walter T. Scheele, also a graduate of Freiburg and major in the Imperial army reserves. Both received a $1,500 annual retainer from the German War Office as industrial spies, in addition to their salaries from Bayer.[387] Schweitzer took the oath of allegiance and became an American citizen in 1894.[388] Throughout a skyrocketing career, Dr. Schweitzer amassed a sizeable fortune, became president of Bayer's subsidiary, the Synthetic Patent's Company, and remained on Bayer's payroll as a consultant.[389] Dr. Schweitzer was also a member of the American Chemical Society from 1892 to the beginning of the war, and was recognized as one of the leading personalities of the industry.[390]

His loyalty to the United States did not supersede that of his home country. He not only became a key intelligence asset of the Secret War Council, but also strongly supported German propaganda efforts in the World War with widely circulated articles such as "Can Germany be starved into Submission?," "Industrial Germany in Wartime," "Military Strategy and the Enemy's Industries," "Industrial Germany in Wartime," and many more. He founded the German Publication Society, was a prominent member of the German University League, and gave several keynote speeches in favor of the German position in the conflict.[391] Citizenship clearly served to complement the agent's cover and allowed for public agitation on the behalf of Germany. American officials described the then fifty-two year-old Dr. Schweitzer on a passport application in 1913 as six feet tall, large forehead, blue eyes, large nose, gray-blond hair, "ruddy" complexion and a full face.[392] A mustache brushed up at the edges like the emperor's, as well as the pince nez on his prominent nose, rounded out the image of a commanding personality, but not without charm and warmth.

Hugo Schweitzer in 1915, courtesy of the Chemical Heritage Foundation

Dr. Schweitzer had impressed Heinrich Albert through his integrity, absolute loyalty to the German cause and intellectual capability. The German pharmaceutical executive theorized early in the war in an article titled, "Chemists' War" that the chemical industry was the key to defeating Germany's enemies.[393] His ideas turned out to have prophetic value, considering the role of chemical and biological weapons used later in the war. After founding the German Publication Society, raising significant contributions from the German-American community, and working with Albert and Dernburg on propaganda projects, Schweitzer wanted to do more. He inundated Albert's office with a barrage of suggestions in the spring of 1915, as the German agents in New York embarked on finding strategic raw materials that could disrupt the American production of explosives, arms, and ammunition.

The business executive and formidable chemist identified a chemical hardly known for its strategic value: phenol, also known as carbolic acid. This chemical compound, which is derived from crude oil, is used in many industrial products, mainly all kinds of polycarbonates and polymers, as well as detergents, and pharmaceuticals such as Aspirin. However, carbolic acid also was a key ingredient in the production of TNT. The price of carbolic acid increased as the American munitions industry boomed. Shortages of this crucial ingredient in Aspirin haunted Bayer's Rensselaer, New York factory that produced this wonder drug. Dr. Schweitzer immediately saw a tremendous opportunity to procure the necessary phenol for the Bayer Chemical Company while, at the same time, removing its availability for the explosives industry. He proposed to Albert and his team in April 1915 to build a factory that processed benzene into phenol and picric acid. This factory would have cost an estimated $100,000, and would have cornered the entire high explosives market in a similar fashion that the Bridgeport Projectile Company tried up the available powder and hydraulic press capacity.[394]

Not ready to invest in a second factory, the idea remained on the back burner while the team explored other options to limit the supply of strategic chemicals. Heinrich Albert hired William Wilke in April 1915, likely a Schweitzer recommendation. The Secret War Council put Wilke in charge of researching the benzene, phenol, and picric acid industries.[395] He was born in Germany in 1874 and worked as an engineer for the German-American Stoneware Works in Buffalo, New York.[396] An American citizen since 1902, his secret service background is yet to be determined.[397] While the documentation on Wilke's background is scarce, he clearly acted under the direction of Dr. Schweitzer, who had been on the German secret service payroll as an industrial spy since before the war. Albert handed Wilke a cashier's check for $30,000 for his mission on May 4th 1915.[398] Three days later, the agent received another $60,000 and a stipend of $600 per month for the next six months.[399] More payments followed later that year and into 1916. In total, Wilke received over $100,000 ($2 Million in today's value) in order to lock up strategic chemicals all over the United States.[400] After a barrage of suggestions and market data on the chemical industry, Schweitzer received orders to corner the high explosives market through purchases of picric acid, a key ingredient of TNT, in June 1915. However, despite serious efforts using Stallforth and various straw men, and despite offering contracts above market price, neither Schweitzer nor Wilke could get a contract with the American picric acid manufacturers.[401]

While Schweitzer's idea for a German-owned factory wound its way through the Secret War Council's decision-making process, another formidable American inventor and entrepreneur chomped at the bit. Suffering from shortages of carbolic acid for his own ventures, Thomas Edison decided to build his own phenol refining plant in Silver Lake, New Jersey. Edison had no designs on participating in the booming war industry. Rather, the inventor of the phonograph urgently needed phenol for his booming vinyl record production company. Naturally, Edison's plans quickly circulated in the chemical industry and reached the ears of Dr. Schweitzer. The Bayer executive immediately entered into negotiations with Edison to secure excess production for his Aspirin production and prevent phenol from reaching explosives manufacturers.

Albert agreed to finance the purchase of Edison's entire annual excess output. Bayer Aspirin, a much-needed product in the domestic U.S. market, became the ideal cover for the project. After the Interior Department gave the green light for the investment, Schweitzer secured 1.2 million pounds of phenol at the end of June, virtually locking down the available U.S. capacities for the entire year.[402] Without phenol, there would be no picric acid. Albert spent $1.3 million ($27.3 million in today's value) on the contract.[403] Schweitzer and Albert created a web of dummy companies to obscure the underlying mechanics of the operation. Edison's phenol went to the Chemical Exchange Association, a post office box brokerage firm in New York. The actual deliveries went to the Heyden Chemical Works in Garfield, New Jersey, a subsidiary of the Chemische Fabrik von Heyden in Radebeul, Germany.[404] As was the case with most German industrial producers, the Heyden concern in Germany had been requisitioned for the war effort and, thus, was under the control of the Interior Department and Albert Ballin. Phenol and derivative products went from Garfield directly to Bayer. Dr. Schweitzer sold off what Bayer did not need to other end-uses not considered detrimental to the German war effort. The action severely affected the U.S. markets, as did cornering the powder market. The price for toluene and picric acid, as well as for all related high explosives, skyrocketed as a result of the German actions.[405] So successful and profitable was the project that Dr. Schweitzer "gave a lavish private dinner at New York's swanky Hotel Astor in honor of Heinrich Albert. It was a happy evening because behind all the backslapping, champagne and cigars lay the knowledge that Schweitzer had pulled off a remarkable coup... Schweitzer now controlled one of the few available sources of phenol in America and was set to make a fortune."[406]

The success of the German team in acting unrecognized behind the scenes of the American munitions industry was not long-lived. It was Albert himself who accidentally broke the seal of silence in the end. He had his briefcase snatched on July 24th 1915. The phenol purchases and the details of ownership of the Bridgeport Projectile Company suddenly graced the first pages of American dailies. Albert, teasingly called "minister without portfolio" in the press, offered to resign and return to Germany as a result, but was turned down flatly. Interestingly, nothing about the clandestine projects was illegal, which prompted the publication rather than legal action in the first place. However, without the secrecy of German finances and management, the continuation of the projects became difficult and public. Aetna refused to deliver after the revelations of Bridgeport's ownership, which resulted in a four-month delay of the first shipment.

The New York team had decided to cancel the order of the remaining four million pounds of powder by the end of 1915. Through the briefcase affair, Schweitzer's phenol purchases had become public. Edison eventually cancelled the deliveries to Heyden and Bayer under pressure. While Albert used his lawyer, Norvin Lindheim, to enforce the signed and legal contracts, the war was rapidly entering a new, more violent stage on the American continent. Despite the setback, the Bridgeport project and the "Great Phenol Plot" remained the most successful German secret missions of the first war year. Heinrich Albert praised Dr. Schweitzer's success in a letter later in the war:

The breadth of highmindedness [sic] with which you at that time immediately entered into the plan has borne fruit as follows: One and a half million pounds of carbolic acid have been kept from the Allies. Out of this one and a half million pounds of carbolic acid four and one-half [sic] million pounds of picric acid can be produced. This tremendous quantity of explosives stuffs has been withheld from the Allies by your contract. In order to give one an idea of this enormous quantity the following figures are of interest: Four million five hundred thousand pounds equals [sic] 2,250 tons of explosives. A railroad freight car is loaded with 20 tons of explosives. The 2,250 tons would therefore fill 112 railway cars. A freight train with explosives consist [sic] chiefly of 40 freight cars, so that the 4,500,000 pounds of explosives would fill three railroad trains with 40 cars each. Now one should picture to himself what a military coup would be accomplished by an army leader if he should succeed in destroying three railroad trains of 40 cars, containing four and a half million pounds of explosives.[407]

Von Papen proudly filed a report on May 18th 1915 to the Imperial War Ministry announcing, "All reports received here – from the English press as well as from the negotiations of the Allies with munitions-makers [sic] here – show that there is a great shortage of ammunition in Russia, and that the needs of the English with their apparently enormous expenditure of ammunition during the last weeks, are nowhere near being met."[408]

CHAPTER 8: OPERATION "PEREZ"

IGHTING A WAR AGAINST THE United States required solid public relations. The Secret War Council had tried hard to turn around the listing propaganda ship throughout the fall of 1914. It proved to be an overwhelming task in the face of a very successful British campaign and continued missteps within the German publicity machine. Bernhard Dernburg, the former German minister of colonial affairs, who had taken charge of the German propaganda efforts in the U.S., managed to enlist William Bayard Hale as a spokesperson and writer. He also created and ran the German Information Bureau, which flooded editorial boards across the nation with continuous updates of the war from a German perspective. The effort showed some modest success among certain minorities, but the general public overwhelmingly sided with the Entente, especially on topics such as the occupation of Belgium and unrestricted submarine warfare.

A shift in the propaganda approach had to take place, not the least because of changing conditions in the United States. Shortly after Hale joined the Press Bureau in October, the American economy rebounded sharply. The price for cotton normalized in November, greatly reducing the efforts of southern politicians to fight the British blockade of Central Europe. Beginning in January 1915, munitions and military supply demands from the Entente all but eliminated unemployment and quieted public discontent. The German government ordered a sabotage campaign against American production and logistics facilities on January 24th 1915 and declared unrestricted submarine war against any ship entering a 'war zone' around the British Isles a week later.[409] The goal of German propaganda now switched from trying to convince the American public of German righteousness to empowering an opposition to exports of war supplies. Simultaneously, her agents actively tried to prevent the flow of goods to the Entente through other clandestine means.

The Imperial War Department authorized the use of 9.45 million dollars for projects in the United States in keeping with the new strategy targeting the United States.[410] Heinrich Albert's bookkeeping shows four new accounts in the spring of 1915, all of which were designated to the War Department's representative in the United States, Military Attaché Franz von Papen: "Von Papen I" contained the expenditures that financed the Bridgeport Projectile project, including a corner on the U.S. smokeless powder market, arms and ammunition for Indian and Mexican revolutionaries, industrial presses, and critical chemicals. Albert disbursed $3.9 million ($82 million in today's value) from this account in 1915.[411] He used $3.3 million to lock up the U.S. smokeless powder market, and $600,000 to pay for contracts on equipment that were mainly hydraulic presses in order to thwart building new munitions factories in the U.S. "Von Papen II" covered purchases of strategic chemicals, mainly phenol. "Von Papen III" comprised propaganda expenditures. This account was separate from the German embassy account Albert kept for propaganda funds. Von Papen's propaganda accounts were comprised of payments to agents and news outlets that agitated on behalf of Germany in the United States.[413] "Von Papen IV" was another account for salaries and commissions for agents that were directly employed by the military attaché's office. "Von Papen V" covered salaries and commissions for employees of the Bridgeport venture, as well as payments to agents involved in the market-cornering activities.[412]

The fact that the War Department now paid for propaganda projects implies that these projects were part of the larger war strategy against the United States. In addition to the War Department, Dernburg's office expenses, as well as those of other new propaganda projects, continued to be accounted for as expenditures of the Foreign Office.[414]

Beginning with the German invasion of Belgium in August of 1914, British propaganda had succeeded in turning American public opinion solidly against the German empire and her allies. Initially, Americans might have had misgivings about the interruption of trade with Central and Northern Europe through the British sea blockade. Many disliked British war ships patrolling American harbors and the publication of ever-increasing lists of conditional and absolute contraband. Lost revenue from cotton trade with Europe in the fall of 1914 wreaked havoc on American growers, especially in the South, and provided a fertile soil for effective pro-German propaganda. If German propaganda could ever have played a role in influencing the course of American politics, it would have been then, in the first months of the war. Trade with England and France made up more than adequately for lost trade with Scandinavia and central Europe by the winter of 1914 and the spring of 1915. The recovery of the American economy and the ensuing boom far outweighed the downside of having cut economic ties with the Central Powers.

During the dark days of August, September, and October 1914, the German propaganda had a unique chance to stress the obvious arguments for upholding freedom of the seas, strict neutrality, and trade with all of Europe. This opportunity went unused. Instead, amateur German propagandists emphasized "German cultural superiority" and published self-righteous treatises justifying the violation of Belgian neutrality, human rights abuses, and militarism. This type of propaganda resonated with the German-American community – but hardly convinced anyone else. Instead, the German message provided Britain with a growing arsenal of arguments with which to embarrass her enemies. Despite the best efforts of the propaganda team in New York, and despite the limited success in suppressing the aggressive Pan-German voices of German-American university professors, the German message drowned in a sea of pro-Entente articles in the mainstream American papers of the day.

The Dernburg office suspected, with good reason, that the British secret service not only exercised a large influence on American editorial boards, but that British funding supported the ever-increasing number of "investigative journalists." The loudest voice of British propaganda was the *Providence Journal* that in the spring of 1915 revealed German clandestine activities in great detail. Editor-in-chief, Australian-born John R. Rathom, received British intelligence as the basis for many of the paper's sensational revelations.[415] He admitted in 1920: "Our direct connection with these Slavic organizations [Emmanuel Voska], however, as far as the anti-German work was concerned, came to us originally from British sources, through which we were first introduced to one or two of the leaders in this important work; and the major part of the documentary evidence which came into our possession came either through the British, Canadian, or American

Government Intelligence sources."[416] The *New York Sun* and the *New York World* also published investigative reports with intelligence provided by the British embassy. The *New York Times* and other large American dailies willingly re-printed these reports of the muckraking press. To the defense of Dernburg and his associates in New York, the German propaganda, like most other efforts on the American front in 1914, suffered from a lack of funding. Instead of prioritizing the meager funds that were available to advance a broader message in the mainstream press, the German press office funded the *Fatherland* and publications of German and pro-German scholars. The English propaganda, with its finger on the pulse of American public opinion, also meagerly funded but properly prioritized, thus moved leagues ahead of the German effort. According to the British newspaper magnate, Lord Northcliffe, his organization alone controlled eighteen leading American papers.[417] The editor of the *London Chronicle* went even further in the fall of 1914: "We have... no better allies in America than the editors of the great papers."[418]

One of the most vocal critics of the German propaganda campaign was the Imperial Ambassador, Count Bernstorff. Having grown up in England and understanding the American psyche from having served as Germany's representative in the United States since 1908, Bernstorff disliked the elitism of German scholars and the blatant, confrontational tone of Viereck's publication. He wrote in his memoirs: "...the American does not care to be instructed. He has no interest in learning the 'truth' which the German Press [sic] communications and explanatory pamphlets were so anxious to impress upon him. The American likes to form his own opinions and so only requires facts..."[419] In the beginning of 1915, through the influence of the ambassador as well as William Bayard Hale, Felix Sommerfeld, and other vocal critics of Dernburg's office, the German propaganda effort shifted visibly. Dernburg increased his public speaking engagements and flooded American mainstream media with articles. In addition, a news bulletin from the press bureau in New York disseminated pro-German information to editorial boards as well as to thousands of private recipients on a daily basis.[420]

The bulletin, about twenty-two by twelve inches in size, was usually five-columned and printed on one side only. The masthead of every issue bore the title, 'German Information Service.' This was followed by 'M. B. Claussen, 30 East 42nd Street, New York City.' To the side, in small print, was a message to the recipient, 'The Managing Editor': The material sent herewith is offered for publication without charge and is released for use upon receipt. This bulletin is issued daily, except Sundays. Its contents come only from reliable sources, chiefly the press of the European capitals. The authority for every story is clearly indicated. In view of the British censorship of war news, it is believed that this sheet will be found an invaluable supplement to the regular news reports, enabling papers to give a more comprehensive picture of events. We shall be glad to supply photographs, mats or cuts of any illustrations appearing in the sheet, upon request, by mail or telegraph. We shall appreciate the courtesy of a place on your exchange list.[421]

Was it successful? "Our mail is dernburged until the postman can scarcely stagger up the front stoop with it. They are systematic those Germans. If you doubt it, send them your postoffice [sic] address," a journalist complained in 1915.[422] Yet, despite the turnaround, more needed to be done.

Count Bernstorff had been pushing to purchase mainstream American newspapers since the beginning of the war. He believed that owning American newspapers and influencing American journalists, maybe even with financial enticements, would be the only solid answer to the effective British propaganda. Count Bernstorff's push to buy American papers had fallen on deaf ears for months, not the least because of lack of funding. Any such undertaking required finances. As early as October 17th 1914, He wrote to Albert and Dernburg in a strictly confidential note, "I was offered to buy *the Washington Post* today for two million dollars with the intention to allow a buy back after the war for one-and-a-half million. A second offer was to put the paper at our complete disposal for two months for $100,000. The paper has significance as it is the only large paper in the capital. What is your opinion with respect to the funding question?"[423] Albert and Dernburg's answers are not archived. Certainly, there was no further discussion on the issue until March 1915, whether as a result of Dernburg not allowing the ambassador to mingle in his business, or, even more likely, because Albert rejected the idea for lack of money. Ambassador Count Bernstorff's idea re-surfaced in the spring of 1915 as the propaganda effort started to show better results, and with outsiders like Sommerfeld, Hale and others pushing for more 'mainstream' efforts. The change of strategy towards the United States and the resulting resolution of the "funding question" was instrumental in the change of attitude.

Since Bernhard Dernburg's failure to raise a loan for Germany in August and September of 1914, Albert had tried his best to find banks that would advance credit or outright funding for his undertakings.[424] He was able to receive small loans and credits to a limited degree that were usually tied to his blockade-running operation. However, the first six months of the German efforts in the U.S. were marred by lackluster financing. Any bank that offered financing for Germany risked losing its business with the English or French government. American banks were increasingly less inclined to risk their business in an effort to help Germany as the American economy relied more heavily on commerce with the Entente. Therefore, not even bankers with strong ties to Germany, such as Hans Jacob Schiff of Kuhn, Loeb and Company, or James Speyer and Max Warburg took up Albert's offer to float war bonds, even forfeiting very favorable commissions. A small brokerage firm, Chandler and Company, with a customer base mostly around Philadelphia and no business with the Entente, offered Count Bernstorff and Albert in November 1914 to underwrite a $10 million issue of German war bonds with an option for another $15 million. Although "Chandler and Co. was not a first class outfit with international repute,... it was ... to be expected that a smaller house would be inspired with much more ambition to make a bond issue into a success..."[425]

Negotiations with Chandler's lawyers, Hays, Kaufmann and Lindheim, continued throughout January and February 1915. When it became clear that none of the larger investment banks were considering taking up a German war bond issue, and when all efforts of bringing together a syndicate of larger banks failed, Albert and Count Bernstorff relented. Chandler and Co. signed a contract on March 26th for a $10 million offering of 5% bonds payable in nine months. Chandler placed $4.5 million with major banks, which offered the bonds to their customers, and $5.5 million were made available to the general public.[427] Chandler and Company sold $3.5 million of the bonds offered to the general public. Most disappointing for Albert was the fact that Warburg, Speyer and other German-American investment bankers refused to take up any of the German bonds. As a result, Chandler could not place most of the bonds it had committed to. After the *Lusitania* crisis in May 1915, with a general American public unwilling to invest in Germany's war effort, Albert was forced to write off $2.8 million.[428] Instead of the envisioned $10 million, Albert had realized what a, for him disappointing, $7.1 million. $2.6 million of the proceeds immediately went to the Central Purchasing account. The German embassy received $500,000, von Papen received $2.5 million for the Bridgeport Projectile Company, and $324,000 went to finance propaganda. Albert and von Papen allocated another $347,000 for projects such as sabotage and arms purchases, and $60,000 paid for coupons, legal fees, and bank expenses. One large chunk of money, $750,000, went to a new account.[429]

In line with the other measures to wage war on the United States, Heinrich Albert suggested to Ambassador Count Bernstorff in February 1915 to rekindle the efforts for the acquisition of American newspapers. He wrote:

> ...True neutrality does not exist...The English have systematically worked long before the war, and especially in the first few weeks when German news was not available here, in order to malign us, and to paint a fake picture of us. We neglected both to gain sufficient influence, and to win the entire American people; exchange professors influence but a small part of the nation; the only means [to influence a broader public is] English printed news papers [sic], which would give the readers, and impregnate them without their knowing or noticing it, German ideas... Following are the most influential papers under E. [English or Embassy?] influence.
> *Times* – Editor is the publisher Ochs (G. [German] Jew.)
> *Sun* – Rinst, German Jew (embittered)

Herald

Evening Post and *Evening Mail*.

German *Staatszeitung*, Ridder, very much read by German Americans, poor German.

Fatherland, special war-sheet, published by Viereck.

Hamburg Fremdenblatt, also saily [sic] correspondence by Hale, published by Dernberg [sic].

We have the feeling now, that lectures and discussions are of little purpose – Dernberg [sic] and his associates have done much good – but no one alters his veins, and things speak for themselves. That the Americans are so wholly pro-Ally is explained by reason of their general ignorance, poor education, no knowledge whatever of business, and of German government... [430]

Count Bernstorff liked the idea. He cabled to the Foreign Office on March 10th 1915:

Main point is no longer organization of news service, but in placing news here. Entire press here, as well as all telegraph agencies, in hands of money interests allied with England. Therefore, although best possible news bureau organized here under Dernburg's direction, news gets only scant circulation, as long as we do not control an important newspaper here which will force other papers to accept German news for sake of their journalistic reputation. Offer for purchase of suitable newspaper under consideration. Urgently request immediate authorization to make initial payment of $325,000. Total sum $1,300,000. [431]

His superiors in the Foreign Office approved the project within days. Heinrich Albert had made contact with a curious thirty-three year-old American businessman from La Porte, Indiana. Dr. Edward Aloysius Rumely, a third generation German immigrant, had studied medicine in Germany. His main source of income was the Rumely Company, a farming implement manufacturing company founded by his grandfather and granduncle. The year of his grandfather's death, 1904, the publicly traded Rumely Company employed three hundred workers. Edward took over from his uncle as chief executive in 1907. That same year he founded a trade school for boys, the Interlaken School. Designed to train the future farming generation in the use of modern agricultural techniques and technology, Rumely employed progressive teaching methods using "a novel learning-by-doing educational model founded in Germany. Many industry leaders lectured there, including Henry Ford and International Harvester's Clarence Funk."[432] Rumely developed a revolutionary kerosene fueled tractor in 1909, the Rumely Oil Pull, nicknamed "Kerosene Annie." It became a resounding commercial success with over 60,000 tractors sold before the World War. According to the chief of the Bureau of Investigations, A. Bruce Bielaski, Rumely took "that corporation from a $3,000,000 corporation up to a $36,000,000 corporation in a very short period of time..."[433] The enterprising doctor modeled his factory after the principles of Henry Ford. Both became good friends in the process.[434]

However, Rumely overextended the business and his company incurred financial woes by 1913. The Board of Directors forced him to resign. Clarence Funk, his successor as Chief Executive, tried his best but could not manage to turn the business around on account of the outbreak of the World War. "In January 1915, the venerable Rumely Co. filed for bankruptcy and the Rumely family lost control of the company it [had] founded in 1853."[435] Without the family in control it still continued under the family name into the early 1930s when Allis-Chalmers took ownership.[436]

A fervent pro-German desperate to steer business towards his fledgling firm, Rumely approached Bernhard Dernburg in November 1915 who introduced him to Albert.[437] The Midwestern entrepreneur proposed to the German commercial representative to employ his political connections and lobby for changes to the English contraband lists.[438] Himself a progressive, Rumely had become close friends with the former American President, Theodore Roosevelt. Through his contacts, Rumely wanted to organize shipments of his tractors, as well as kerosene and oil to Germany via Denmark, Holland, Italy and Sweden.[439] In turn, he envisioned importing potash, and dye stuffs. The export dreams of Rumely, however, did not materialize. Despite having concluded a contract with Albert to export tractors, the tightening British blockade ruined his efforts.[440] Thus the bankruptcy filing.

Apparently, Albert took a liking to the bespectacled, intellectual medical doctor and businessman during their conversations. Albert was closely acquainted with Edmee Reisinger, the widow of Hugo Reisinger and Busch empire heiress. Reisinger, with whom Albert carried on an affair, owned the majority of the Mail and Express Corporation, which owned the *New York Evening Mail*.[441] Her son, Kurt, served on the Board of Directors.[442] Rumely, who owned some stock in the newspaper, as well, had tried since the fall to push the ailing New York paper towards a more pro-German point of view.[443] Albert and Count Bernstorff decided to use Rumely with money available from the sale of war bonds and with the blessing of the War Department and the Imperial Foreign Office. The entrepreneur offered lots of business experience, great connections to American industry, Wall Street, and politicians. Staunchly pro-German, he was young, "with a good appetite and not much to do."[444] A perfect fit. Not wanting to appear as the outright owner of the daily, Albert made a secret agreement with Rumely to act as the front man for the German government. He paid Rumely $100,000 ($4.2 million in today's value) on both March 15th and April 1st 1915, for what would be the first installments for buying the *New York Evening Mail*, code-named "Perez."

On May 15th, $707,500 moved from Albert's accounts to Rumely, coded "Perez matter."[445] Another $78,664 followed on June 11th, and $75,000 on September 20th.[446] Two payments of $7,500 and $75,000 completed the sale in 1916.[447] The total cost of the *New York Evening Mail* for the German Empire came to $1.2 million ($24 million in today's value).[448] The paper secured, Rumely moved to New York and took the post as editor-in-chief. Throughout the fall of 1914 and spring of 1915 the paper had become the public mouth-piece of Theodore Roosevelt, who used the platform to voice his severe criticism of President Wilson's foreign policy towards Germany. It landed the former American President on a list of "German sympathizers" compiled by the Bureau of Investigations.[449]

Rumely had partnered with the Irish immigrant, Samuel McClure, a muckraker of the first order. S. S. McClure had fearlessly taken on Standard Oil and John D. Rockefeller, in particular, as editor of the *McClure's Magazine*.[450] Lincoln Steffens, a fellow muckraker and close friend, published numerous exposés in *McClure's Magazine* on the rampant corruption of municipal government around the country.[451] The articles gained national acclaim. McClure, as well, made it his mission to fight corruption in the United States. His model for a successful local form of government was that of Germany. McClure's editorials, in part as a result of his Irish heritage but also as a student of Germany's political system, took on a distinct pro-German tinge that, as the war broke out, rivaled only George Sylvester Viereck in audacity.[452] McClure became the public face of the paper's editorials. Famous editors, such as H. L. Mencken and John E. Cullen, as well as reporters of the stature of John Reed, joined the pro-German editorial staff.[453]

Despite the German ownership of the paper, Rumely made some effort to portray a sense of neutrality. However, the message in the paper's editorials mirrored that of the *Fatherland*: "England's blockade violates international law," "Germany has a right to defend itself with submarines," "the United States should be militarily better prepared (therefore using available arms and munitions for its own forces rather than selling them to the Entente)," and "the U.S. should intervene in Mexico and create order." One significant difference was the absence of scholarly contributors, especially the German-American professors that cluttered the pages of the *Fatherland* with their intellectual treatises week after week.[454]

The sinking of the *Lusitania* on May 7th 1915 severely affected the potential for success of the German-owned paper. The public sentiment in New York caused subscription rates for Rumely's venture to deteriorate within months of the sinking. The *Evening Mail* slid into the red by the fall of 1915. The German embassy, unwilling to give up on its investment, supported the paper financially until the entry of the United States into the war. Over and over, a steady stream of German funds flowed across to the McClure Newspaper Corporation, Rumely and McClure's partnership.[455] According to the *New York Times*, the total financial support of the embassy amounted to $626,000, although Albert's books reflect payments of $273,000 coded to "Hays-Perez." Other payments are coded "Kaufman- P. matter," which likely covered another project.[456]

1916							
Oct.	13	By payment of 10% on account of SS Brynhilda,					$20,000.
" "	13	" to Hays Kaufmann & Lindheim for legal services up to Sept. 30, 1916					31,600.
" "	13	Payment to Hays for account of Imperial German Embassy re "Perez" matter,					30,000.
" "	26	Payment to Hays for account of Imperial German Embassy re "Perez" matter,					30,000.
Nov.	3	" "	" "	" "	" "	" "	32,000.
" "	20	" "	" "	" "	" "	" "	20,000.
" "	28	" "	" "	" "	" "	"	20,000.
Dec.	4	" "	" "	" "	" "	" "	18,000.
" "	6	" "	" "	" "	" "	" "	30,000.

457

Rumely finally was arrested on July 8th 1918, on charges of perjury and trading with the enemy, since he had lied about the true ownership of the newspaper to government investigators.

The purchase of the *Evening Mail* would not be the only investment of the German propagandists. One of the mainstays of German-American newspapers was the *New Yorker Staats-Zeitung*. More than 547 German language publications existed in cities all over the North and West of the United States in 1914.[458] Fifty-three of these publications were newspapers, many of which served the German-American communities of Wisconsin, Ohio, and Illinois.[459] The *New Yorker Staats-Zeitung*, however, was the largest and one of the oldest. Owned by Herman Ridder, the paper had a significant influence on the war reporting in the mainstream American press. More often than not, the *New York Times* and others quoted articles that had first appeared in Ridder's *Staats-Zeitung*. Naturally, the German embassy considered the paper an important outlet to communicate with the German-American community of New York. Herman Ridder, the senior owner, unexpectedly died in January 1915. He left to his sons a paper that was indebted up to $300,000 ($6.3 million in today's value). Afraid of having to declare bankruptcy, the Ridders appealed to the German ambassador for help. Count Bernstorff estimated the cash needs of the paper to be around $550,000 ($11.5 million in today's value) and urged the German government to provide immediate help of at least $200,000 ($4.2 million in today's value) in a telegram.[460]

Dernburg and Albert knew for a while that the *Staats-Zeitung* was in dire straits. Adolph Pavenstedt of G. Amsinck and Co., the primary banking connection for Albert in 1914, admitted in 1917 that Dernburg supported the ailing paper financially. Pavenstedt, a member of the Board of Directors of Ridder's concern up to the outbreak of the war, knew the Ridders personally.

> Perely Morse ...made public today testimony given by Adolph Pavenstedt former head of the banking house of G. Amsinck and Company to the effect that he loaned $20,000 to the late Herman Ridder, publisher of the *New Yorker Staats-Zeitung*... Pavenstedt's testimony showed $15,000 of the payment came from Dr. Bernhard Dernburg, former German colonial minister, and director of German propaganda in this country but that neither Mr. Ridder nor any member of his family ever knew of Dernbrug's [sic] connection with the transaction. Mr. Ridder came to him about the time the European war began, Pavenstedt said and asked for a loan of $20,000. Without Mr. Ridder's knowledge Pavenstedt went to Dernburg and told him the situation. He said he told Dernburg the Ridder's 'have always followed a very good course for the 'German interests here.' 'Then I asked hi mif [sic] he would put up the money.' Pavenstedt testified. Dernburg replied that because he wanted him (Pavenstedt) 'interested,' he would give $15,000 if Pavenstedt would give $5,000 advance money. 'I talked to my partners about it and the firm of Amsinck and company first advanced the $5,000 with the $15,000 of Denburg' [sic] but I afterward personally took the money from my account because the partners objected ... None of Mr. Herman Ridder's sons, nor any one [sic] connected with them on the *Staats* [sic] knew Pavenstedt had not advanced his own money.[461]

The witness produced the copy of a check for $20,000 from Pavenstedt to Ridder, dated October 12th 1914.[462] The small loan did little to save the paper when the extent of Ridder's financial problems came to light in January 1915. The Imperial Foreign Office agreed to prop the

Ridders up with a $200,000 credit in response to Count Bernstorff's emergency request. Rather than disbursing the money, Pavenstedt organized an issue of $200,000 worth of preferred stock. The shares raised the required cash and the paper remained in business given the German government's guarantee in the background.[463] The *Staats-Zeitung* and the *Fatherland* constituted the two main German language dependencies in the United States until the entry of the United States into the war.

In addition to mainstream papers, the German propaganda effort also covered a wide range of smaller publications that served other minority communities considered to be pro-German or susceptible to German propaganda. The Irish-American papers, *Bull*, edited by Jeremiah A. O'Leary, Sinn Fein's news outlet, the *Gaelic American*, edited by John Devoy, and the *Irish Press and News Service* organized by James K. McGuire, received ample support from the propaganda funds of the German War Department. A. Bruce Bielaski, the Bureau of Investigations chief testified in 1918 before a U.S. Senate subcommittee:

> James K. McGuire, who organized this Irish Press and News Service for the Germans, was also the author of two books... in whose publication he was financially assisted by Dr. Albert's office... McGuire is the owner of the following newspapers and publishing companies: *The Syracuse Printing and Publishing Co.*, the *Wolff-Thomas Publishing Co.*, New York; the *National Catholic*, New York; the *Light*, Albany; the *Truth*, Scranton; the *Sun*, Syracuse. He also furnished Irish news to a number of other Catholic papers. He sent out through this news service bulletins two or three times a week to 18 or 20 papers in which he had been interested, and to the daily newspapers. The number of copies he sent out varied according to the importance of the subject matter. He would send out 50 or 60, sometimes two or three hundred.[464]

McGuire, the former mayor of Syracuse, received $14,800 for his venture on June 19th 1915 ($310,000 in today's value).[465]

The bookkeeping of Heinrich Albert contains a second

newspaper purchasing account under the code "Perez II." This second account shows a $220,000 ($4.6 million in today's value) investment in a "Jewish Newspaper."[466] The Foreign Office had dispatched two German Zionists, Dr. Isaac Strauss and Arthur Meyerowitz with a translator in the fall of 1914 to specifically target the American-Jewish community. They were to promote a pro-German message and collect donations "for the needy Jews in Eastern Europe."[467] Albert's accounting does not show any disbursements to the two propagandists in the fall of 1914. Still, likely with funds of their own, the German agitators engaged in propaganda activities that Bernhard Dernburg lauded in November 1914: "Relations with the American Jewish press had 'come off to a good start' and were being carefully cultivated."[468] Dr. Isaac Strauss received $20,000 from Albert on January 14th 1915. Another payment of $25,000 followed later that year.[469] Von Papen's propaganda accounts show monthly stipends of $1,500, $2,000, and $3,000 to Strauss at the same time.[470] He received another $7,500 and $12,000 in 1916.[471] Strauss received over $100,000 ($2.1 million in today's value) from Albert in total.

Albert's books, as well as Count Bernstorff's memoirs, are silent as to the identity of the "Jewish Newspaper" that they purchased. The project could, in fact, have been the publication of a new, monthly periodical, the *American Jewish Chronicle*, owned by Isaac Strauss.[472] It first appeared in May 1916 and does not seem to have produced the desired impact Albert had envisioned. According to historian Doerries, the investment had been a mistake, and Strauss refunded the full amount to the German government. Count Bernstorff wrote to Chancellor von Bethmann Hollweg later that year: "May I ask you to treat this transaction as nonexistent, especially also when dealing with Jewish circles."[473] Strauss refunded the $100,000 in two payments on September 21st and 23rd 1916, coded "Payment by J. Simon, Dr. Strauss."[474] Since John Simon was one of Albert's most important trade connections, it cannot be said for sure whether this credit reflected a true reimbursement or whether Albert simply re-coded the investment from the Foreign Office to his commercial accounts, so that Count Bernstorff's superiors would be content. The Strauss venture did not amount to $220,000, which leads to the suspicion that there were other, secret investments into Jewish publications.

Albert's accounts show two mysterious payments in his temporary advance account. Coded "Steamship 'Perez'," Albert paid $190,000 to an unknown recipient on May 27th 1915. There was no steamship *Perez*, of course, nor was this payment related to the purchase of the *New York Evening Mail*, which had already been paid on May 15th.[475] Another strange payment went to a Leo Wallerstein on September 17th 1915, coded "Perez matter." Wallerstein was the inventor of a brewing technique that revolutionized industrial beer production. His involvement with the *Perez* project is unknown. It is certain, as a result of the coding and timing of the payment, that the payment to Wallerstein, as well, had nothing to do with the *New York Evening Mail*.[476] Again, no explanation regarding what these funds supported can be found. It is very likely, however, that some of these payments covered the $220,000 investment in the mysterious "Jewish Newspaper," which Albert shows under the code "Perez II."[477]

478

One of the preeminent Jewish journalists and editors in New York was Herman Bernstein. He founded the Yiddish daily *Der Tag* in October of 1914 with unknown funding, just around the time the German Press Bureau was ramping up operations.[479] He remained its editor until 1916, when he founded another Jewish daily, the *American Hebrew*. According to Bernstein's own, somewhat subjective opinion, he wrote to a potential investor in the venture in May 1915: "The *Day* has achieved the greatest success that a Jewish newspaper has ever achieved anywhere in the world... We have attained in six months a daily circulation of over seventy thousand, more than *The Jewish Daily News*, established thirty years ago, and as big a circulation as the *Wahrheit* [truth], established about ten years ago..."[480] Bernstein's hostility towards Russia and his scathing editorials against this arch enemy of Germany were fully in line with Dernburg and Strauss's propaganda goals towards the Jewish-American minority. "Yiddish newspapers, like Herman Berstein's [sic] *Der Tag*, reported on atrocities and massacres committed by Russian troops in occupied territories against the Jewish population ... Although Russia and her allies tried to gain the favor of the American Jewry with origins in Eastern Europe, this part of the Americans of Jewish faith for a long time saw a better alternative in a victorious Germany."[481]

Correspondence of Bernstein with Strauss and his colleague, Arthur Meyerowitz, in 1915 suggest that there was quite a substantial interaction between the journalist and the German propagandists, especially Meyerowitz.[482] Strauss mentioned *Der Tag* as "our paper" in a letter to Bernstein dated December 14th 1914.[483] Meyerowitz wrote to Bernstein in a letter dated January 17th 1915, while the "Perez" project was feverishly discussed in the Press Bureau, "Today I wrote to Mr. Schiff in great detail about the conversation I had yesterday with Gr. B. [Count Bernstorff] and would ask you urgently, not to do anything until Tuesday afternoon and also not to write anything. I hope that Gr. B. [Count Bernstorff], to whom I announced your visit of today in writing yesterday, gave you a friendly reception this morning. We have to discuss all questions in detail before [underline in original] you face public discussion... Professor [illegible] introduced me to Mr. Schapiro whom I liked quite well..."[484] David Shapiro, Hans Jacob Schiff, and Max Warburg bought a majority interest in the paper for $75,000 on May 15th. Bernstein had to raise the remaining $30,000 for the agreed capitalization of $100,000.[485] He raised the main portion of this money through Julius Rosenwald of Sears and Roebuck, and Julius Goldman.[486] The meetings between Meyerowitz and Ambassador Count Bernstorff, as well as between Count Bernstorff and Schiff indicate that money from Albert found its way via Jewish bankers in New York to support *Der Tag* at the same time. How Albert accounted for the funds is not clear in his bookkeeping. The obvious link seems to be Leo Wallerstein, who received a one-time payment of $75,000 in September, coded "Perez."

The German propaganda agents' involvement with Bernstein also offers a telling glimpse into the mechanics of the Press Bureau and their influence on editors of newspapers and magazines. Bernstein was inundated with articles, clippings, books, and pamphlets from the German propaganda agents. Strauss sent the following "intelligence" to Bernstein for consideration on December 14th 1914:

"A friend of our paper, who is well informed on the German side of the conditions along the eastern theater of war writes to us: On Saturday, December 12th you featured news from London as a leading article, which claimed that the Jews of Lodz, Kutno, and Mlawa were not only mistreated by the Russians but also suffered a lot at the hands of German soldiers. This report does not... represent the truth. Notwithstanding the fact that looting, as it has been reported from the region of Kutno, are impossible as a result of the discipline for which the German gentleman [probably a type meaning army – Herr versus Heer] is known..."[487] On the cover of his letter, Strauss wrote, "If you consider it appropriate, could you please feature the attached note. Best regards, your subservient Straus[sic]."[488] Meyerowitz was less subtle about his requests. He wrote to Bernstein on November 16th 1914, "I am sending you attached the Austrian *Wochenschau* and the *Israelist*. Also I am sending you an article about the war and the emigration issue. Can you tell me if you will feature this? In this case it would have to be translated... I would ask you... not [underlined in the original] to mention my name."[489] Meyerowitz followed up on December 5th 1914:

> Dear Mr. Bernstein: -
>
> For the past weeks I have sent you a great number of smaller and greater notes and articles for publication in your valued paper. I did this for two reasons. In the first place, it seems to me, the publications of these articles will be of great advantage to the general Jewish cause, and in the second place I had put same at your disposal exclusively with a view to help your young enterprise along. To my regret, only a few of these articles have appeared so far. I realize perfectly, that at the present time you will have so much material on hand, that I cannot reasonably ask you to publish all I have sent you.
>
> ... In [the] future I would request in our mutual interest that you return in a day or two that material, which you cannot print. Otherwise a great deal of work and endeavor will be to no avail and I do not accomplish the purpose I have in view...[490]

Meyerowitz offered to Bernstein in another letter, "I would rather read the proof myself and am willing to come to the printer late at night, so that there will be no mistakes... "[491] In addition to free proof reading, the German agent also gave the Jewish editor regular summaries of "newspaper articles dealing with Jewish issues from the German press."[492] The German Information Service that handled a similar news summary for the Irish press in America obviously cut clippings for the Jewish press, as well.

Marcus Braun, the Hungarian-American editor of the magazine, *Fair Play*, also received support through the German propaganda organization. After Count Bernstorff had publicly commended the pro-German reporting of the magazine in March 1915, he directed Heinrich Albert to pay Braun a monthly stipend of $1,200 ($25,200 in today's value) for a few months in 1915.[493] Braun received $3,574.20 ($75,000 in today's value) in January 1916, to go away after he had tried to milk the German embassy for more.[494] Albert's accounts are not entirely clear on other payments to smaller publications. Two entries in October 1916 show $18,000 and $5,000 withdrawals from Albert personally coded, "Press matter." Where the money ended up cannot be surmised. The Hearst Press reported the German side of daily events with more than casual sympathy. Whether or not Albert or Dernburg financially "rewarded" individual reporters is not documented, but highly likely.

Edward Lyell Fox, a correspondent of the Wildman Syndicate, went to Germany in 1915 to report on the German war effort and dispel negative reports on German atrocities in Belgium. His work was widely printed in the Hearst press. Fox was actually a paid agent of the German government. He not only reported in the German interest, he also did camera work for German propaganda films destined for the U.S. market. Fox was uncovered when English search parties confiscated Franz von Papen's luggage at Falmouth, England, in January 1916. The editorial head of Germany's press office in New York, William Bayard Hale, received an assignment from Hearst in 1916 to report from Germany, while he was still on the payroll of the German government.[495] Karl Alexander Fuehr, the German propaganda chief after Dernburg left the United States in June 1915, commented in 1916, "Only the following papers can be described as really neutral [pro-German]:

The New York Evening Mail, *The Milwaukee Free Press*, *The Washington Post*, *The Chicago Tribune*, and the Hearst Papers: *New York American, New York Journal, Chicago Examiner, Evening American, Boston American, Atlanta Georgian, San Francisco Examiner, Los Angeles Examiner,* and the *Evening Herald.*"[496] Possible examples for undue influence are disbursals that went to Ernst A. Schirmer, who worked for *Pearson's Magazine.* He received several payments in 1916 amounting to $1,500 ($31,500 in today's value), either for influencing his reporting or for smuggling German propaganda films to the United States, or both.[497] In addition to the already pro-German papers and magazines of the Irish-American, German-American, and Indian-American communities, historian Hirst documented that by 1916 German influence on editorial boards of mainstream American magazines and newspapers covered several dozen publications all across the United States.[498]

The films Schirmer brought to the United States document another, fascinating propaganda project of Heinrich Albert's. Following the establishment of the German press office under Dernburg's direction, the German propaganda organizers decided to send American journalists to Germany in order to obtain direct information from Americans, which catered to an American audience. Two American journalists, Edward Lyell Fox and Albert Knox Dawson, went to Germany in November 1914 as war correspondents. Fox officially worked for the *Wildman Magazine*, while Dawson worked as a freelancer.[499] Initially, the German government reacted coolly to the assignment of the two Americans. However, after Matthew Claussen, the member of Dernburg's staff responsible for publicity and film, sent a more forceful message to Germany, the two were allowed to start their work embedded with the German army. Claussen wrote: "Repeat urgently earlier suggestion about photographer Dawson and war correspondent Fox. It would be most undesirable if both should leave without accomplishing anything. Moving pictures by Dawson, with Fox's cooperation, in which, if possible, correspondents themselves appear, urgently desired. Costs would be covered by big newspapers here."[500]

A familiar face of American cinematography joined the two journalists in Germany, Frank N. Thayer.[501] He had directed the American blockbuster *And Starring Pancho Villa as Himself* for the Mutual Film Company in 1914. The team went to the Western Front with several cameramen and staff and started shooting footage of the war. Over

2,500 feet of film from the front made its way to New York in March 1915. Albert incorporated the American Correspondent Film Company on April 12th 1915 in keeping with the other investments in propaganda projects.[502] The straw man of the operation was Ernst Reinhold Felix Malitz who reported to Matthew Claussen. Malitz, who was born of a German father and Italian mother in Brandenburg, Germany in 1876, worked with Albert on sourcing and exporting rubber from the United States to Germany.[503] He had arrived in New York from Germany on August 3rd 1912 and lived in lower Manhattan with his wife, Martha.[504] He still was a German citizen at the time when he engaged in business with Albert.[505] The initial funds, two payments to Claussen on June 21st for $23,500, came from von Papen's propaganda account.[506] Albert paid $50,000 on October 5th 1915 to the "American Correspondence [sic] Film Company," which financed the launch of nine feature films in October, November, and December.[507] Albert added another $12,000 to the company in March 1916.[508] According to the *New York Tribune*, Albert invested a total of $72,000 ($1.5 million in today's value) in the film production company. Possibly, the payments to Claussen only in part went to this project, but it is far more likely that in excess of $86,000 ($1.8 million in today's value) went to Malitz and his colleagues to finance the European trips and production expenses.[509]

Although historians have discounted the German effort as inconsequential, Albert's efforts require a closer look. The company published and screened nine movies in 1915 and 1916, all of which had been shot in Europe.[510] Dawson and Fox assembled one-hour movies from footage of German military cameramen, as well as their own cinematography. The reels found their way to the United States via Schirmer, Fox, Dawson and others. The movies received English subtitles in studios in Connecticut.

The Battle and Fall of Przemysl was a full-length (four reels at twelve minutes each) feature film that debuted in American theatres in November 1915.[511] Historian van Dopperen described the content:

> Although most of the footage in Dawson's film appears to have been taken behind the front lines, it showed some amazing aspects of warfare: Austrian brigade headquarters are seen being hit by a Russian shell; a pilot takes off in his plane to locate the enemy's

battery; high above Przemysl, the artillery's position is marked on a map and the guns are finally destroyed. Such a clear-cut sequence is rather exceptional for a World War I film, since scenes were often edited without much attention to continuity. Dawson's film pictured the Austrian soldiers cheerfully enjoying camp before Przemysl. Then, in Part 3, the siege guns are put into action while a group of machinegunners [sic] move forward into the fight. As a climax, soldiers are seen rushing up the heights around the river San in their attempt to storm the forts of Przemysl. According to Edward Lyell Fox, Dawson nearly lost his life while filming this scene. Some may have had their doubts as to its authenticity, but the trade paper Variety was strongly impressed. 'It is so well photographed,' explained a reviewer, 'that one might for a minute suspect it was staged for the benefit of the camera, but this is overshadowed when one sees the dying kicks of one poor devil who fell as his comrades stroke [sic] into the rain of bullets. The manner in which he falls and his dying convulsions are enough to convince the most skeptical [sic].'[512]

The film magazine, Billboard, hailed the movie as a first-class production. "It was generally agreed by those present that the films were the most remarkable of the many battle pictures so far shown in this country."[513] Motion Picture News commented on the film, "A valuable attraction."[514] Other full-length movies followed, such as Warring Millions (1915), System – The Secret of Success (1915), The Battles of a Nation (1916), and The Fighting Germans (1916).

It would be too easy to discount these efforts as inconsequential. Dernburg had hired experienced professionals in Thayer, Fox, and Dawson as part of the strategy to make a more "American" targeted propaganda. To be able to shoot original footage, assemble, publish, and distribute it all within a twelve-month time span in no way lagged behind the active and successful film propaganda the English produced for the U.S. market. The manner of distribution of these movies is also impressive. Despite the animosity towards Germany and the repercussions for American companies for working with the German government, the propagandists in New York managed to enlist the Mutual Film Company, which had distributed the very successful Pancho Villa movies and was about to become Charlie Chaplin's platform. Hearst agreed to take on the German films, as well, during negotiations with Ambassador Count Bernstorff. This arrangement, however, did not cover all productions in all regions. Additionally, Dawson and retired general Samuel A. Pearson traveled all along the East Coast, South, Midwest, and West showing the films and "offering supplemental lectures."[515] The press office in New York achieved a remarkable amount of work in a short period of time, for a total investment of less than $100,000. The German propaganda in itself, nonetheless, could not prevent the fallout of the sinking of the *Lusitania* and the highly effective English propaganda from shifting the weight of public opinion towards the Entente. However, starting in the spring of 1915, that had not been the objective. Film propaganda was designed to help keep the U.S. out of the war as long as possible, thus supporting the other projects directed against the United States. It was successful in that regard.

Besides the marked change in strategy and efficiency in 1915, the personnel attached to the war propaganda office raises important questions. A mystery man appeared in the meeting notes of the German press committee. Customarily, the protocols of the Press Office meetings contained only the principal members, Dernburg, Meyer, Meyer-Gerhardt, Hale, Viereck, Fuehr, Cronemeyer, and Claussen. However, there were more participants in these meetings. Witnesses testified in 1918 that Rumely had attended from time to time. Count Bernstorff also mentioned in his memoirs, *My Three Years in America*, "a small committee nominated by himself [Dernburg] and consisting, in addition to Herren Albert, Meyer, Gerhardt and Fuehr, of a few American journalists and business men."[516] These American journalists were unmasked in the testimony of A. Bruce Bielaski before the U.S. Senate in 1918: Edward Lyell Fox of the American Correspondent Film Company, James F. J. Archibald, another war correspondent arrested in England on the way to Germany, who had letters from Franz von Papen in his possession, and Edward Emerson.[517] Bielaski does not mention the "businessmen" in Count Bernstorff's description. These definitely included Edward A. Rumely who had tried throughout the fall to instill a pro-German influence in *The New York Evening Mail*. Frederico Stallforth also seems to be a candidate. He wrote a letter to Heinrich Albert on January 26th 1915, in which he mentioned giving Albert a medal from Dernburg.[518] Albert wrote to an investor in German war bonds on November 3rd 1915, "I know Mr. Stallforth superficially, being formerly acquainted with him. He represents the German-American Bank and has also had dealings with Dr. Dernburg."[519] The nature of Stallforth's "dealings" with Bernhard Dernburg is not known, but likely involved propaganda work.

A third businessman, who as a naval intelligence spy had obvious reasons for staying in the background, was Felix A. Sommerfeld. Sommerfeld had shown interest in Dernburg's work, helped him with the introduction to William Bayard Hale, and was well connected to newspaper editors in the city through his work for Madero, Carranza, and Villa. A highly skilled press manipulator, the German agent intimately knew influential American editors from his time in Mexico, David Lawrence of *The New York Evening Post* (like Hale a confidante and special envoy of President Wilson), William Willis of *The New York Herald*, Chris Haggerty of *Associated Press*, Timothy Turner on assignment in Europe, Jimmy Hare on assignment in Europe, Frank Thayer of the Mutual Film Company, and many more. Another among his contacts from his work on the Mexican border was Fred B. Warren, now a vice president of the Goldwyn Film Corporation and former owner of *The St. Louis Star*.[520] William Randolph Hearst, so close with Count Bernstorff that his associates called the German ambassador "Hans," also knew Felix Sommerfeld.[521] Sommerfeld negotiated with Venustiano Carranza and Pancho Villa to save Hearst's 1.6 million-acre ranch, Babicora, in Chihuahua from confiscation.[522] Though revolutionary irregulars looted the ranch multiple times, the land remained in the family until 1953. The newspaper mogul, therefore, owed some measure of gratitude to the German agent who mediated on several occasions on his behalf. To the delight of German propagandists, Hearst's outrage at President Wilson's foreign policy vis-à-vis Mexico translated into editorials that were highly critical of the American administration. Sommerfeld also had excellent connections with the Wilson administration, as well as former government officials, such as Secretary of State Philander Knox.

Heinrich Albert mentioned a curious set of initials in an undated letter to Count Bernstorff, believed to have been drafted in January or February 1915, in which Albert supported purchasing American newspapers: "M.M.'s work very great, and responsible; but the cooperation of all is excellent. The great confidence of the Embassy, makes him attractive to everybody, as well as Boy-Ed and v. Papen; for Dernburg discusses everything with him... "[523] This mystery person, who appeared only once in Albert's papers, seems to have taken charge of the direction of the propaganda strategy sometime in the first months of 1915. None of the archival records dealing with Dernburg, Albert, the German embassy, and propaganda contain a name with the initials M. M.[524] This person, who had attached himself closely with Dernburg, was acceptable to Count Bernstorff and the two military attachés. The German propaganda chief wrote in a secret message sent to Admiral Henning von Holtzendorff on May 10th 1915: "...Through my friend, Felix A. Sommerfeld, German citizen... "[525] There were not many people in Bernhard Dernburg's circle to whom he would refer as "my friend." While no definite proof exists, there is significant circumstantial evidence that Felix Sommerfeld indeed was M. M.

The influence of this mysterious M. M. on German propaganda was profound. He coordinated the interests of the Foreign Office with those of the German War and Interior Departments. He also balanced the influence of strong personalities who did not always get along, namely, Count Bernstorff, Albert, Dernburg, Fuehr, von Papen, and Boy-Ed. Sommerfeld's influence became noticeable with the hiring of his friend, William Bayard Hale. This marked the end of the tiring and ineffective messaging of German cultural superiority and militarism in the American mainstream press. It extended to the acquisition of the *New York Evening Mail*, the pro-German editorials in many of the large dailies, such as the *Boston Globe*, the *New York Herald*, the *New York Evening Post*, and the *Washington Post*. Finally, the Dernburg office made use of completely new media: movies.

Without question, German propaganda efforts made a significant leap in the spring of 1915. Dernburg's speeches started to have a positive impact. Mainstream publications, especially the Hearst press, used more and more information of the press offices' news service. American correspondents, such as Fox, began to bring back news items that were not controlled by the British. Then, the unspeakable happened: The *Lusitania* sinking in May 1915. Within days, the German propaganda machine lay in shambles. Desperate attempts by Dernburg and others to explain away the savagery of the German action with legal arguments dug the hole for German propagandists deeper. Dernburg was on his way back to Germany within a month of the sinking. While the press bureau continued its work, and many of the projects of the spring of 1915 came to fruition in the latter part of that year, German propaganda never fully recovered from this single setback. Albert described his definition of the United States to his wife on May 13th 1915, one week after the demise of the *Lusitania*, "I feel like a sane person who is watching with uneasiness whether a grown, powerful brat with an atrophying brain is able to become healthy again or whether he will harm those next to him or living with him while he is recovering."[526]

It is easy for historians to judge the German efforts as a complete failure from start to finish. Undoubtedly, the German propaganda with the express goal of convincing the American public to support the German cause had been ineffective between August and November 1914. Amateur propagandists with a complete lack of plan and focus clumsily botched the few, but existing, chances to make a case for "true neutrality" by German definition. "The Germans seemed determined, not only to counter Allied interpretations, but to provide Americans with so much information that they could not fail to see the justice of the German cause. That this procedure would induce the United States to pursue a kind of neutrality that ruled out aid or encouragement to the Allies, was the obvious hope."[527] This hope was clearly dashed in the spring of 1915, when the American economy hummed with British, Russian, and French orders financed by J. P. Morgan. There was no chance, and Count Bernstorff, Dernburg, Albert, von Papen, Boy-Ed, and others in the German team in the U.S. had no doubts about it, that the U.S. would voluntarily embrace an embargo and return to a resulting economic recession. Albert noted in his diary on April 8th 1915, "Press session. Important communications from H. [Hale] which coincide with my view that there is no hope at all for energetic action on the part of the United States against England."[528] This would have been political suicide for the Wilson administration, one year before presidential elections.

Designed to complement the war effort against the United States, German propaganda continued on its mission to buy time after the *Lusitania* sinking until the United States eventually entered into the European war. Albert commented to his wife about the frustration, but also the resolve, that followed the sinking of the ocean liner: "We are starting from scratch again. We are constantly filling the barrel of Sysiphos [sic – slight mix-up of Greek mythology], because it won't change anything... But it would be ridiculous to despair now. You know that is not the way I am. We just have to keep working."[529]

Albert and his colleagues diligently kept up the work. Political divisions over the course of American foreign policy that followed the *Lusitania* sinking caused the resignation of Secretary of State William Jennings Bryan. The United States also started to ramp up for the presidential elections of 1916. Cunningly, German agitators talked up and supported the candidacy of the republican candidate, Charles Evens Hughes. Bryan's wing of the Democratic Party also served as a tool of German agitators to split public opinion over Wilson's foreign policy. It is hard to measure exactly to what extent German propaganda drove these developments on the American political scene. However, without question, divisions in the political landscape supported the express German goal of delaying decisive action by the United States government. President Wilson won the elections of 1916 with the slogan "He kept us out of war." The implication was that his election would guarantee a continuation of this course. Despite the fact that by the time of the election President Wilson had most likely already decided that war with Germany was inevitable, it required a huge propaganda effort lasting months, after his decision was made to secure public support for a war.

The German propaganda changed its purpose after November 1914, and especially with the proper funding from the Imperial War Department starting in February 1915. The motto now read: Make it as difficult as possible for the U.S. to enter the war against the Central Powers. Against this background, the propaganda effort made a steep turn-around, albeit with a wholly different set of goals. By the time the German government sent orders to New York to start deliberate acts of war in the United States on January 24th 1915, and declared unrestricted submarine warfare against commercial shipping on February 4th, the propaganda organization in the U.S. was well staffed, its efforts focused, and its projects funded. Despite the setbacks, investments in minority publications, pro-German movies, editors in mainstream papers, and more targeted, subtle messaging, showed results. There was never a chance of turning the United States' public decidedly against the Entente, and the members of the Secret War Council never kidded themselves about this fact. However, from the spring of 1915 until the fall of 1916, German propaganda became the most effective it would be during the whole war period. British observers agreed, including Sir Horace Plunkett, who in April 1916 sent a memorandum to Sir Cecil Spring Rice, claiming that the Germans were using various kinds of news "superbly," and that "the British were being bested in this area."[530]

The American government worked hard to balance the economic benefits of supplying the Entente with the resulting repercussions of attracting the war to American shores. This balancing act lost President Wilson the support of his political ally and Secretary of State, William Jennings Bryan. He, as well as law enforcement and clandestine services of the American government, saw how a storm was brewing among German agents, German sympathizers, and pro-German minority groups within the country. Albert and his colleagues, von Papen and Boy-Ed of the military and naval branches of the Imperial War Department, had received clear orders in January 1915: Stop the flow of munitions to the Entente with all means at your disposal. Thus, while the German propaganda pushed for "true neutrality," "arms embargo," "peace," and "freedom of trade," German agents now planned and executed the most egregious acts, targeting the officially neutral United States.

It would be a mistake to try to separate the German propaganda from the ensuing sabotage campaign, market-cornering efforts, missions to create a war between the U.S. and Mexico, and the destabilization of the American workforce. Albert did not switch hats from 'propaganda agitator' with the goal of American neutrality to 'throat-cutting mastermind' in his responsibility as paymaster of sabotage agents. One set of responsibilities complemented the others. The purpose of German propaganda after January 24th 1915 was to prevent the exportation of munitions, while dragging out the eventual entry of the United States into the war. By the spring of 1915, no one was in doubt as to the disposition of the United States towards the German Empire. The supply of the Entente with arms and ammunition had made her into a combatant from the German point of view, and that of William Jennings Bryan, scores of American politicians, and leaders of minority communities. The munitions supplies had to be stopped, and the New York team had authorization to use any means at its disposal, propaganda being one of them. The Imperial War Department footed the bill as a logical consequence. Just as Albert, Dernburg, and Count Bernstorff closed the deal on the *New York Evening Mail*, a host of agents armed with generous funds, germs, plans for building bombs, and causing civil unrest swarmed out from New York, Baltimore, Newport News, New Orleans, Detroit, and San Francisco to wreak havoc on the country that had become the vital supply backbone for Germany's enemies.

CHAPTER 9: RUDDER BOMBS

THE FIREBOMB CELL IN NEW Jersey under Walter T. Scheele was but one of a host of clandestine groups that worked on sabotaging factories, harbors, and ships. Also with a mission to sink freight ships on the East Coast of the U.S. was the secret agent Lieutenant Robert Fay. He arrived in New York on April 24th from Rotterdam.[531] The twenty-four year-old infantry officer caught the attention of his superiors in February 1915, while serving on the Western Front in France. Fay, who himself had suffered from the lethal rain of American-made artillery munitions, proposed a time-bomb design that disabled rudders on munitions ships traveling from the United States to Europe. Fay showed his idea to the battalion commander. Impressed with the details, Fay's superior alerted the army intelligence office in Berlin who invited and interviewed the young soldier.[532] Not only did Fay have a design that seemed like a good idea, he had also worked at the Submarine Signal Company in Boston before the war and spoke English fluently.[533] His brother-in-law, Walter E. Scholz, eight years older than Fay, still lived in New Jersey. The trained mechanic worked as a draftsman for railroad companies. Rudolph Nadolny of the General Staff, Department IIIB, Political Section, gave Fay a fake Scottish passport under the name of H. A. Kearling and $4,000 ($84,000 in today's value) for a sabotage mission in the U.S. He was to report directly to Military Attaché von Papen in New York and proceed with his plans.[534] Von Papen, not sure what to think of the much older-looking, lanky soldier with sunken cheeks, prominent nose, receding hairline, and black mustache, sent him to talk to Franz Rintelen, who was working hard on getting the Scheele conspiracy back on track.[535]

Rintelen claimed in his book that he paid Fay to develop a contraption designed to sink merchant ships. Von Papen told the Mixed Claims Commission in the 1920s that he and Boy-Ed suspected Fay to be an English spy and sent him away. Fay himself told investigators that he received contacts from von Papen to help him source explosives and build his bomb. His statements square with the protocols of his co-conspirators. Whether or not Rintelen played a role in Fay's work from the onset remains unclear. It is likely that Rintelen told the truth about his connection with Fay since he was in charge of the bomb plot in New York at the time when Fay first reported to von Papen. Like the Scheele project, Fay's mission hung in the balance from the beginning because the bomb only worked theoretically. Fay's idea of a timed explosive sounded promising to von Papen, but it was a complicated design.

> A brief description of the contrivance reveals the mechanical ingenuity and practical efficiency of Fay's bomb. A rod attached to the rudder[,] at every swing the rudder gave[,] turned up by one notch the first of the beveled wheels within the bomb. After a certain number of revolutions of that wheel it in turn gave one revolution to the next and so on through the series. The last wheel was connected with the threaded cap around the upper end of the square bolt and made this cap slowly unscrew until at length the bolt dropped clear of it and yielded to the waiting pressure of the strong steel spring above. This pressure drove it downward and brought the sharp points at its lower end down on the caps of the two rifle cartridges fixed below it like the blow of a rifle's hammer. The detonation from the explosion of these cartridges would set off a small charge of impregnated chlorate of potash which in turn would fire the small charge of the more sluggish but stronger dynamite and that in turn would explode the still more sluggish but tremendously more powerful trinitrotoluol.[536]

The resulting explosion, Fay argued, would be strong enough to blow the stern of a ship off and sink it. American investigators, who looked at Fay's design after his arrest, agreed with the claim.[537]

The German agent established his workshop in his brother-in-law's garage in Weehawken, New Jersey. Initially, and with the help of Rintelen's agent, Otto Wolpert, Fay bought one hundred pounds of potassium chlorate. However, he needed more. Through von Papen, Fay met the nephew of a wealthy financier by the name Max Breitung. Fay asked Breitung for help. The young financier, anxious to prove his worth to the German government, had met the New York factory representative of a German cuckoo clock manufacturer on a transatlantic voyage. They had kept in contact through the German Club in New York. The acquaintance was Dr. Herbert O. Kienzle, a thirty year-old engineer from the town of Scheveningen in the Black Forest area of Germany. Kienzle had been a keen supporter of the Secret War Council's propaganda efforts. He had written several articles on Dum Dum [hollow point] bullets for the German-owned paper, *Fatherland*, and New York's German language daily, *New Yorker Staats-Zeitung*. His investigative journalism also appeared in large American dailies. The war had ground his clock business to a halt. He made several futile attempts to diversify the product line, getting into lamps, linens, and crafts, but the prospective American customers stayed away from his exclusive store on Park Place. Like Edward Rumely, the managing editor of the German-owned *New York Evening Mail*, and others that engaged with the Secret War Council's projects, the engineering PhD had time on his hands and holes in his pocket.

While researching his articles, he had found a patent the Remington Arms Company had filed recently regarding Dum Dum bullets. This type of hollow point bullet disintegrates on impact and causes horrible wounds in its victims. The Hague Convention of 1899 outlawed this particular design for use in war. German outrage understandably flared when the illegal rounds suddenly appeared on the battlefields in Belgium and France. German authorities suspected U.S. manufacturers as the source. Emperor Wilhelm II vehemently protested to President Wilson in the fall of 1914. The President denied any U.S. production. Von Papen subsequently received orders to start an investigation into the matter. Kienzle took on the assignment. He traveled to Bridgeport, Connecticut, with an acquaintance from Germany, Paul Daeche, to find the truth. Indeed, the two came up with the evidence with the help of a German-American employee at Remington.[538] Von Papen was delighted and sent the illegal bullets to the German ambassador as evidence. The success of Kienzle's Dum Dum investigation prompted von Papen to assign the ambitious businessman and engineer to the Fay project.

Breitung and Kienzle secured 336 pounds of potassium chlorate for Fay, but it took until June to get it.[539] The source, a German-American chemist, was compromised. The U.S. Secret Service had noticed the movement of these explosive chemicals and sent a mole to Breitung's supplier. Through Breitung, Fay became acquainted with Kienzle and Daeche, who joined the team in the beginning of May 1915. The four, Fay, Scholz, Kienzle, and Daeche worked feverishly on the bomb design, all the while reporting back to Rintelen on the progress. Kienzle had a small motorboat, which he sold to Fay. Together, the saboteurs toured the New York harbor and checked out the large transatlantic steamers lined up to transport their deadly cargo to Europe. Security did not seem to be an issue, since guards were checking who was coming onto the ships, but not the little boats scurrying around in the harbor.

Back in the garage, the conspirators experimented with the two necessary explosives, potassium chlorate and TNT. Kienzle had a friend who worked in road construction. The clock maker's friend worked on the grounds of a sanatorium in Butler, New Jersey, where Kienzle had spent some "quiet time" in the past.[540] Builders in 1915 dynamited their way through the countryside in lieu of using heavy earth-moving equipment to prepare a roadbed. The contractor friend had lots of dynamite. When Fay went to Butler to "look that place over," he met the contractor, a German-American named Englebert Bronckhurst, who supplied him with twenty sticks.[541] Fay built a wooden replica of a ship's rudder in the backyard of Scholz' property. Fay and Scholz worked over the course of several weeks on the spring mechanism, the waterproof container for the explosives, the attachment to the rudder, and all other important details that would make the design viable. Kienzle likely did, but never admitted to having looked over the design from a technical standpoint. Since the winding spring mechanism came straight out of clock mechanics, it is hard to imagine that the trained clock maker did not have any input.[542] Sometime in June, Rintelen demanded to see a demonstration of the bomb. The team made four attempts, but the bomb did not work as designed.[543] The container with the potassium chlorate kept getting wet, the firing mechanism still had quirks, and even the dynamite did not have the envisioned result.[544] When Rintelen left for Europe in August, the project came to a grinding halt. American investigators, meanwhile, had discovered the 'cigar' bombs, and were canvassing the waterfront for any hint as to who was behind it.

Fay's next moves are not documented in detail. The four saboteurs kept working on the bombs. However, it seems that money was in short supply. According to Fay, von Papen sent him to Kentucky to bomb a manufacturing plant.[545] Fay went to the Midwest in September 1915, and canvassed the factory in question. A female witness in Chicago reported to investigators that Fay "fleeced her out of eleven hundred and fifty dollars, representing himself to be employed by German Secret Service whose draft for salary and expenses had been delayed."[546] After Fay returned to New York, he asked Kienzle to get him one hundred pounds of TNT for the factory demolition. Kienzle went to his previous source in New York. However, the chemist was now under U.S. Secret Service surveillance and did not have access to TNT. The Secret Service shadow posed as a supplier in a classical sting operation, and offered to provide the dynamite. The agent found out about the other members of the German sabotage cell during the process, and after meeting Fay, had him, Paul Daeche, and Walter Scholz arrested.

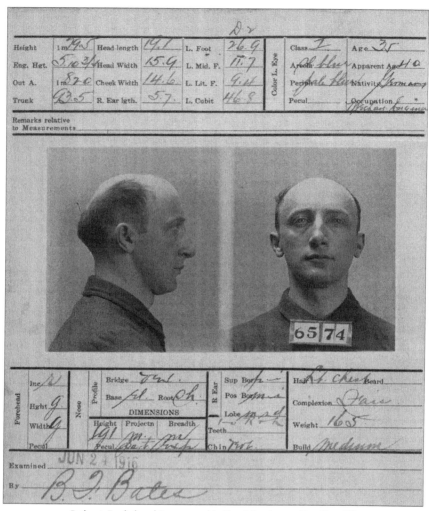

Robert Fay's booking record in the Atlanta penitentiary.[547]

The American authorities had stopped a dangerous plot that, without ever damaging a single ship or factory, had come close to fruition. When authorities searched the garage, they found four finished rudder bombs and two hundred in process.[548] Fay received an eight-year sentence; Scholz four years; and Daeche, Kienzle, and Breitung two years each. Fay's adventures in the war did not end there. The German government disavowed the agent after his exposure. A desperate nationalist, Fay could not imagine spending the rest of the war behind bars instead of the frontlines of the European war. He escaped from the federal penitentiary in Atlanta in August 1916. Von Papen supplied him with some money via Paul Koenig in a meeting in Philadelphia shortly after the escape. The agent hid in Chicago, receiving additional funds from Koenig.[549] He crossed the border into Mexico near San Diego a few months later and, with financial aid from the German legation in Mexico, made it all the way to Spain. There, his trip ended. Spanish authorities refused to let him return to Germany. He finally gave himself up to American authorities in 1918.

CHAPTER 10: THE WOLF AND THE TIGER

NVESTIGATORS, POLITICIANS, AND HISTORIANS HAVE long grappled with deciphering the true mission of Franz Rintelen. While the sabotage projects are well documented, Rintelen's role in setting up Dr. Scheele's operation, directing the efforts of Robert Fay, and having a hand in a variety of activities, such as attacks on Canada, cornering the black powder market, blowing up factories, even causing the sinking of the *Lusitania*, and the explosion of Black Tom Island, are largely exaggerated claims.[550] Rintelen published two books in the 1930s. The publicity of his claims had the purpose of boosting book sales.[551] He enjoyed the limelight and exploited the unwillingness of the German government to come clean after the war. His public feuds with Franz von Papen, Erich Hossenfelder, Heinrich Albert, Johann Heinrich Count von Bernstorff, and others, which he inflamed with outrageous claims in media interviews, earned him book sales but skewed historical treatment of his true activities for many decades.[552]

The facts of his mission are quite different from his embellished version. He received a limited amount of funds, namely $508,000 ($10.5 Million in today's value) from Karl Boy-Ed, to whom he reported.[553] Dr. Scheele's mission did not originate from him, but had been afoot months earlier. Rintelen did organize the distribution of the firebombs, an action that landed him in penitentiary. As far as archival sources show, he had nothing to do with hiring, organizing, or financing the group of agents that blew up Black Tom Island in 1916, although he personally knew some of the perpetrators. He briefly worked with the main naval intelligence agent in 1915, who destroyed the Black Tom, in order to distribute Dr. Scheele's bombs. The fires and explosions at major factories occurred long before, and long after his presence in the U.S. All evidence indicates that Boy-Ed and von Papen organized the cells that executed the sabotage missions without any measurable input from Rintelen. His problems with von Papen and Albert resulted from his lack of team spirit, brash arrogance, insubordination, and desperate need for publicity, which contributed to his eventual downfall. In short, he became a rogue agent when he worked in the United States in 1915. Rintelen had not just been recalled to Germany as a result of Boy-Ed and von Papen's complaints, but rather high-tailed it out of the country after American and British secret services had uncovered him on information from the German agent, Felix Sommerfeld.[554]

The German government maintained throughout the 1920s and 30s that Rintelen's mission was largely peaceful. While 'peaceful' is a word begging for definition in this circumstance, Rintelen did spend almost all his funds on disturbing labor relations at U.S. ports and munitions factories, not on sabotage. One could call that 'peaceful' in the sense of 'non-violent.' Although there is no question that Rintelen handled the Scheele mission for Boy-Ed, archival evidence suggests that his primary mission indeed consisted of creating labor unrest. The imperial German government had developed an interesting and progressive relationship with labor within the empire. Strictly opposed to the socialist movement – the Social Democratic Party and the Communist Party of Germany – Chancellor Prince von Bismarck and his successors co-opted the political aspirations of the German labor movement through the creation of a social security network that included old-age pensions, accident insurance, state sponsored medical care, and unemployment insurance in the decades before the war. The resulting social contract kept the left-of-center parties at bay until the end of World War I.

The idea of infiltrating labor and nationalistic movements around the world with the purpose of hurting the enemy became a priority for German war planners immediately at the onset of the war. Various connections to Irish, Indian, and Jewish minorities in the United States provided fertile ground to co-opt their aspirations for the war effort. For example, German secret agents Strauss and Meyerowitz came to the United States in the fall of 1914 to specifically cater to the Zionist movement. Count Bernstorff, Albert, von Papen, Boy-Ed, and Dernburg spent a lot of effort and funds on the minority press, as well as projects such as weapons for the Indian independence movement against Great Britain, or organizational support for the Irish revolution. Von Papen, in particular, was obsessed with the notion that German-American and German citizens produced weapons for the Allies. As soon as the Entente began buying significant amounts of munitions in the U.S., von Papen and Boy-Ed asked regional German consulates to assemble lists of German and German-American workers in factories that produced war material for the Allies. The military attaché sent out a circular to the German consulates and to German citizens in April 1915 that had been identified as working "for the enemy," and threatened them with prosecution in Germany.[555] The effort extended to propaganda articles in the German language press that pronounced any German citizen supporting the Entente war effort a traitor.[556]

Issuing threats to the German citizens, as well as to German-Americans, produced more resistance than support, to the chagrin of its organizer. The German vice-consul of New Orleans, Dr. Paul Roh, asked von Papen a few months later, in August 1915, to tone down his rhetoric as his threats "made in earlier publications... have been... commented on [by the German citizens working in factories producing for the Allies] with snide, even scorn..."[557] Grudgingly, von Papen agreed to back down and, instead, asked the consulate to find industrial companies not involved in munitions production to take over German workers.[558] The "snide and scorn" had its roots in the increasing difficulty of any German citizen or German-American to find employment, in general. The German diplomatic corps had little chance of motivating industrial workers to quit their jobs simply for 'the cause' without offering any alternatives. The recognition of this fact bore fruit. That same month, August 1915, von Papen tasked Hans Libau and Frederico Stallforth to organize a labor placement organization for workers that quit their jobs in munitions factories. This effort proved to be wildly successful.

However, before the new placement office came into existence, the Secret War Council targeted a much larger, low-hanging fruit, that would sabotage the war production for the Entente. Count Bernstorff and Bernhard Dernburg, especially, had long worked on contacts to the American Federation of Labor president, Samuel Gompers, as well as leaders of various minority groups in the United States, such as Jeremiah O'Leary, John Devoy and Har Dayal. While the German efforts yielded some sympathy with a few of the union leaders, a measurable effect on war production lacked entirely. Rintelen took over the labor project in May 1915 on orders of the War Ministry in Berlin. Rather than focus on minorities, he targeted American union workers, in general, with the aim of disrupting deliveries to Europe, and building enough political pressure to create an export embargo in the process.

The key contact for this endeavor was Thomas C. Hall, an American theology professor. Hall, an avowed socialist, had studied in Germany and headed the Union Theological Seminary in New York. He also joined the German University League and became one of the out-spoken intellectuals who publicly supported the German cause at the onset of the war.[559] His links to the German propaganda organization brought him close to Bernhard Dernburg and the rest of the Secret War Council. He contributed dozens of articles to Sylvester Viereck's *Fatherland*. He co-authored the book, *Germany's Just Cause*, together with Bernhard Dernburg and William Bayard Hale in the fall of 1914. Hale, himself a seminarian, and his wife, engaged very energetically in the American peace movement. Hall joined in the cause with a number of intellectuals and scholars. A member of the Intercollegiate Socialist Society, Hall established important connections to the International Workers of the World (IWW), as well as important union leaders including Samuel Gompers, the president of the American Federation of Labor (AFL).[560]

While the members of the Secret War Council had a variety of contacts to labor and peace movements, Rintelen needed political access to realize an audacious plan: Infiltrate peace and labor move-ments in order to instigate strikes in the munitions industries. Hall suggested an acquaintance who had political connections and whose public persona was large enough to allow Rintelen to hide in its shad-ows.[561] Like Edward Rumely, the businessman Heinrich Albert selected to head the *New Your Evening Mail*, David Lamar, the notorious "Wolf of Wall Street," had maneuvered himself into a desperate situation: He faced an indictment for impersonating a public official, and his financial house of cards was on the verge of total collapse. Lamar, however, represented a different caliber of character from Rumely, who had sold his soul to the German cause by sheer conviction. Lamar came to Rintelen following the pervading scent of easy money and for a chance to hurt his nemesis, J. P. Morgan and his U.S. Steel Corporation. George Plochmann of the Transatlantic Trust Company,

Rintelen's banker in New York, warned the German agent about using Lamar: "I said to him that he was the last person I would have anything at all to do with."[562] Lamar was a crook of the first order with a reputation in and around Wall Street that should have raised a forest of flags for Rintelen and his peers in the Secret War Council.

> Lamar was then in desperate straits. Bad luck had followed him in the Street for two years, and had crowned his misfortunes with this expensive trial [for impersonating A. Mitchell Palmer] and threatened imprisonment. He owed money everywhere for personal expenses; the merchants with whom he traded had stopped his credit; he had descended to borrowing from his friends in sums as small as two dollars at a time. Then he met Rintelen, who was on fire with a passion that blinded him to consequences and who flourished before the eyes of the famished Wolf a half million dollars of real money. He was manna fallen from heaven.[563]

Everyone knew from numerous newspaper exposes, that Lamar had a host of American politicians in his pocket. Maybe it was the political access that attracted Rintelen to the notorious "Wolf of Wall Street," or a deeper sense of kindred souls since both men seemed to be cut from the same cloth.[564] In the beginning of May, Thomas Hall introduced Lamar to Rintelen. The meeting allegedly occurred in the offices of Frederico Stallforth, who then shared his space with railroad investor Andrew D. Meloy.[565] The group discussed ways to promote a munitions boycott. Lamar thought he could finagle the introduction of a bill in Congress, and buy the votes to pass it. He also thought that a Supreme Court judge could be bribed into challenging the legal basis on which America traded with the enemy. Finally, the Wall Street juggler proposed to found a union and place politicians with a labor constituency on its board. Plochmann testified in later years, "Rintelen, talking of him, would say that he was a man of a great deal of push and force. In fact, I was under the impression that David Lamar, to hear Rintelen talk, was stronger than the United States Government, or any government on the face of the globe, for that matter..."[566] Rintelen was ecstatic and, according to Plochmann, compelled with "an eagerness too great for caution."[567]

David Lamar's background and history remains dotted with question marks and unsolved mysteries to this day. U.S. agents, who had the task of shadowing him, described the Wall Street scoundrel as "... about 5 feet 10, weighs probably 180, and is always dressed in the extreme of fashion, with a decided preference for coats with wide skirts and silk hats. His skin is swarthy, his nose prominent and his hair, which he brushes straight back from his forehead, is as black as a raven's wing. His mustache would do credit to a policeman of the old school."[568]

Lamar himself told Senator Lee S. Overman of North Carolina in 1913, that his last name was an alias and that his past was his to guard.[569] Rumors regarding his family background included the possibility that his father was an important industrialist or a Wall Street mover-and-shaker. Others thought that he was the black sheep of the prominent Lamar family of Ruckersville, Georgia. Supreme Court Justice Joseph Rucker Lamar emphatically denied in 1914 that the "Wolf of Wall Street" had any relation to his family.[570]

The office of Frederico Stallforth, Andrew Meloy, and Franz Rintelen in 1915. Behind the desk is Frederico Stallforth; sitting, his brother-in-law, Alfred Risse. Third man is unknown. Photo courtesy Prevo Collection.

Franz Rintelen, approximately 1915, copyright expired

David Lamar in 1913[571]

Just like Rintelen, who told anyone in the United States willing to listen that he was related to the Hohenzollern family and that his father was "Imperial Minister of Finance," Lamar, as well, was an imposter.[572] The Bureau of Investigations case file characterized Lamar as being...

...endowed by nature with a fascinating personality and with a brilliant mind which he had enriched by study, a man capable of great things, he was possessed by that strange perversity which often afflicts men of exceptional cleverness --- he would rather make one dollar by adroit crookedness than a million by unexciting honesty. Perhaps his origin affected his character --- he admitted, sometimes boasted, that he was the illegitimate son of a Spanish Jewess and a Gentile banker whose name is a household word in America and the world over.[573]

While he stirred the rumor mill about his potential high-class background, the truth might have been the opposite. His background may well have been lower class, if manners and education are any indication. Lamar's real name was David M. Lewis, as people who knew him in Omaha, Nebraska in the 1890s identified him in New York.[574] His surname, Lewis, seems to have been derived from Levy.[575] His age is disputed. U.S. prison records in 1916 noted his age as fifty-two (birth year 1864). Census data in 1910 list him as having been born in 1870. Obituaries in 1934 gave his birth year as 1868.[576] The *Reading Eagle* reported in Lamar's obituary, "he refused to give his real name to authorities, but his brother Henry signed his name to a legal document as Henry M. Levy."[577] Also, quite notorious was Lamar's brother-in-law, Bernard Smith. He purchased a beach house for Lamar in Eastwood, New Jersey, in 1900. The original owners sued Lamar and Smith between 1902 and 1907 in order to get the property back after the two had defaulted on mortgage payments.[578]

David Lamar appeared in New York in 1899, just as the listing for David M. Lewis disappeared in Omaha. His rise to stardom in New York's financial circles became legendary. In a mix of awe, fear, and disgust, New York papers frequently reported on the "Wolf of Wall Street," his face-offs with Rockefeller and Morgan, and the millions he made in his bear raid attacks. The 1910 census listed him as living in Manhattan with his first wife, Marie, and two Irish immigrant servants.[579] He had one daughter with his first wife.[580] After the First World War and on-going brushes with the law, the fifty-seven year-old Lamar divorced in 1924 and re-married Edna French, a twenty-one year old Broadway dancer, a few months later.[581] He died of a heart attack, alone and broke on January 13th 1934 in a New York hotel. By then he was so down- and-out that it took days for anyone to even claim his body.[582]

One noteworthy brush with the law that exemplifies Lamar's personality occurred in 1903 when the driver of Lamar's carriage lost the family dog, and "Lamar struck him several times with his cane."[583] The driver "took the cane away… and knocked him [Lamar] down with it."[584] Lamar fired him but did not leave it at that. He "[the driver] was attacked a few nights later."[585] The fight escalated even further. The beaten coach driver went to the police and reported the attack. After questioning and admitting his involvement, Lamar was arrested and released on bail. The dispute now went to trial. Hours before the chauffeur was scheduled to testify in court, he was attacked again, beaten mercilessly, and stabbed on the steps of the court house. Witnesses identified the assailants as William Delanoy, alias "Monk" Eastman, and Joseph Brown, a member of the notorious Eastman Gang.

Suspecting Lamar had something to do with the attack, the investigation confirmed that, indeed, the Wall Street broker had hired the men and Lamar's brother-in-law, Bernard Smith, had pointed out the victim to the gangsters. Lamar, his brother-in-law and co-conspirator in the attack, Bernard Smith, Eastman and Brown all went to court in a closely and very publicly observed trial. Despite Eastman turning on Lamar, and accusations flying in all directions, and despite the overwhelming proof of Lamar hiring Eastman to commit the vicious attack, all four defendants went free.[586]

The "Wolf of Wall Street" could not be caged, building on an already enlarged ego of audacity and recklessness. Lamar's financial specialty was 'Bear Raids.' He would buy especially cheap stocks and talk them up. Then, he would get investors to join him. The value would go up further. He would dump his holdings at the highest point. The stock would slump as a consequence and "investors ended up sitting on piles of worthless paper. Lamar's enemy list, as well as his shady reputation, extended from the Rockefellers, whose scion, John junior, he helped relieve of a million dollars,[587] and to the Morgans, whose U.S. Steel Corporation he actively tried to destroy.[588]

Lamar was convinced that the Morgan-owned U.S. Steel Corporation had given preferential prices to Great Northern and Northern Pacific railroads in which J. P. Morgan had financial interest.[589] The unfair trade advantage ruined stock prices in railroad companies in which Lamar had invested. Subsequent lawsuits failed, mainly because Lamar brought fake witnesses to court who were quickly exposed.[590] He tried everything in his power to draw attention to this issue, but the Morgan lobby in Washington proved more powerful than his. Lamar boasted to investigators in 1915 that he actually had written the Stanley Resolution of 1909. The act initiated an investigation into the affairs of U.S. Steel Corporation.[591] During the course of the fight between Lamar and J. P. Morgan, the Senate Lobby Investigating Committee attempted to call one of Lamar's associates to testify. Lamar impersonated then-Representative A. Mitchell Palmer in a phone call to sabotage the effort.[592]

The Wolf had gone too far. The episode earned him a highly publicized Senate investigation, trial, and conviction for impersonating a U.S. official. His senate testimony in 1913 crowned the headlines of American dailies for weeks. *Investor's Monthly Magazine* commented, "... the amazing audacity of Mr. Lamar's testimony in Washington, in which he admitted everything that had been charged against him and boasted of his malign influence in Washington, makes Baron Maunchausen [sic] look like an amateur besides him."[593] U.S. Secret Service agents finally caught up with Lamar in the Waldorf Astoria in New York in November 1914, after he had eluded capture for months.[594] The "Wolf" had appealed his conviction, posted $10,000 bail ($210,000 in today's money), lost virtually all his customers, was so bankrupt that he borrowed single digit dollar amounts from friends, and was fighting to stay out of prison when Rintelen met him in May 1915.[595]

The greatest frustration of the military planners in Germany, as well as the Secret War Council in New York, was the fact that the Imperial Foreign Office, and Ambassador Count Bernstorff, in particular, had not been able to influence Congress to pass an arms embargo against the Allies. It was not for lack of effort on the part of the German ambassador. Count Bernstorff tried to enlist German-American senators and congressmen for a legislative effort to stop American munitions shipments. The German-American press and German propaganda chimed in with the chorus of the genuine American peace movement, led by prominent American politicians including Secretary of State William Jennings Bryan, to produce a groundswell of popular support for an embargo. The proposal had a limited chance of success from the onset. Labor leaders, especially Samuel Gompers, preferred full employment to the recession of the previous fall and winter. German-American politicians feared for their re-elections if they attracted attention for pro-German agitation. Despite the efforts of the German-friendly press, including the Hearst papers, the *Fatherland*, the *New Yorker Staats-Zeitung*, and Bernhard Dernburg's press mailings, the effort lacked popular support and political will.

Frustrated and impatient with the slow grinding mill of propaganda and political agitation, Dernburg, likely without the knowledge of Ambassador Count Bernstorff, attempted to shut down loading docks in the major Atlantic harbors in April of 1915 through strikes. German agent Matthew F. Cummings of Boston, Massachusetts, approached William Dempsey of the Longshoremen's Union in New York with an introductory letter from the German propagandist and Dernburg associate, Edmund von Mach.[596] Cummings offered to pay $10 per week for a maximum of six weeks to 22,000 dockworkers, most of whom were of Irish descent and staunchly anti-British, if they walked off their jobs.[597] When T. V. O'Connor, the president of the national Longshoremen's Union, got wind of the negotiations, he went straight to William F. Flynn, Chief of the U.S. Secret Service.[598] The discussions with Cummings continued for a few weeks with the Secret Service watching every move. However, the offer coincided with the sinking of the *Lusitania* on May 7th 1915. Dernburg, in a gross miscalculation of public sentiment, caused a huge scandal with inflammatory speeches that sought to justify the German atrocity. Ambassador Count Bernstorff, after securing safe conduct from the English authorities, sent Dernburg back to Europe in the latter part of May to protect the former German Minister of Colonial Affairs from almost certain legal troubles in the U.S. Dernburg's departure effectively ended the plot.[599] O'Connor went public a few months later.[600]

Lamar's proposals to Rintelen had a slightly different bent. What was missing in the effort, according to the "Wolf of Wall Street", was a measure of corruption to turn the tide for an embargo. Anybody had a price and, in Lamar's opinion, that included American Federation of Labor president Samuel Gompers, other labor leaders, and especially politicians. According to Lamar, Congress could be bought to pass legislation that curbed exports of arms and munitions to Europe.[601] Communication between the Imperial War Department and Rintelen or his superior Boy-Ed does not reveal an authorization to move ahead with the political effort that, in all fairness, was Count Bernstorff's domain. However, Rintelen maintained that he received a green light.[602] The claim appears plausible, although the go-ahead probably came through Karl Boy-Ed around May 15th 1915, and not directly from Berlin.[603] Count Bernstorff steadfastly denied after the war having had any knowledge of the effort. However, it is possible that he and Boy-Ed conferred on the issue and decided to let Rintelen move ahead. Speaking against the ambassador's involvement is the fact that Rintelen's mission overrode the arguably slower and ineffective diplomatic effort of the German ambassador to influence American politics, as well as Bernhard Dernburg's effort to dabble in American labor relations. Lamar made it sound easy: It was just a question of money. That, the "Wolf" learned from the "Dark Invader," Franz Rintelen, was not a problem. "Lamar told Rintelen that Congressman Buchanan [of the Seventh District of Illinois – Northern Chicago] was the most available man to be used; that he could be bought for $12,500 [$260,000 in today's value]... "[604]

Buchanan had been president of the International Association of Bridge and Iron Workers for several years.[605] He was one of a group of politicians that, together with Lamar, had fought large American trusts since 1900. A preeminent labor representative in Congress and a prominent member of one of David Lamar's creations, the Anti-Trust League, he also had supported Lamar in the past in his effort to pass legislation against the U.S. Steel Corporation. Another member of Congress, Representative Henry B. Martin of the 15th District of New York, was also in the pockets of Lamar. Born in Fillmore County, Minnesota, in 1858, Martin grew up on the frontier. After becoming a house painter and moving to Iowa, he rose through the ranks of the Knights of Labor to become a member of the executive board and editor of its paper.[606] He moved to New York in 1894, and became a key political ally for Lamar against American steel trusts. As national secretary and main agitator of Lamar's Anti-Trust League, Martin represented the league in Congress starting in 1902.[607] A representative from New York, he was Lamar's main warrior in the battles against J. P. Morgan, William R. Hearst, and John D. Rockefeller.[608] Martin had been the intermediary between Lamar and U.S. Representative Augustus O. Stanley of Kentucky in writing and passing the Stanley

Resolution of 1909.[609] Stanley subsequently led an anti-trust investigation against Morgan's U.S. Steel Corporation.

According to Bureau of Investigations detectives, it only took an initial bribe of $5,000 in "... five $1,000 bills" from Martin to get Buchanan's attention.[610] Martin also was supposed to enlist Federation of Labor (AFL) president Samuel Gompers into the organization. However, in a spat over policy, Martin ran afoul with the AFL in 1897.[611] Thus, unbeknownst to Rintelen, Martin's relations with Gompers were strained, at best. A third member of Lamar's core group was Representative Hiram Robert Fowler of the 24th district of Illinois. The trained lawyer and longtime member of the Illinois state legislature ran for national office on a democratic ticket in 1910.[612] A member of the Claims Committee, he only served two terms in Congress. Fowler lost his re-election bid in the 1914 election and, "out of a job... [is] trying to connect with someone."[613] That someone turned out to be David Lamar. Frank S. Monett, and retired Attorney General of Ohio, Herman J. Schulteis, a lawyer and Anti-Trust League officer, all battle-hardened fighters in Lamar's war with U.S. steel trusts, also joined the team.

Buchanan and Fowler managed to enlist several high-profile labor leaders to join in executive positions of Lamar's new organization. Jacob C. Taylor, a progressive politician and labor leader in New Jersey, ran the Cigar Makers' Union in Newark. He eventually succeeded Frank Buchanan as president of the "Peace Council." Milton Snelling, the vice-president of the International Union of Steam and Operating Engineers of America, became the organization's vice president. The group recruited Ernest Bohm as treasurer, who was the current secretary of the Central Federated Union, and a former member of the Knights of Labor union.[614] C. H. Gustafson, president of the Nebraska Farmers' Union, was supposed to recruit farmers to the organization that had been disenchanted with the British blockade, which prevented food shipments to Central Europe. New York lawyer Charles A. Oberwager, as well as a former U.S. ambassador to Spain, and personal friend of William Jennings Bryan, Hannis Taylor, provided knowhow for international law and foreign policy.[615] A distraction to most, but certainly an easy way to add to the meager membership count, were leaders of various Midwestern German-American organizations, such as G. F. Hummel, national president of the Teutonic Sons of America.

Lamar's plan went into immediate action. Armed with funds from Rintelen, the "Wolf" sent Buchanan to talk to Samuel Gompers, and to get his endorsement for a national labor organization promoting world peace through an arms embargo. Gompers declined. Lamar then sent Congressman Martin with an offer of $50,000 ($1 Million in today's value).[616] Apart from the unwise choice of messenger, the bribe did not sway the labor leader, either. Instead, the group aroused Gompers' suspicion that the money had its origins in Germany, which he immediately claimed publicly.

The group now tried to go around the AFL with Gompers out of the equation. Proposing a new union, the "Labor's National Peace Council," Buchanan, Fowler, Martin, Monett, and Schulteis enlisted labor activists in the various peace organizations all across the nation to support their idea.[617] The new union planned a large event in Washington D.C. in the end of July 1915 that was to include a meeting with representatives of the Wilson administration. Lamar's puppets offered an all-expenses-paid trip for that purpose to the capital for anyone who wanted to attend. Although the offer sounded too good to be true, the membership drive showed initial results. Gompers, who now publicly discredited the new organization, stood by helplessly as Buchanan organized several large events to promote his new peace organization.

Buchanan addressed a national peace conference at Carnegie Hall in New York on June 19th with the former Secretary of State and peace activist, William Jennings Bryan, who had just resigned his office in protest to the latest *Lusitania* note.[618] The event lent tremendous legitimacy to Buchanan's efforts. Hannis Taylor, as one of Bryan's old friends, was probably instrumental in securing his appearance.[619] The conference passed a call for general strike in a unanimous vote:

> The resolution, which call upon the 2,000,000 organized workers of this nation to band together in a determined effort to perform the task that President Wilson and his administration has shirked in forbidding the selling of foodstuffs and war materials, reads as follows:
>
> 'Whereas the frightful European war has aroused the peoples of all countries to a sense of duty in devising ways and means to demand and enforce immediate peace; and
>
> 'Whereas the Central Federated Union of Greater New York and vicinity, representative of over 300,000 organized men and women, fully cognizant of these conditions, has decided to make an effort for peace and appeals for co-operation to the American people; and
>
> 'Whereas labor furnishes the fighting material and pays the expenses and produces all materials for the conflict; therefore be it
>
> 'Resolved. That we call upon organized labor throughout the United States to seriously consider at once the proposition of a general strike among those industries employed in the production of ammunition and food supplies; and be it further
>
> 'Resolved. That we favor the authorization of a labor delegation of three to visit the labor centers of the belligerents and confer with them upon the best positive method in concluding this awful catastrophe.[620]

Three days later, on June 22nd, the Labor's National Peace Council formally appeared as a new force on the American political horizon. The logo of a handshake had a "Three Musketeer" tagline: "An injury to one is the concern of all."[621]

A delegation of the union led by its president, Frank Buchanan, requested a meeting with President Wilson the next day.[622] The president politely declined but offered the group to meet with Secretary of State Robert Lansing, who had just taken over for William Jennings Bryan. Lansing saw the delegation on July 6th and accepted their petition urging the U.S. government not to allow ships laden with munitions to "clear port."[623] Major dailies, including the *New York Times*, immediately fingered David Lamar as the force behind the new organization.[624]

The membership drive now went into high gear. Lamar's agitators attended an AFL meeting in St. Louis on June 30th. The group, this time including Franz Rintelen, who stayed in the background, invited union members in Baltimore on July 7th and 14th for a meeting in Washington, D.C. later that month. Also on July 14th, Labor's National Peace Council organizers pressed union members in New Orleans to pass an embargo resolution. Former Attorney General of Ohio Monett spoke at an AFL meeting in Cleveland the next day, on July 15th, while Frank Buchanan went to Bridgeport, Connecticut in the same week to verbally ignite a volatile situation in the munitions industry. The large orders for munitions and supplies had precipitated a virtual explosion of manufacturing capacity. Shortages of labor fueled competition for workers between manufacturers. Women, even children, joined the workforce. Work conditions in factories bursting at the seams with order backlogs worsened by the day. Despite full employment, wages remained low. Union efforts to organize thousands of non-union workers triggered an immediate, violent response from management. The AFL, by and large, refused to support local unions' efforts to confront low wages, long work hours, and unsafe working conditions. Dissatisfaction among the workforce simmered at dangerous levels. All that was needed was a lit match...

Three weeks after the founding of the Labor's National Peace Council on July 15th, and at the height of the efforts to sign up supporters, the *Chicago Day Book* reported on a strike in Bridgeport, Connecticut. Most notably, the strike occurred without authorization of the AFL, a stated policy of Buchanan and Lamar after Gompers' refusal to join.

MILITIA HELD IN READINESS IN BRIDGEPORT ARMS STRIKE

Bridgeport, Conn., July 15. Samuel Gompers, president of [the] American Federation of Labor, expected to reach Bridgeport today in [an] effort to avert [a] general strike among employes [sic] ... [that] would tie up manufacture of war munitions for European belligerents. Four companies of the Connecticut coast artillery, with headquarters here, awaited the call today to take charge of the situation. About 300 men were on strike today, mostly millwrights and hod carriers, working on the new addition to the Remington plant. At a secret meeting of the central labor union [sic] last night the advisability of calling out the 18 branches of the allied metal trades' was considered.[625]

It was not just the strike alone that prompted Gompers to rush to Connecticut, but the presence of Frank Buchanan on the ground, whose "advent on the scene was marked by an immediate turn for the worse in the situation."[626] The strike escalated in the next days, quickly threatening a complete shutdown of Remington Arms Company, and a host of Bridgeport's munitions and supply factories. The machinist union, with which Frank Buchanan in his previous union jobs had been closely aligned, joined the truckers, garment workers, and bricklayers. Some twenty thousand workers, including several thousand women had walked out across the Northeastern manufacturing belt, the heart of America's export industries, by July 17th.[627] The strikes expanded from Connecticut to New York, New Jersey, and Pennsylvania, and included five plants in Bridgeport: the Tidewater Oil Company factory (belonging to Standard Oil) in Bayonne, New Jersey; the General Chemical Company in Hackensack, New Jersey; the Baldwin Locomotive Works in Eddystone, Pennsylvania; and a host of smaller outfits.[628] The strike also turned violent. The police in Bridgeport clashed with picketing workers on July 21st, and in Bayonne three workers died a few days later when panicked guards of the plant shot into the crowd.[629] The strikers demanded eight-hour workdays, better work conditions, overtime pay, and higher wages. Ominous newspaper reports gave voice to the worst fears of the government and industrialists.

ALL ARMS FACTORIES MAY BE CLOSED BY STRIKE

Bridgeport, Conn., July 17.- - Bridgeport was quiet today. Union leaders, directing the proposed strike that may tie up the great Remington arms and munitions factories, said it was the lull before the storm that will break early next week unless the company agrees to let the millwrights work in its shops under machinists' union rules. Every factory in Bridgeport must grant the eight-hour day also, they said. 'The machinists will strike the first of the week unless the companies capitulate,' said J. J. Keppler, international vice president of the machinists' union, today. 'That is final.'[630]

Frank Morrison, one of Gompers' lieutenants, immediately accused the strikers to be infiltrated by German agents. "... It was to be expected that German agents would attempt to interrupt the manufacture of munitions in this country," he argued in an interview.[631] Gompers clearly identified the Labor's National Peace Council as the force behind the strikes. "Mr. Gompers by strong inference served notice, in his statement, on Frank Buchanan, of Illinois, and his labor peace council, that organized labor as a body not only is not in favor of his propaganda ostensibly for the promotion of peace, [but] actually to prevent shipments of arms to Great Britain, France and Russia, but that he regards Mr. Buchanan's activities with suspicion and the purpose of the organization with distrust."[632] Within days, however, pushed to the sidelines by Buchanan, the AFL grudgingly and publicly voiced support for the strikers no matter "whether German gold started the Bridgeport strike."[633] Gompers, who Bureau of Investigations agents were shadowing, quickly disappeared from the list of instigators of the massive strikes.[634]

While workers picketed all over the American Northeast, and while U.S. investigators desperately tried to find the source of the sudden unrest, the American Embargo Conference in Washington with the attendance of former Secretary of State William Jennings Bryan attracted two hundred men and women on July 24th 1915. Again the organizers attempted to speak with the American president, and he declined. Joseph P. Tumulty, President Wilson's secretary wrote,

July 24, 1915

Dear Mr. Buchanan,

I am genuinely sorry to say that the President was so rushed during his brief stay in Washington that there was no opportunity to take up with him your request for an appointment for a committee from your organization. As you doubtless will realize, the President has been so completely absorbed during the past week in the consideration of matters of pressing importance that he literally has had no time for anything else. I know you will understand and bear with me.

Sincerely yours,

J. P. Tumulty

Secretary to the President[635]

Buchanan promptly fired off a furious letter to the president:

My Dear Mr. Tumulty:

Your favor of the 24th inst, duly received, and to put the situation mildly, was decidedly disappointing in character. The information it contained, though courteously phrased, could not and did not alter the inference forced by the statement made. Your intimation that the President's time was so fully taken up with matters of pressing importance that he could not grant an audience to representatives of labor, that has made the United States of America the proud nation that it is, in order to permit them in person to demonstrate that the subsidized press, representing organized dollars In America, which is seeking to serve as the volunteer adviser of the President, was misrepresenting labor's attitude In the present crisis, is tantamount to a declaration that the President is more concerned about the desires of big business, that he is to discover the heartfelt sentiment of the common people... I thank you, Mr. Tumulty, for your candor. My duty to those I serve leaves me no alternative but to say that so long as they, the people whom I serve, continue to be united in their belief that progress and prosperity is dependent upon of the scriptural admonition. 'And they shall beat their swords into plow shares and their spears into pruning hooks; nation shall not life [sic] up sword against nation, neither shall they learn war any more.' Just so long shall I continue to rap at the door of the President's private chambers to secure admittance for a delegation of workers who not only desire peace but peace abroad as well.

I again urge upon you to kindly present to the President my desire for a conference, and inform him that if I am to be denied the courtesy so liberally extended to speaking for Big Business, I shall be reluctantly forced to advise the public of my position in the premises through the medium of an open letter.

Awaiting your reply, I have the honor to be very truly yours.

Frank Buchanan.[636]

The congressman, emboldened by the success of his agitation in Bridgeport, fundamentally accused President Wilson of being under the influence of "big business" interests. This did not sit well with the administration.[637] The leaders of the Labor's National Peace Council also called for the resignation of New York Collector of the Port, Dudley Field Malone, threatened law suits against British shipping giant Cunard and others to mandate a stop to munitions shipments, lobbied investigations into the Federal Reserve for allegedly financing the war effort of the Entente, and demanded the nationalization of all U.S. munitions factories.[638] None of these proposals had much chance of garnering political support but insured that the Peace Council remained in the national headlines through July and August of

1915. All governmental eyes became fixed on the financial background of this new "labor" movement, partly because of the sudden and noticeable increase in disposable income for the Council's organizers, partly because of the attacks on the Wilson administration, but mostly because of the widespread outbreak of labor unrest. In addition, the backlash from the attacks of the Peace Council showed immediate results. Gompers and the AFL "discouraged" any associated labor leader from supporting the Peace Council, correctly suggesting that German money was behind the effort.

A relatively small group of fifty people came to the long anticipated meeting in Washington D.C. on July 30th.[639] Buchanan and Fowler, in the face of a miserable recruitment result, hyped the support base of the Peace Council for public consumption. The *New York Sun* reported on August 2nd that the union claimed "to speak for at least 1,000,000 labor voters, 4,600,000 farmers and a large number of businesses and civic organizations..."[640] In reality, the President had refused to see the Peace Council's delegation. The membership drive and the huge publicity effort had yielded fifty delegates, and, to top off the bad news, vice president Milton Snelling resigned one week before the meeting under protest, claiming that he was made the tool of German propagandists.[641] Snelling's resignation, the lackluster support of labor, and the powerful opposition of the AFL leadership and the Wilson administration guaranteed that the organizing effort fizzled. The "Dark Invader", Franz Rintelen decided to flee the United States on August 3rd 1915, as he was about to be discovered. Reports all over national papers that German money was behind the organization sealed the Peace Council's fate.[642]

Despite serious efforts by Department of Labor mediators, and negotiations between the labor unions and management representatives, the strikes continued until the end of August and into September.

WHOLE CITY ON STRIKE

BRIDEPORT, Conn., Aug. 26.—Bridgeport is strike bound with practically 10,000 men, women and children out of work.

They are all demanding a raise in wages and an eight-hour day. Half a dozen industries in the city are tied up.

Girls in three corset factories struck today. A thousand clerks, most of whom are girls, have tied up the department stores, while 8,000 munitions workers walked out.

In addition the employes of the New Haven railroad here are out. Laundry workers and the barbers have struck.

GERMAN

NOTE IS

LARRY SULI WALKS! IT THE FIRST

By E. A. Peters

"Gee, I'd like to get outside of a big, juicy beefsteak!"

Propped up in a softly pillowed wheelchair, enjoying the cool air of a screened porch at the county hospital, Larry Sullivan yesterday afternoon gave voice to the first desire that he has expressed since his operation.

"When I get out of this hospital, I'm going to hobble to the nearest restaurant and order the biggest porterhouse they have in stock. I've got such an appetite that I could eat planked horse meat and relish it. I never was so hungry in my life, and you bet a hospital diet isn't my hobby, by a long ways," said he.

Stands Alone for First Time.

Larry is recovering from one of the most unusual operations ever performed at the county hospital. His two paralyzed, helpless limbs have been stiffened with artificial bone, until the boy is able to stand upright on them. Yesterday, for the first time in his life, the cripple stood alone

longer, but covering an his much-de the middle

M

"They tr and I haven world," he a pital food i an appetite of a cripple, like a real before in m

Larry is smiles. Th and orderli model patie

"All that to get out a a regular "I'm going when I get won't disap who helped tion and w me up in b

Comm

Mayor Fa Humane Of trict Nurse and Mrs. J. lake has

President Wilson had to insert himself personally in the situation on September 13th, and threatened serious repercussions for "lawless and faithless employees."[644] Rather than further escalating the situation, management had to give in to virtually all the demands of the unions in the end. Workers received the coveted eight-hour workday, also higher wages, overtime pay, better work conditions, and guaranteed rights to organize. Historians disagree to this day on whether the strikes constituted a German plot or legitimate labor agitation. Based upon the available sources, it was probably a combination of both. The results of the strikes would have been a resounding success for Frank Buchanan, a vindication for his efforts to establish a competition to the powerful AFL. However, by the end of the strikes, publication of his involvement with Franz Rintelen and David Lamar had surfaced. The extent of German financial involvement in the plot became apparent within weeks. Buchanan resigned his position with the Peace Council and attempted to stem the tide of public outrage at his activities. After all, he was an elected official in the legislative branch.

A grand jury handed down indictments to the conspirators Rintelen, Lamar, Buchanan, Fowler, Martin, Schulteis, Monett, and [Jacob C.] Taylor on December 27th 1915, for violating the Sherman Anti-Trust Act.[645] Legal troubles, incarceration, and bad publicity dogged the accused for years to follow. After Rintelen came back to New York under extradition orders in 1917, the organizers of one of the largest industrial strikes in the history of the United States were convicted. Despite the serious implications for the participants, the German backers of the unrest should have been content with the results. The strikes effectively disrupted shipments of war supplies to the Allies for months. Sporadic strikes in Bridgeport and other industrial centers continued throughout the neutrality period of the war as a result of the resounding success for the unions. Additionally, after the strikers settled for increased pay, supplies had become more expensive for the European belligerents, another stated goal of the German war strategy.

Without a doubt, David Lamar and Franz Rintelen's brainchild had little political impact on the surface. A few naïve politicians, with William Jennings Bryan as their flag bearer, rose to the occasion and spoke out in favor of this concocted peace movement. Buchanan and Fowler, who craved public attention, basked in the limelight of national headlines for a brief two months. However, the Labor's National Peace Council never gained any political clout that could have pushed through an arms embargo against the Entente. Virtually all of the American labor leaders supported the status quo of a "neutral" United States that benefitted from the tremendous windfall of Allied industrial orders. It is no surprise that Lamar and his cronies failed to sign up Sam Gompers and the other major labor leaders in the United States. While German propaganda portrayed Gompers as a tool of the British (he was actually born and raised in London), he not only immediately recognized the likely backers of the movement, but also maintained that supporting an embargo was not in the interest of the American worker or its union representatives. Gompers testified in court in 1917, "labor in this country had been greatly benefited [from the munitions industry], because the days of unemployment during the early part of the war had been followed by a time of full employ-ment."[646] What the labor leader failed to recognize, however, was the fact that the war situation had empowered the labor movement to make a quick and successful push for the eight-hour day. Separating the AFL from the "rogue" strikes, and branding the strikers as tools of German agitation, cost the union's reputation dearly. Gompers and his labor leaders briefly stood on the wrong side of history in one of the greatest achievements of organized labor in the annals of the United States: The introduction of the eight-hour workday.

It is unlikely that Lamar, Rintelen, Buchanan, and the others ever considered an arms embargo achievable. Rather, the true mission of the organization was twofold: Gain maximum publicity with scan-dalous attacks on the Wilson administration, which hopefully would rally the existing but fragmented peace movement led by William Jennings Bryan. The second goal was to exploit the chaos the explo-sion of war production had caused in the Northeast. The Secret War Council in New York knew all about the labor market in Bridgeport. Rintelen's effort coincided with the successful German attempts to hire workers away from Remington Arms and others for the new, German-owned Bridgeport Projectile Company, and in the process, raising wages to inflate prices for Entente war supplies.

The precise impact of Rintelen and Lamar's effort on the strikes in the major industrial centers in the Northeast that summer is virtually impossible to gauge. Unrest was certainly pre-programmed as war profiteering largely benefitted the large corporations, while workers suffered under long shifts, mediocre pay, and horrid working conditions. Giving inflammatory speeches to the workers, as Buchanan undoubtedly had done in Bridgeport, and supplying cash for strike actions, accounts for the strikes to have occurred when they did. Evaluating the Peace Council project, together with the German purchase and construction of the Bridgeport Projectile Company, leaves little doubt that Germany's attack on American labor relations delivered a serious blow to the Allied supply effort. The U.S. Secret Service concluded in August 1918, "The strikes at the Remington Arms plant, Bridgeport, was [sic] probably caused by Rintelen. He attempted to bring about a strike on the Atlantic Coast through the Longshoreman's Union. He is mentioned in connection with strikes at the Remington Arms, Ilion, N. Y.; the General Electric at Schenectady, N. Y.; the Keystone Watch Case, N. Y.; etc..."[647]

After Rintelen's arrest and debriefing in England, the Labor's National Peace Council disintegrated at the end of September 1915.[648] Big questions remained as to where Rintelen's half million dollars had gone. Seventy-five thousand dollars ($1.6 Million in today's value) stayed in New York with Frederico Stallforth, who financed sabotage missions after Rintelen's departure.[649] The continuing fire bombings of ships through the fall of 1915 seem to support the allegation. The remainder of Rintelen's funds has not been fully accounted. The American Bureau of Investigations retrieved Rintelen's account ledgers from the Transatlantic Trust Company in the fall of 1915. Rintelen wisely had destroyed the incriminating check stubs but the dates and amounts of disbursements allow for some interesting observations.[650] Rintelen had deposited $300,000 ($6.3 Million in today's value) with Transatlantic Trust on May 20th 1915, which came from the German Naval Attaché Karl Boy-Ed.[651] This marked the time when Rintelen and Lamar decided to create the Labor's National Peace Council. Lamar cashed "one of von Rintelen's checks for $15,000 ($315,000 in today's value)," likely a retainer to start getting active on May 15th.[652] Rintelen wrote a check for $30,000 ($630,000 in today's value) on June 1st.[653] These checks coincided with the hitherto financially downtrodden "Wolf of Wall Street" suddenly being flush with cash. Rintelen spent another $20,000 on June 12th, $25,400 on the 18th, and $26,500 on the 21st.[654] Rintelen wrote a check for $5,500 on June 30th.[655] At the exact time, Frank Buchanan had allegedly received $5,000, which his co-conspirators claimed he spent for himself and was supposed to repay.[656] Federal investigators had traced $200,000 "of funds credited to Captain Rintelen into the hands of a notorious scoundrel [Lamar]…" by November 1915.[657] Rintelen spent $170,000 ($3.6 Million in today's money) from this E. V. Gibbons and Company account between May and July 1915.[658] Comparatively, the cost of Rintelen's firebombing project was relatively low.[659] Frederico Stallforth, who recalled "seeing" these large checks, testified, "I think one time he [Rintelen] put it [the $25,000 check] in an envelope and sent it to the bank, and they always brought it in a package… Afterwards, when I went in [to Rintelen's office], I saw the package on Mr. Lamar's coat lying [sic]."[660] The large checks in June and July 1915 indeed went to Lamar and, to a large degree, financed the labor unrest in Connecticut, New York, Pennsylvania, and New Jersey.

According to the Bureau of Investigations Lamar received at least another $100,000 from Rintelen. According to a memo Frederico Stallforth, who took over Rintelen's projects after August 3rd, drafted on August 11th 1915, "in a perfectly legitimate way $100,000 had already been paid out [by Lamar] for the … organization against the United States Steel Company…"[661] With $75,000 left of Rintelen's funds and approximately $200,000 traced to Lamar, $77,000 traced to the firebomb plot, there is a deficit of over $125,000. According to George Plochmann, Lamar got "money out of him [Rintelen] to 'bear' the market so as to pay him back the money he had used."[662] Whether Lamar indeed used money from Rintelen for speculation is unknown but highly doubtful since Heinrich Albert had to sign off on any expenditure over $10,000. Also, how much money actually ended in the pockets of David Lamar and his cronies, and how much trickled down to strike organizers on the ground, may never be discerned. The results of this attack on American labor relations were well worth the expense in the eyes of the German government and of David Lamar, even if the strikes cost $325,000 ($6.8 Million in today's value). Despite the fact that Lamar and his cronies seemed to have delivered on their promises, Rintelen, and likely Heinrich Albert, grew weary of the Wolf's insatiable appetite for cash. According to George Plochmann, the "Dark Invader" "would throw up his hands and say [,] this fellow [Lamar] cost me hundreds of thousands of dollars, and I don't know how to get away from him."[663] Jealous of Lamar and hoping to score a slice of the German financial cake for his own schemes in Mexico, Rintelen's office mate, Andrew Meloy, hired the Mooney and Boland Detective Agency to shadow Lamar.[664] Nothing is known about the results of the investigation which points to the possibility that the detectives did not come up with anything tangible on the wily Wall Street operator.

Not only did the organizers of the Peace Council feel serious repercussions. American munitions manufacturers decided to accelerate the layoff of thousands of workers with Central European background as a result of German sabotage activities, and the capture of Austrian documents that pointed to an effort to use Austro-Hungarian minority workers for work disruption. Albert's group in New York quickly countered the lay-offs. Under the auspices of Franz von Papen, Hans Liebau, and Frederico Stallforth, the Secret War Council organized an employment office that placed laid-off workers with non-war material-producing industries. The net result of the decision to lay off 'Teutonic' workers might have prevented some instances of sabotage, but more importantly, removed a significant amount of skilled labor from the rapidly expanding industrial plants. Expensive retraining, as well as serious lapses in quality and production safety, added further to the inflationary prices for war materials and, in some instances, resulted in explosions without the necessity of dispatching a sabotage agent.

CHAPTER 11: JUNTA "X"

ESIDES SABOTAGING ALLIED MUNITIONS SHIPS and financing labor unrest, Franz Rintelen also interfered in the already shaky relations between Mexico and the United States. Since the Great War had started in August 1914, altercations between the U.S. and Mexico occurred in the winter of 1914/1915, when fighting between Carranzista and Villista forces spilled across the border at Naco, Arizona. Felix A. Sommerfeld had helped broker a ceasefire and thus averted a renewed American military intervention. President Wilson turned Veracruz over to Venustiano Carranza after a seven-month occupation in November 1914. However, the Mexican border was by no means quiet. Lawlessness, banditry, shifting battle lines, and arms-smuggling kept U.S.–Mexican relations at a tense simmer. German war planners kept a close watch on the southern border of the U.S. As German activities in the United States took on a distinctly more violent character in 1915, Mexico presented both a military target and a distinct opportunity to create troubles for the United States. The military target was the oil-producing region around Tampico. Most of the wells belonged to British and U.S. interests and fueled the sizable British fleet in Atlantic waters to a large degree. The German admiralty also ordered the Secret War Council to disrupt the oil production there by authorizing sabotage against U.S. munitions production.

The newly appointed German minister to Mexico, Heinrich von Eckardt, had supported the viewpoint of German businessman Eugen Motz in early January 1915, namely that "the Tampico oil fields could and actually should be almost completely in German hands… "[665] The German envoy seemed to endorse a more peaceful approach to keeping Mexican oil from the British fleet, namely financing a clandestine takeover of the oil fields with German capital and interrupting supplies through strikes.[666] However, the War Department in Berlin, probably realizing that there was absolutely no chance of acquiring the Mexican oil wells in a short period of time, ordered them dynamited, instead. German records indicate that von Eckardt met "middlemen" who represented attachés von Papen and Boy-Ed in Galveston on February 22nd and in New Orleans on February 24th 1915 to finalize the sabotage plans against Tampico.[667] However, the Imperial Admiralty instructed Captain Boy Ed to call off the action in an ambiguous communication on March 11th: "Significant military damage to England through closing of Mexican oil resources not possible. Thus no money for such action available."[668] Apparently, the Admiralty was expecting the Standard Oil Company, which had strong financial ties to the Mexican Petroleum Company, "to show itself favorable" to the German government.[669] The Admiralty's expectations seemed to upset Captain von Papen's simultaneous arrangements to have an agent named Carlos von Petersdorf "create the greatest possible damage through extensive sabotage of tanks and pipelines."[670] Added von Papen, "given the current situation in Mexico, I am expecting large successes from relatively little resources."[671] Nevertheless, no noteworthy acts of sabotage occurred in Tampico during 1915 and 1916, perhaps due to Standard Oil's intentions, or perhaps due to competing interests within the Imperial War Department.

While the Secret War Council received orders to sabotage oil production in Mexico, which then were countermanded, a relatively unknown American businessman from New York named Andrew Meloy approached the German government with an outlandish scheme. The Irish-American business promoter had boarded a ship in New York with his wife, Alice, on January 16th 1915, and sailed to Germany. He stayed in Berlin in the beginning of February and travelled around Europe until the middle of March.[672]

Meloy met with representatives of the Deutsche Bank in Berlin. Through his involvement with the Mexican National Railways which were in part financed through this bank, Meloy had contacts high up, possibly even to its director, Franz Rintelen's father. A report the American ambassador to England, Walter Hines Page, prepared for the U.S. Secretary of State illuminated Meloy's plan: "Meloy's repeated statements [which Meloy made after his arrest in England in August 1915]... are to the effect that his business in Berlin is to obtain financial support of the Deutsche Bank for a coalition of Mexican leaders... "[673] Immediately following the meetings in Berlin, Meloy traveled to Geneva and Paris where he conducted further negotiations with the former Mexican Secretary of War under Victoriano Huerta, Manuel Mondragón.[674] "I decided then to make the trip to Berlin, confer with the Deutsches [sic] Bank and then come to Paris and arrange with Mondragón whatever was feasible."[675] Obviously, the information he received for his scheme in Berlin had been positive enough to warrant further negotiations with Mexican exiles.

Mondragón, who was living in Spain in exile, was working on a plan to raise an army against both Venustiano Carranza and Pancho Villa to take back control of Mexico. Mondragón had been in contact with his old comrades, Victoriano Huerta, also exiled in Spain, as well as exiled General Aureliano Blanquet, and Félix Díaz for that purpose. These four had overthrown the democratically elected government of Mexico in the spring of 1913. The putschists murdered the Mexican president Francisco Madero and his vice-president José Maria Pino Suarez in the process. A powerful coalition of Mexican revolutionaries sprung up under the leadership of Venustiano Carranza, and with the financial support of important U.S. interests, as the usurper-president Huerta sought to consolidate his dictatorship. Huerta's government finally capitulated in July 1914 during a furious and violent war that lasted fifteen months and caused the United States to occupy the harbor city of Veracruz. The First World War was just about to begin.

Despite the success of the revolutionaries, Mexico did not stabilize. Power struggles among the revolutionary leaders, most notably Francisco *Pancho* Villa, Emiliano Zapata, and Venustiano Carranza continued to tear Mexico apart. The foreign community stood by helplessly as the revolution destroyed whatever remained of the sizeable foreign investments in mining, banking, ranching, and commerce. Andrew Meloy was among the distraught American investors. He owned rail lines in the mining areas of Northern Mexico together with a group of financiers.[676] "All are familiar with the terrible ruin which has swept over Mexico during the past four years. No bank, no railroad, no property of any kind has escaped the burden of this ruin... My own personal affairs in common with the personal affairs of the Stallforths and other railways and banks have been compelled to endure the burden of this progressive ruin. My own personal investment in Mexico is more than $350,000 [7.3 Million in today's value]. The total investment of my immediate friends through my office is more than $1,700,000 [$35.7 Million in today's value]..."[677] If Meloy could convince banks and businesses such as the powerful railroad companies that he had a realistic plan to pacify Mexico, he believed he could raise the money needed for such an endeavor.

Barcelona, Paris, Havana, New Orleans, San Antonio, and New York became centers of intrigue at this time, with exiled members of the Mexican political elite plotting to enter the fray. Thousands of refugees, displaced civilians, former federal soldiers, and especially Orozquistas (who Pancho Villa executed mercilessly if captured) led lives of destitution in every major American border city. The Mexican general, Félipe Ángeles, who had served in the federal army under Presidents Porfirio Díaz and Francisco Madero, then as Secretary of War under Carranza, and finally as the strategic genius behind Pancho Villa's most successful military campaigns, moved to Boston, Massachusetts after a falling-out with Villa in May 1915. He remained in close touch with Mexican expatriates in New York City. Newspapers in the summer of 1914 had briefly traded his name as a potential candidate for the Mexican presidency.

Also in New York was Eduardo Iturbide, a polo-playing social-ite who had basked in the gratitude of the American colony in Mexico City, which he had protected from revolutionary furor in 1914. One of his best friends was Leon Canova who had smuggled him out of Mexico and who had meanwhile become the head of the Latin American desk in the State Department. Although Iturbide had lit-tle or no real influence in Mexican politics, his sway with the State Department helped keep his name in the mix of potential saviors for Mexico. Félix Díaz, the nephew of the former President of Mexico, cooled his heels in Havana but came to New York periodically to try to raise money for military expeditions against Carranza.[678] Most of the powerful Madero family lived in New York and San Antonio: the deposed president's father, his former Secretary of Finance, his for-mer Secretary of Interior, two of Francisco Madero's uncles, as well as his widow. They kept a fairly low profile because of the large invest-ments that they hoped to recover one day in Mexico. However, not much went on with respect to Mexican conspiracies that the Maderos did not know about.

Whoever wished to listen to these expats would hear of gran-diose plans to retake power in Mexico and finally create order. The only thing that seemed to be perpetually missing was money. Neither the American, nor French, nor British governments showed much willingness to support ever-new revolutions and counter revolutions in Mexico in the spring of 1915. The members of Huerta's deposed government, in particular, stood no chance of receiving American support, since President Wilson had endorsed the powerful opposition that defeated the usurper. Wilson was holding out for an eventual Mexican unity government that could count on popular support. The choice clearly lay between Villa and Carranza, not Huerta, Díaz, or Mondragón.

Andrew Meloy had made powerful connections not only with these latter exiled Mexican factions spoiling for a fight but also with the Carranza representatives in the U.S., through his longtime friend, lawyer, and lobbyist Charles A. Douglas, and Villa's envoy in the U.S., Felix A. Sommerfeld. Charles Douglas, in turn, was closely connected to the Counselor of the U.S. State Department, Robert Lansing. Lansing had mingled in Mexican affairs as a legal advisor to then President Victoriano Huerta before he joined the State Department.[679] Ever an optimist, Meloy believed that he could combine the interests of all these factions with the goodwill of the American government and the finance of German, as well as, American banks.

Initial talks between Meloy, Sommerfeld, and Douglas in the winter of 1914/1915 seemed to have given Meloy the impression that a grand coalition of the different Mexican factions was indeed possible. By then, Villa and Carranza started to fight against each other in earnest, virtually guaranteeing a perpetuation of the civil war in Mexico for years to come. "When the Villa–Carranza split occurred... the finances of Villa were directed in New York by Mr. Felix Summerfield [sic] and Frederick [sic] Stallforth. These two men came to wield a very considerable influence over Villa and immediately in my plans for a reorganization of Mexico assumed a position of great importance."[680] Frederico Stallforth, ever the promoter, promised to "cultivate with Villa the possibility of an arrangement [to join Mondragón's group]."[681] Indeed, Meloy hoped, a new insurgency that was well financed, thus having a powerful military presence, and was supported by the majority of the political factions in Mexico, would eventually receive the stamp of approval from the American government.

Sommerfeld and Stallforth seemed to have kept Meloy in the belief that such an alliance between Huerta, Mondragón, Blanquet,

Díaz, Iturbide, and Villa would be possible. There certainly was a large incentive to keep this impression alive as long as possible: Intelligence. It was crucial for both agents to remain in the know of what the exile community was planning. The same held true for the representative of Carranza in the United States, Charles Douglas. He, as well, seemed to have egged on the naiveté of Meloy. "...I had conferences with him [Douglas] of exactly the same character as my conferences with Stallforth...," Meloy stated to American investigators.[682] The situation in Mexico in the spring of 1915, and the personal disposition of both Carranza and Villa towards these exiles, made Meloy's scheme seem unrealistic on the surface. Carranza in particular had no reason whatsoever to veer from his track of gaining total control of Mexico. His main commander, Álvaro Obregón, was continuously gaining ground against Villa. In April 1915, Villa had suffered his hitherto most devastating defeats in the two battles at Celaya. In another engagement in the first week of June, at the battle of León, Obregón again won decisively against Villa's Division of the North.

Observers noted admiringly that Obregón had studied German techniques in the battles raging in France. The German influence in the Mexican general's techniques came into the open through a Hearst reporter embedded with the Carranzistas. He handed a report from Captain Juan Rosales, a Carranzista, meanwhile living in El Paso, to the B.I.:

> General Obregón had his arm shot off early in the fifth, and then Krum [sic] Heller took charge. He had five German officers with him. None of them went into the field, but as every Mexican officer had been instructed by Obregón to obey Heller, he and his Germans sat in a little tent away from the firing line and made maps. On several occasions they rode out to hills and looked at everything through their field glasses. Then they would return to their tent. I was attached to Col. Heller's staff. Late that night Col. Heller sent for every Carranzista officer. Some of them regarded them as foolish and threatened to disobey, but Heller again produced an order signed by General Obregón commanding every Carranzista officer to obey him (Heller)

[.] That settled the matter and the fight soon began. It did not last long. Villa was whipped and then retreated. Heller gave more instructions and our army advanced. Villas [sic] was whipped again and retreated. Heller again followed him and whipped him again. This was the end of Villa's army.[683]

Arnold Krumm-Heller was a German agent, of course, a former personal physician of President Madero, and the head of the Mexican Freemasons. Obregón lay in his tent and reportedly contemplated suicide as a result of his debilitating injury. His commanders had to place guards at his bedside to keep the general alive. Meanwhile, a group of German officers formed a command center from which they conducted Obregón's battles. Reality defies imagination!

Krumm-Heller had been dispatched to both Zapata and Villa a few months earlier, in January 1915, to offer military trainers to the revolutionaries, but both had declined. Villa not only rejected him, but asked the messenger who submitted Krumm-Heller's offer to tell him, "I give him [Krumm-Heller] 24 hours to get out of my country. If he is found here after that I will have him shot."[684] Krumm-Heller and his officers then went on to decisively defeat Villa's one-dimensional tactic of frontal cavalry assaults without keeping sufficient reserves. Villa came to regret rejecting the German offer. As these battles decimated his forces, Carranza had no incentive to even consider sharing power in Mexico with the old garde.

However, Meloy's efforts seem less strange under scrutiny. Members of the State Department backed, maybe even concocted, Meloy's plan. President Wilson issued an ultimatum to the various Mexican factions on June 2nd to come to an agreement or the U.S. would intervene militarily.[685] A flurry of action started within the State Department as a result. William Jennings Bryan resigned on June 9th as Secretary of State over his frustration with Wilson's foreign policy towards Germany, which he believed would eventually drag the United States into the conflict.

Robert Lansing, the Counselor of the State Department, who had advised the President on a stricter course towards Germany, came in his place. However, Lansing also believed that the continuation of the Mexican Revolution posed a national security risk for the United States.[686] His main advisor on Mexico was Leon Canova, the recently appointed head of the Latin American desk at the State Department. He had served as a special envoy to Mexico before his appointment. During Christmas 1914, Canova had incurred the ire of both Francisco Villa and Emiliano Zapata for smuggling the conservative chief of police for the Mexican capital, Eduardo Iturbide, out of harm's way. Villa, who pursued the consul all the way up to the U.S.-Mexican border, vowed to kill Canova if he ever set foot into Mexico again. This man now headed the Latin American desk and advised the Wilson administration on Mexican policy.

Canova belonged to a group of American businessmen and exiled Mexican politicians who believed that, in the end, only an American military intervention or a faction of Mexicans with the full financial and political support of the United States could end the ongoing civil strife south of the border. This group included such men as the former Mexican Foreign Secretary Manuel Calero, Félix Díaz, and Aureliano Blanquet – two of the conspirators who had overthrown President Madero in 1913 – and Villa's main military advisor, as well as the former secretary of war for Carranza, Félipe Ángeles. Manuel Esteva, the Mexican consul in New York under Porfirio Díaz, and Victoriano Huerta, whom Carranza had fired in the fall of 1914, Andrew Meloy, and Frederico Stallforth all belonged to this group. Sherburne G. Hopkins, the powerful lobbyist for Madero, Villa, and Carranza in Washington D.C., and Felix Sommerfeld at least shared the group's ideas on resolving the Mexican civil war. Leon Canova, with the silent blessing of Robert Lansing, became the group's spokesman in the State Department.

In a proposal to Secretary of State Bryan dated May 1915, Canova claimed that Villa was ready to lay down his arms, and a newly configured faction would be able to absorb his forces and pacify Mexico.[687] Canova stated that he was able to enlist former federal officers (represented by Blanquet, Mondragón, and Ángeles), rally the support of the Catholic Church (represented in the group through Félix Díaz and Eduardo Iturbide), receive financial support from the American oil and railroad industry (represented by Andrew Meloy, Charles Douglas, and Sherburne Hopkins), and mount this new opposition force quickly and effectively. Mexico would be pacified by eliminating both Carranza and Villa.

The plan Canova submitted to Secretary Bryan, and the plan Andrew Meloy pursued, are almost identical. After his arrest in England, Meloy described his ideas for pacifying Mexico to the American Ambassador, Walter Hines Page. Meloy's statement matched Canova's plan almost verbatim.[688] The American business-man claimed that, through Sommerfeld and Stallforth, he had assur-ances that Villa would step aside, that Meloy had broad support from different factions in Mexico: members of the old federal army, the Catholic Church, and important American financiers and industrialists. Even the information Meloy gave regarding Carranza's refusal to be part of any unity government closely matched the known information about the Pan-American Conference that took place from July 15th to August 8th. Charles Douglas apparently told Meloy, as well as Lansing and Canova, after meetings in Veracruz, that Carranza would not yield or participate in any unity government.[689] President Wilson not only personally followed Douglas's meetings; he had given Secretary Lansing instructions for the lawyer to talk to Carranza. "I understand that Judge Douglas is going to start for Vera Cruz on Monday. Would it not be well to have a talk with him (not at your office, but at your house and as privately, as much away from the newspapers, as pos-sible) [parentheses in the original] and let him go down with a full understanding of our position, namely that Carranza must meet every honest advance half way if he expects to win our confidence, and that he must win our confidence, at least in some degree, if he hopes for ultimate recognition."[690] Certain that he would win the revolutionary war, Carranza refused to negotiate.[691]

Further linking the Canova plan to Meloy, the arrested busi-nessman perplexed the American ambassador in London by claiming repeatedly that Mr. Charles A. Douglas of Washington was "Counselor to the Department of State for Latin American affairs."[692] That title belonged to Leon Canova. The embarrassment for Canova to have been involved in a scheme, in which German agents also participated, grew in the months to come. The head of the Bureau of Citizenship in the State Department told Canova in September 1915, "It appears to me that Meloy is engaged in a scheme of considerable proportions to foment a new revolutionary movement in Mexico, with German aid."[693]

Meloy pursued his plan in good faith with all the Mexican fac-tions, and with the sympathetic knowledge of key members of the U.S.

State Department, throughout the spring of 1915. The various Mexican factions all waited for whatever advantage they could gain from the scheme. German agents, meanwhile, plotted to use Meloy's idea as a smokescreen for introducing more strife into the border region than already existed. The American businessman traveled three times back and forth to Europe and met with exiles in his office in New York. Boy-Ed wrote to Heinrich Albert in July 1915, "I have repeatedly conferred with him [Meloy] and have received the impression that he is an honorable, trustworthy man. If he has a commercial failing, according to my observation, it is this one, that he is entirely too confiding and is easily made the victim of tricky businessmen."[694] The arrival of Rintelen in April and his participation in the plot at the behest of Boy-Ed in the beginning of May 1915 made a laughingstock of the naïve Meloy.

Rintelen's opportunity to subvert the plot for his purposes arose when Mondragón proposed to arrange the purchase of U.S. rifles from government surplus through a Russian military attaché in Paris, Colonel Ignatieff. Since the U.S. government would not sell arms directly to belligerents, Mondragón offered to arrange for the purchase.[695] However, Mondragón's plan seems to have been to deliver these rifles to Mexico and support his envisioned military campaign. The Mexican general traveled to New York in April to make final arrangements, just around the time when Franz Rintelen arrived. Through Meloy or Stallforth, the two men met. Posing as a wine merchant with the name Edward V. Gates, Rintelen proposed to finance the purchase.[696] He had hoped to entice the Russian government into placing more orders with his front company. Taking down payments and then defaulting on the contracts would not only have hurt the Russian government financially, but also would have tied up American munitions plants with dummy orders as, indeed, Albert and his agents were already doing while this plot unfolded. U.S. Ambassador to Britain Page mused, "Ignatieff was being used as a catspaw [sic] to supply the money for the purchase of the rifles which were not to go to Russia via Sweden as Ignatieff desired, but in reality to Mexico."[697]

Little over one week after the arrival of Franz Rintelen, ex-president Victoriano Huerta, Manuel Mondragón, Enrique Creel, the former governor of Chihuahua, and Huerta's Secretary General José Delgado stepped off the steamer *Antonio Lopez* in New York on April 12th 1915. Even before the ship docked in the harbor, Enrique

Llorente, Villa's representative in Washington who reported to Sommerfeld, filed a protest with the Wilson administration. He alleged what most believed to be true at the time: that the former dictator of Mexico came to insert himself in Mexican affairs once again.[698] Before letting Huerta enter the United States, immigration officials made the exiled dictator give an oath to the effect that he would stay out of Mexican affairs.[699] Despite the oath and public pronouncements, New York's newspapers continued to speculate about the true purpose of Huerta's trip.[700] The general smilingly informed reporters that he was on a "pleasure trip" and had no intention of mingling in Mexican affairs. He settled in a suite on the fifth floor of the Hotel Ansonia, Broadway and 73rd street in New York. Reporters watched closely as Huerta received hundreds of visitors, generals of the Porfirio Díaz era, former governors, and exiled politicians, all hoping to join the new movement.[701] The old dictator basked in the attention, freely granted interviews with journalists, and smilingly ignored direct questions as to his purpose in New York. Claiming that he had "fallen in love with this country," Huerta rented a large villa in the Hamptons in the beginning of May. His wife and children, as well as a flock of servants, joined him in the new home, a household of thirty-five.[702]

Huerta's private secretary José C. Delgado, Victoriano Huerta, and his confidential agent in the U.S., Abraham Z. Ratner, in New York, April 12th 1915.[703]

The line of Mexican luminaries visiting the ex-dictator did not decrease. One of Huerta's secret visitors was General Pascual Orozco. The notorious revolutionary had first supported President Madero, then participated in uprisings against him.[704] Sommerfeld had hunted the former mule driver turned revolutionary general for years without success. Orozco's followers, known as "Red Flaggers" because of their identifying red bandanas in battle, constituted the largest group of potential fighters in a new revolution. The Mexican revolutionary was the arch-enemy of Pancho Villa and his faction of revolutionaries.

Orozco came to Meloy's offices sometime in May and met with Franz Rintelen.[705] Stallforth describes what happened next: "...a peculiar incident occurred, that required considerable maneuvering on his [Stallforth's] part to keep Summerfeld [sic] who was in his office from coming into contact with Orozco... being in the office of Meloy at the same time, knowing that Villa and Huerta followers were at the same time dead enemies."[706] With Orozco on board, Huerta, Mondragón, and Blanquet, and the seemingly agreeable Villa and Ángeles, "Meloy told Stallforth that he had all of the factions in Mexico under his control except Carranza's party, but he hoped perhaps to bring pressure to bear on Carranza through Germany in some way."[707] Félix Díaz, despite his fruitless entreaties with Villa in the past, also became part of the group and arrived in New York sometime in June. Díaz supposedly had financial support from the Roman Catholic Church of Mexico. Father Francis Clement Kelley had founded a seminary on the outskirts of San Antonio with the purpose of organizing Mexican clergy to countermand the anti-clerical undercurrent of the Mexican Revolution.[708] In the end, however, Father Kelley did not, or could not, support the Huerta plot financially.

Evidence that Felix Sommerfeld (and by extension, Pancho Villa) did not support the Huerta-Orozco-Mondragón plot surfaced in El Paso in the first week of May 1915. Sommerfeld had traveled to the border in total secrecy where he still operated Villa's secret service on the American side.[709] His intelligence chief in El Paso was Hector Ramos who worked hand in hand with federal agents of the Bureau of Investigations. The well-known soldiers-of-fortune, Sam Dreben and Emil Holmdahl, as well as retired policeman, Powell Roberts, even former agents of the Bureau of Investigations, filled the ranks of this powerful organization.[710] It is unknown whether Sommerfeld had come to confer with Villa, but he certainly came to focus his secret service organization on sabotaging the "Científico" plot. American agents of the Bureau of Investigations reported on May 3rd, "... Felix Sommerfeld and [illegible], both very active heretofore in revolutionary matters, had been seen a few days ago, just about daylight, coming from the direction of the foothills north of El Paso."[711]

The effort to dismantle the plot paralleled the cooperation between Sommerfeld's people and U.S. authorities in 1912. Dreben, Roberts, Ramos, and many more had fought another Orozco uprising and had brought it to its knees at that time.[712] A satisfied U.S. official reported to B.I. Chief Bielaski, "I am assured the hearty cooperation of mayor, sheriff, and United States military. All are working harmoniously together. Villa agents rendering valuable assistance..."[713] Here again, Sommerfeld's men covered every angle of the conspiracy, submitted daily written reports to the U.S. authorities, pointed out suspects, and in some cases arrested them and turned them over to U.S. authorities.[714] The organization Sommerfeld had created, with the help of Villistas from Ciudad Juarez, identified suspects and places where arms, munitions, and explosives were stored in an all-out war against the conspirators. The suspects ended in jail, and on several occasions, the secret service men stole the supplies and took them across the river to the Villa garrison.[715] Lázaro De La Garza, who worked with Sommerfeld and the Maderos in Villa's supply operation, gave intelligence on the conspirators in New York, while Sherburne Hopkins worked the Washington side with reports going directly to the U.S. State Department.[716] The noose around Huerta's conspirators was tight.

There is little doubt that Villa opposed any plot that included Orozco or Huerta. The day Sommerfeld had been spotted near El Paso, Huerta's chief arms buyer in New York, Abraham Ratner, disparaged Villa in the press, "'General Huerta,' he said, 'had ordered Villa executed, and when Villa was brought before him he stretched himself at General Huerta's feet and made a piteous appeal for mercy. He caught General Huerta around the legs, tried to kiss him, and humbled himself in every possible way. 'Please, please spare me,' he whined as he cringed before the General,' said Ratner."[717] Comments such as this did not play well to the man who had raised an army of forty thousand men, defeated Huerta on the battlefield, and helped send him into exile. Villa and his men in the United States, with Felix Sommerfeld as their main spokesman, now did anything in their power to foil the conspiracy.

The Huerta-Orozco-Mondragón plot featured prominently in the headlines of New York's papers for weeks. And it was real. Federal agents all along the border checked every nook and cranny for conspirators, money, arms, and ammunition. The Secretary of War personally addressed the issue with the Attorney General on May 6th in a memorandum,

> Sir:
>
> I have the honor to quote for your consideration and such action as you deem advisable, the following extract from a letter I received from the Intelligence officer, U.S. forces at Douglas, Arizona:
>
> 'Indications in El Paso point to the assembling there of many supporters of the Cientificos composed mostly of soldiers and officers who came across the line after the battle of Ojinaga. A large part of these men are at present in El Paso and can be seen any day at the Hotel El Paso… The Villa forces at Juarez have been fearing that an attack might be made and it is thought that should Villa be unsuccessful a new revolution will be launched at or in the vicinity of Juarez with the object of taking that port from the Villa faction. All of this points to preparations for General Huerta to re-enter Mexico.'
>
> Very respectfully,
> (signed) Lindley M. Garrison
> Secretary of War[718]

The fact that Secretary Garrison admonished the Justice Department to do something is significant. Military Intelligence had filed only a few reports on the issue in April. Felix Sommerfeld seems to have been the source of the most pertinent information. The week before he went to the border, on April 23rd, he wrote to his personal friend, the American Secretary of War: "I was very sorry not to have had the pleasure of seeing you in Washington last week, but I hope to see you in the near future, in order to tell you all I know about the latest developments in Mexico."[719] The timing of Garrison's note to his colleague coincided exactly with Sommerfeld's return from El Paso.

The entire group of conspirators arrived in New York in the middle of June. Manuel Mondragón, who had gone to Europe in May, returned together with Aureliano Blanquet on June 15th.[720] Félix Díaz came from New Orleans. Andrew Meloy arrived on the 21st from Europe. Feeding rumors about a split between him and Villa, Félipe Ángeles turned up in New York, as well, to confer with the Maderos and members of the former Madero cabinet. Naturally, papers speculated that he, maybe even Villa himself, contemplated joining the Huerta movement.[721] Pascual Orozco also came briefly around the 20th and returned to El Paso on the 24th.[722] He mostly stayed at the border frantically organizing the incursion and supplies for the conspirators.[723] Rumors of fantastic supplies or arms and ammunition ran rampant all along the border. However, these were supplies going to Villa and Obregón's forces in most instances, not the "Científico" opposition.[724]

According to British intelligence, intensive meetings occurred with and around Huerta that involved Franz Rintelen, Franz von Papen, and Karl Boy-Ed. Boy-Ed, who steadfastly claimed never to have met Huerta other than in Mexico in 1914, might not have been personally involved, but still professed his sympathies with the exiled dictator in his memoirs.[725] "His forced removal by the Americans I always thought it [the ousting of Huerta] to be a calamity for Mexico," he wrote in 1920.[726] During these meetings, which very likely involved Franz von Papen, it became clear that the Meloy "Peace Plan" for Mexico was failing miserably. First Chief Carranza had publicly announced that he would have no negotiations with Pancho Villa, Huerta, or anyone else for that matter, from the beginning. His chief of the artillery and secret service agent, Arnold Krumm-Heller, who was the head of the order of Freemasons in Mexico, went as far as expelling Huerta, Díaz, "and about eighty other Mexicans, who have been prominently identified with the political affairs of Mexico" from the Grand Masonic Lodge.[727] Carranza sent an official document to Washington D.C. and had it published, signed the "Masonic Grand Orient..." bearing the Masonic seal of "Progreso y Libertad Órden de Mexico."[728]

While no one showed much surprise that Carranza refused to participate in the negotiations, other leaders bailed, as well. Both Félipe Ángeles, who may never have been committed to the insurgency, and Manuel Mondragón, the centerpieces of Meloy's plan, quit. U.S. State Department agents, who analyzed Rintelen's correspondence after his arrest in England, concluded that "Mondragón had refused the offer [of the Catholic Church to finance him] because the idea of re-establishing the power of the Catholic Church in Mexico was futile. He had also refused 100,000 dollars and the Secretaryship [sic] of War, which he was offered if he would accompany Huerta to the border... apart from Mondragón, Díaz and the Catholic Church will remain impotent."[729] Meloy's idea had come apart at the seams.

Despite these setbacks, Huerta and Orozco kept pushing their plot. Throughout May and June, significant amounts of supplies poured into the border region, consigned to small arms dealers in and around Texas. Sommerfeld's activities and enlistment of his friend, the Secretary of War, the sudden influx of military materiel, combined with the rampant rumors that a conspiracy was afoot, caused great alarm among the American officials and the Villista secret service.[730] It was very difficult to separate these shipments from deliveries to Villa and Obregón. Both imported millions of cartridges for the more than sixty thousand soldiers in active duty. The source of weapons and munitions, as well as the finances behind them, became the looming question. Felix Sommerfeld was sending millions of cartridges from the Western Cartridge Company, Peters Cartridge Company, and Winchester Arms Company to the border throughout the preparation period of this plot.

Felix Sommerfeld pointed to a large cache of arms and ammunition that the Mexican government had supposedly bought in 1913 in an interview with B.I. Agent Cantrell.[731] According to him, this cache had been stored in the Navy Yard of New York ever since Huerta's demise and belonged to the Mexican government. According to Sommerfeld, Huerta had laid his hands on these supplies and shipped them to the border through the Ratners and the Russian-Jewish-Mexican merchant, Leon Rasst. U.S. State Department documents somewhat support the main facts of Sommerfeld's claim. The SS *Monterrey* stopped in New York in April 1915.[732] Customs officials impounded a large load of rifles, machine guns, and ammunition, and stored them in the New York Navy Yard. Leon Rasst, a shady businessman who worked with any faction as long as it was profitable, tried to have the impounded shipment released. However, U.S. authorities determined that the true owner was Abraham Ratner. He subsequently received the rights to the arms.[733] Officials in El Paso tried to find out on May 12th who had received eight carloads of munitions matching approximately the size of Ratners's cache. The Villista secret service further confirmed that the consignment had not been theirs.[734]

U.S. authorities and Sommerfeld's organization tried their best to stop the conspiracy. Despite their efforts and the lack of support from the other Mexican factions, Victoriano Huerta and his immediate followers decided on June 24th to go ahead with their plan. The exiled general and a group of his closest advisors took a train to San Francisco on that day, ostensibly to visit the World Fair exhibition. However, in Chicago they switched trains and headed to Kansas City, where they changed destinations again, and headed for El Paso.[735] The train stopped right across the Texas border near Newman, New Mexico, a small hamlet between New Mexico and Texas, and only twenty miles from El Paso on the early morning hours of June 27th. Pascual Orozco and a small group of Huertistas waited at the station with two cars to take their leader across the Mexican border. However, the El Paso Customs Collector and intelligence agent Zach Lamar Cobb, with a detail of soldiers from Fort Bliss, arrested Orozco and his men at the station. Huerta greeted Orozco as the train stopped on the Texas side of the border, just before U.S. authorities arrested him, as well.[736] Huerta seemed completely surprised. The American public was not as surprised. Even before agents arrested Huerta, New York papers had reported that the general was on a train bound for El Paso to start a new revolution.[737]

Huerta and Orozco posted bail within hours and remained in El Paso, freely continuing to plot their insurgency. Orozco escaped from house arrest on July 3rd 1915. Reports indicated that he entered Mexico where three hundred of his followers awaited him. He went into hiding on the American side of the border, as it turned out, without men, or equipment, or money. An American posse hunted him and four companions down, and shot them dead on August 30th.[738]

Huerta, who had been re-arrested after Orozco's escape, remained incarcerated at Fort Bliss. A lifelong alcoholic, the death of Orozco caused him once more to seek solace in cognac and other spirits. After falling ill, being released, rearrested, and falling ill again, he died on January 13th 1916. The official cause of death read cirrhosis of the liver, an entirely reasonable explanation. However, reports of two botched medical operations leading to his final decline fueled conspiracy theories ever since that someone, maybe even the American government, had murdered him.

The border remained unsettled for months to come. Félix Díaz launched his own, unsuccessful insurrection from New Orleans in the coming months. The Bureau of Investigations also uncovered several small filibustering operations in August. About $10,000 worth of arms and ammunition fell into the hands of American officials.[739] However, the plot of the "Científicos" under the leadership of Huerta and Orozco had effectively ended with the arrests near Newman, New Mexico.

Félipe Ángeles conducted meetings in July with Secretary of the Interior Franklin K. Lane and Hugh Lenox Scott, Wilson's Chief of the Army. Ángeles proffered former members of the Madero administration as candidates for a unity government in Mexico during these meetings.[740] He also reiterated the stated commitment of Villa that he would go into exile if Carranza did the same.[741] Secretary Lane thought enough of Ángeles' foray that he informed President Wilson of the conversations.[742] Wilson had been especially impressed with Ángeles and considered him a potential candidate for the Mexican presidency. None of the Mexican factions shared his admiration. *The New York Herald* reporter Alexander Williams phrased the likelihood of an Ángeles administration in Mexico a few months later: "Félipe Ángeles is the enemy politically of every faction in Mexico other [than] that headed by Villa. Every other faction considers him a traitor. None of the important Mexicans would under any conditions affiliate with him."[743] However, Ángeles presented a new approach to the Wilson administration, one that revived the idea of a unity government without either Villa or Carranza as its head. Sommerfeld and Army Chief of Staff Hugh Lenox Scott supported Ángeles' foray. It would have been a sensible solution had Secretary Lansing and Leon Canova not shifted gears by then. Both were now pushing for a government under Carranza's auspices in the face of a continuing decline of Villa's power in Mexico, and despite their shared belief that Carranza was impossible to deal with.

The details of the Huerta-Orozco-Mondragón plot and many of the facts remain obscured to this day. The links between Meloy and the State Department, and Leon Canova in particular, have never fully come to light. Secretary of State Robert Lansing certainly knew of Canova's activities, even if he did not participate in meetings with the Mexican exile groups, their lawyers, and lobbyists. Leon Canova suddenly seemed absent from the front lines of policy-making as soon as the arrest of Andrew Meloy in August 1915 uncovered the fact that he had been linked to German agents. This fact is particularly apparent because there was a flurry of activity regarding Mexico in August and September 1915. Several meetings of the Pan-American Conference occurred. The U.S. government also engaged in tough negotiations with Pancho Villa over confiscated American property. The conniving Canova remained at his post in Washington, quietly manipulating the fluid situation in Mexico to his ends. By the middle of September 1915, Villa's fate was sealed. Secretary Lansing and his head of the Mexican desk had convinced President Wilson to recognize Venustiano Carranza as the de-facto president of Mexico over Pancho Villa's faction. The decision would have grave consequences for the United States.

English propaganda helped Lansing and Canova sweep their embarrassing link to German secret service activities under the rug. Instead of embarrassing the U.S. government, the pro-English press went into high gear to sensationalize once more a plot of the "Huns" trying to hurt the United States. Since the failure of the conspiracy coincided with the arrest of Franz Rintelen and the resulting feeding frenzy of the American press, most historical treatments of the plot are fraught with factual mistakes. Nearly all historians dealing with this topic repeated claims of the *Providence Journal* and other British propaganda, with the notable exceptions of Reinhard Doerries and Alan Knight.[744]

The English misinformation campaign started with a report in the *New York Times* on August 4th beginning with the ominous words, "The *Providence Journal* will say tomorrow morning..."[745] The *Providence Journal*, of course, was the British propaganda counterpart to George Sylvester Viereck's, German-financed, *Fatherland*.

The article went on, "Large sums of money have been paid to Huerta since his arrival in this country directly through German hands, and it is known that some of this money was used for the purchase of rifles which were subsequently sent by water from New York to Yucatán."[746] Most importantly, there are no records in German archives that substantiate Barbara Tuchman's claim, parroted in virtually every book on the conspiracy since: "Eight million rounds of ammunition were purchased in St. Louis... and a preliminary sum of $800,000 deposited to Huerta's account in the Deutsche Bank in Havana as well as $95,000 in a Mexican account."[747] These 'facts' came from the *Providence Journal* and have never been corroborated with any archival evidence. While the German financing of the Secret War Council, transfers of funds to Boy-Ed, Albert, and Count Bernstorff are all well documented in German archives, the funding of the Huerta plot is nowhere to be found.[748] Also Rintelen's correspondence, which British authorities confiscated in August of 1915, contained evidence to the effect that he was trying to find sources of funding for Mondragón, but did not have them at the time. Investigators of the State Department summarized the information in the letters with respect to the Mexican plot: "He [Rintelen] doubts whether the Germans will want to extend their investments in Mexico just now."[749] Also, "he [Rintelen] was working [note the inference that he had not achieved that at this time] to provide arms for Mexican revolutionists."[750]

Considering that Rintelen's accounts showed an unexplained deficit of $125,000 in August, it is theoretically possible that some of this money financed the Huerta-Orozco-Mondragón plot.[751] However, according to the testimony of Rintelen's banker Plochmann, the "Wolf of Wall Street" David Lamar "tried to get money out of him [Rintelen] to 'bear' the market so as to pay him back the money he had used," a more likely explanation where Rintelen's funds could have ended.[752] Neither the Bureau of Investigations, nor the investigators of the Justice Department in the 1917 trial of Rintelen, nor the lawyers of the Mixed Claims Commission that closely investigated the Rintelen mission in the 1920s and 1930s, could come up with a single check or money transfer between Huerta, his co-conspirators, and Rintelen, Boy-Ed, or Franz von Papen.

The arms buyer for von Papen was Hans Tauscher. His records indicate that, indeed, he owned a large cache of U.S. army surplus rifles that were supposed to have gone to Indian independence fighters. However, U.S. authorities impounded those supplies in June 1915 when the arms of the *Annie Larsen* came to light.[753] Investigators looking into Tauscher's affairs determined that he had significant amounts of munitions in storage in New York in 1917.[754] Tauscher also shipped "500 cases of 7 millimetre [sic] cartridges... consigned to the Guatemalan government" around the middle of August 1915.[755] Whether the shipment to Guatemala found its way to Mexico, and if so, to whom, is not documented. Despite all the allegations, British propaganda claims, and multiple investigations for decades, the only documented money Rintelen disbursed for the Huerta-Orozco-Mondragón conspiracy was $10,000 ($210,000 in today's value), paid on July 16th 1915.[756] This relatively small check to Andrew Meloy could have covered expenses for bribing officials and paying recruits or defectors, which happened on a large scale.[757] It was too small for significant munitions purchases. Many other possibilities for Meloy receiving this money exist, such as the business promoter paying himself for various services he had provided to Rintelen.

The U.S. Justice Department solved the mystery of where most of Huerta's funds had originated on July 7th 1915: Huerta himself.[758] Huerta had cashed several hundred thousand dollars of his own money, as Felix Sommerfeld had explained to B.I. Agent Cantrell a few days earlier. According to Sommerfeld, this money came from Mexican bonds Huerta had on deposit in New York. Agents of the B.I. confirmed Sommerfeld's allegations, namely that Huerta sold Mexican bonds to finance his conspiracy.[759] According to the captain of the German warship that took Huerta to Jamaica into exile in 1914, "Huerta and General Blanquet were well supplied with travelling money, and the women similarly with jewelry. Huerta had roughly half a million marks in gold with him. In addition, he had a much greater amount in checks and other paper [i.e. treasury bonds]."[760] José Vasconcelos, Mexican lawyer, and member of the Madero and Gutiérrez governments, testified on June 30th, "When he [Huerta] left Mexico it was estimated that he took out with him around five million [in] gold [approximately $2.5 million, which in today's value would be $52 million]."[761] In short, Sommerfeld and Vasconcelos both estimated that Huerta had access to millions of dollars of his own money while in New York.[762]

The arrest of Huerta on June 27th, and the collapse of the

"Científico" conspiracy, brought to light some astonishing facts about the Secret War Council. Sommerfeld, Bernhard Dernburg, and very likely Karl Boy-Ed made the decision around the beginning of May that the Huerta-Orozco-Mondragón plot was not worth supporting. This decision stood in stark contrast to the continued efforts of Franz Rintelen, Frederico Stallforth, and Andrew Meloy, as well as those of the "Oliver North of the State Department," Leon Canova, to push on with the plot.[763] The extent of Robert Lansing's knowledge or involvement in the plot is unknown. Clearly, he supported a solution that eliminated Villa and Carranza as players in a pacified Mexico. He knew Huerta, and had worked for him as a lawyer several years before. It is still unlikely that he actively involved himself in the plot or took a special interest in it.[764]

Felix Sommerfeld worked closely with Boy-Ed through the fall of 1914 and in the spring of 1915. His regular intelligence reports to the naval attaché attest to Sommerfeld's job description as a German naval intelligence agent.[765] It is highly unlikely to assume that Sommerfeld acted without approval from Boy-Ed when he took apart the Huerta plot at the border. When Rintelen inserted himself into Mexican affairs, a much larger and much more effective German clandestine project was under way. Sommerfeld, whom the American government considered an honest broker, who had personal access to the highest levels of the Departments of Justice, War, and State, and whose connections to the American business elite greatly exceeded those of Andrew Meloy and Rintelen combined, undertook the most ambitious German project of the period: Create a war between the United States and Mexico through the manipulation of U.S. government officials, American businesses, and the only real power in Mexico to cause this war: Pancho Villa. Sommerfeld proposed to create an intervention in Mexico to the German admiralty through Bernhard Dernburg on May 10th 1915. "He [Sommerfeld] is completely sure that an intervention of the United States in Mexico can be provoked... let Mr. Sommerfeld through me [Dernburg] have a clear 'yes' or 'no.'"[766] When Sommerfeld received a clear "yes," Rintelen stood in the way.[767]

Sommerfeld took him out without hesitation. He leaked Rintelen's identity to James F. McElhone of the *New York Herald* on May 17th, two weeks after he went to the border, and the week after he conferred with Lindley Garrison.[768] McElhone's boss was

Editor-in-chief William Willis, one of Sommerfeld's closest friends.[769] Willis not only published his reporter's scoop on the German agent, but also reported Sommerfeld's information to the Chief of the U.S. Secret Service, William Flynn.[770] The *New York Sun* carried an article on May 26th, mentioning a mysterious German agent named "Hansen" (Rintelen's alias).[771] Not knowing how he had been identified, Rintelen closed his office and moved in with Meloy and Stallforth at 55 Liberty Street. Sommerfeld reportedly was a frequent visitor there. According to witnesses, Sommerfeld not only watched Rintelen's every move, but also "advised" him. Rintelen had presented Sommerfeld a letter of introduction from Peter Bruchhausen. Bruchhausen, a German commercial attaché attached to the legation in Argentina, was Sommerfeld's intelligence handler in Mexico between 1911 and 1913.

As the American secret service began to close in on Rintelen, the German agent himself participated in his own downfall. Rintelen had contracted the publicity agent, John C. Hammond, for $10,000 to spread propaganda against the Allies as early as the end of April.[772] The effort to show Bernhard Dernburg and the others in the German Press Office how propaganda was done backfired badly. Hammond reported Rintelen's identity, as well as his activities, to President Wilson's secretary, Joseph Tumulty.[773] Rintelen also blundered in his social activities. He invited Anne L. Seward, a young and pretty schoolteacher who he knew from Berlin, on several dates in the first week of June. Rintelen spoke of "unlimited funds" at his disposal and made disparaging remarks about the "policy of the United States and the action of the President," in order to impress her and other dinner guests.[774] The niece of former Secretary of State William Seward found "the actions and general conduct of Captain Rintelen... so suspicious that... she determined to and did write the President upon the subject."[775] This letter, as well, went to President Wilson's secretary, Joseph Tumulty.

Rintelen had become a rogue agent and a tremendous liability for the Secret War Council in New York by the time the Huerta affair came to light. British and American agents began to hone in on his location and activities. French police discovered the first 'cigar' bombs on the *SS Kirk Oswald* in Marseilles on May 10th. The New York Bomb Squad was hot on the heels of Rintelen's sabotage team. Likely upon the request of his direct superior, Karl Boy-Ed, the German Admiralty issued an order for Rintelen's recall on July 2nd.[776] The strike at Bridgeport began on July 15th and aroused further suspicions about this mysterious agent in New York. Heinrich Albert "lost" his briefcase in the New York "El" on July 24th, exposing most intelligence operations the Secret War Council was conducting. The pavement was getting too hot for Rintelen. Without the ability to obtain a new passport, the agent booked a voyage back to Europe on the SS Noordam. He had decided to use the Swiss passport with which he had come to America. Meloy, his wife, and his secretary joined the German agent on his trip. Even then, on the voyage back to Europe, Rintelen could not keep his mouth shut and aroused suspicions from other passengers. British patrols took "The Dark Invader" off the ship during a routine check at Ramsgate on August 13th.

Initially able to successfully hide his true identity under questioning, he caved after a few days. The British government interned him as a prisoner of war until 1917, when the American government won his extradition. Frederico Stallforth alluded to the real attitude in the Secret War Council concerning the Huerta-Orozco-Mondragón plot in a report to Heinrich Albert in the middle of August. Celebrating the fact that Meloy had accompanied Rintelen to Europe, Stallforth wrote, "All that which might have been especially suspicious has vanished and we have put out of the way all relating to the Mexican business... Perchance [sic] you will decide... to hold our friend M[eloy] over on some pretext or other so that he will not again make such a furor [referring to the discovery of the Huerta plot] here. You can imagine how well everything is going here since he [Meloy] has been eliminated from this stage [and gone to Europe]."[777]

Half-hearted German efforts to affect a prisoner exchange for Rintelen in 1918 did not work, mainly because a few months after his arrest in England the German government, through Ambassador Count Bernstorff, disavowed him.[778] When Rintelen came back to the U.S. in 1917, the war between Germany and the United States he had so carelessly provoked, was in full swing. Since his offenses occurred in the neutrality period, New York courts convicted Rintelen of several felonies and passed sentences aggregating to four years of incarceration for procuring a false passport, conspiracy, firebombing ships, and causing labor unrest.[779] The Huerta plot did not figure into his conviction. There simply was not enough evidence of a German-Mexican conspiracy.

CHAPTER 12: DISCOVERY AND REPERCUSSIONS

UGUST 13TH 1915 MARKED A day that shook the Secret War Council to its core. Two major events occurred simultaneously that put in question the very purpose of its mission. British authorities had arrested Franz Rintelen, the German sabotage agent, on his way to Germany, along with his travel companion Andrew Meloy and his wife, as well as Meloy's secretary. British investigators found incriminating papers, many pointing to Frederico Stallforth, Rintelen's confidante and Meloy's business partner in New York, when they searched Meloy's luggage. The second event, one that the members of the Secret War Council dreaded even more, was the discovery that the contents of Heinrich Albert's briefcase had found their way to the newsroom of *The New York World*.

After secret service agent Frank Burke had duped the German commercial agent into losing his satchel three weeks earlier, on July 24th, German officials in New York had desperately tried to identify the culprits. Never quite establishing that the U.S. Secret Service was behind the theft, Paul Koenig informed Albert that an "independent newspaper writer" named George Calvert had proffered a selection of the papers to the *World* editor, Timothy Walsh.[780] Calvert, according to Koenig, had links to the Treasury Department. Indeed, Calvert likely was Frank Burke's cover identity. The German secret service agent listed all the names of journalists involved in handling Albert's papers and their addresses.[781] Although Koenig did not specifically mention it, one can easily deduct that between August 2nd and August 13th his agents scoured New York in attempts to lay their hands on these documents through any means possible. However, all the while the papers rested safely and protected in the U.S. Treasury Department. Initially not sure who had taken the briefcase, Albert placed an ad in the *New York Evening Telegram* on July 27th: "Lost on Saturday. On 3:30 Harlem Elevated Train, at 50th St. Station, Brown Leather Bag,

Containing Documents. Deliver to G. H. Hoffman, 5 E. 47th St., Against $20 Reward."[782] Nobody, of course claimed the reward nor returned the briefcase to Albert's secretary, Georg Hoffmann.

After examining the contents of the briefcase, the American government decided on August 2nd 1915 to give them to the *New York World*. The newspaper notified Albert on August 13th, the day of Rintelen's arrest, that they had his papers in its possession. Desperately trying to thwart the publication, the German embassy sent the sixty-six year-old Second Counselor of the German Embassy in Washington, a member of the royal aristocracy of Prussia, and former member of the German parliament, Hermann Prince von Hatzfeld zu Trachenberg, to speak with Secretary of State Robert Lansing.[783] The unsuspecting German diplomat did not realize that Lansing knew all about the issue since he had arranged for the *World* to get the documents. The entreaty came to naught. The *World* ran first page exposés on Albert and the activities of the Secret War Council between August 15th and 18th.

Albert's papers revealed the German ownership of the Bridgeport Projectile Company, the investments in American munitions, market-cornering efforts, investments in newspapers, bribes to American politicians, links of the Deutsche Bank representative, Hugo Schmidt, to the German operation, and payments of the German government to George Sylvester Viereck and the *Fatherland*.[784] Every day new headlines seemed to top the ones of the day before. A. Bruce Bielaski, Secretary of State Lansing, and President Wilson convened emergency meetings to figure out how to react to the revelations.[785] German Ambassador Count Bernstorff found himself cornered by anxious journalists wherever he went.[786] The articles smothered whatever goodwill the general American public could still muster for Germany after the sinking of the *Lusitania*. English propaganda wallowed in the revelations that had found their way from Albert's satchel to the headlines of American dailies.[787]

Editorials both damned and pitied the German efforts. A *New York Evening Globe* editorial titled, "Insult to the American People," compared the German support of the American peace movement to an insult "as much as if she [Germany] had deliberately fired at our flag."[788] The *New York Evening Post* wrote, "The pro-Germans have a right to carry on a propaganda [sic], to establish legitimate press bureaus and circulate news; the difficulty of it is that they have gone about it so badly... Here the boasted German efficiency has utterly failed. Germans are wonderful as organizers and soldiers, but in the higher realms of psychology and the spirit, Heaven [sic] knows, there are none to compare with them for wrecking their own cause."[789] Even the Secret War Council's own, *The New York Evening Mail*, pondered, "If she [Germany] charged England with having incited the German propaganda in America by subtle intrigues, she would bring a charge against her enemy which, if true, would show what a dangerous and intelligent foe England is."[790] The *Brooklyn Eagle* demanded serious consequences: "The documents published by the *New York World* prefer such a serious indictment against agents of the German government that action should at once be taken in Washington."[791]

Albert himself confided to his wife, "*The Evening Sun* speaks of 'bovine stupidity' [with respect to the letters and checkbooks English officials confiscated from von Papen in January 1916]... I for instance do not feel at all insulted at the 'bovine stupidity'; I am obliged rather to admit frankly that this reproach is not so entirely unjustified, applying not to v. P. [von Papen] alone but myself too. For, no matter how valid excuses you may give for the disappearance of a brief-case [sic] or few carrying letters which get seized, it is the result after all which determines and marks such things as 'bovine stupidity.'"[792] Albert's self-flagellation seemed appropriate. The revelation of his papers made virtually the entire portfolio of German secret service activities in the United States public. Albert, Boy-Ed, and von Papen became household names in the American press. The U.S. Secret Service listened in on their phone conversations; British, Czech, and American agents shadowed their every move.

793

Albert's *faux pas* was the proverbial straw that broke the camel's back. Public opinion had already sharply turned against Germany in the beginning of May as a result of the sinking of the *Lusitania*. President Wilson sought to calm emotions and to plot a political course that would keep the United States from entering the war in Europe. He gave an infamous speech at a naturalization ceremony in the Convention Hall in downtown Philadelphia on May 10th 1915, three days after the sinking of the *Lusitania*. "The example of America must be a special example. The example of America must be the example not merely of peace because it will not fight, but of peace because peace is the healing and elevating influence of the world and strife is not. There is such a thing as a man being too proud to fight. There is such a thing as a nation being so right that it does not need to convince others by force that it is right."[794] In stark contrast, Bernhard Dernburg spoke at the Hollenden Hotel in Cleveland on May 8th, defending the German atrocity of the ocean liner's sinking, and stoking the divisions within the American public. The timing of Dernburg's speech, apart from its content, could not have been worse. He spoke of Germany's right to self-defense, while bodies were still being identified in Ireland.

The German propaganda effort in the United States completely derailed as a result of the sinking and the callous German response to it. The *New York Evening Mail*, now identified as a German-owned paper, lost most of its subscriptions and became virtually defunct. Ambassador Count Bernstorff ordered Dernburg back to Germany before the American government could expel him. However, it was not only German propaganda that suffered severe setbacks. The German Admiralty decided to halt the submarine war in its entirety on September 18th 1915, following restrictions on submarine commanders, which were designed to prevent another incident involving passenger liners.[795] Hermann Bauer, the submarine force commander, described the restrictions that had provoked an uprising within the fleet. "The orders included all ships that could carry passengers. Within this category were all steamers with more than one funnel, with more than 14 mph speed, with a promenade deck, with several rows of side windows or with a large number of [life] boats. This protected also the valuable enemy ships against submarine attacks. Against attempts of surfaced U-boats to stop these ships, they had their speed and armaments."[796]

More and more details of German activities came to light in the United States: Rintelen's projects, the ship bombings, labor strikes, propaganda efforts, and alleged fomentation of border troubles with Mexico, were all revealed or were about to be. Publicity agent and informer of the Bureau of Investigations, J. C. Hammond, confirmed the identity of Franz Rintelen in the end of July. Sommerfeld, of course, had already leaked Rintelen's name a month earlier. Also in July, Samuel Gompers linked the strike in Bridgeport, Connecticut to the efforts of German agents and implicated David Lamar and his political cronies. New York Bomb Squad Chief Thomas Tunney was hot on the heels of Rintelen and his sabotage crews since 'cigar' bombs had been found on the steamer *Kirk Oswald* in May, and meanwhile, on several other ships originating from New York.[797] It had been high time for Rintelen to leave on August 3rd, barely escaping arrest, if only for ten days.

The news of Rintelen's arrest did not reach the editing rooms of American dailies until the first week of September.[798] As he sailed into the trap that American and British agents had set for him, the U.S. government was well aware of German secret service activities in the United States. Agents of the Bureau of Investigations had documented meetings between either Karl Boy-Ed or Franz von Papen and General Huerta in June. Although no definite links could be established, the U.S. government, with the support of Sommerfeld, reacted swiftly in squelching the plot. The five-month Odyssey of the *Annie Larsen* ended at Grays Harbor in Hoquiam, Washington, on June 29th 1915, two days after the arrest of Huerta. The local customs collector impounded the ship, including what remained in her hold. He found 4,000 rifles and one million cartridges worth $25,000.[799] Two weeks earlier, on the 14th of June 1915, American investigators arrested Hans Tauscher as he organized the loading of German-paid arms on the steamer, *Djember*, in New York.[800] The story made the headlines in the beginning of July. Tauscher was summoned to court a few weeks later. He refused to implicate Franz von Papen under cross-examination. However, the damage was done. The U.S. government had clearly traced the weapons of the *Annie Larsen* and the *Djember* to Hans Tauscher and suspected Franz von Papen since he was his superior.[801]

The arrival of the *Annie Larsen* in Washington State also pointed to the entire German naval intelligence cell on the West Coast under the command of Consul General Franz Bopp in San Francisco. While the consul remained in the shadows a short while longer, the role of the flamboyant socialite and San Francisco shipping tycoon, Frederick Jebsen, came into public view. Rather than face arrest for violating the neutrality laws of the Unites States, he decided to escape the dragnet of the American authorities. He made his way to Germany in disguise at the end of June and volunteered for service on the submarine *U 36*. She sank on July 24th 1915 off the Shetland Islands, shot to pieces by the English Q-ship, *HMS Prince Charles*, a warship disguised as a freighter.[802] The revelations of German aid to Hindu groups in the United States and India brought the German consul, Franz Bopp, and his attachés squarely into the crosshairs of American authorities. Bopp and his Vice-Consul Eckhart H. von Schack were indicted in February 1916 after a lengthy investigation that also revealed German sabotage missions in Canada.[803]

The revelations contained in Albert's briefcase, of which the Wilson administration had possession in the last week of July 1915, supported the mounting evidence of German secret service missions targeting the United States. Despite protestations of innocence by Ambassador Count Bernstorff, Secretary of State Robert Lansing became convinced that decisive action had to be taken. Together with Secretary of the Treasury William McAdoo, Lansing had carefully sifted through Albert's documents and decided which of these to make available to the *World*.[804] Of course, both Lansing and McAdoo, whose responsibility the Secret Service fell under, knew much more than what they gave to the newspapers for publication. Secretary Lansing had been briefed on Franz Rintelen after J. C. Hammond had given a full report to the Bureau of Investigations at the end of July.[805] Lansing had convinced President Wilson by August 4th that the "country was 'honeycombed with German intrigue and infested with German spies.'"[806]

Changing the President's attitude was not an easy task. Wilson still strongly believed in 1915 that he could broker peace between the Central and the Entente powers. The revelations of the Rintelen mission and of the Albert papers started to turn the tide. To top the string of bad news, the German submarine *U 24* sank the White Star passenger liner *SS Arabic* on August 19th close to where the *Lusitania* had met her fate three months earlier. Forty-four passengers, among them three Americans and three crew members, died in the attack. The American president's strategy on dealing with Germany and the maintenance of "neutrality" received a bad lashing as a result, from both supporters and detractors of the administration. "Too proud to fight" became a rallying cry against a president who was up for reelection in 1916.

However, President Wilson did not change his mind for purely political considerations. Responding to the actions of the Secret War

Council within the borders of the United States became a matter of national security for the first time since the war in Europe had begun. Although American authorities failed to apprehend Rintelen before he boarded the *Noordam*, the State Department received an extensive report on Rintelen, his papers, and associates on September 15th.[807] The source of Rintelen's funding remained unknown until October, when investigators interviewed George Plochmann, who fingered the German Naval Attaché, Boy-Ed, as the source.[808] The arrest of Robert Fay on October 24th 1915, and the discovery of his bomb-making materials, unraveled the ship-bombing plot, as well as further evidence of German attacks on U.S. property. It did not make much difference to the American government that Count Bernstorff disavowed both Rintelen and Fay as not acting on orders of his government. The evidence of German government involvement in the organizing, financing, and execution of missions to cause labor unrest, border troubles, and sabotage of American factories was overwhelming.

The American response to these discoveries was swift and comprehensive. President Wilson announced an increase of the U.S. army by 140,000 troops in November.[809] The Justice, Treasury, and State Departments negotiated the creation of a "Central Intelligence" agency comprised of the secret services of the three branches in early December.[810] Both efforts were clear signals that national security considerations motivated the Wilson administration to act. The increase in troop strength that Army Chief of Staff Hugh Lenox Scott had sought for years mainly shored up the American border with Mexico, which was still reeling from the Huerta-Orozco-Mondragón plot.[811] Domestically, a centralized intelligence organization clearly targeted perceived needs for homeland security. The U.S. Secret Service tapped the phones of Heinrich Albert, his girlfriend Mrs. Edmee Reisinger, Franz von Papen, Karl Boy-Ed, Hans Tauscher, Paul Koenig, the German Club, George Sylvester Viereck, and several others starting in August 1915.[812] Unbelievably, Felix Sommerfeld, Frederico Stallforth, and Paul Hilken's phones were not included.[813]

The government also decided to bring German agents to trial. The German navy supply scheme was the only fully investigated plot that could be effectively litigated at the time. The real target of the proceeding was German Naval Attaché Karl Boy-Ed, who the American government made great strides to implicate as the organizer of the plot.[814] Since he enjoyed diplomatic immunity, prosecutors made an example of Dr. Carl Buenz, the seventy-three year-old director of HAPAG. Buenz and several other managers went on trial on November 24th 1915, for supplying German warships in the fall of 1914 from U.S. soil using false manifests. Buenz received a sentence of two years imprisonment on December 17th. After fighting his conviction all the way to the Supreme Court, he was finally compelled in 1918 to serve in the federal penitentiary in Atlanta together with other felons, such as Franz Rintelen and Charles von Kleist. Both von Kleist and Buenz died in prison. Rintelen subsequently, and in honor of his fallen friend, took the pen name Franz Rintelen von Kleist. [815]

The HAPAG trial was a clear shot across the bow for the German officials in the United States. Robert Fay and his associates, Daeche and Scholz, were convicted in short order for attempting to sabotage ships. Werner Horn and Paul Koenig, including several of his men, stood trial in December 1915 for the attacks on the Welland Canal.[816] Also, American prosecutors hauled dozens of witnesses in front of jurors in a New York grand jury proceeding to testify in the Rintelen conspiracy in the beginning of October 1915. Frederico Stallforth refused to appear in front of the Grand Jury in a daring case of passive resistance, and got away with it – at least for a time.[817]

Felix A. Sommerfeld was among the witnesses the Grand Jury called.[818] Fairly self-assured that he could remain above suspicion, he answered the prosecutors' questions without giving much information. It helped that he had outed Rintelen's name and was on record for opposing the Huerta plot. He also was instrumental a month earlier in helping the U.S. State Department wrest millions of Dollars of confiscated money and property from Pancho Villa, and return it to American companies.[819] However, despite the fairly benign questioning before the Grand Jury, American officials gave Sommerfeld some additional scrutiny a few weeks after his testimony. New York police arrested him in the Hotel Astor, handcuffed him in front of the guests, and hauled him off to jail on October 28th 1915. The pretense was an old warrant from 1898, when Sommerfeld had stolen $250 from his brother's landlord, a German-American by the name of Hans Zimmermann.[820]

Boy-Ed immediately tried to get the German Consulate General to exert pressure on the accuser. "Since the possibility exists that...

Zimmermann made his accusations against Sommerfeld with best intentions (because he also erroneously thought that Sommerfeld was an enemy of the German cause) [Parentheses in the original], I would like to inquire with the Imperial General Consul whether this private Zimmermann could not be approached tentatively and inconspicuously to suppress this disruptive and for the German reputation unfavorable affair."[821] Hossenfelder, the acting German Consul General in New York, who had a less than cordial relationship with the naval attaché, responded, "[S]ince your Excellency declare that German interests are touched by this case, I assume that over there [the Naval Department] more is known about Sommerfeld... I therefore subserviently suggest informing me in detail about the facts of the case."[822] Of course, the naval attaché had no intention of briefing the consul general on details of Sommerfeld's job.

Sommerfeld hired a high-powered law firm and quickly beat the charges. The accuser, however, did not vanish. He blackmailed Sommerfeld for years hence.[823] While Sommerfeld tried to talk his way out of the New York police department's holding cell, agents of the Bureau of Investigations rifled through his possessions in his Astor suite. It must have been a disappointing outcome that they found no incriminating evidence. This is not to say that there was none. Sommerfeld's uncle, Ed Rosenbaum, commented on the episode in 1916: "Felix Sommerfeld was arrested in New York City on an old charge for the purpose of detaining him while they went through his room and searched for his private papers... they were not smart enough for Felix."[824]

The evidence the American government had gathered against both von Papen and Boy-Ed in the course of their investigations caused Secretary of State Lansing to demand their recall on December 2nd 1915.[825] The State Department publicly alluded to the false manifests and passport fraud as the reasons.[826] However, Boy-Ed's financing of Rintelen, as well as evidence of von Papen's involvement in the cornering of munitions and sabotage, pointed to their leadership roles in the German secret service organization, and figured prominently in the decision to declare both attachés *personae non gratae*. Secretary Lansing wrote to Ambassador Count Bernstorff on December 5th, "the relation of the two attachés to persons engaged in illegal or questionable practices was known. I will mention Von Wedell, Ruerode,

Rentlen [sic., meaning Rintelen], Stegler, Buenz, Archibald [a captured messenger for Austrian ambassador Dumba and von Papen]...''[827] The Austrian Ambassador Dr. Konstantin Count Dumba had already received his passports in September after a captured messenger had revealed letters in which the ambassador had expressed support of a strike of Austro-Hungarians in American munitions factories.[828] The papers included a letter from von Papen to his wife in which he referred to the American public (or newspaper editors as he later specified) as "those idiotic Yankees."[829]

CHAPTER 13: THE "DARK INVADER" IN THE LIGHT OF HISTORY

ESPITE THE ABILITY OF AMERICAN investigators to move in on the various German cells of saboteurs in the latter half of 1915, and despite positively identifying the links of sabotage to the German government, the elimination of von Papen and Boy-Ed did not end German clandestine activities in the U.S. Most German agents remained undeterred, in part because of a lack of cooperation between U.S. government agencies that prevented the coordination of evidence, but also in part because the American legal system was wholly unequipped to deal with the clandestine war fought on its territory. The brief arrests of Hans Tauscher, Paul Koenig, Felix Sommerfeld, Frederico Stallforth, and other key German spies in 1915 generated mostly publicity but did not end the German clandestine war. The American prosecutors could not get the convictions necessary for removing these second tier agents and prevent them from wreaking further damage on the United States. The legal tools to stop the German attacks came only in June of 1917 with the Espionage Act, after the American entry into the war, and after the German secret service had largely moved out of the country.

Rintelen sued the German government after returning to Germany in 1921, for damages for the four years he spent in the Atlanta penitentiary. Disenchanted and bitter about the war, Rintelen wrote his memoirs called *The Dark Invader* in the late 1920s.[830] The German government tried to stop its publication. After years of wrangling, a British publisher finally accepted the manuscript in 1933. Fearing for his life when Franz von Papen and then Hitler became chancellors of Germany, Rintelen moved permanently to Great Britain in 1931 and renounced his German citizenship. *The Dark Invader* became a great success once it hit the stands in Great Britain and the United States. Rintelen followed up his first book in 1935 with *The Return of the Dark Invader*.[831] His books, as well as multiple interviews he gave to promote them, contained exaggerations that even exceeded those spread in the British propaganda of World War I. He claimed to have been in charge of literally everything: propaganda, sabotage, thousands of agents, even the sinking of the *Lusitania*, and sabotage acts that happened a year after his departure.[832] An honest discussion of what really happened in the United States in the spring and summer of 1915 did not come forth because of the ongoing legal action between Germany and the United States through the 1920s and 30s. It would have affected Germany's position in the negotiations.

In a final analysis, Rintelen had serious personality issues that thwarted his career and put those assigned to work with him in danger. The navy commander might have suffered from an inferiority complex that caused him to constantly exaggerate his importance. Adopting a false title of nobility, he claimed to Americans that he was a member of the imperial family.[833] Like Horst von der Goltz, another megalomaniac character of the time, Rintelen insisted that he reported to the Kaiser who had personally sent him.[834] He swore to Bernhard Dernburg during a spat that he would make sure that the Kaiser never received him again.[835] Dernburg was a personal friend of Wilhelm II and a former cabinet member. Rintelen seemed to honestly believe that if he could just get in front of President Wilson, he could convince him to institute a weapons embargo against the Allies. While still in Berlin and desperate for the attention of his superiors, he attacked two of the most powerful players in the German empire, Max Warburg and Albert Ballin.[836] He hid under the coattails of Secretary von Tirpitz when the backlash whipped him, and recklessly invoked his boss' power. While his superiors in the admiralty seemed to have considered this youthful daredevil useful, his activities in Berlin were but a foreshadowing of the damages he caused when he came to the U.S.

Impulsive action and reckless ambition defined Rintelen's career. His main failure was not to follow the orders under which he had come to the U.S., namely to create labor unrest and stop munitions shipments. The more egregious failure was his indiscretion and lack of respect for the people and projects the Secret War Council had so carefully put in place. He told anyone who wanted to listen that his powers exceeded those of the German ambassador.[837] He believed he could do a better job than Dernburg, Albert, Boy-Ed, and von Papen combined, and as a result, he inserted himself into their projects.

The outcomes were disastrous. Not only was he discovered within weeks of his arrival, but anybody who came in contact with him in the three months of his stay found himself in the interrogation rooms of American authorities shortly thereafter. The expulsion of Karl Boy-Ed in December 1915 resulted to a large degree from Rintelen's discovery. The government found out in October 1915 that the $508,000 Rintelen had at his disposal came from the naval attaché. Two months later, Boy-Ed received his passport.

Rintelen's brashness and miscalculation of power and influence would haunt him all his life. No one came to his rescue while he served out his prison sentences in a Georgia penitentiary. When he returned to Germany, he received a medal for his wartime service but otherwise was shunned. The recognition he so desperately craved remained elusive. The only place where he could be the hero he wanted the world to see was in his books. His chosen country of residence, Great Britain, arrested Rintelen in 1940 and interned him for the duration of the Second World War bringing his career to a tragic conclusion. A U.S. Secret Service agent remarked: "The causes of his failure were typically Prussian – he had no understanding of men and conditions and he thought he was a superman."[838] His friend and co-conspirator in New York, George Plochmann, had an even better characterization of Rintelen: "Excellent talker, with the cast of a man who lives his life as in the penny dreadful novel. He lives in that kind of style at home or wherever he goes. Either he does something exceedingly foolish, or can pull off a very big task."[839] Indeed, his actions were "exceedingly foolish" causing the downfall of this German agent in 1915. Franz Rintelen died in London on May 30th 1949 of a heart attack.

CHAPTER 14: BIOLOGICAL WARFARE

RINTELEN'S UNFINISHED BUSINESS FELL INTO Frederico Stallforth's lap. Stallforth had lost his investments in Mexico in the Revolution and was in desperate financial straits in the summer of 1915. He eagerly took the job, hoping for Heinrich Albert's financial support.[840] The German-Mexican banker sent $10,000 to London for Rintelen's defense as a first action after the arrests in England.[841] Heinrich Albert continued to support the arrested agent's legal defense both in England and the United States after his extradition in 1917. All payments from Albert went through Frederico Stallforth. He testified in 1917, "I have received several times small amounts from ten to fifteen thousand dollars... in connection with the Rintelen matter..."[842] Stallforth was an unlikely spy and, maybe because of that, so good at what he did. He was an amateur with serious liabilities, such as his chronic shortage of cash, and a history of questionable business ventures. Constantly trying to raise money for his defunct Mexican family business, he networked with anyone who could help him, including a host of influential German-Americans. Certainly, he was not always successful in his efforts. Oren Sanford, a wealthy magnate in Winchester, Massachusetts, denied him funding because "Life is uncertain at best and should you be killed in that machine of yours [Stallforth owned a car] some fine day I should have much trouble getting my money back..."[843]

Stallforth had paid his dues in the eyes of Albert and Boy-Ed, despite his apparent weaknesses, and maybe especially for his excellent networking skills and daring persona.[844] The Mexican-German banker had recruited multiple agents for Albert, von Papen, and Boy-Ed to carry mail to Germany during 1914 and 1915.[845] Stallforth also had skillfully managed Albert and Boy-Ed's links to German agents Hugo Schmidt, Paul Hilken, Felix Sommerfeld, Franz Rintelen, and David Lamar. He had cultivated several financial backers and agents for the Secret War Council, such as Rudolph Pagenstecher (propaganda, newspapers), Dr. Wilhelm Wirbelauer (dye stuffs), and his best personal friend, Hans Stoehr (wool). It was only logical for Albert to extend Stallforth's responsibilities since he was the only member of the Secret War Council, other than Albert himself, who was familiar with the existing financial structures and agent networks.

Frederico Stallforth, unknown date (approximately 1925).
Picture courtesy Prevo Collection

Stallforth's connections went way beyond knowing a few sympathetic German-Americans. After Rintelen's arrest and Albert's briefcase incident, the German-Mexican had become one of the few viable options to provide funds to agents in charge of clandestine operations. Stallforth admitted to investigators in 1918 that he indeed paid a German agent in Boston: "Mr. Albert delivered the money to me and I turned it over."[846] Through Rintelen he personally knew naval intelligence agents Bode, Wolpert, Hilken, and Hinsch, the group in charge of firebombing commercial ships.[847] The latter two also had the task of blowing up the Black Tom loading terminal in the New York harbor from whence the majority of American munitions were shipped to the Entente. Erich von Steinmetz, who brought biological warfare agents to the United States in March 1915, Carl "the dynamiter" Wunnenberg, dispatched to blow up American factories, Paul Koenig, von Papen's secret service chief, and Franz Wachendorf, alias Horst von der Goltz, the sabotage agent under arrest in England at the time, rounded out the agents Stallforth admitted to knowing.[848] However, there were more.

Amazingly, the German-Mexican banker remained largely undisturbed, even after Rintelen's mail disclosed Stallforth's involvement with German secret service activities. Letters Meloy carried for the banker revealed the latter as the German government's contact to the Deutsche Bank. Weeks later, investigators found out that Stallforth had sublet office space to Rintelen. Despite these revelations, American investigators considered the German-Mexican banker too small a fish to fry. A smooth talker, brilliantly networking in American, German, and Mexican circles, he elevated disarming the American authorities with his innocent charm to an art form. Though considered corruptible and out for personal gain, he appeared harmless to investigators, more like a David Lamar or an Andrew Meloy, not the dangerous and battle hardened type of agent, as Hans Tauscher, Paul Koenig, or Franz Rintelen.

Frank L. Polk, the Counselor of the U.S. State Department and agent for its intelligence service, interviewed the German agent in March 1916. Stallforth had refused to appear before the Grand Jury investigating German activities in the U.S., for which he was slapped with contempt of court. His lawyer opined after the meeting, "the authorities of the United States have stated to us that they were satisfied that you [Stallforth] were not connected with nor guilty of any violation of any laws of the United States, and of your thorough and sincere desire to promote the friendly relations between this country and Germany, and that you have to that end made every effort in good faith."[849] A. Bruce Bielaski, the B.I. chief, wrote in August 1917, "I have a sort of feeling about Stallforth that he never has been absolutely fair with us, but, of course, have nothing tangible with which to support this feeling."[851] Despite mountains of circumstantial evidence placing the German-Mexican banker in close relations with convicted sabotage agents, nothing stuck to Stallforth. He seemed invincible.

Stallforth met with Captain Wolpert and Paul Hilken in New York the day after Rintelen's arrest in England.[852] Wolpert, the HAPAG superintendent in New York Harbor, and Hilken, the North German Lloyd manager in Baltimore, had been in charge of the firebombing project and other sabotage under Rintelen. Stallforth wrote in his report to Albert, "To-day [sic] Capt. Wolpert came and gave me a report. From the same it is to be seen that during the last weeks very many horses have been shipped over there and among them en route a tremendous number have been stricken, almost 25 to 30%..."[853] Stallforth continued, "The whole United States is upset to-day [August 13, 1915] because the horses are becoming sick. Here in Yonkers during the past few weeks over a thousand horses must have fallen to the ground."[854] Apart from the evidence Stallforth provided for the claim that the sabotage group around Wolpert now worked under his direction, the report indicated the fruition of another sabotage effort: Biological warfare. Despite the testimony of Dr. Scheele claiming that the glanders and anthrax germs von Steinmetz had brought from Germany in the spring of 1915 arrived dead, German agents worked hard on developing another source. Stallforth testified in 1917,

> "Rintelin [sic] was interested in getting horses sick and I think Henbiel [Hilken] in Baltimore. I cannot tell [you] about the other two captains. If they were interested or not... I can tell you all the names but I cannot tell you which ones [sic] were interested. Menchel [Hinsch], Wolpert, Bode, Shaley, Schimmel and Fay, the man in Boston, I don't remember his name, -- Sternberg [Steinberg]... The plan was that he [Rintelen] tried to get some serum of any kind that could be inoculated in

one horse and that this horse would contaminate the
rest of them... When Rintelen left he said that he had
some serum and that nothing was done with it. I don't
know how Mr. Rintelin [sic] got that serum."[855]

The serum Rintelen claimed to have had in his possession might have
been from a source in the U.S. However, it seems far more likely that it
was another one of his infamous exaggerations. There is no evidence
whatsoever that the German secret service used anthrax or glanders, given the documented failure of the Steinmetz germs and the
arrival of a new agent with new spores in the fall of 1915. The German
General Staff made a renewed effort to prevent equine shipments
from the United States to Europe in the summer of 1915 as a result
of the failed Steinmetz mission. Unlike the Mexican revolutionaries
who fought their engagements along railroad lines that carried the
troops and animals, most European war theatres were far removed
from modern logistics. Horses were a key component to supplying the
front lines and transporting troops and equipment. Most importantly,
Great Britain almost entirely relied on American supplies of equines.
England possessed a total of 25,000 horses at the outbreak of the war.
The British military possessed 591,000 horses, 213,000 mules, 47,000
camels and 11,000 oxen by 1917.[856]

Anton Dilger's passport photo June 8th, 1917.[857]

A trained medical doctor, born and raised in rural Virginia of German parents, stepped off the SS *Noordam* in New York, the same ship that had carried Franz Rintelen two months earlier to imprisonment on October 7th 1915.[858] Dr. Anton Dilger had studied medicine at Johns Hopkins University in Maryland and later at the University of Heidelberg. Specialized in microbiology and tissue culture research, the thirty year-old Dilger volunteered as a field surgeon in the German army when the war began. Sometime in the summer of 1915, the General Staff of the Army called Dilger to Berlin where he received orders from Rudolf Nadolny, the head of the General Staff, Political

Section IIIb, to introduce glanders and anthrax into horse transports from the United States.[859] After the American doctor arrived in the U.S. in the beginning of October, he and his brother, Carl, grew the bacteria in an apartment in Chevy Chase, Maryland and created the means to distribute them. "Four phials [sic] were carefully wrapped inside the velvet padding - one labeled 'B' for Bos (Latin for cattle) and one labeled 'E' for Equus (Latin for horse)... All was set up to grow large amounts of Bacillus anthracis (causing anthrax) and Burkholderia mallei (then called Bacillus mallei, causing glanders)."[860] Dilger supplied the bacteria to Friedrich Hinsch between October and December 1915 who, in turn, distributed them to agents in New York, Philadelphia, and Baltimore. Frederico Stallforth, through Paul Hilken in Baltimore, acted as paymaster for the operation. Hilken was questioned in 1918 on the financing of his war time activities.

> "Q. Were Bode and Stallforth paying you any funds at that time? A. Stallforth and Rintelen were closely associated and it is possible that through Stallforth I was getting money to give to Captain Hinsch or Dilger. That I don't remember, but it is possible. Q. Well, do you think that is probable? A. Probable, yes... Q. Your best recollection is that you had been getting money from Stallforth or Rintelen to give to Dilger or Hinsch, or both of them? A... I did give money to Dilger and Hinsch. Q. Money that you got from Stallforth or Rintelen or both of them? A. Yes... Q. Do you know at this time what they [the payments] were for? A. Yes. Q. What were they for? A. For the Anthrax germs at Norfolk... Q. You must have gotten some payments from Stallforth after that time [when Rintelen had left the country]? A. I think, I did."[861]

Friedrich Hinsch had been one of Rintelen's point men for the delivery of incendiary devices onto steamers. With the departure of the sabotage agent on August 3rd 1915, Hinsch became "department chief of the German secret service."[862] Despite the ambiguous title and job description, Hinsch seemed to have taken over the German sabotage campaign in Baltimore, Maryland, as well as in Newport

News, and Norfolk, Virginia.[863] One of his assistants, Edward Felton, testified in 1930, "My first work with these fire things [cigar bombs] for Capt. Hinsch commenced some time [sic] early in 1915. From then on for about a year or two I was receiving regularly things for use in starting fires. I was also receiving expenses and an allowance of money of about $150 to $200 a week, which I used in paying other men to distribute these fire things... I remember once after he [Hinsch] had been up in New York he said things were getting too hot for him up there."[864] Paul Hilken's diary supports the assumption that the discovery of unexploded cigars in Marseille in the middle of June might indeed have made New York too hot for the German agent.[865]

According to Hinsch's own testimony, he started making his own "dumplings" (firebombs) on the interned German ship he commanded before the war, the SS *Neckar*, starting in the summer.[866] Other than Hinsch's statement to that effect, there is no evidence that this was the case. Scheele's bomb design remained the standard for the German sabotage agents through 1915 and into 1916. All chemicals came from Dr. Scheele's laboratory in Hoboken. The assembly of the 'cigars' took place on the German cruiser SMS *Kaiser Friedrich der Grosse*. When Captain Tunney of the New York Bomb Squad finally discovered the bomb makers in March of 1916, the German government had already sent the sabotage agent, Frederick L. Herrmann, to Baltimore to deliver more bombs to Hinsch.[867] The money needed to distribute the bombs first came from Franz Rintelen then from Frederico Stallforth through Paul Hilken.[868] Although Hinsch steadfastly denied having anything to do with sabotaging American factories in the fall of 1915 and spring of 1916, Ed Felton recalled that Hinsch "often spoke of other fires in factories and warehouses..."[869] The well-documented fires at Aetna, DuPont, Roebling's and Sons, Bethlehem Steel, Baldwin Locomotive, and other munitions plants in the fall of 1915 have never been solved. However, many of these fires occurred in the region Hinsch covered for the German Secret Service, and where he admittedly had dozens of men occupied with sabotage acts.

While Hinsch's crews of dockworkers busied themselves with placing firebombs into the holds of Allied ships, he evidently also undertook a campaign of sabotaging horse and mule shipments. American investigators wrote in 1918, "He was engaged in an active sabotage campaign in this country [United States] involving attempts

'to infect horses and mules transports [sic] with anthrax germs'...
These activities started 'in May 1915 after [he] talked with Rintelen
personally...'"[870] Despite Rintelen's departure and subsequent arrest
on August 13th 1915, the firebomb plot was in full swing in the fall
of that year. Stallforth took control of approximately $75,000 ($1.6
Million in today's value) of Rintelen's remaining funds.[871] The German
sabotage cells in Baltimore and New York wreaked havoc on international trade with Stallforth reluctantly financing the effort (Hilken
called him a "miser").[872] Stallforth's personal fortunes also seemed
to have radically improved that fall. He signed an expensive lease on
an estate in White Plains, New York on September 4th 1915, the same
time he made Hilken beg him for funds. The annual lease was $2,000
(approximately $42,000 in today's value).[873]

Hinsch freely admitted in 1930 that the following testimony
of Edward Felton with respect to infecting horses and mules was
accurate:[874]

> A few months after I commenced work on trying to
> start fires Capt. Hinsch explained to me that he had
> some further work for me to do in connection with
> some germs to start disease among the horses that
> were being collected at different shipping points. That
> work commenced, as near as I can remember, about
> the late summer or early fall of 1915. From then on for
> a period of nearly a year I was working regularly under
> Capt. Hinsch in also distributing disease germs. I did
> this work in Norfolk, Newport News, and in New York
> City... The germs were given to me by Capt. Hinsch in
> glass bottles about an inch and a half or two inches
> long, and three-quarters of an inch in diameter, with a
> cork stopper. The bottles were usually contained in a
> round wooden box with a lid that screwed on the top.
> There was cotton in the top and bottom to protect the
> bottles from breaking. A piece of steel in the form of a
> needle with a sharp point was stuck in the under side
> [sic] of the cork, and the steel needle extended down
> in the liquid where the germs were. We used rubber
> gloves and would put the germs in the horses by

pulling out the stopper and jabbing the horses with the sharp point of the needle that had been down among the germs... We did a good bit of the work by walking along the fences that enclosed the horses and jabbing them when they would come up along the fence or lean over where we could get at them. We also spread the germs sometimes on their food and water that they were drinking... Capt. Hinsch gave me the instructions as to where I would find the horses and also gave me the bottles of germs and the money. I used a good many of the same men on this work that I did on starting the fires. I had about ten or twelve men working on these matters for me. We would work at it sometimes at night and sometimes in the daytime. A good many of the men were also doing other work and they made this extra money on the side... Capt. Hinsch was accustomed to giving me brown paper packages filled with these tubes and with the fire things. Sometimes he would give me these at his apartment in Baltimore [on Charles Street] and sometimes he would meet me at New York, Norfolk or Newport News.[875]

Despite one of the firebombs going off in Ed Felton's pants in Newport News, the African-American stevedore and his crew worked undetected until 1917. The generous pay of $15 per day (approximately $350 in today's value) obviously made it worth the risk. Hinsch commented on his stevedore's work in 1930, "Eddie Felton was a smart fellow, always on the job from morn [sic] to night, who got the best out of his negroes and who worked hard and did not hesitate to take a hand himself..."[876]

The known facts and admissions of the main players establish that Dr. Dilger, his brother Carl (who transported the germs from Chevy Chase, Maryland to Hinsch), and the stevedores under Captain Hinsch's command indeed carried out the scheme of infecting horses. The connection between the Baltimore cell and Frederico Stallforth is clearly documented: Paul Hilken's diary for 1915 mentions meetings with the German-Mexican banker on nine occasions, starting with an introduction through Rintelen on June 23rd.[877] Hilken had meetings with

Stallforth concerning funds as soon as Rintelen had left the country. "Thursday 5 [5th of August] see St. – 500."[878] Then on September 1st: "'Biltmore' meet B & St. nothing doing [no money forthcoming]."[879] "Tuesday 21 [21st of September] Get 500 fr. St. [from Stallforth] after much trouble..."[880] Hilken's diary entries also support the fact that Hinsch received his firebombs from New York. What investigators mistakenly took for meetings with Dr. Dilger ("Dr.") in August 1915, were indeed meetings with Dr. Scheele and the leaders of the fire bombing campaign in New York, Captains Wolpert and Bode.[881] Entries for frequent meetings and phone calls with "K" throughout the summer and fall of 1915 allow the conclusion that the Baltimore cell also was in contact with Paul Koenig, Franz von Papen's intelligence chief in the New York.[882]

However, the effects the "bio war" campaign had on the British and French supply chain are much harder to establish. There are virtually no reports of glanders, charbon (same sickness), or anthrax in newspapers of the time. The only reports of horses dying while being transported on ships are related to submarine attacks and to a barge sinking in the Hudson River in December of 1915, killing over five hundred horses.[883] The barge apparently sank as a result of sabotage (the drain plugs had been removed) and could well have been the work of German agents, maybe even Friedrich Hinsch's men. Notable are also reports of stampeding horses that press reports blamed on German agents.[884] However, the incidents had nothing to do with poison and infection. Only one report recounted an incident in December 1914, in which a German agent allegedly poisoned horses bound for Italy while sailing on a steamer. Although 336 horses reportedly died, the cause seemed to have been lack of water rather than poison.[885]

Author Robert Koenig asserted in the biography of Anton Dilger called *The Fourth Horseman*, that 6,600 horses died on Atlantic transports between 1915 and 1917.[886] This number includes all instances of horses dying. An expert on the use of biological weapons, the trained pathologist Dr. Martin Furmanski researched the Dilger mission extensively and concluded that there simply was not enough data to prove one way or another how effective the effort was. He doubted that Dilger had the means of effectively weaponizing glanders and anthrax.[887] The delivery of biological agents through amateurs, such as the stevedores under Ed Felton, made it very likely that the cultures never created any serious mass infections on animal transports. Other disease, mostly forms of pneumonia and pulmonary failures caused by stress, accounted for most of the losses of equines at sea.[888] Disputed numbers on how many equines were actually infected underline to this day the difficulty of identifying the biological agents and the causes of death of these animals. However, it may be established that only a small fraction of animals died of glanders or anthrax.

German efforts to disturb the flow of horses from the U.S. to Europe had the purpose of causing delays and additional cost, as was the case with the firebombed ships. Corrals were typically not well guarded in the beginning of the war, as Ed Felton had described, making it easy to infect the animals. Allied buyers increased security and care for animal transports as the war progressed. There was a safe and effective test for glanders by 1915. The Bureau of Animal Industry distributed Ophthalmic Mallein to ranches in the Midwest and West for testing for glanders bacteria in June 1915 without any connection to the German "bio war" efforts. Infected animals had to be killed and disposed of immediately to reduce chances of infection of other animals.

Statistics of shipments of horses and mules between 1915 and 1917 tell an interesting story that may very well indicate a tangible success of the German "bio war" campaign. British and French horse shipments dropped by nearly fifty percent when the German effort could have shown first results in 1916 (Dilger did not arrive until October 1915), but picked back up to 1915 levels in 1917 until American troop transports reduced the Allied shipping capacity and effectively ended the supply effort.[889] Could an extensive testing regimen and quarantine of animals have caused the supply effort to slow significantly? Neither the English nor the American governments have publicly acknowledged any change in procedure.

Despite the widespread conviction that the Dilger plot had no real impact on the Allied war effort, Stallforth, Hilken, Dilger, and Hinsch undoubtedly complicated the loading and transporting of war supplies for the Allies, considering the concurrent firebombing of ships. The growing activities and importance of the Baltimore cell also evidenced the rise of a new cadre of German secret agents. The main members of the Secret War Council, immobilized, discredited, and under tight surveillance in the fall of 1915, stayed largely in the background. Then, the New York cells of sabotage agents had been either discovered or knew that they were being closely watched. Still, links between the Baltimore group and the Albert office existed: Hilken noted in his diary on August 31st "Out to Plainfield…"[890] Two weeks later, Heinrich Albert wrote to his wife Ida, "Here again a tremendous heat has set in, from which I have fled for a few days again to the guest-free house of Hagedorn in Plainfield."[891] What better place to meet with sabotage agents than at the New Jersey country estate of the wealthy German-American cotton broker and Albert business partner, Adolf G. Hagedorn, far away from the prying eyes of American and British secret agents? Only days later, with the blessing of Albert and Boy-Ed, Frederico Stallforth began disbursing Rintelen's funds and began financing the entire Baltimore operation.[892]

Hilken, Dilger, and Herrmann went back to Germany and received new instructions in Berlin to organize the most ambitious project in the war in the spring of 1916. The group had the task of blowing up the Lehigh Valley Railroad Company's loading terminals on Black Tom Island, under the cover of establishing a commercial submarine service between Germany and the United States. The German General Staff had chosen the Baltimore cell over their sabotage cells in California and New York, largely because of their independence and efficiency. Stallforth became the link between Albert and the terror cell. The Dilger plot was but a warm-up for a new and final chapter in Germany's clandestine war on the United States.

EPILOGUE

THE GERMAN AGENTS IN NEW York and Baltimore, Sommerfeld, Stallforth, Krumm-Heller, Hilken, and Hinsch, as well as Witzke and Jahnke on the West Coast, carefully plotted their next moves, undisturbed and undetected by American authorities, despite the many clues of their connection to the Secret War Council. These plots would cause the United States to provision its military, and send all but one division of the regular army, together with over one hundred thousand national guardsmen, to the border with Mexico by the summer of 1916. German agents blew to smithereens the loading terminals of Black Tom Island in the New York harbor, causing an earthquake that measured 5.5 on the Richter scale, in July 1916. The freedom of action that allowed German plotters to thrive seems baffling in hindsight. However, arrests in the summer and fall of 1915 had created a false sense of accomplishment within American law enforcement.

The New York Bomb Squad realized that more conspirators had been active as a result of Fay's arrest in the fall of 1915. The investigation into the sugar cargoes, and who loaded them, led to the lighter captains. Officials re-opened an investigation into von Kleist from there, who, in the meantime, had had a falling out with Scheele and was disgruntled. Just a few months after he had started his job at the fertilizer plant, the U.S. Secret Service introduced one of their own undercover agents as a down-and-out, far-related family member who was looking for a job. The goodhearted nobleman took him in and got him a job in the plant.[893] However, the agent could only find evidence of contraband smuggling. The result was a warehouse raid whereby the police seized seventy-five bags of fertilizer. As close as they had gotten, the lawmen never penetrated the secret of the firebombs. Playing another ruse on the gullible nobleman, an undercover agent of the Secret Service posed as a German agent (he did not even speak German) in March 1916. Von Kleist, who Scheele had fired a month earlier without paying his last wages, told the undercover agent everything and was promptly arrested by the New York Bomb Squad.[894] Tragically, the U.S. government made an example of the old man who, according to Scheele, had not been privy to much of the conspiracy. He was prosecuted, convicted to penitentiary, and died of complications from influenza in the federal prison in Atlanta in January 1919.

Just before von Kleist's arrest, after a warning from von Papen's successor, Wolf von Igel, Dr. Scheele chose to temporarily disappear. The Secret Service trap snapped shut in the beginning of April 1916. Von Kleist, Wolpert, Bode, Becker, the three sailors on the *Kaiser Friedrich der Grosse* and their supervisor, first engineer Carl Schmidt all had to appear before the magistrate in handcuffs. Scheele, von Steinmetz, and Schimmel had gotten away. While the eight conspirators received stiff sentences – von Kleist even died in prison – the American authorities assumed, for the longest time, that the chemist had made it back to Germany. Finally, in 1918, after letters between Dr. Scheele and his wife surfaced, American agents found him living under a false name in Cuba. He was extradited in March 1918. Scheele, fearing that he would be sentenced to death in a court martial, offered to switch sides, just as Fay had offered his inventions to the American Department of War in return for a lighter punishment. The deal was sealed when chemists of Thomas Edison's laboratories debriefed the doctor. They could not believe their eyes when the German agent showed his notes and designs while he told all he knew.[895] Abandoned by his government and branded a traitor, the "brain of the [firebomb] conspiracies" became an American agent.[896] He worked on multiple bomb designs, air propelled artillery shells, and a host of other inventions he had in his repertoire until the end of the war. The chemist settled in Hackensack, New Jersey after the war without ever having to serve a single day in jail.[897]

It will never be possible to positively identify every ship that the German sabotage agents targeted in 1915 and 1916. The American government accused Wolpert, Bode, and von Kleist to have fire-bombed thirty-five ships valued at $10 Million ($210 Million in today's value) between January 1st 1915 and their arrest on April 13th 1916.[898] Approximately $12 Million ($252 Million in today's value) of damages

occurred at the same time, as the result of fires in war industry factories. It is impossible to ascertain exactly which fires resulted from
sabotage, and which did not. Factory fires, especially where combustibles were involved in the production, happened as a matter of course.
However, overall fire damages in the U.S. actually declined nation-
ally, as well as in New York in 1915.[899] Other statistics also illustrate
the difficulty of assessing the size of the German campaign against
factories. Nineteen factories, which in 1915 would have been among
the war material producers, reported fires in 1914.[900] The total damage
from these fires for the calendar year was estimated at $10 Million.
Twenty-seven fires destroyed approximately $12 million worth of land,
equipment, and goods during the twelve months after the sabotage
campaign commenced.[901] Many of the latter fires had been attributed
to the German sabotage campaign, although the Mixed Claims
Commission awarded only a tiny fraction of these damages to claim-
ants. Considering the fact that factories sprung up like mushrooms in
1915, and that the war production required manufacturers to enter
into the production of explosives, munitions, metal milling, and other
fire-prone processes, the outbreak of large fires in munitions facilities
does not seem surprising. However, it was certainly possible and fit-
ting for saboteurs to cause fires in such facilities and remain undetected. The real number of arsons will never be known. However, the
destruction of major American factories, such as Bethlehem Steel,
John A. Roebling and Sons, Baldwin Locomotive Company, DuPont,
Aetna, and others certainly occupied the top spots on the German military attaché's target list.

The firebombed ships provide much better data to analyze.
The group of saboteurs around Dr. Scheele freely admitted their
crimes and put numbers to their efforts. The thirty-five ships the
group stood accused of having firebombed are documented. An additional group of thirty-nine ships that also suffered suspicious fires in
the same time period brings the number of targets to seventy-four.
Embarrassed U.S. authorities downplayed, and tried to hide the fact
that German sabotage agents obviously had breached navy yards in
New York, New Jersey, and Pennsylvania. Five American warships suffered fire damages. The USS Oklahoma and USS New York, two new
battleships in construction, were almost completely destroyed.[902]

American, British, and French authorities found 'cigars' on

thirteen ships in the time period between January 1915 and April 1916, most notably on the SS *Kirk Oswald* in Marseille on May 10th 1915. The *Kirk Oswald* was not the first ship in which authorities discovered bombs. The SS *Cressington Court*, the SS *Lord Erne*, and the SS *Lord Downshire* all had bombs in their holds when they docked in Le Havre. However, the French government sent only the incendiary devices found in Marseille to New York. Captain Tunney of the New York Bomb Squad used these bombs to uncover first the lighter captains, who had arranged the placement of the bombs, and later the entire plot.

The statistics for ship fires are much more revealing than for factories. In the calendar year 1914, ten ships reported fires in the hold, five of these before the war started. Three of these fires seemed suspicious: one occurred on a sugar transport in the end of October 1914; one was on a coal tender to supply the British fleet also in the end of October; and the third concerned a horse transport in the beginning of November. These three fires seem to have had a connection with the war. They likely represented early attempts of sabotage the German military attaché von Papen organized. Even considering all ten fires in 1914 as the "statistical baseline," sixty-six fires in 1915 stand out in stark contrast to the baseline.[903] The fires occurred in sugar shipments in fourteen cases, leading American investigators to the German captains operating the inner harbor delivery carriers. Sugar does not have a history of accidental combustion. Coal, cotton, and hay are all materials that are well known to combust accidentally, especially in combination with moisture. Thirty-five ships that went up in flames originated in New York, all of them near, or next to the piers where German ships were interned. Fifteen ship fires entered the news between January and May 1916, ten of which originated in New York. Five fires occurred on ships from June to December, one determined accidental. A potentially larger number of ship fires besides the reported incidents, never made it into the news because the crews managed to extinguish the blazes.

The sabotage campaign, although alive and well in 1916 and 1917, shifted focus from attacking ships to sabotaging major installations such as harbors and large factories. Although there is insufficient evidence to prove German agents' involvements the fires in the port of Norfolk in May 1916, San Francisco and Baltimore in June, and the Black Tom terminal in July caused tens of millions of dollars in damages to installations, finished goods, and shipping. Despite many arrests and the expulsion of diplomats, the American government could not root out the saboteurs in this vast country. The sabotage campaign of the German Empire that started in the end of January 1915 made it painfully clear to the U.S. government that, over the long haul, America would have to join the Allies. The German actions against the United States after January 1915 – the submarine war against commercial shipping, the cornering of American industries, the firebomb campaign, even the attempt to introduce biological weapons of mass destruction into the mix – presented a massive and imminent threat to the national security of this country. President Wilson, although keeping up the pretense of neutrality, while remaining unwilling or unable to reduce the flow of supplies to the Entente at the same time, prepared for the worst. Although still eighteen months away, war with Germany seemed to turn into a self-fulfilling prophecy.

Several important facts stand out in the sabotage campaign of 1915. Dr. Scheele's involvement in the firebomb plot, which officially accounted for the destruction of thirty-five Allied steamers loaded with munitions, started much earlier than Franz von Papen and Franz Rintelen, the two main conspirators, wanted the world to believe. The fingerprints of the Secret War Council in New York, and, by extension, those of the German government in Berlin were all over the sabotage campaign. Rintelen received $500,000 from Karl Boy-Ed from the funds of the Imperial Navy. Hans Böhm, whom the German sabotage cables mentioned by name, received $50,000 from Boy-Ed to undertake a massive campaign against railroad installations in the U.S. and Canada in the weeks after the sabotage order. Werner Horn's employment by von Papen is well documented. He used vials of nitroglycerin. Dr. Scheele, a sleeper agent stationed in the United States for decades before the war, showed investigators in 1918, that he had developed special formulations of nitroglycerin.[904] The vials, the Sheriff of Vanceboro commented, looked nothing like anything he had ever seen before.

The Secret War Council in New York set so many sabotage missions afoot that multiple tomes have been written about the subject. Consul Franz Bopp and his associates on the West Coast attacked targets in Canada and the U.S. A dynamite-laden barge in Seattle harbor blew up in May 1915, causing a massive fire and destroying a large portion of the loading piers. The saboteur that American authorities captured was a German agent who worked for von Papen. Even without being able to prove the dozens of serious factory fires that caused tens of millions in damages in 1915, one such fire that occurred in 1916 is well documented. The Black Tom Island loading terminals blew up in July, causing such vast destruction on U.S. soil that only the attacks on Pearl Harbor in 1941 and on New York and Washington in September 2001 would surpass it.

The question of the effectiveness of Germany's strategy to wage a hot war within the United States in 1915 looms large. Moderate voices of the times, such as that of the German Ambassador Count Johann Heinrich von Bernstorff, have long held that the effort was a massive failure. The arguments supporting this assertion maintain that the hardened stance of the American government against Germany precipitated the eventual participation of the United States on the side of the Entente. The last embers of public support for the German cause died out in 1915 with the ships and factories German agents incinerated that year. American supplies to the Allies, however, did not materially slow down. The U.S. entered the war on the side of the Allies in the end, and the result is well known. Indeed, if the German strategy would have had the goal of keeping the United States out of the war, the sabotage campaign represented a massive miscalculation and blunder on the part of the Imperial General Staff and Admiralty. However, the assumption of this goal as the basis for analysis of Germany's strategy is misguided. All archival documents on the subject point to the fact that German hardliners, including the Secret War Council in New York, considered the entry of the U.S. into the war inevitable, and to some, even preferable. Understanding that the goal of Germany's military leadership in Berlin was to shift U.S. attention to its own affairs and thus sabotage the ability of the U.S. to pledge resources to Europe, the results of the sabotage campaign appear in a completely different light.

The German sabotage campaign of 1915 created a national climate that reveals many parallels to the Al Qaeda attacks on the United States in 2001. The most prevalent means of mass transportation in 1915 was ocean travel. The most common means of transportation to and from the United States were ships. Ships, like airplanes one hundred years later, were easy targets for terrorists. The horrible scenes of innocent victims drowning in cold oceans then, just like airplane passengers falling from the sky now, received lots of media attention. The resulting pressure on American government agencies to provide security would come at a staggering price. It is thus not surprising that the German strategy targeted shipping more than factories. The effects, measured in the number of ships damaged or destroyed, were miniscule, just like the material cost of demolishing the twin towers in relation to the American economy does not register. However, the true cost to the American economy then and now was, and is, tremendous.

Every freighter from any harbor in the United States had to be inspected, and every cargo certified by officials. Frederico Stallforth assessed the success of the ship bombing campaign in a report to Heinrich Albert on August 13th 1915, "What has been done with the money... is extraordinarily well expended. Consider the following points: The anxiety over the ships. Every chest which is transported to-day [sic] from here to England must be held up at the dock and searched over. This makes an enormous cost, and in addition extra policemen and watchmen have been installed, and this costs the Allies a great sum."[905] In addition to the security cost, smaller shipping lines that could not afford war insurance refused to transport war materials. Thousands of security guards patrolled the piers. The cost of war materials for the Allies exploded, in part because of German market-cornering efforts, in part because of the high cost of security, insurance, and shipping.[906] While the majority of sabotage incidents took place in New York and the surrounding area, German saboteurs lurked all around the country in the minds of American citizens. Newspapers naturally hyped the public's worst fears to the point that virtually any factory or ship fire had been set by a 'Hun.'

Clearly, the German campaign was one of premeditated terror. Neither von Papen, Boy-Ed, Rintelen, nor Albert had any qualms about the fact that the campaign would not yield a decisive blow against the actual flow of goods. What they did hope, however, was to create a climate of such insecurity and outright panic that the U.S. government would be forced to either restrict the flow of munitions to the Allies, or to build up its own military in defense against "the enemy within." The latter was the case. The buildup of the American military presented an opportunity for Germany to take advantage of in 1916, but became a curse in 1917 and 1918 when it had not done so. Critics have long maintained that the campaign produced nothing but ill will. Authorities scooped up the main saboteurs in effective dragnets within months. The American government expelled Boy-Ed and von Papen by December 1915, as a result of their connections to the conspiracies. However, the seeds that precipitated the largest, most serious attacks against the U.S., had been sown in 1915. The remaining conspirators faithfully continued their work. Friedrich Hinsch and Paul Hilken in Baltimore directed ever-larger firebomb attacks.[907] Kurt Jahnke and Lothar Witzke in San Francisco operated undetected in the shadows of Consul General Franz Bopp's arrest. Frederico Stallforth in New York handled the financial transactions between Albert, Boy-Ed, and Rintelen, while learning to elude the probing eyes of American investigators. Felix Sommerfeld in New York was a master in disguising his past as a spy, and rested comfortably under the protective shadows of high-powered American friends. Carl Heynen, an organizational genius, remained undetected and active. Dr. Schweitzer directed missions from New York until his death in 1917. All these agents suffered their trial by fire in 1915. Battle hardened, they were determined to defeat the United States on the home front. The submarine war, the sabotage campaign, the market-cornering efforts, and the sinking of the Lusitania underlined the existence of a de facto state of war between Germany and the U.S. in 1915.

German agents carried on with their missions in 1916. In the summer of that year, virtually the entire U.S. army and National Guard defended the border to Mexico against persistent raids. These raids were for the most part the work of German agents. That summer, the German clandestine campaign had briefly eliminated the possibility of a military intervention of the U.S. in the European War. The motivation and activities of the Secret War Council do fit into the larger picture of German war strategy. The sabotage campaign, the incitement of labor strikes, and the creation of border troubles were but a prelude to a massive campaign against commerce shipping through unrestricted submarine warfare. However, Germany changed its mind in 1916 and, in the process, allowed the United States to arm and train its soldiers. The military intervention in 1918 dealt a quick and devastating defeat to the German Empire. By then Sommerfeld, Stallforth, Heynen, Schmidt and a host of others awaited the end of the war at

Fort Oglethorpe, Georgia as "interned enemy aliens." All continued with their careers in the 1920s. Stallforth became a prominent banker and surfaced here and there with Sommerfeld in the U.S., Mexico, and Germany. Rintelen, von Kleist, Fay, and other convicted agents served out their prison sentences in federal penitentiary. Von Kleist and the former HAPAG chief in the U.S. Karl Buenz died while incarcerated. Walter Scheele switched sides and remained a respected member of his New Jersey community after the war. Franz Wachendorf also did not serve a prison term in return for his testimony against Rintelen and von Papen. The leaders of the Secret War Council, Heinrich Albert, Bernhard Dernburg, Count Johann Heinrich von Bernstorff, and Franz von Papen rose to prominent posts after returning to Germany. Only Karl Boy-Ed's career had eclipsed during the war.

APPENDIX: FIREBOMBED SHIPS

Ship Name	Sailing Date	Accident Date	Proven Incendiaries	Reporting Date	Origination
Grindon Hall	2/2/1915	2/7/1915		2/7/1915	Havana
Regina d'Italia	2/17/1915	2/16/1915		2/17/1915	New York
La Touraine	2/27/1915	3/7/1915	Proven	3/9/1915	New York
San Guglielmo	3/16/1915	4/11/1915	Proven	4/11/1915	Galveston, TX
Devon City	4/27/1915	4/27/1915	Proven	5/12/1915	New York
Cressington Court	4/29/1915	5/5/1915	Proven	5/13/1915	New York
Lord Erne	4/29/1915	5/5/1915	Proven	5/13/1915	New York
Kristianiafjord	5/1/1915	5/7/1915		5/17/1915	Bergen
Lord Downshire	5/1/1915	5/9/1915	Proven	5/15/1915	New York
Kirk Oswald	5/2/1915	5/10/1915	Proven	5/20/1915	New York
Samland	5/1/1915	5/13/1915	Proven	5/13/1915	New York
Chiyu Maru	1-May-15	5/15/1915		5/17/1915	San Francisco
Bankdale	5/8/1915	5/16/1915	Proven	5/24/1915	New York
Strathtay	5/8/1915	5/20/1915	Proven	6/2/1915	New York
Anglo-Saxon		5/21/1915		5/21/1915	New York
Penlee	6/12/1915	6/12/1915	Proven	6/13/1915	Philadelphia
USS Alabama		7/1/1915		7/21/1915	
USS New Jersey		7/1/1915		7/21/1915	

Ship Name	Destination	Source	Comments
Grindon Hall	London	NYT	Came into Norfolk harbor ablaze
Regina d'Italia	Naples	NYT	Cotton caught on fire, had passengers, oil and munitions
La Touraine	Le Havre	NYT	Burned for three days
San Guglielmo	Naples	NYT	Stopped in New York before crossing Atlantic, 6000 bales of cotton destroyed
Devon City	Le Havre	NYT	Caught fire at docks
Cressington Court	Le Havre	NYT	Bombs discovered, loaded at South Brooklyn Piers next to HAPAG ships
Lord Erne	Le Havre	NYT	Bombs discovered, loaded at South Brooklyn Piers next to HAPAG ships
Kristianiafjord	New York	NYT	1300 passengers
Lord Downshire	Le Havre	NYT	Bombs discovered, loaded at South Brooklyn Piers next to HAPAG ships
Kirk Oswald	Marseille	NYT	4 Bombs discovered, loaded at South Brooklyn Piers next to HAPAG ships
Samland	London	NYT	Caught fire at sea
Chiyu Maru	Yokohama	NYT	7,000 ton freighter
Bankdale	Le Havre	NYT	Bombs discovered, loaded at South Brooklyn Piers next to HAPAG ships
Strathtay	Marseille	NYT	Caught fire at sea
Anglo-Saxon	London	Landau	Bombs Found
Penlee	Le Havre	NYT	Burned in harbor, two fires, sabotage suspected
USS Alabama	in dock	NYT	Incendiary fires all at the same places, close to powder magazines
USS New Jersey	in dock	NYT	Incendiary fires all at the same places, close to powder magazines

Ship Name	Sailing Date	Accident Date	Proven Incendiaries	Reporting Date	Origination
USS San Francisco		7/1/1915		7/21/1915	
Minnchaha	7/4/1915	7/7/1915	Proven	7/15/1915	New York
Cragside		7/12/1915	Proven	7/25/1915	New York
USS Oklahoma		7/19/1915	Proven	7/20/1915	Camden, NJ
Knutsford		7/20/1915	Proven	7/20/1915	New York
Vulcan		7/20/1915		7/20/1915	Portsmouth, ME
Cragside		7/24/1915	Proven	7/25/1915	New York
Mystery Ship		7/25/1915		7/26/1915	New York
Arabic	7/27/1915	7/27/1915	Proven	11/5/1915	New York
Asunción de Larinaga		8/9/1915	Proven	8/9/1915	
Williston		8/13/1915	Proven	8/13/1915	
Rotterdam	8/21/1915	8/25/1915	Proven	9/3/1915	New York
Dixie	8/27/1915	8/27/1915	Proven	8/27/1915	New York
FFF	8/27/1915	8/27/1915	Proven	8/30/1915	New York
Sant' Anna	9/8/1915	9/12/1915	Proven	9/13/1915	New York
Lapland	9/16/1915	9/15/1915	Proven	9/16/1916	New York
Athinai	9/16/1915	9/19/1915	Proven	9/19/1915	New York
San Guglielmo	9/27/1915	9/27/1915	Proven	11/5/1915	New York
Colorado	10/23/1915	10/25/1915		10/26/1915	Charleston, SC
Euterpe	11/2/1915	11/2/1915	Proven	11/5/1915	New York
Rio Lages	10/31/1915	11/4/1915	Proven	11/9/1915	New York

Ship Name	Destination	Source	Comments
USS San Francisco	in dock	NYT	Incendiary fires all at the same places, close to powder magazines
Minnehaha	London	NYT	Had to be towed to Halifax, munitions cargo destroyed
Cragside	Marseille	NYT	Bombs discovered, loaded at South Brooklyn Piers next to HAPAG ships
USS Oklahoma	in dock	NYT	Burned with two separate fires at opposite ends of the ship, no cause found, ship badly damaged
Knutsford		NYT	Caught fire at sea
Vulcan		NYT	Coal Fire
Cragside	Gibraltar	NYT	Burned in harbor, entire cargo of sugar destroyed
Mystery Ship	Unknown	NYT	Ship could not be identified, sank, no survivors
Arabic	London	NYT	Two sticks of dynamite found
Asunción de Larinaga		Landau	Caught fire at sea
Williston		Landau	Bombs found
Rotterdam	London	NYT	Caught fire at sea, carried red cross donations for Germany
Dixie	in dock	NYT	Caught fire at docks, lighter for cargo ships
FFF	in dock	NYT	Caught fire at docks, lighter for cargo ships
Sant' Anna	Marseille	NYT	Caught fire at sea, 1700 Italian reservists on board, 18 bombs found, $100,000 cargo destroyed, burned in Brooklyn pier exactly one year before
Lapland	Liverpool	NYT	Bombs discovered dockside
Athinai	Constantinople	NYT	Caught fire at sea, 470 passengers
San Guglielmo	Naples	NYT	Bombs found at dock, dynamite
Colorado	New York	NYT	Cotton cargo burned
Euterpe	in dock	NYT	Started burning in seven places simultaneously, 8564 bags of sugar entirely destroyed
Rio Lages	Queenstown	NYT	Caught fire at sea, sugar, loaded at Yonkers, destroyed

Ship Name	Sailing Date	Accident Date	Proven Incendiaries	Reporting Date	Origination
USS Prairie		11/7/1915		11/7/1915	New York
Ancona		11/7/1915			
Rochambeau	11/1/1915	11/8/1915	Proven	11/21/1915	New York
Livieta	11/9/1915	11/9/1915		11/12/1915	Port Arthur, TX
Barkdale	11/15/1915	11/26/1915	Proven	11/27/1915	New York
Lord Ormonde	11/24/1915	11/28/1915	Proven	12/20/1915	New York
Tyningham	12/1/1915	12/5/1915	Proven	12/12/1915	New York
Virginia	12/18/1915	12/17/1915		12/18/1915	Richmond, VA
Alston		12/24/1915	Proven	12/24/1915	
Inchmoor	12/26/1915	12/26/1915	Proven	12/26/1915	New York
Manchuria		12/26/1915			

Ship Name	Destination	Source	Comments
USS Prairie		NYT	Fay arrest, supposed attempt made
Ancona		Landau	Caught fire at sea
Rochambeau	Bordeaux	NYT	Caught fire at sea, no cause determined, 418 passengers, coal bunker fire, 13,000 GRT
Livieta	Buenos Aires	NYT	Oil tanker exploded as a result of a bomb
Barkdale	Bordeaux	NYT	Caught fire on sea, 100 bales of cotton burned
Lord Ormonde	Bordeaux	NYT	Horses and sugar, caught fire at sea
Tyningham	Liverpool	NYT	Two separate fires at sea, sugar cargo destroyed
Virginia	New York	NYT	Barge with horses sank after sabotage, 600 horses drowned in Hudson
Alston		Landau	Dynamite found while at sea
Inchmoor	in dock	NYT	Sugar cargo caught on fire
Manchuria		Landau	Caught fire while at sea

ENDNOTES

1. Statements as to their support of unrestricted submarine warfare are found in their memoirs and wartime commentary.

2. Albert's treasurer and member of the German clandestine cell in New York, Carl Heynen, first coined the term "Secret War Council" in 1915.

3. Karl Alexander Fuehr's disposition towards the submarine campaign and sabotage has been questioned and often portrayed him as being more moderate and in line with Count Bernstorff. His diaries from his time in New York, however, do not support this view. See for example NA RG 65 Albert Papers, Box 12, "Translation of Dr. Fuehr's Yearbook for 1915," Entry for October 5, 1915: "Count v. Bernstorff submits note in the submarine question in which we give in, very little. Without a doubt the wisest thing we could do. Unfortunately much time lost."

4. Sabotage agent Franz Rintelen, Karl Boy-Ed, the German Naval Attaché, and Franz von Papen, the German Military Attaché in the United States and future German chancellor, German Ambassador Johann Heinrich Count von Bernstorff, Horst von der Goltz, and pro-English secret agent Emanuel Voska are but a few of the eyewitness accounts published in the 1920s and 30s..

5. Document re-printed in Doerries, Reinhard R., *Prelude to the Easter Rising: Sir Roger Casement in Imperial Germany*, Frank Cass Publishers, Portland, OR, 2000, p. 75.

6. Ibid.

7. Ibid., pp. 72-82.

8. Ibid., p. 81.

9. NA RG 76 Mixed Claims Commission, Box 2, cables, Nadolny to Foreign Office, January 24, 1915.

10. Ibid.

11. NA RG 242 Captured German Documents, T 141, Roll 19, von Papen to Nadolny, March 17, 1915.

12. Ibid.

13. NA RG 65 Albert Papers, Box 19, Albert to Secretary of Interior, April 20, 1915.

14. See NA RG 65 Mixed Claims Commission, Box 11, Memorandum of German witness [Nadolny]. "He admits being responsible for authorizing sabotage in this country as

contained in his intercepted message of January 26, 1915, but alibis this authority by suggesting that he knew German officials in this country would pay no attention to the authorization and further assures the Commission that no subsequent steps were taken by him looking to the carrying out of the authorization thus given." Also Ibid., Box 14, "Denials by German Officials of Sabotage Activities During the Period of Neutrality."

15.   NA RG 65 Albert Papers, Box 24, Amsinck Account 1915.

16.   Ibid.

17.   Hirst, David Wayne, *German Propaganda in the United States, 1914-1917*, Northwestern University PhD. Dissertation, Evanston, IL, 1962, p. 66.

18.   Stallforth Papers, private collection, Correspondence 1915.

19.   NA RG 65 Albert Papers, Box 24, G. Amsinck and Company Accounts.

20.   Ibid., Box 24, Albert Diary, entry for February 6, 1915.

21.   Ibid., entry for January 23, 1915.

22.   Boy-Ed, Karl, *Verschwörer?* Verlag August Scherl GmbH, Berlin, Germany, 1920.

23.   Picture of unknown origin, approximately 1873, public domain.

24.   Library of Congress Prints and Photographs Division Washington, D.C., public domain.

25.   NA RG 131 Alien Property Custodian, Entry 199, Box 131, File 3221, Boy-Ed Accounts; for example "January 31 [1915], G.A. (secret agent) and February 3 [1915] G.A. (secret agent)."

26.   NA RG 131 Alien Property Custodian, Entry 199, Box 131, File 3221, Boy-Ed Accounts; for example, April 8 and April 15 [1915], "Commander Boy-Ed traveling expenses."

27.   NA RG 65 Albert Papers, Box 7, Boy-Ed Accounts; Boy-Ed disbursed $3,000 per week in cash.

28.   NA RG 65 Albert Papers, Box 7, Boy-Ed Accounts.

29.   NA RG 65 FBI Case Files, M1085, File 8000-925, statement of Walter Scheele.

30.   Hirst, *German Propaganda in the United States, 1914-1917*, p. 61.

31.   NA RG 65 FBI Case Files, Roll 877, File 8000-925, Memo to A. Bruce Bielaski, March 28, 1918.

32.   NA RG 36 Passenger and Crew Lists of Vessels Arriving at New York, New York, 1914, T715, Roll 2364, page 47, line 20. Also NA RG 65 Albert Papers, Box 23, diary entry for August 26, 1914. The Allied Property Custodian determined on August 13, 1918 that Albert arrived on the *SS Oskar* on August 11, 1914 and listed visiting a "friend," Mr. Reisinger. Neither the diary nor the arriving vessel documentation corroborates that claim. See NA RG 131 Alien Property Custodian, Entry 199 Box 38 File 907. As an irony

of history, *Oskar II* not only carried the most powerful German spymaster to the U.S. to command the German clandestine operations there, it also became Henry Ford's peace expedition ship in 1915.

33.   Baccalaureate in Germany is the so-called *Abitur*, which allows a graduating student to be admitted to college.

34.   "Good" would translate to "B" in the American grading system.

35.   Reiling, Johannes, *Deutschland: Safe for Democracy?* Franz Steiner Verlag, Stuttgart, Germany, 1997, pp. 15-16. Reiling could not find any evidence of Albert having finished a PhD. However, he mistakenly argues that only Americans accorded him an academic title. His passport issued in Hamburg August 1914 read: *"Bearer of this identification, Dr. Heinrich F. Albert goes as private secretary to the director of the Hamburg-America Line Mr. Ecker via Copenhagen to the United States of America."* NA RG 65 Albert Papers, Box 23. It is not clear whether Albert did or did not earn the academic title.

36.   *Geheimrat* was a title bestowed upon bureaucrats in the German and Austro-Hungarian empires before 1918. It has nothing to do with "secret" (literal translation) or even an allusion to secret agent as some writers have alleged. Rather, the word *geheim* can be translated in this case as "trusted." The *Geheimrat*, therefore, has the meaning of trusted advisor to the court, a purely bureaucratic title.

37.   Clemens Delbrück was a cousin of Hans Delbrück, the accomplished scholar. In 1916, the Emperor accorded Clemens the status of Baron.

38.   NA RG 65 Albert Papers, Box 23, Letter to Ida, January17, 1916.

39.   Arndt von Holtzendorff was the brother of Admiral Henning von Holtzendorff who commanded the Imperial High Seas Fleet before World War I. Emperor Wilhelm II appointed him Commander of the Navy in 1915. He was a big proponent of unrestricted submarine warfare. Although archival links showing cooperation between the two influential brothers is hard to find, it is significant to keep in mind the important fact that one brother ran the military, the other the civilian (and government controlled) fleets of the German Empire during the World War. Further research into this relationship is certainly warranted.

40.   There is very little information about the backgrounds and responsibilities of Ecker and Polis during the war. This author is firmly convinced that the two wartime managers had intelligence responsibilities. U.S. authorities neither suspected nor even questioned these HAPAG managers, despite the well-known fact that they had supervisory control of Heinrich Albert, and that the Hamburg-America building where they worked became the headquarters of German clandestine operations in the war.

41.   NA RG 65 Albert Papers, Box 23, Letter to Ida, January17, 1916.

42.   For example, historian Barbara Tuchman.

43.   NA RG 85, Immigration and Naturalization, T715, Roll 2364, page 47, line 20.

44.   NA RG 131 Alien Property Custodian, Entry 199, Box 48, file 1123, Statement of Karl Neumond.

45.   Ibid., Box 38 file 907, Alien Property Custodian to Francis B. Garvan, October 6, 1918.

46.   Library of Congress, Prints and Photographs Division Washington, D.C., LC-G432-1381, 1916, public domain.

47.   NA RG 65 Albert Papers, Box 19, "Military War Supplies," February 11, 1915.

48.   NA RG 65 FBI Case Files, M1085, File 8000-925, Department Memorandum, April 19, 1916.

49.   U.S. Census, 1910, T 624, Queens Ward 2, Queens, New York, Roll 1067, page 25B.

50.   City Directory of Albany, New York, 1891, "Walter Scheele, chemist, 32 Eagle." City Directory of New York, all boroughs, 1894. "Scheele Walter T. chemist, 76 William, h Bay Ridge, L.I."

51.   For example U.S. Patent Office, Patent #744413 (varnish manufacturing process, 1903), Patent #707646 (food preservation, 1902), Patent #820442 (food preservation through liquid air, 1906), Patent #818979 (food preservation, 1906)

52.   U.S. Census, 1910, T 624, Queens Ward 2, Queens, New York, Roll 1067, page 25B.

53.   NA RG 65 FBI Case Files, M1085, File 8000-925.

54.   Ibid.

55.   Ibid.

56.   Ibid.

57.   Landau, Henry, *The Enemy Within: The Inside Story of German Sabotage in America*, G.P. Putnam's Sons, New York, NY, 1937, p. 44.

58.   Ibid.

59.   NA RG 65 FBI Case Files, M1085, File 8000-925.

60.   Ibid.

61.   Ibid.

62.   Ibid.

63.   Some scholars also credit Scheele with the invention of mustard gas. While Scheele did not invent it, he possibly found a process or formulation that allowed the mass production of the nerve agent or changed its properties in some fashion. Francis Galvan, the Allied Property Custodian who investigated Bayer, Heyden, and other German chemical companies started the claim in 1919, that Scheele invented mustard gas. Countless studies have taken this unsubstantiated rumor as fact. What exactly Scheele had invented with respect to poisonous gas is not clear. The formula of the German mustard gas used on the battlefield originated from a lab accident of Hans Thatcher Clarke, an English chemist who studied in Germany in 1913. It is possible that Dr. Scheele participated in some fashion in creating a formulation for the safe mass

production of the accidentally created nerve agent. He did make several valuable contributions to the battlefield, however, which are documented. The sheer amount of products and formulae the German agent created in the first years of the World War have astonished contemporaries and historians alike.

64.   Ibid. The file contains the debriefing of Scheele in 1918 when he detailed his knowledge to American agents.

65.   NA RG 65 Albert Papers, Box 1, Folder2. Also Ibid., Box 8, Folder 26, Lemke to Albert, July 21, 1915. Also Ibid., Lemke to Lindheim, July 22, 1915, "74 bags of Para Rubber stored in Campbell Stores, Hoboken.

66.   Ibid., Box 8, Folder 26, Lemke Affair. Also Ibid., Box 24, Full Accounting. Lemke, who had leased several steamers, worked through the "Fiske Trading Corporation," the "Southern Products Trading Corporation," the "W. L. Green Commission Company." He ended in a legal battle with Albert in July, 1915.

67.   Ibid., Box 7, Check dated November 4, 1915.

68.   Reiling, *Safe for Democracy?* p. 135. Albert's bookkeeping is unclear as to the exact amounts.

69.   NA RG 65 Albert Papers, Box 21, Folder 106, von Jagow to Count Bernstorff, May 2, 1916.

70.   NA RG 65 Albert Papers, Box 7.

71.   Voska, Emanuel Victor and Irwin, Will, *Spy and Counter-Spy*, George G. Harrap and Co Ltd., London, 1941, p. 112. It is not entirely clear what the separation material really was. Some accounts mention aluminum, others lead, zinc, paraffin, or copper. It is safe to assume from the various U.S. agents' reports that the first separators consisted of paraffin that sometimes did not deteriorate, thus making the bomb a dud. Later, Scheele seemed to have used aluminum plates of different thicknesses that corroded in sulfuric acid. NA RG 65 FBI Case Files, File 8000-925. According to Scheele's debriefers in 1918, the chemicals used were hexamenthylene tetramene on one side, and powdered sodium peroxide on the other. Tunney, Thomas J., *Throttled: The Detection of the German and Anarchist Bomb Plotters in the United States*, Small Maynard and Company, Boston, MA, 1919, p. 138. Tunney of the New York bomb squad described the chemicals as potassium chlorate on one side and sulfuric acid on the other.

72.   Investigators and witnesses of the time coined the descriptive words "cigar" and "pencil" when describing the firebombs.

73.   NA RG 65 FBI Case Files, M1085, File 8000-925, Department Memo, April 22, 1916. Scheele purchased lead pipes that were delivered on January 13, 1915.

74.   NA RG 76 Mixed Claims Commission, Docket No. 8103, "Brief for the Claimant, June 1928, p. 59.

75.   NA RG 65 FBI Case Files, File 8000-925, Envelope #5 contained in confiscated materials from Scheele's laboratory.

76. NA RG 76 Mixed Claims Commission, Box 7, Exhibit 2.

77. NA RG 65 FBI Case Files, M1085, File 8000-925.

78. NA RG 65 Albert Papers, Box 10, "habe ich im Frühjahr 1915... in New York die New Jersey Chemical Agricultural Comp. gegründet..." Also NA RG 65 FBI Case Files, M1085, File 8000-925. Scheele associate Carl von Kleist gave to protocol, that the money was "to start this bomb factory."

79. NA RG 65 Albert Papers, Box 23, Financials.

80. Ibid., full accounting starting May 9, 1915. Also Reiling, *Safe for Democracy?*, p. 130.

81. NA RG 242, Captured German Documents, T 141, Roll 19, von Papen to Nadolny, geheim, March 17, 1915.

82. *The New York Times*, February 28, 1915, "Six Liners Sail Under Six Flags. Also Bonsor, N. R. P., *North Atlantic Seaway: An Illustrated History of the Passenger Services Linking the Old World with the New*, Volume 2, Brookside Publications, Wheat Ridge, Colorado, 1978, p. 657. Here, the sailing is listed for the beginning of March, which seems to be in error.

83. *The New York Times*, March 7, 1915, "500 Miles off Irish Coast."

84. Ibid., March 10, 1915, "France Inquires into Touraine Fire." Also Ibid., April 15, 1915, "His Real Name Schwind, 'Swoboda' Now Admits." Also Ibid., April 1, 1915.

85. Ibid., March 7, 1915, "500 Miles off Irish Coast."

86. NA RG 65 FBI Case Files, File 8000-925, von Kleist interrogation.

87. Ibid., belongings of Walter Scheele, envelope #5.

88. Tunney, *Throttled*, p. 128. The *Hennington Court* appears to have caught on fire in February 1916. The *Orton*, *Lake Erie*, could not be found as having burned in January 1915. The *Carlton* also could not be verified.

89. *The New York Times*, February 8, 1915.

90. Ibid., April 13, 1916, "Von Papen named in Plot."

91. Ibid., April 11, 1915, "Big Cotton Cargo Burnt."

92. Ibid., January 20, 1915, "Spy Hint in Roebling Fire."

93. Landau, *The Enemy Within*, p. 36. The Metal Industry Magazine reported the fire to have occurred in February. See *Metal Industry Magazine*, Volume 13, January to December 1915, The Metal Industry Publishing Company, New York, NY, 1916, February 1915.

94. *Metal Industry Magazine*, Volume 13, January to December 1915, The Metal Industry Publishing Company, New York, NY, 1916, February 1915.

95. *The New York Times*, November 21, 1915, "Munition Plant Fires Laid to Incendiaries."

96.   *Metal Industry Magazine*, Volume 13, January to December 1915, The Metal Industry Publishing Company, New York, NY, 1916, April 1915.

97.   NA RG 65 FBI Case Files, M1085, File 8000-925.

98.   www.v-kleist.com, viewed 2-10-2013, cites a text in the official family history about von Kleist: „*Dazu ist er viel zu bescheiden trotz seiner Zugehörigkeit zu einer der ältesten aristokratischen Familien In Deutschland und hat seinen eigenen Weg gemacht. Schiffsjunge auf einem alten Kahn, Maat, Kapitän. Er hätte bei der Garde-Kavallerie in Potsdam eintreten können, aber er wollte nicht.*"

99.   Ibid.

100.   Tunney, *Throttled*, p. 161.

101.   Strictly speaking, Otto Wolpert worked for the Atlas line, a subsidiary of HAPAG.

102.   US Census 1910, T 624, Roll 893, Page 2B, Jersey City, Ward 12, Hudson, New Jersey.

103.   United States Senate, *Brewing and Liquor interests and German and Bolshevik Propaganda*, Report and Hearings of the Subcommittee on the Judiciary of the United States Senate, Government Printing Office, Washington D. C., 1919, p. 2675.

104.   NA RG 65 FBI Case Files, M1085, File 8000-174, Agent Cantrell to Department, July 23, 1915.

105.   NA RG 131 Alien Property Custodian, Entry 199, Box 131, Boy-Ed Financials. There are numerous disbursements mentioning Bode in Boy-Ed's records.

106.   Marineschule Mürwick, Flensburg, Germany, Marine- Verordnungsblatt (Personalveränderungen), 1913. His navy rank was Leutnant zur See (Lieutenant Junior).

107.   NA RG 65 FBI Case Files, M1085, File 8000-925, Scheele interrogation, "Destruction of Livestock." For his estimated arrival see NA RG 76 Mixed Claims Commission, Box 13, Folder 2.

108.   Ibid., Interrogation of Walter T. Scheele.

109.   NA RG 76 Mixed Claims Commission, Box 13, File 2.

110.   NA RG 65 FBI Case Files, M1085, File 8000-3089, Stallforth to Albert, Captured document from Stallforth's office, entry for August 13, 1915.

111.   NA RG 76 Mixed Claims Commission, Box 13, File 2.

112.   NA RG 65 FBI Case Files, M1085, File 8000-925, "Information Given by Dr. Scheele concerning list of Names and Incidents submitted by Mr. Offley."

113.   Ibid., Department memo, April 26, 1916.

114.   Library of Congress Prints and Photographs Division Washington, D.C., LC-DIG-ggbain-21460 and 21459, public domain.

115. Ibid.

116. Ibid., interrogation of Charles von Kleist.

117. Ibid., Bielaski to Pendelton, undated memo.

118. The Bridgeport Projectile Company became a dummy factory in Bridgeport through which German agents could acquire powder, munitions, and critical parts in order to hurt other munitions manufacturers.

119. *The New York Times*, March 7, 1915, "5 Killed in Powder Mill."

120. Landau, *The Enemy Within*, p. 305.

121. See, for example, NA RG 131, Alien Property Custodian, Entry 199, Box 165, which contains the phone transcripts of von Papen, Boy-Ed and Albert's offices. Also Tunney, *Throttled*, and Voska, *Spy and Counter Spy*, describe the efforts of the New York bomb squad to shadow the German officials.

122. Captain Rintelen von Kleist, Franz, *The Dark Invader: Wartime Reminiscences of a German Naval Intelligence Officer*, Lovat Dickson Ltd, 1933.

123. See Whitcover, Jules, *Sabotage at Black Tom: Imperial Germany's Secret War in America, 1914-1917*, Algonquin Books of Chapel Hill, Chapel Hill, NC, 1989, p. 54.

124. See von Feilitzsch, Heribert, *The Secret War Council*, Henselstone Verlag LLC, Amissville, VA, unpublished manuscript, 2015, for more information on activities in 1914.

125. Document printed in full in Doerries, *Prelude to the Easter Rising*, p. 75.

126. NA RG 76 Mixed Claims Commission, Box 14, Generalstab der Armee, Abt. IIIB to Foreign Office, January 24, 1915.

127. The sabotage teams will be covered in detail later in the book.

128. NA RG 65 Albert Papers, Box 24, Albert to Delbrück, May 10, 1915.

129. Horne, Charles F., editor, *Source Records of the Great War*, Vol. III, National Alumni, New York, 1923.

130. The Story of the Great War, Volume V., Francis J. Reynolds, Allen C. Churchill, Francis Trevelyan Miller, eds., John A. Collier & Son Company, New York, 1919.

131. Count von Bernstorff, Johann Heinrich, *My Three Years in America*, Skeffington and Son Ltd., London, 1920, p. 112. Also Justus D. Doenecke, *Nothing Less Than War: A New History of America's Entry into World War I*, The University Press of Kentucky, Lexington, KY, 2011, p. 63.

132. Senator Thomas P. Gore introduced a bill to deny passports to any American seeking to travel on a belligerent ship. The bill did not pass. However, it reflected the fear that Americans traveling on belligerent ships would eventually drag the U.S. into the war, which is what ultimately happened. See discussion in Doenecke, *Nothing Less than War*, p. 162.

133.   *The New York Times*, March 13, 1915, "Germany's Submarine War."

134.   NA RG 65 Albert Papers, Box 22, Chapter III. Albert received $1.1 million ($23.5 million in today's value) between 1914 and 1916 from British shipment reimbursements.

135.   www.uboat.net, viewed 2-2012.

136.   Koerver, Joachim, ed., *German Submarine Warfare 1914-1918 in the Eyes of British Intelligence: Selected Sources from the British National Archives, Kew*, Schaltungsdienst Lange, Berlin, Germany, 2010, p. xix, Table 6. 14 submarines served on coastal patrols and were not fit for ocean service.

137.   Scheer, Reinhard, *Germany's High Sea Fleet in the World War*, Cassell and Company, London, 1920, p. 36.

138.   Bauer, Hermann, *Als Fuehrer der U-Boote im Weltkriege: Der Eintritt der U-Boot-Waffe in die Seekriegsfuehrung*, Koehler und Amelang, Leipzig, 1941, p. 44. Translation by the author.

139.   Churchill, Winston S., *The World Crisis, 1911 to 1918*, Odhams Press Limited, London, 1939, p. 278.

140.   As quoted in Koerver, *German Submarine Warfare 1914-1819 in the Eyes of British Intelligence*, p. LVI.

141.   Bauer, *Als Fuehrer der U-Boote im Weltkriege*, p. 57.

142.   Admiral Fisher had raised the specter of British starvation in the face of an effective blockade in 1903.

143.   Schroeder, Joachim, *Die U-Boote des Kaisers: Die Geschichte des deutchen U-Boot-Krieges gegen Grossbritanien im Ersten Weltkrieg*, Bernard und Graefe, Lauf a. d. Pegnitz, 2003, p. 56.

144.   Carlisle, Rodney P., *World War I*, Facts on File Inc., New York, 2007, p. 73.

145.   Koerver, *German Submarine Warfare 1914-1918 in the Eyes of British Intelligence*, p. xviii, Table 4.

146.   *The Northern Mariner/Le marin du nord*, XVII, No. 3 (July, 2007), "The Attacks on U.S. Shipping that Precipitated American Entry into World War I," by Rodney Carlisle, p.46.

147.   *The New York Times*, June 10, 1915, "British Liner Flew The American Flag." The article explains that the British navy ordered the flag ruse.

148.   As quoted in Koerver, *German Submarine Warfare 1914-1919 in the Eyes of British Intelligence*, p. XLIV.

149.   Koerver, *German Submarine Warfare 1914-1919 in the Eyes of British Intelligence*, p. XXV-XXVI. The estimates of U-boats in actual service ranges from 14 to 34. See Roessler, Eberhard, *Die Unterseeboote der Kaiserlichen Marine*, Bernhard und Graefe Verlag, Bonn, Germany, 1997, pp. 73 and 84. The actual numbers show eight ocean-going (diesel motorized) U-boats in service at the outbreak of the war (U-19, U-20,

U-21, U-22, U-23, U-28, U-29, U-30). Another 7 came into service during 1914 (U-31, U-32, U-33, U-34, U-35, U-37, U-38). Five more came into service in February of 1915 (UB-1, UB-2, UB-4, UB-5, UB-10). 7 submarines with gas engines were used for patrols in the English Channel. These numbers also match Bauer's account. See Bauer, *Als Fuehrer der U-Boote im Weltkriege*, p. 192.

150.   *The New York Times*, February 9, 1915, "Washington Officials Silent."

151.   *Lewiston Evening Journal*, February 17, 1915, "German Submarine Sank British Ship."

152.   *The New York Times*, February 21, 1915, "Submarine helped save men." Also Bauer, *Als Fuehrer der U-Boote im Weltkriege*, p. 200.

153.   Churchill, *The World Crisis*, Odhams Press Limited, London, 1939, p. 735.

154.   *The New York Times*, June 4, 1915, "Germany Offers to Pay."

155.   NA RG 65 Albert Papers, Box 19, Folder 104, file 142.

156.   Bauer, *Als Fuehrer der U-Boote im Weltkriege*, p. 201.

157.   Ibid., pp. 266-267.

158.   www.uboat.net:8080/wwi/ships_hit/losses_year.html?date=1915-03&string=March+1915, viewed 12-2012. The fleet consisted of U-6 (listed in Bauer), U-9 (not listed in the source but listed in Bauer), U-10, U-12, U-17 (listed in Bauer), U-20, U-23, U-27, U-28, U-29, U-33 (listed in Bauer), U-34, U-35, and U-37.

159.   *The New York Times*, April 4, 1915, "Defends *Falaba* Sinking; Germany Holds that the Submarine Had No Time for Rescues."

160.   *Bay Of Plenty Times*, March 31, 1915, "Sinking of *Falaba*, Callous Germans Jeer drowning people." Also *The New York Times*, March 31, 1915, "Photographs taken on Sinking *Falaba*."

161.   www.uboat.net:8080/wwi/ships_hit/losses_year.html?date=1915-03&string=March+1915, viewed 12-2012.

162.   www.uboat.net:8080/wwi/ships_hit/losses_year.html?date=1915-03&string=April+1915, viewed 12-2012. The U-boats used that month were U-5, U-6, U-10, U-22, U-24, U-26, U-30, U-32, U-33, U-35, U-37, U-38, UB-4, UB-5, UB-10.

163.   Bauer, *Als Fuehrer der U-Boote im Weltkriege*, p. 289.

164.   Ibid., pp. 289-290.

165.   Von Tirpitz, Alfred, *Erinnerungen*, K. F. Koehler Verlag, Berlin 1927, p. 348.

166.   NA RG 65 Albert Papers, Box 24, diary for 1915.

167.   *Lusitania's* sister ship, *Mauretania*, which served in the navy as a troop transporter, the *Aquitania* (also a troop transporter), the *Britannic*, and the *Olympic* (both on transatlantic line service).

168.   *The Fatherland*, Volume II, Number 14, May 12, 1915, "The Incident of the *Gulflight*."

169.   Preston, Diana, *Lusitania: An Epic Tragedy*, Walker and Company, New York, NY, 2002, p. 76.

170.   *The New York Times*, February 21, 1915, "Submarine Sinks British Steamer Without Notice."

171.   Her sister ship, *Mauretania*, took the Blue Riband from *Lusitania* in 1909. However, the *Mauretania* was a troop ship. The German liners *Vaterland* and *Imperator* were interned, leaving the *Lusitania* as the only superliner in the transatlantic service.

172.   Boy-Ed, *Verschwoerer?*, p. 74. The day of the publication is obscured by the date the embassy wrote on the warning, "April 22, 1915." As a matter of fact, the warning appeared only once in the *New York Times*, namely on May 1, 1915. See *The New York Times*, May 1, 1915, "German Embassy Issues Warning." The intention had been to have it appear in the *Washington Post* and other papers for three weeks. That never happened. See NA RG 65 FBI case files, M1085, File 8000-174, Haniel to unknown in New York (presumably Dernburg), April 22, 1915, "…once a week during the next three or four weeks."

173.   *The New York Times*, May 1, 1915, "German Embassy Issues Warning."

174.   Preston, *Lusitania*, p. 94.

175.   Bailey and Ryan, *The Lusitania Disaster*, p. 96.

176.   Deutsches Bundesarchiv, Institut für Meereskunde, Access number, Bild 134-C1831, public domain.

177.   Bauer, *Als Fuehrer der U-Boote im Weltkriege*, p. 290.

178.   Ibid., p. 291.

179.   Bailey and Ryan, *The Lusitania Disaster*, p. 137.

180.   www.archives.gov/exhibits/eyewitness/html.php?section=18, viewed 12-2012.

181.   Ibid.

182.   Boy-Ed, *Verschwoerer?* pp. 78-79.

183.   NA RG 65 Albert Papers, Box 24, Albert to Delbrück, May 10, 1915.

184.   Von Bernstorff, *My Three Years in America*, p. 115.

185.   NA RG 65 Albert Papers Box 12, Folder 67 "Translation of Dr. Fuehr's Yearbook for 1915," also Box 24, "Albert diary 1915."

186.   Katz, Friedrich, *The Secret War in Mexico: Europe, The United States and the Mexican Revolution*, University of Chicago Press, Chicago, 1981, p. 334.

187.   Ibid., p. 74.

188.   NA RG 65 FBI Case Files, M1085, File 8000-174, Haniel to unknown in New York, April 22, 1915.

189.   NA RG 65 Albert Papers, Box 24, Albert diary 1915.

190.   See for example the New York Times, May 1, 1915, The New York Tribune, May 1, 1915.

191.   The Washington Times, May 1, 1915.

192.   NA RG76 Mixed Claims Commission, L. M. Cantrell to Department, July 19, 1915.

193.   Doerries, Imperial Challenge, p. 82.

194.   Churchill, The World Crisis, p. 731.

195.   The New York Times, September 1, 1915, reports from Lloyd's Register that 77 British ships with 180,713 GRT were sunk between May and August 1915.

196.   Koerver, German Submarine Warfare 1914-1819 in the Eyes of British Intelligence, p. XXII.

197.   Ibid.

198.   Ibid., XVI.

199.   Bauer, Als Fuehrer der U-Boote im Weltkriege, p. 252. Bauer lists 19 submarines lost in 1915, 22 in 1916, 63 in 1917, and 69 in 1918.

200.   Ibid., pp. 169ff.

201.   Ibid., p. 245.

202.   Broadberry, Stephen and Howlett, Peter, "The United Kingdom during World War I: Business as usual?" June 2003, www2.warwick.ac.uk/fac/soc/economics/staff/.../wp/wwipap4.pdf , viewed 12-2012, p. 39. Also French, David, British Economic and Strategic Planning 1905 to 1915, Routledge Library Editions, Abingdon, Great Britain, 2006, pp. 98-99

203.   Koerver, German Submarine Warfare 1914-1819 in the Eyes of British Intelligence, p. LVIII.

204.   Stallforth Papers, private collection, interview of F. Stallforth by State Department Councilor Polk, March 15-16, 1916.

205.   NA RG 60 Department of Justice, File 9-16-12-5305, Agent Offley to A. Bruce Bielaski, January 19, 1918.

206.   NA RG 65 Albert Papers, Box 23, Albert to Delbrück, May 10, 1915.

207.   Bauer, Als Fuehrer der U-Boote im Weltkriege, pp. 171-172.

208.   NA RG 65 Albert Papers, Box 23, Albert to Delbrück, May 10, 1915.

209.   NA RG 76 Mixed Claims Commission, Box 14, Generalstab der Armee, Abt. IIIB to Foreign Office, January 24, 1915, "Secret. For Military Attaché. For sabotage in United

States and Canada... In the United States sabotage can be extended on all sorts of factories for war supplies..." Despite denials, the German military attaché pursued the order. See NA RG 242 Captured German Documents, T 141, Roll 19, progress report back to Section IIIB, dated March 17, 1915: "Sabotage against factories here did not progress much, since all factories are watched by hundreds of secret agents..."

210.   "The Dark Invader" refers to Rintelen's book about his time in the United States, published in 1933 in England.

211.   NA RG 76 Mixed Claims Commission, Box 13, Folder 2. NA RG 85 Passenger and Crew Lists of Vessels Arriving at New York, New York, T715, Roll 2404.

212.   NA RG 65 FBI Case Files, M1085, File 8000-174.

213.   NA RG 76 Mixed Claims Commission, Box 13, Franz von Rintelen, Memorandum on Activities. The word 'legal' does not have to have been contained in Rintelen's original instructions. Rintelen, *The Dark Invader*, p. 74. Rintelen remembers his instructions to have been "to buy what I can and to destroy anything else." NA RG 65 Albert Papers, Box 19, von Papen to von Falkenhayn, April 9, 1915. Von Papen wrote to the general that he understood Rintelen's mission to "curtail the supplies of war material for our enemies in every way [emphasis by the author] possible." Also, Geissler, Erhard , *Biologische Waffen – Nicht in Hitlers Arsenalen: Biologische und Toxin-Kampfmittel von 1915 bis 1945*, LIT Verlag, Münster, Germany, 1999, pp. 83-84. According to a General Staff document dated March 18, 1915, Rintelen's instruction stated verbatim, "to prevent and delay the exportation of war materials, especially ammunition, by all means."

214.   Friedrich Rintelen was born in Arnsberg, Westphalia in 1836. A powerful banker and politician in imperial Germany, Friedrich Rintelen studied law at the Universities of Bonn and Heidelberg. He became a judge and administrator in imperial Germany in the 1880s. He also represented the Catholic Center Party in the Prussian parliament for two years. He became president of the German version of the Court of Appeals in 1896.

215.   *The World's Work*, Volume 36, Doubleday Page and Company, New York, 1918, p. 305.

216.   NA RG 85, Immigration and Naturalization, T715, Roll 501. Also, Board of Trade: Commercial and Statistical Department and successors: Inwards Passenger Lists, BT26, Part 243, Item 30; Rintelen arrived in England on the SS *Teutonic* von New York on June 8, 1905.

217.   Ibid.

218.   *The Financier*, Volume 114, New York, August 1, 1919, p. 235.

219.   NA RG 65 FBI Case Files, M1085, File 8000-174, Agent Frank (illegible) to Bielaski, September 17, 1915.

220.   NA RG 76 Mixed Claims Commission, Box 13, Folder 2.

221.   National Archives of the UK, Kew, Surrey, England, Board of Trade, Commercial

and Statistical Department and successors, Inwards Passenger List, Series BT 26, File 274.

222. NA RG 76 Mixed Claims Commission, Box 13, Folder 2.

223. NA RG 65 FBI Case Files, M1085, File 8000-174, Agent Frank (illegible) to Bielaski, September 17, 1915.

224. Rintelen did not take Friedrich Rintelen's position at the Deutsche Bank after his father's passing in 1907 and, only twenty-nine years old, became the youngest director in the history of the prestigious banking house, as has been rumored in government documents and several historical works. See, for example, NA RG 76 Mixed Claims Commission, Box 13, Folder 2.

225. Rintelen, *The Dark Invader*, foreword by Reinhard Doerries, endnote 5, p. XXXIII.

226. Starke, Holger, *Vom Brauereihandwerk zur Brauindustrie, Die Geschichte der Bierbrauerei in Dresden und Sachsen, 1800-1914*, Böhlan Verlag, Köln, Germany, 2005, p. 446.

227. Marineschule Mürwik, Verlustlisten 1914-1915, MIM381, KAI17 040 (Band 3), Number 51B. Also Rintelen, *The Dark Invader*, foreword by Reinhard Doerries, endnote 5, p. XXXIII.

228. NA RG 76 Mixed Claims Commission, Box 13, Folder 2.

229. Ibid.

230. NA RG 65 Albert Papers, Box 24, Diary entry for August 10, 1914 mentions the agreement with Kuhn, Loeb and Company of which only $500,000 became available. Rintelen sent this amount. See BAMG, Freiburg, RM3, File 7934, memo "ganz geheim" dated August 24, 1914.

231. Bundesarchiv für Militärgeschichte, Freiburg, RM 3, File 7934. The file contains memos signed by Rintelen transferring funds via Warburg, Kuhn, Loeb and Company, HAPAG, and the Reichsbank.

232. Ibid., Schmidt of Deutsche Bank to Staatssekretär von Tirpitz, July 31, 1914.

233. Ibid., Rintelen to von Tirpitz, September 19, 1914.

234. Ibid., Rintelen to HAPAG, August 10, 1914.

235. Ibid.

236. Ibid., Diskonto Gesellschaft Berlin to Reichsmarineamt, August 22, 1914 and September 1, 1914.

237. Ibid., Schmidt to von Tirpitz, August 24, 1914.

238. Ibid., Reichsbank to von Tirpitz, September 12, 1914.

239. Ibid., Deutsche Bank to von Tirpitz, August 29, 1914 and September 12, 1914.

240. Ibid., Deutsche Bank to von Tirpitz, September 17, 1914.

241. NA RG 76 Mixed Claims Commission, Box 13, Folder 2.

242. Ibid.

243. Stallforth Papers, Private Collection, diary entry May 23, 1915.

244. Bundesarchiv für Militärgeschichte, Freiburg, RM 3, File 7934. See several memos between Warburg and Tirpitz mentioning "Oberleutnant Rintelen."

245. Ibid., Warburg to von Tirpitz, August 26, 1914. Also Ballin to von Tirpitz, August 27, 1914.

246. Rintelen, *The Dark Invader*, p. 82. Rintelen claims that he had known Boy-Ed socially and worked with him "for several years."

247. Ibid.

248. NA RG 76 Mixed Claims Commission, Box 13, "Memorandum Re Rintelen," February 18, 1939.

249. Rintelen, *The Dark Invader*, p. 80.

250. NA RG 85 Passenger and Crew Lists of Vessels Arriving at New York, New York, T715, Roll 2404.

251. NA RG 65 FBI Case Files, M1085, File 8000-174, Rintelen to Sullivan March 26, 1915; Sullivan to Charles Harrah, April 12, Sullivan to Rintelen, April 14, 1915, referring to Rintelen's visit with the family.

252. NA RG 65 FBI Case Files, M1085, File 8000-174, Count Bernstorff to Rintelen, April 13, 1915.

253. Ibid., Agent Benham to Department, March 29, 1916, interview with Bernhard Siedenburg.

254. NA RG 76 Mixed Claims Commission, Box 13, "Memorandum Re Rintelen," February 18, 1939.

255. Ibid.

256. Ibid., Box 14, Denials of German officials. Also Ibid., Box 13, Folder 2. Documents in the Mixed Claims Commission file on Rintelen show that he deposited his first funds with Plochmann's bank on April 7, 1915. These funds came from Albert and Boy-Ed and had to be deposited after they met.

257. Ibid., Statement of Boy-Ed, February 14, 1928.

258. NA RG 65 Albert Papers, Box 7, Boy-Ed to HAPAG, October 23, 1914.

259. NA RG 87 U.S. Secret Service, A1, Entry 65, "Synopsis of Franz von Rintelen Mission."

260. NA RG 76 Mixed Claims Commission, Box 13, Folder 2, "Memorandum on Activities." The listed deposit amount, less the money Rintelen had brought himself and deposited. See also Rintelen accounts in NA RG 65 FBI Case Files, M1085, File

8000-174.

261. There are no archival documents showing a registration as a business. Rintelen might have just worked with a P.O. Box and a letterhead. He wrote the first checks from this company on April 22, 1915.

262. NA RG 76 Mixed Claims Commission, Box 13, "Memorandum Re Rintelen," February 18, 1939.

263. NA RG 65 Albert Papers, Box 45.

264. Ibid., Folder 3, Agent Offley to Department, June 28, 1915.

265. NA RG 65 FBI Case Files, M1085, File 8000-174, Agent Benham to Department, October 2, 1915.

266. NA RG 65 Albert Papers, Box 19, von Papen to von Falkenhayn, April 9, 1915.

267. Ibid.

268. Ibid.

269. Ibid.

270. Ibid.

271. NA RG 76 Mixed Claims Commission, Box 13, Folder 3. See also NA RG 65 FBI Case File, M1085, File 8000-174, Agent Benham to Department, January 3, 1916. Rice was president of Donald W. Macleod and Co. in New York, a linen and flax importer trying to do restart a factory in Courtrai, Belgium.

272. Rintelen, *The Dark Invader*, p. 84.

273. This was the claim of all the German officials after the war.

274. *The New York Sun*, May 26, 1915, "Even British Ships Broke Own Blockade."

275. NA RG 65 FBI Case Files, M1085, File 8000-174, Agent Benham to Department, January 3, 1916.

276. The Rice-Meloy connection is documented through letters found in Meloy's luggage when he was arrested in August 1915. See NA RG 65 FBI Case Files, M1085, File 8000-174, Rice to Meloy, July 24, 1915. Rice met with Rintelen in Meloy's house on July 17, 1915. See also Heribert von Feilitzsch, *In Plain Sight: Felix A. Sommerfeld, Spymaster in Mexico, 1908 to 1914*, Henselstone Verlag LLC, Amissville, VA, 2012, chapter 6.

277. NA RG 65 FBI Case Files, M1085, File 8000-174, Department Memo undated.

278. Rintelen was *Korvettenkapitän zur See* (Second Lieutenant Commander), equal to Major of the Army, Boy-Ed was *Korvettenkapitän* (Lieutenant Commander), equal to Lieutenant Colonel of the Army, von Papen was *Hauptmann* (Captain of the Army), Scheele was *Major* (Major of the Army), one rank above von Papen.

279. NA RG 87 U.S. Secret Service, A1, Entry 65, "Synopsis of Franz von Rintelen Mission."

280. NA RG 65 FBI Case Files, M1085, File 8000-925, Statement of trucker Heine.

281. Ibid.

282. Ibid., statements of Preidel, Garbade, and Paradis.

283. Ibid., Statement of Georg Preidel.

284. Ibid., Statement of Wilhelm Paradis.

285. Tunney, *Throttled*, p. 130.

286. NA RG 65 FBI Case Files, M1085, File 8000-925, Memo to Department, April 22, 1916. Also Ibid., Statement of Georg Preidel. Preidel told investigators that the production of the bombs started in March or the beginning of April, which, if true, would place the establishment of the "bomb factory" on the steamer before the arrival of Rintelen, another indication that the whole project was well underway when he arrived.

287. Ibid.

288. Ibid., Statement of von Kleist.

289. Ibid., Statements of Garbade, Paradis, and Preidel.

290. Ibid., Statement of Dr. Scheele.

291. *The New York Times*, April 15, 1916, "Bomb Plot Men, Deserted in Jail, May Name Chiefs."

292. *The New York Times* had a weekly column called, "Sailings for War Zone," which detailed not only the sailing dates, but ship names and even the cargo. See, for example, *The New York Times*, February 28, 1915, "Take Big Cotton Cargoes: Vessels leaving Galveston...", also *The New York Times*, April 2, 1915, "Seven Big Grain Cargoes Shipped from Baltimore."

293. NA RG 87 U.S. Secret Service, A1, Entry 65, "Synopsis of Franz von Rintelen Mission."

294. Ibid.

295. NA RG 65 FBI Case Files, M1085, File 8000-174, Statement of Friedrich Henjes.

296. *The New York Times*, August 29, 1915, "Six Arrested Here for Ship Fire Bombs."

297. NA RG 65 FBI Case Files, M1085, File 8000-925, Timeline.

298. *The New York Times*, August 29, 1915, "Six Arrested Here for Ship Fire Bombs."

299. NA RG 65 FBI Case Files, M1085, File 8000-925, Scheele Interrogation.

300. Ibid.

301. Ibid. Bode and Scheele met Connors repeatedly in a hotel in New Orleans. Scheele paid $2,500 on April 28, and another $2,500 on April 30.

302.   Ibid., Memos to Bielaski, April 1916.

303.   NA RG 131 Alien Property Custodian, Entry 199, Box 131, File 3221, Boy-Ed Financials.

304.   NA RG 65 FBI Case Files, M1085, File 8000-174, Statement of Friedrich Henjes. Also Ibid., Statement of Paul Hilken.

305.   Millman, Chad, *The Detonators: The Secret Plot to Destroy America and an Epic Hunt for Justice*, Little, Brown and Company, New York, 2006, pp. 33-34.

306.   NA RG 76 Mixed Claims Commission, Box 7, Paul Hilken Diary 1915.

307.   As quoted in Koenig, Robert, *The Fourth Horseman: One Man's Mission to Wage the Great War in America*, Public Affairs, 2006, p. 95.

308.   *Rangliste der Deutschen Marine für das Jahr 1914*, Ernst Siegfried Mittler und Sohn, Berlin, Germany, 1914, p. 279.

309.   Ibid.

310.   NA RG 76 Mixed Claims Commission, Box 7, Paul Hilken Diary 1915.

311.   NA RG 65 FBI Case Files, Miscellaneous file 8000-174, von Papen to von Igel, April 24, 1915.

312.   Ibid.

313.   *The New York Times*, calendar year 1915, survey of articles containing steamer, ship, or fire in the headlines.

314.   *The Philadelphia Evening Ledger*, July 21, 1915, "Nine Compartments Damaged By Flames on Great Warship."

315.   *The New York Times*, June 14, 1916, "4 to 10 Die in Blast and Grain Pier Fire."

316.   NA RG 76 Mixed Claims Commission, Box 8, Folder 1, copyright expired.

317.   NA RG 65 Albert Papers, Box 20, military reports.

318.   NA RG 65 Albert Papers, Box 19, Sommerfeld to Boy-Ed, November 11, 1914.

319.   NA RG 65 Albert Papers, Box 19, Sommerfeld to Boy-Ed, November 29, 1914

320.   NA RG 65 Albert Papers, Box 19, Boy-Ed to Count von Bernstorff, December 18, 1914.

321.   NA RG 65 Albert Papers, Box 19, Tauscher to von Papen, January 4, 1915.

322.   NA RG 65 Albert Papers, Box 19, von Papen to von Falkenhayn, April 9, 1915.

323.   NA RG 65 FBI Case Files, M1085, File 8000-174, von Papen to War Department, Military Report, March 30, 1915.

324.   NA RG 65 Albert Papers, Box 19, Papen to Secretary of War, draft, co-signed by Albert, undated (estimated February 11, 1915). Antimony is mixed into the lead to

make it harder. Lead-based bullets tend to deform and disintegrate without antimony as a hardener when accelerated in a barrel.

325.   Hamilton, Douglas T., *Shrapnel Shell Manufacture*, The New Industrial Press, New York, NY, 1915, p. 4.

326.   NA RG 65 Albert Papers, Box 20, Secretary of War to von Papen, March 20, 1915.

327.   NA RG 65 FBI Case Files, M1085, File 8000-174, von Papen to War Department, Military Report, March 30, 1915. The effort to tie up delivery contracts was already underway, according to the report.

328.   The numbers vary from 3.5 million pounds to five million pounds. The actual contract was indeed for 4,450,000 pounds, NA RG 65 Albert Papers, Box 5, Memorandum of Carl Heynen, August 31, 1915, also memorandum titled, "Powder Contracts."

329.   NA RG 65 Albert Papers, Box 20, von Papen to War Department, March 30, 1915.

330.   NA RG 36 Passenger and Crew Lists of Vessels Arriving at Baltimore, M255, Roll 44, page 4.

331.   NA RG 36 Passenger and Crew Lists of Vessels Arriving at New York, M237, Roll 557, page 1559.

332.   NA RG 36 Passenger and Crew Lists of Vessels Arriving at New York, M237, Roll 631, entry August 29, 1894.

333.   NA RG 60 Department of Justice, file 9-16-12-5, December 16, 1918.

334.   www.facebook.com/topic.php?uid=127204100643003&topic=108,   viewed 10-2010, Pearl-Edgar Family Tree; Also NA RG 60 Department of Justice, file 9-16-12-5, George Clynes to Norvin Lindheim, August 1, 1917.

335.   NA RG 60 Department of Justice, file 9-16-12-5, W. H. Campbell to Norvin Lindheim, August 22, 1917.

336.   *The Mexican Yearbook 1912*, McCorqudale and Company Limited, London, 1912, p. 71.

337.   *The Bankers Magazine*, Volume 77 (July to December 1908), Bankers Publishing Company, New York, 1908, p. 611.

338.   AA Mexico II Paket 17, von Rieloff to Foreign Secretary, February 4, 1909.

339.   Ackerman, Carl W., *Mexico's Dilemma*, George H. Doran Company, New York, 1918, p. 98.

340.   *The Massey-Gilbert Blue Book of Mexico for 1903: A Directory in English of the City of Mexico*, The Massey-Qilbert Company, Sucs., Mexico, D.F., 1903, p. 107 (American Club members) and p. 129 (Deutscher Verein members).

341.   NA RG 60 Department of Justice, file 9-16-12-5, W. H. Campbell to Norvin

Lindheim, August 22, 1917.

342.   Ibid.

343.   AA Mexico IV Paket 29, von Rieloff memorandum, March 7, 1912.

344.   NA RG 60 Department of Justice, file 9-16-12-5, George Clynes to Norvin Lindheim, August 1, 1917.

345.   NA RG 60 Department of Justice, file 9-16-12-5, F. J. O'Keefe to P. H. Campbell, August 23, 1917; Also ibid., John Hanna to Department, October 6, 1919.

346.   NA RG 36 Passenger and Crew Lists of Vessels Arriving at New York T715 Roll 2378, page 157.

347.   NA RG 60 Department of Justice, file 9-16-12-5, Heynen to Swiss Legation, December 16, 1918.

348.   NA RG 76 Mixed Claims Commission, Box 2, January 24, 1915. The sabotage order does not mention Mexico; however, von Papen reported on March 17, 1915 that he had sent sabotage agents to Tampico, see NA RG 242 T141 Roll 19, von Papen to Generalstab der Armee, March 17, 1915. The effort was cancelled before it was fully executed. Also, see *The New York Times*, October 25, 1915, "Mexico Hears of Raiders." The article claims that "all" oil for the British fleet came from Tampico at that time.

349.   NA RG 60 Department of Justice, file 9-16-12-5, Heynen to Swiss Legation, December 16, 1918.

350.   NA RG 76 Mixed Claims Commission, Box 7, Memorandum by H. Martin, December 28, 1935.

351.   See below, Hugo Schmidt activities.

352.   NA RG 65 Albert Papers, Box 18, chapter 5.

353.   NA RG 65 Albert Papers, Box 24, G. Amsinck Accounts, February 3, 1915. Albert also purchased two sailing vessels.

354.   NA RG 65 Albert Papers, Box 18, chapter 5.

355.   NA RG 165 Military Intelligence Division, file 9140-878, Frederico Stallforth, list of agents. No immigration record for that date can be found, most likely because Schmidt traveled undercover.

356.   Gerard, James W., *Face to Face with Kaiserism*, George H. Doran Company, New York, 1918, p. 278.

357.   NA RG 65 Albert Papers, Box 24, G. Amsinck Accounts, from September 1914 to February 28, 1915.

358.   NA RG 65 FBI Case Files, M1085, File 8000-3089, Statement concerning Hugo Schmidt, undated (1918).

359.   NA RG 65 FBI Case Files, M1085, File 8000-3089, Quotations, August 19, 1915.

360. Ibid.

361. Ibid.

362. NA RG 131 Alien Property Custodian, Entry 199, Box 28, file 654, Statement of Friedrich A. Borgemeister.

363. NA RG 65 Albert Papers, Box 3, Albert to Secretary of Treasury, Statement No. 111. Of the $7,121,500 of treasuries sold, $62,000 were deducted for fees (i.e. commissions).

364. NA RG 65 Albert Papers, Box 3, Folder 10, Cohn to Albert, November 3, 1915.

365. NA RG 65 Albert Papers, Box 10, Albert to Secretary of Interior, April 10, 1915.

366. NA RG 65 Albert Papers, Box 5, Statement of George W. Hoadley, October 30, 1918.

367. NA RG 65 Albert Papers, Box 5, Statement of George W. Hoadley, October 30, 1918.

368. NA RG 65 Albert Papers, Box 5, Memorandum on Bridgeport Project, August 10, 1915.

369. NA RG 65 Albert Papers, Box 5, Statement of George W. Hoadley, October 30, 1918.

370. NA RG 65 Albert Papers, Box 5, Papen I, Accounts for Bridgeport, payments March 26 and April 2, 1915 (10,000 and 30,000 cash payments to Hoadley and Knight). *The New York World* reported that the down payment was $140,000. See *The New York World*, August 18, 1915, "Hoadley's Promised Larger Contracts to Aetna Company." The *World* seems to have been mistaken.

371. *The New York Times*, November 23, 1915, "Amazing Contract."

372. NA RG 76 Mixed Claims Commission, F. B. McMillin to H. H. Martin, July 26, 1930.

373. NA RG 65 Albert Papers, Box 5, Memorandum of Carl Heynen, September 30, 1915. The specific mention of Bethlehem Steel in NA RG 65 Albert Papers, Box 19, Papen Military Reports, April 24, 1915.

374. *The New York Times*, November 23, 1915, "Amazing Contract."

375. NA RG 65 Albert Papers, Box 5, Memorandum of Carl Heynen, September 30, 1915.

376. *The New York Times*, November 17, 1915, "Tied up Munitions by German Trick."

377. NA RG 76 Mixed Claims Commission, F. B. McMillin to H. H. Martin, July 26, 1930.

378. Douglas T. Hamilton, *Shrapnel Shell Manufacture*, The New Industrial Press, New York, NY, 1915, p. 29.

379. NA RG 65 Albert Papers, Box 5, Memorandum of Carl Heynen, September 30,

1915.

380.   NA RG 65 Albert Papers, Box 5, Riano to Bernstorff, May 28, 1915.

381.   NA RG 65 Albert Papers, Box 5, Memorandum of Carl Heynen, September 30, 1915.

382.   NA RG 65 Albert Papers, Box 45, Bridgeport Projectile Company accounting.

383.   NA RG 65 Albert Papers, Box 5, Memorandum titled "Powder Contracts," undated (March 1916).

384.   NA RG 65 Albert Papers, Box 5, Memorandum of Carl Heynen, September 30, 1915.

385.   NA RG 65 Albert Papers, Box 10, Albert to Secretary of Interior, April 20, 1915.

386.   Staatsarchiv Hamburg, Band, 373-7 373-7 I, VIII (Auswanderungsamt I), Roll 1740.

387.   NA RG 65 FBI Case Files, Roll 877, File 8000-925.

388.   New Jersey State Archives, V227, Roll 54, Page 64.

389.   Jeffreys, Diarmuid, *Aspirin: The Remarkable Story of a Wonder Drug*, Bloomsbury Publishing, New York, NY, 2005, p. 110. Dr. Schweitzer also held multiple patents, for example U.S. Patent Office, Washington, D.C., Patent number: RE13550, Filing date: January 29, 1913, Issue date: April 1, 1913; Patent number: 1009796, Filing date: August 1, 1911, Issue date: November 28, 1911; Patent number: 539550, Filing date: February 12, 1895, Issue date: May 21, 1895.

390.   *Electrochemical and Metallurgical Industry*, Volume 7, 1909, editors Eugene Franz Roeber, Howard Coon Parmelee, New York, NY 1909, p. 149, "Schweitzer Celebration." Also *Journal of the American Chemical Society*, 1892, Volume 14 (2), p. 23.

391.   Ibid., p. 111.

392.   NA RG 59, State Department, M1490, Roll 176, File A1 534.

393.   NA RG 131 Alien Property Custodian, APC Entry 277, Box 1.

394.   NA RG 65 Albert Papers, Box 2, file 4, Report dated April 9, 1915.

395.   RG 65 Albert Papers, Box 2, file 4.

396.   NA RG 65 Albert Papers, Box 2, file 4.

397.   NA RG 36 M1674, Roll 285.

398.   NA RG 65 Albert Papers, Box 2, File 4.

399.   Ibid.

400.   Ibid., $24,000 in July, 1915, June 1916 $5,500, December 1916, $4,000. Also, see NA RG 65 FBI Case File, M1085, File 8000-174, Schweitzer to Albert, August 26, 1915 "Payments to American Oil and Supply Company [for carbolic acid], July 2 to August

23 $33,637."

401.   NA RG 65 FBI Case Files, M1085, 8000-3089, Stallforth to William J. Kindgen, July 26, 1915.

402.   NA RG 65 Albert Papers, Box 5, Folder 17, Contract between Schweitzer, Albert, June 23, 1915. Also Box 2, File 4, Papen to War Department, June 23, 1915. Payments for the Phenol contract were accounted under the Papen II account.

403.   NA RG 65 Albert Papers, Box 5, contract Albert with Schweitzer, June 23, 1915.

404.   *The New York Times*, July 30, 1918, "German Chemical Plant is Seized." The German ownership of the plant did not come into the open until 1918.

405.   NA RG 65 Albert Papers, Box 19, Military Report, May 18, 1915.

406.   Jeffreys, *Aspirin: The Remarkable Story of a Wonder Drug*, p. 113.

407.   United States Senate, Committee of the Judiciary, *Alleged Dye Monopoly*, Resolution 77, Government Printing Office, Washington D.C., 1922, p. 224.

408.   NA RG 65 Albert Papers, Box 19, Munitions Report, May 18, 1915.

409.   Horne, Charles F., ed., *Source Records of the Great War*, Vol. III (New York, NY: National Alumni, 1923).

410.   NA RG 65 Albert Papers, Box 10, Folder 39, Albert refers in a memo to the Department of War dated April 20, 1915 to the authorized $9,450,000.

411.   NA RG 65 Albert Papers, Box 45, Papen Accounts.

412.   NA RG 65 Albert Papers, Box 3, Folder 16, "Verzeichnis der Belege."

413.   NA RG 65 Albert Papers, Box 5, Folder 20, "Propaganda v. P. III" dated July 20, 1915.

414.   NA RG 65 Albert Papers, Box 3, Folder 10, Accounting of the Imperial German Embassy, October 1915.

415.   Voska, Emanuel Victor, Irwin, Will, *Spy and Counter-Spy*, George G. Harrap and Co Ltd., London, 1941, p. 73.

416.   *The Nation*, Volume 111, November 17, 1920, p. 557, "The Confession of John R. Rathom (Providence Journal)."

417.   Hirst, *German Propaganda in the United States, 1914-1917*, p. 158.

418.   As quoted in Ibid.

419.   Von Bernstorff, *My Three Years in America*, p.46.

420.   Ibid., p. 47.

421.   Hirst, *German Propaganda in America, 1914-1917*, p. 72.

422.   NA RG 65 Albert Papers, Box 5, Folder 20 "About Dernburging."

423.   NA RG 65 Albert Papers, Box 3, Folder 10.

424.   Dernburg had instructions to raise $150 million to fund the German efforts in the United States during the war, i.e. propaganda, purchasing of supplies, financing of insurance etc. See NA RG 65 Albert Papers, Box 22 "Kapitel III: Die Geldbeschaffung."

425.   NA RG 65 Albert Papers, Box 22, "Kapitel III: Geldbeschaffung."

426.   NA RG 131 Alien Property Custodian, Entry 199, Box 28, File 654 Statement of Frederick A. Borgemeister.

427.   NA RG 65 Albert Papers, Box 22, "Kapitel III: Geldbeschaffung."

428.   NA RG 65 Albert Papers, Box 3, Folder 10, "Utilization of Treasury-notes," August 25, 1916.

429.   Ibid., Folder 16, Statement to the Secretary of the Imperial Treasury, May 15, 1915.

430.   NA RG 65 Albert Papers, undated letter to "his Excellency," date estimated around February 1915 (definitely before the attempts to buy American papers in March 1915 and before the *Lusitania* sinking in May). His characterization of the American public in itself reflected an attitude that would make a more sensible propaganda impossible.

431.   United States Senate, *Brewing and Liquor interests and German and Bolshevik Propaganda*, Report and Hearings of the Subcommittee on the Judiciary of the United States Senate, Government Printing Office, Washington D. C., 1919, pp. 1453-1454.

432.   Hume, Sherwood, "The Rumely Revolution, From industrial revolutionary to rusty relic: Rumely remembered 150 years later," www.farmcollector.com/tractors/rumely-revolution.aspx , March 2003.

433.   United States Senate, *Brewing and Liquor interests and German and Bolshevik Propaganda*, Report and Hearings of the Subcommittee on the Judiciary of the United States Senate, Government Printing Office, Washington D. C., 1919, p. 1452.

434.   *The New York Times*, August 3, 1918, "Ford Aided Rumely, Says George Harvey."

435.   Hume, "The Rumely Revolution."

436.   University of Oregon, Edward A. Rumely Papers.

437.   Reiling, *Deutschland: Safe for Democracy?* p. 187.

438.   NA RG 65 Albert Papers, Box 5, Folder 18, Rumely to Albert, January 30, 1915. Historian Reiling documented an earlier contact of Rumely's with Dernburg, ostensibly for the same purpose.

439.   NA RG 65 Albert Papers, Box 5, Folder 18, Rumely to Albert, January 30, 1915.

440.   Reiling, *Deutschland: Safe for Democracy?* p. 187.

441.   United States Senate, *Brewing and Liquor interests and German and Bolshevik*

Propaganda, Report and Hearings of the Subcommittee on the Judiciary of the United States Senate, Government Printing Office, Washington D. C., 1919, p. 1422.

442.   *The New York Times*, July 11, 1918, "Rumely's Case Goes to the Grand Jury."

443.   See Mencken, H. L., *My Life as Author and Editor*, Alfred E. Knopf, New York, 1992.

444.   United States Senate, *Brewing and Liquor interests and German and Bolshevik Propaganda*, Report and Hearings of the Subcommittee on the Judiciary of the United States Senate, Government Printing Office, Washington D. C., 1919, p. 1452.

445.   NA RG 65 Albert Papers, Box 3, Folder 16, To the Secretary of the Imperial Treasury, May 15, 1915.

446.   Ibid., Box 24, Temporary Advance Account.

447.   Ibid., Verzeichnis der Belege. These last payments may have been to prop the newspaper up financially but were booked under newspaper purchases in Albert's files. See also Ibid., Box 3, Folder 10, Trial Balance October 14, 1915. Perez 861,164 (missing the two 1916 payments of $7,500 and $75,000.

448.   Ibid., Utilization of Treasury Notes, August 25, 1916.

449.   NA RG 65 Albert Papers, Box 12, File 67.

450.   McClure, Samuel S., *My Autobiography*, Frederick A. Stokes Company, New York, NY, 1914, p. 238.

451.   Ibid., pp. 242-243.

452.   Rumely, Edward A., *The Gravest 366 Days, Editorials Reprinted from the Evening Mail of New York City*, The New York Evening Mail, New York, NY, 1916.

453.   Mencken, *My Life as Author and Editor*, p. 194.

454.   Ibid. One exception is John Burgess, who wrote on questions of international law in the fall of 1915.

455.   NA RG 65 Albert Papers, Box 3, Folder 16, Entries marked Hays-Perez in amounts in amounts ranging from $18,000 to $40,000 in 1916. Albert lists three outlays in the final accounting of 1916, which seem to reflect the sum of the Hays-Perez entries.

456.   *The New York Times*, July 9, 1918, "Arrest Rumely; Say Germany owns the Evening Mail." Also see NA RG 65 Albert Papers, Box 3, Folder 16 and Box 24, German Embassy Account 1916.

457.   NA RG 65 Albert Papers, Box 24, Imperial Embassy Account.

458.   Wittke, Carl, *The German-Language Press in America*, University of Kentucky Press, Louisville, KY, 1957, p. 243

459.   Ibid.

460.   Doerries, p. 51. According to Major Humes of the U.S. Justice Department,

Ridder's debts were closer to $300,000. See United States Senate, *Brewing and Liquor interests and German and Bolshevik Propaganda*, Report and Hearings of the Subcommittee on the Judiciary of the United States Senate, Government Printing Office, Washington D. C., 1919, p. 2773.

461.   *Bisbee Daily Review*, October 21, 1917, "More Intrigue Unearthed for Many Doublers."

462.   *The New York Times*, October 21, 1917, "Dernburg Money Helped to Finance Staats-Zeitung."

463.   United States Senate, *Brewing and Liquor interests and German and Bolshevik Propaganda*, Report and Hearings of the Subcommittee on the Judiciary of the United States Senate, Government Printing Office, Washington D. C., 1919, p. 2775.

464.   Ibid., p. 1396.

465.   NA RG 65 Albert Papers, Box 24, Temporary Advance Account.

466.   Doerries, p. 63.

467.   Doerries, p. 62.

468.   Doerries, pp. 63-64.

469.   NA RG 65 Albert Papers, Box 24, Temporary Advance Account. Also RG 131 Allied Property Custodian, Entry 199, Box 28, File 654. This payment is referenced in the statements of the Allied Property Custodian as "commission for the sale of the *SS Atlantic*." The Allied Property Custodian questions this charge, which seems to have been a payment to Strauss for something else.

470.   NA RG 65 Albert Papers, Box 5, File 20, Report July 20, 1915.

471.   NA RG 65 Albert Papers, Box 24, Temporary Advance Account.

472.   NA RG 131 Allied Property Custodian, Entry 199, Box 28, File 654.

473.   As quoted in Doerries, p. 269.

474.   Ibid.

475.   NA RG 65 Albert Papers, Box 24, Temporary Advance Account.

476.   NA RG 65 Albert Papers, Box 24, Temporary Advance Account.

477.   NA RG 65 Albert Papers, Box 3, Folder 16, "Utilization of Treasury Notes," August 25, 1916.

478.   NA RG 65 Albert Papers, Box 3, Folder 16, "Utilization of Treasury Notes," August 25, 1916.

479.   YIVO Institute for Jewish Research, New York, Record Group 713, Papers of Herman Bernstein, Folder 250.

480.   Ibid., Bernstein to Lewisohn, May 21, 1915.

481. Löwer, Thomas, *American Jews in World War I - German Propaganda Courting the American Jewry*, Munich, GRIN Publishing GmbH, 2004, p. 8.

482. YIVO Institute for Jewish Research, New York, Record Group 713, Papers of Herman Bernstein, Folder 213 and 191.

483. Ibid., Folder 213, Straus to Bernstein, December 14, 1914.

484. Ibid., Meyerowitz to Bernstein, January 17, 1915.

485. Ibid., Folder 250, Schapiro and Aronson to Bernstein, May 15, 1915.

486. Ibid. Also NA RG 65 Albert Papers, Box 23, Albert Diary, Entry for April 23, 1915. It is an interesting fact that at the end of April, Heinrich Albert noted in his diary, "Dinner at Goldmann's [sic]." Purely circumstantial, the entry does indicate that there could be another connection between the German government and the funding of "The Day."

487. Ibid.

488. Ibid.

489. Ibid., Folder 713, Meyerowitz to Bernstein, November 16, 1914.

490. Ibid., Meyerowiz to Bernstein, December 5, 1914.

491. Ibid., undated letter Meyerowitz to Bernstein.

492. Ibid., for example Meyerowitz to Bernstein, February 2, 1915.

493. NA RG 65 Albert Papers, Box 24, Temporary Advance Account. For von Bernstorff's commendation see NA RG 131, Alien Property Custodian, Entry 199, Box 129, File 3103, Bernstorff to Braun, March 15, 1915.

494. Ibid.

495. Hale had a contract with the German press office for $15,000 per year from the fall of 1914 until 1918.

496. United States Senate, *Brewing and Liquor interests and German and Bolshevik Propaganda*, Report and Hearings of the Subcommittee on the Judiciary of the United States Senate, Government Printing Office, Washington D. C., 1919, p. 1588.

497. NA RG 65 Albert Papers, Box 24, Temporary Advance Account, 1916. The entries are made for Ernst A. Scherer, Ernst A. Schiamer, E. A. Scherer, and Schirmer, which all seem to be transcribing mistakes by the B.I. Also NA RG 65 FBI Case Files, M1085, File 8000-174, Schirmer appeared to have carried letters from Albert to the German government in March 1916.

498. See Hirst, *German Propaganda in the United States, 1914-1917*, pp. 87-91.

499. *Film History*, Volume 4, No. 2 (1990), pp. 123-129, "Shooting the Great War: Albert Dawson and the American Correspondent Film Company, 1914-1918," by Ron van Dopperen, p. 124.

500.   Ibid.

501.   Ibid.

502.   Ibid., p. 125. Also Hirst, *German Propaganda in the United States, 1914-1917*, p. 77.

503.   United States Census, 1920, Roll T625, Page 4.

504.   Staatsarchiv Hamburg, Band 249, page 1875, Roll K 1824.

505.   NA RG 85 Petitions for Naturalization from the U.S. District Court for the Southern District of New York, 1897-1944, M1972, Roll 156.

506.   NA RG 65 Albert Papers, Box 24, Temporary Advance Account.

507.   Hirst, *German Propaganda in the United States, 1914-1917*, pp. 77-78. Hirst mentions another seven movies that likely were incorporated into the features, but also screened separately.

508.   NA RG 65 Albert Papers, Box 24, Temporary Advance Account.

509.   NA RG 65 Albert Papers, Box 24, Temporary Advance Account, June 1915 $23,500, October 1915 $50,000 ($1 million in today's money), March another $12,500. The *New York Tribune* reported that he invested $72,000, which is believable. There are multiple payments of $10,000 with only propaganda coding that could have made up for the missing amount. See *The New York Tribune*, May 7, 1918, "Malitz, German Spy Paymaster, Gets Two Years." Also Hirst, *German Propaganda in the United States, 1914-1917*, p. 77. This author claims that the company received a total of $140,000. See, as well, Ron Van Dopperen, Cooper C. Graham, *Shooting the Great War*, p. 66, in which he also mentions the $140,000 and an additional 9,000 German Reichsmark that Dawson received directly in Germany.

510.   Library of Congress, Catalogue of Copyright Entries, Part 4, Volume 10, Government Printing Press, 1916, p. 579. Malitz registered copyrights for six movies in October, November and December 1915.

511.   See the Imperial War Museum, object IWM 1039-1. Van Dopperen wrote that the movie came to American theatres in July 1915, which this author could not verify.

512.   *Film History*, Volume 4, No. 2 (1990), pp. 123-129, "Shooting the Great War: Albert Dawson and the American Correspondent Film Company, 1914-1918," by Ron van Dopperen, pp. 127-128.

513.   *Film History*, Volume 4, No. 2 (1990), pp. 123-129, "Shooting the Great War: Albert Dawson and the American Correspondent Film Company, 1914-1918," by Ron van Dopperen, p. 127.

514.   As quoted in Van Dopperen, Graham, *Shooting the Great War*, p. 81.

515.   Hirst, *German Propaganda in the United States, 1914-1917*, p. 78.

516.   Johann Albrecht Count von Bernstorff, *My Three Years in America*, p. 42.

517.   *The New York Times*, December 7, 1918, "Lays Bare German Plots." Also NA RG

65 Albert Papers, Box 45, Falmouth Papers, letter from E. L. Fox to von Papen, July 28, 1915.

518. NA RG 65 Albert Papers, Box 34, Stallforth to Albert, January 26, 1915.

519. Ibid., Box 3, Folder 10, Albert to Robert Cohn, November 3, 1915.

520. NA RG 65 FBI Case Files, M1085, File 8000-174, James F. McElhone to Bielaski, October 27, 1915.

521. *The New York Times*, December 21, 1918, "Bernstorff told Propaganda Plan at a House Party."

522. Sommerfeld intervened on behalf of Hearst with Madero, Carranza and Villa. While Villa confiscated large landholdings in Chihuahua from Terrazas and other large landowners, Hearst's ranches remained largely intact. This is, to a large degree, through the influence of Felix Sommerfeld.

523. Ibid., Box 5, Folder 20.

524. There was a Vice President and Director of the Foreign Department at the Guaranty Trust Company, the major financial partner of Albert's with the name of Max May. Though possible, no connection between Max May and the propaganda effort or a personal connection to Dernburg could be found.

525. NA RG 242 Captured German Documents, Roll 377, File 735, Dernburg to von Holtzendorff, May 10, 1915.

526. NA RG 65 Albert Papers, Box 23, Letter to Ida, May 13, 1915.

527. Hirst, *German Propaganda in the United States, 1914-1917*, p. 238.

528. NA TG 65 Albert Papers, Box 23, Albert Diaries, Entry for April 8, 1915.

529. NA RG 65 Albert Papers, Box 23, Letter to Ida, May 13, 1915. It is difficult to find a good translation for Albert's prose, "...Aber es wäre noch schöner, wenn wir verzweifeln wollten..."

530. As quoted in Hirst, *German Propaganda in the United States, 1914-1917*, p. 247.

531. NA RG 85 Immigration and Naturalization, T715, Roll 2407, Page 153.

532. *The New York Times*, September 30, 1916, "Fay's Companion is Caught Here."

533. NA RG 65 FBI Case Files, M1085, File 8000-174, Statement Friedrich Henjes. Also *The New York Times*, November 10, 1915, "Breitung Ignorant of Plot, Uncle Says."

534. NA RG 76 Mixed Claims Commission, Box 12, Memorandum on the Activities of Franz von Papen, June 7, 1932.

535. Ibid., Fay recalled that he met Rintelen around the time when the *Kirk Oswald* bombs had been discovered. That would have been in the middle of June. It is not known whether Fay just remembered incorrectly, or whether he worked on his own for one-and-a-half months before Papen sent him to Rintelen. The latter seems highly

improbable since Rintelen was in charge of the bomb plot from mid-April on.

536.   *The World's Work*, Volume 35, May to October 1916, Doubleday, Page and Co., New York, NY, 1916, p. 669.

537.   NA RG 65 FBI Case Files, M1085, File 8000-376.

538.   Ibid., Statement of Walter E. Scholz.

539.   NA RG 131 Alien Property Custodian, Entry 199, Box 119, File 3121, Statement of Robert Fay.

540.   NA RG 65 FBI Case Files, M1085, File 8000-376, Statement of Herbert O. Kienzle.

541.   Ibid.

542.   Ibid.

543.   Ibid., Statement of Walter E. Scholz.

544.   Ibid.

545.   NA RG 131 Alien Property Custodian, Entry 199, Box 119, File 3121, Statement of Robert Fay.

546.   NA RG 65 FBI Case Files, M1085, File 8000-376, Mrs. Schroer to Secretary of State, November 11, 1915.

547.   The National Archives at Atlanta, RG 129, Inmate Case Files, National Archives Identifier 607937.

548.   Landau, *The Enemy Within*, p. 39.

549.   NA RG 131 Alien Property Custodian, Entry 199, Box 119, File 3121, Statement of Robert Fay.

550.   See Rintelen, *The Dark Invader*, pp. 80-186.

551.   *The Dark Invader* (1933), and *The Return of the Dark Invader* (1935).

552.   Rintelen sued the German government for damages arising from his incarceration in the United States. Hossenfelder, von Papen, Albert, and von Bernstorff did what they could to refute Rintelen's claims. In the end, Rintelen moved to England in the late 20s. He feared for his life when, first von Papen, then Hitler became chancellors. Post war publication of blacklists indeed showed that in the plans to occupy England, Rintelen would have been arrested.

553.   NA RG 65 FBI Case Files, M1085, File 8000-174, Rintelen accounts. This amount is minute if Rintelen's mission indeed would have been to buy up munitions in the US in order to create shortages. The German government knew by then that the price tag for cornering munitions was over $20 Million and had denied the funding to Albert's team.

554.   Both Rintelen and von Papen claimed after the war that Rintelen's recall that precipitated his arrest in England was the result of complaints by the German officials

in New York. It seems that, in any case, Rintelen had to leave in a hurry whether recalled or not, because of his impending arrest in the U.S.

555.   NA RG 65 Albert Papers, Box 33, Militärbericht, June 2, 1915.

556.   Ibid.

557.   Ibid., Paul Roh to Franz von Papen, August 16, 1915.

558.   Ibid., Franz von Papen to Paul Roh, August 31, 1915.

559.   United States Senate, *Brewing and Liquor interests and German and Bolshevik Propaganda*, Report and Hearings of the Subcommittee on the Judiciary of the United States Senate, Government Printing Office, Washington D. C., 1919, p. 2783.

560.   Ibid.

561.   NA RG 65 FBI Case Files, M1085, File 8000-174, Statement of George Plochmann.

562.   Ibid.

563.   Ibid., document 149, assessment of Rintelen and Lamar.

564.   The term was accorded to him by the *New York Evening Mail* in 1913.

565.   www.fas.org/irp/ops/ci/docs/ci1/ch3c.htm: National Intelligence Center, CI Reader, Volume 1, Chapter 3.

566.   NA RG 65 FBI Case Files, M1085, File 8000-174, Statement of George Plochmann.

567.   *The World's Work*, Volume 36, p. 314.

568.   *Manufacturer and Financial Record*, Vol. II, No. 3, Detroit, MI, July 19, 1913, "Lamar, The Mystery Man of Wall Street."

569.   United States Senate, Subcommittee of the Committee of the Judiciary, S Res. 92, Volume 2, June 13 to July 10, 1913, Government Printing Office, Washington, D.C. 1913, p. 1726.

570.   *The New York Times*, January 30, 1914, "Lamar A Senate Topic."

571.   *The World's World*, Volume 36, Doubleday Page and Company, New York, 1918, p. 306.

572.   NA RG 65 FBI Case Files, miscellaneous file 8000-174, undated, "In Re: Franz Rintelen."

573.   Ibid.

574.   *The New York Times*, August 24, 1902. Lamar worked for the Law Office of Gregory, Day and Day in Omaha, Nebraska in the early 1890s. The city directory listed a "David M. Lamar, clerk" in Omaha between 1894 and 1899.

575.   Lamar was buried on January 17, 1934 in Manhattan's Riverside Chapel, a Jewish funeral home.

576. *The Montreal Gazette*, January 15, 1934, "David Lamar Dies in New York Hotel."

577. *The Reading Eagle*, January 13, 1934, "'Wolf of Wall Street' Dies."

578. Gabrielan, Randall , *Rumson: Shaping a Superlative Suburb*, Arcadia Publishing, Charleston, SC, 2003, p. 75. Also *The New York Times*, February 15, 1907, "Spalding Evicts Lamar."

579. U.S. Census 1910, Manhattan Ward 22, District 1319.

580. *The Palm Beach Daily News*, January 16, 1934, "No One has Claimed Body of David Lamar."

581. *St. Petersburg Times*, September 21, 1924, "'Wolf of Wall Street' Picks Follies Bride, Broadway Hears."

582. *The Palm Beach Daily News*, January 16, 1934, "No One has Claimed Body of David Lamar."

583. *The New York Times*, July 30, 1903, "Held As Hired Thug, He Threatens Lamar."

584. Ibid.

585. Ibid.

586. *Law Notes*, Volume 7, April 1903 to March 1904, Edward Thompson Company, Northport, Long Island, NY, 1904, p. 142.

587. Collier, Peter and Horowitz, David, *The Rockefellers, An American Dynasty*, Summit Books, New York, NY, 1989, pp. 89-90.

588. *Manufacturer and Financial Record*, Vol. II, No. 3, Detroit, MI, July 19, 1913, "Lamar, The Mystery Man of Wall Street."

589. *The New York Times*, June 7, 1911, "Steel Trust Heads Face Criminal Trial."

590. *The Reading Eagle*, January 13, 1934, "'Wolf of Wall Street' Dies."

591. *Manufacturer and Financial Record*, Vol. II, No. 3, Detroit, MI, July 19, 1913, "Lamar, The Mystery Man of Wall Street."

592. *The New York Times*, September 12, 1913, "Lamar Arrested for Personation [sic]." Palmer became Attorney General after World War I.

593. *Moody's Magazine: The Investors' Monthly*, Volume 16, 1913, p. 24.

594. *The New York Times*, November 7, 1914, "Lamar Arrested at the Waldorf."

595. *The New York Times*, June 24, 1915, "See Lamar's Hand In 'Labor' Peace Move."

596. *The New York Times*, September 14, 1915, "Foiled German Plot to Tie Up Docks." According to O'Connor, Cummings referred to "his 'principal' as the 'big man,' and O'Connor got a very definite impression that this was Dr. Dernburg."

597. *The Seattle Star*, April 10, 1918, "German Money Turned Down by Longshoremen."

598. *The Tonawanda Evening News*, January 28, 1916, "German Agents Wanted Strike."

599.   *The New York Times*, September 14, 1915, "Foiled German Plot To Tie Up Docks."

600.   *Ibid.* Also *The Daily Capital Journal*, September 15, 1915, "German Money Used to Cause Longshoremen to Engage in Strike."

601.   NA RG 65 FBI Case Files, Miscellaneous file 8000-174, "In Re: Franz Rintelen."

602.   Ibid., Rintelen-Schmidtmann Interview, August 20, 1918.

603.   Ibid., Agent Benham to Department, October 1, 1915. Rintelen had dinner at the Yacht Club in New York with Boy-Ed that day. Two days later, he took Thomas C. Hall, the man who connected Rintelen with Lamar, to the Yacht Club.

604.   Ibid., "In Re: Franz Rintelen."

605.   Ibid., Agent William Benham to Department, April 13, 1916.

606.   *The Minneapolis Journal*, November 4, 1902, "Martin is Running: A Former Minneapolis Labor Man Trying to Get into Congress." Also *St. Paul Daily Globe*, December 14, 1893, "Free the White Slave."

607.   *The Omaha Daily Bee*, November 5, 1902, "Congress Goes Republican." Also *The Commoner* (Lincoln, Nebraska), September 27, 1901, "Demand for Trust Investigation."

608.   See for example *The Commoner* (Lincoln, Nebraska), December 8, 1911, "The Steel Trust in the House." Also *Los Angeles Herald*, November 3, 1906, "Hughes' Victory is now Assured."

609.   *Moody's Magazine: The Investors' Monthly*, Volume 19, February, 1916, "The History of the U.S. Steel Corporation" by Arundel Cotter, chapter XII, p. 79. Also, *The Daily Missoulian*, July 4, 1913, "Mulhall's Papers Presented."

610.   NA RG 65 FBI Case Files, Miscellaneous file 8000-174, Testimony of Mr. Canode, undated.

611.   *The Evening Star* (Washington D. C.), April 26, 1897, "Fight Between Labor Bodies."

612.   *The Salt Lake Herald-Republican*, November 23, 1910, "Chapman Loses Out."

613.   NA RG 65 FBI Case Files, Miscellaneous file 8000-174, Memo to Chief Bielaski, July 18, 1915.

614.   Ibid., statement of Ernest Bohm, October 24, 1916.

615.   Hannis Taylor served in Spain from 1893 to 1897 under President Grover Cleveland.

616.   NA RG 65 FBI Case Files, Miscellaneous file 8000-174, undated Memo.

617.   Luff, Jennifer, *Commonsense Anticommunism: Labor and Civil Liberties between the World Wars*, University of North Carolina Press, Raleigh, NC, 2012, p. 37.

618.   *The Bisbee Daily Review*, August 21, 1915, "Labor's Peace Council."

619.   *The New York Sun*, August 1, 1915, "'Labor' Men Cheer Attack on Wilson."

620.   NA RG 65 FBI Case Files, Miscellaneous file 8000-174, Agent William Benham to Department, February 3, 1917.

621.   Ibid., Letterhead of Labor's National Peace Council.

622.   *The Washington Times*, June 24, 1915, "Peace Advocates Seeking President."

623.   *The Washington Herald*, July 7, 1915, "Peace Agitators Want to Keep Ships at Home."

624.   *The New York Times*, June 24, 1915, "See Lamar's Hand in 'Labor' Peace Move."

625.   *The Day Book* (Chicago, Illinois), July 15, 1915, "Militia Held in Readiness in Bridgeport Arms Strike."

626.   *The Washington Herald*, July 18, 1915, "German Agents Incite Trouble."

627.   *The Washington Times*, July 18, 1915, "Gompers Hints at Bribes By Germans."

628.   *Ibid.*, July 20, 1915, "Standard Oil Strikers Riot Near Plant; Brick Strikes Police Inspector." Also *The Omaha Daily Bee*, July 21, 1915, "Few Machinists at Bridgeport Strike." Also *The New York Sun*, August 28, 1915, "Hackensack Strike Ends."

629.   *The Virginia Enterprise* (Virginia, Minnesota), July 23, 1915, "Three Killed in Oil Strike Riots in New Jersey."

630.   *The Day Book* (Chicago, Illinois), July 17, 1915, "All Arms Factories May Be Closed By Strike."

631.   *The Evening Public Ledger* (Philadelphia, Pennsylvania), July 21, 1915, "Unrest in Labor Circles Here Due to War Contracts."

632.   *The Washington Herald*, July 18, 1915, "German Agents Incite Trouble."

633.   *The Washington Times*, July 20, 1915, "Federation of Labor Backs Bridgeport Strike Despite German Gold."

634.   NA RG 65 FBI Case Files, M1085, File 8000-174, Case 11784-1915 Scheele et al., unnamed agent to Chief Bielaski, July 18, 1915.

635.   *The Washington Times*, August 9, 1915, "Tumulty Resents Attack on Wilson by Frank Buchanan."

636.   *Ibid.*

637.   *The Washington Herald*, August 10, 1915, "An Attack Labor Should Repudiate."

638.   NA RG 65 FBI Case Files, Miscellaneous file 8000-174, Statement of Charles Oberwager, November 1916.

639.   *New York Tribune*, August 1, 1915, "Peace Congress Belies Its Name."

640.   *The New York Sun*, August 2, 1915, "'Labor' Would Oust Dudley F. Malone."

641. *The New York Times*, August 11, 1915, "Quits Labor's Peace Council in Disgust."

642. See, for example, *The Labor Advocate* (Cincinnati, Ohio), July 17, 1915, "Well Merited Rebuke." Also *The Washington Herald*, August 1, 1915, "False Colors Hauled Down."

643. *The Tacoma Times*, August 26, 1915, "Whole City on Strike."

644. *The Watchman* (Sumter, South Carolina), September 18, 1918, "Labor Slackers Censured."

645. *The New York Evening World*, December 28, 1915, "Congressman Buchanan, Lobbyists and Labor Leader Indicted in Strike Plots."

646. *The New York Times*, May 3, 1917, "Rintelen's Agent Warned Tumulty."

647. NA RG 87 U.S. Secret Service, A1, Entry 65, Synopsis of the Franz von Rintelen Mission.

648. NA RG 65 FBI Case Files, M1085, File 8000-174, Statement of Ernest Bohm, October 24, 1916.

649. Ibid., Statement of George Plochmann. Plochmann testified that $40,000 remained in the Transatlantic Trust Company. NA RG 165 Military Intelligence Division, File 9140-646, Van Deman to Chief Bielaski, April 12, 1918. Rintelen told MID agents that he had $75,000 in funds in the United States. NA RG 65 FBI M1085 Case Files, file 8000-3089, Statement of Frederico Stallforth, April 22, 1917. Stallforth testified that he retained an additional $12,000 and $25,000 in two other bank accounts of Rintelen's. Stallforth's role in the explosion of Black Tom Island in 1916 will be covered in later chapters. Also, NA RG 59 Department of State, File 341.112 M49/39, Walter Hines Page to Robert Lansing, March 22, 1916, "He stated that he had some $75,000 to his credit at the bank in question."

650. NA RG 65 FBI Case Files, M1085, File 8000-3089, Statement of Frederico Stallforth, April 22, 1917.

651. *The New York Times*, May 2, 1917, "Rintelen Spent $508,000 In His Plot."

652. Ibid.

653. NA RG 65 FBI Case Files, M1085, File 8000-174, Accounting Ledgers of E. V. Gibbons, May, June, July 1915.

654. Ibid.

655. Ibid.

656. Ibid., Statement of Ernest Bohm, October 24, 1916.

657. Ibid., Chief Bielaski to T. C. Willis, November 11, 1915.

658. Ibid., Accounting Ledgers of E. V. Gibbons, May, June, July 1915.

659. NA RG 76 Mixed Claims Commission, Box 14, Memorandum, August 3, 1938.

H. H. Martin estimated that "Scheele received $20,000 from Rintelen and Papen... Wolpert received $57,000 from Rintelen."

660.   NA RG 65 FBI Case Files, M1085, File 8000-3089, Statement of Frederico Stallforth, April 22, 1917.

661.   Ibid., Stallforth Memo (to Boy-Ed?), August 11, 1915.

662.   Ibid., Miscellaneous File 8000-174, Testimony of George Plochmann.

663.   Ibid.

664.   Ibid., File 8000-3089, Memorandum, undated (1917).

665.   Eckardt to Bethmann Hollweg, October 12, 1915, as quoted in Katz, Friedrich, *The Secret War in Mexico: Europe, the United States, and the Mexican Revolution*, The University of Chicago Press, Chicago, IL, 1981, p. 389.

666.   *The World's Work*, Volume 36, May to October 1918, Doubleday, Page and Company, New York, NY 1918, "German Intrigue in Mexico," by George MacAdam, pp. 495-500.

667.   NA RG 242, Captured German Documents, T141, Roll 20, von Eckardt to Foreign Office, July 30, 1915.

668.   As quoted in Doerries, *Imperial Challenge*, p. 167.

669.   As quoted in Katz, *The Secret War in Mexico*, p. 343.

670.   NA RG 242, Captured German Documents, T141, Roll 19, von Papen to General Staff, March 17, 1915.

671.   Ibid.

672.   NA RG 59 Department of State, Passport #4875, issued in Berlin, February 6, 1915. Also, NA RG 59 Department of State, Passport #3138, issued in Berne, February 20, 1915. Passports at the time were issued for a specific travel location. Meloy's travel plans obviously changed abruptly on February 6th, because he went to the American Embassy and asked for an emergency paper to travel to Switzerland. Another emergency passport issued on February 20th allowed Meloy to visit more European countries. It mentioned that the "merchant" desired "to return to the U.S. via France, England, or Italy or Holland." The American consul in Berne hand wrote on the document, "good for six weeks." He left from Liverpool, Great Britain on March 17th and arrived back in New York on the 28th of the month.

673.   Ibid., File 341.112 M49/17, Walter Hines Page to Robert Lansing, September 10, 1915. No documentation of a direct link exist but the timing of Meloy's first trip coincided with the foundation of the "Mexican Peace Assembly," a group of influential Mexican exiles who were publicly appealing to all warring factions in Mexico to end the civil war. Meloy's plan of forming a coalition that could force an end to the strife seemed to be a logical extension of the "Peace Assembly." See Meyer, *Huerta*, p. 219.

674.   Ibid., File 341.112 M49/40, Statement of Juan Petit Hampson, August 21, 1915.

675. Ibid., File 341.112 M49/17, Walter Hines Page to Robert Lansing, September 10, 1915, Statement of Andrew D. Meloy.

676. Ibid. He owned stock in the Mexico North Western and Mexico Western Railways.

677. Ibid.

678. See, for example, NA RG 85 Immigration and Naturalization, T715, Roll 2263, entry for arrivals from Havana, February 21, 1914.

679. *The New York Times*, September 8, 1915, "Lansing's Mexico Service."

680. NA RG 59 Department of State, File 341.112 M49/17, Walter Hines Page to Robert Lansing, September 10, 1915, Statement of Andrew D. Meloy.

681. Ibid.

682. Ibid.

683. NA RG 65 FBI Case Files, M1085, Roll 866, File 232-1266, Statement of John Roberts.

684. Ibid.

685. Ibid., Roll 856, File 232-101, President Wilson to all chiefs of factions in Mexico. Also, *The New York Times*, June 4, 1915, "Wilson will set limit for Mexico."

686. Katz, Friedrich, *The Life and Times of Pancho Villa*, Stanford University Press, Stanford, CA, 1998, p. 529. Also, Lansing, Robert, *War Memoirs of Robert Lansing, Secretary of State*, The Bobbs-Merrill Company, New York, NY, 1935, p. 308.

687. Katz, *Life and Times of Pancho Villa*, pp. 506-507.

688. NA RG 59 Department of State, File 341.112 M49, Statement of Andrew D. Meloy, London, August 23, 1915.

689. Ibid.

690. Ibid., File 812.00/15286½, Woodrow Wilson to Robert Lansing, June 18, 1915.

691. *The New York Times*, August 4, 1915, "Says Germany Used Huerta Against Us."

692. NA RG 59 Department of State, File 341.112 M49, Statement of Andrew D. Meloy, London, August 23, 1915.

693. Ibid., File 341.112 M49/17, Counselor Warren to Leon Canova, September 15, 1915.

694. NA RG 65 Albert Papers, Box 13, Boy-Ed to Albert, July 21, 1915.

695. NA RG 59 Department of State, File 341.112 M49/17, Walter Hines Page to Robert Lansing, September 10, 1915.

696. NA RG 165 Military Intelligence Division, File 9140-878/129, Memorandum, March 19, 1918.

697. NA RG 59 Department of State, File 341.112 M49/17, Walter Hines Page to Robert Lansing, September 10, 1915.

698. *The New York Times*, April 11, 1915, "Villa Men Want Huerta Barred." Also *The New York Tribune*, April 1, 1915, "Huerta on Way for New Revolt."

699. *The New York Tribune*, April 13, 1915, "Exiled Dictator Silent on Mexican Affairs."

700. *The New York Times* and other papers reported when Huerta left Spain. See *The New York Times*, April 1, 1915, "Gen. Huerta on Ship Bound to West Indies."

701. *The New York Times*, May 6, 1915, "Huerta Will Make Future Home Here."

702. *New York Tribune*, May 6, 1915, "Huerta for Long Island."

703. Library of Congress, Photographs and Prints Division, LC-USZ62-97991, copyright expired.

704. *The New York Times*, May 6, 1915, "Huerta Will Make Future Home Here."

705. NA RG 59 Department of State, File 351.112M49/46, Assistant Attorney General Warren to Secretary of State Lansing, September 15, 1915. Reference is made to a letter Rintelen wrote to Charles Douglas, in which he claims he "has been in Orozco's confidence."

706. NA RG 65 M1085, FBI Case Files, Roll 864, Agent Cantrell to Chief, September 30, 1915.

707. Ibid.

708. Lozano, Ann, "Seminary of St. Philip for Mexican students." Handbook of Texas Online (http://www.tshaonline.org/handbook/online/articles/iws01), accessed October 25, 2013. Published by the Texas State Historical Association.

709. See von Feilitzsch, *In Plain Sight*, chapter 13, "The Sommerfeld Organization."

710. NA RG 65, FBI Case Files, M1085, Roll 859, File 232-162, Agent Beckham to Chief, May 6, 1915. Sommerfeld still controlled his former employees, Powell Roberts, Hector Ramos, Sam Dreben, and Emil Holmdahl who all were providing information on the conspirators to the American government.

711. NA RG 65, FBI Case Files, M1085, Roll 859, File 232-162, Agent Beckham to Chief, May 3, 1915.

712. See von Feilitzsch, *In Plain Sight*, chapter 13. Also Meyer, Michael C, *Mexican Rebel: Pascual Orozco and the Mexican Revolution, 1910-1915*, University of Nebraska Press, Lincoln, NE, 1967, p. 82.

713. NA RG 65 FBI Case Files, M1085, Roll 859 file 232-162, Agent Beckham to Chief, April 24, 1915, re. Científico Movement.

714. Ibid., Agent Beckham to Chief, May 12, 1915.

715. Ibid., Roll 858, file 232-162, Agent Stone to Chief Bielaski, August 14, 1915.

716.   For example Ibid., Roll 859, file 232-164, Sherburne Hopkins to Chief Bielaski, July 13, 1915.

717.   *The New York Times*, May 3, 1915, "Gen. Huerta's Aid to Open Bank Here."

718.   NA RG 65 FBI Case Files, M1085, Roll 859, File 232-162, Sec. War to Attorney General, May 6, 1915.

719.   NA RG 165 Military Intelligence Division, File 5761-1091/6, Sommerfeld to Secretary Garrison, April 23, 1915.

720.   NA RG 85 Immigration and Naturalization, T715, Roll 2417.

721.   *The New York Times*, June 24, 1915, "Villa Agent at Capital."

722.   Harris, Charles H., III and Sadler, Louis R., *The Secret War in El Paso: Mexican Revolutionary Intrigue, 1906-1920*, University of New Mexico Press, Albuquerque, NM, 2009, p. 197.

723.   Ibid.

724.   See, for example, NA RG 65, FBI Case Files, M1085, BI reports dated May 2, 1915, May 6, 1915, May 27, 1915, June 7, 1915. Also NA RG 59 Department of State, File 812.113/3674, Cobb to Secretary of State, June 4, 1915, "Statement of arms and ammunition exported from El Paso, April 12 to June 4, 1915 ... Villa has consumed half of above."

725.   Boy-Ed, Karl, *Verschwörer?* Verlag August Scherl GmbH, Berlin, Germany, 1920, p. 83.

726.   Ibid.

727.   *The Washington Times*, May 2, 1915, "Masons Expel Huerta, Félix Díaz, and Others."

728.   Ibid.

729.   NA RG 59 State Department, File 341.112M49/40, Walter H. Page to Robert Lansing, April 3, 1916.

730.   NA RG 65 FBI Case Files, M1085, Roll 859, file 232, BI reports from May 20-24.

731.   Ibid., file 232-162, Agent Cantrell to Chief Bielaski, July 3, 1915.

732.   NA RG 59 Department of State, File 812.113/3644, 3645, 3646, 3647.

733.   Ibid.

734.   NA RG 65 FBI Case Files, M1085, Roll 859, file 232-162, Agent Beckham to Chief Bielaski, May 12, 1915.

735.   Michael C. Meyer, "The Mexican-German Conspiracy of 1915," *The Americas*, Volume XXIII, July, 1966, No. 1, p. 86. Also, Chalkley, John F., *Zach Lamar Cobb: El Paso Collector of Customs and Intelligence During the Mexican Revolution, 1913-1918*, Southwestern Studies, No. 103, University of Texas Press, El Paso, TX, 1998, p. 30.

736.   Ibid., p. 31.

737.   *The New York Tribune*, June 27, 1915, "New Huerta Plot Afoot on Border."

738.   See Meyer, *Huerta*, pp. 226-227 for a more detailed discussion.

739.   Harris and Sadler, *The Secret War in El Paso*, pp. 203-209.

740.   Ibid., p. 510.

741.   Ibid., p. 509.

742.   Ibid., p. 510.

743.   NA RG 65 FBI Case Files, M1085, Roll 858, File 232-162, Agent Benham to Department, November 6, 1915.

744.   See Jones and Hollister, Landau, Tuchman, Katz, Meyer, Harris and Sadler.

745.   *The New York Times*, August 4, 1915, "Says Germany Used Huerta Against Us."

746.   Ibid.

747.   Tuchman, Barbara, *The Zimmermann Telegram*, Macmillan Company, New York, NY, 1958, p. 76.

748.   Rintelen's supposed trip to Spain before he came to the United States is also not factual. Rintelen was in Belgium before he came to the U.S. There are no reports that he went to Spain in 1915 nor that he had any meetings with Huerta in Europe. See Bundesarchiv für Militärgeschichte, RM 3, 7934, War financing.

749.   NA RG 59 State Department, File 341.112M49/40, Page to Lansing, April 3, 1916.

750.   Ibid., File 341.112M49/15.

751.   See previous chapter.

752.   NA RG 65 FBI Case Files, M1085, file 8000-174, Testimony of George Plochmann, undated (October 1915).

753.   *The Washington Times*, July 2, 1915, "Consignment of Arms Intended for Batavia are Confiscated in Brooklyn." Also, *The New York Sun*, July 2, 1915, "Shipment of Arms Reported Seized."

754.   NA RG 65 FBI Case Files, M1085, Roll 855, File 232-37, W. Stokes Kirk to Howard P. Wright, January 6, 1917.

755.   NA RG 131 Alien Property Custodian, Entry 199, Box 38, File 902, Winchester Repeating Arms Co.

756.   NA RG 76 Mixed Claims Commission, Box 13, Memorandum, August 3, 1938. "July 16, 1915, Rintelen paid Meloy $10,000 through Stallforth."

757.   NA RG 65 FBI Case Files, M1085, Roll 859, file 232-162, Agent Pinckney to Chief Bielaski, July 7, 1915, list of Huerta recruits with sums paid to each of them.

758. Ibid., Agent Barnes to Chief Bielaski, August 14, 1915.

759. Ibid., Agent Cantrell to Chief Bielaski, July 3, 1915

760. As quoted in Katz, *The Secret War in Mexico*, p. 248.

761. NA RG 65 FBI Case Files, M1085, Roll 859, file 232-162, Statement of José Vasconcelos, June 30, 1915.

762. Ibid., Agent Cantrell to Chief Bielaski, July 3, 1915.

763. Katz, *Life and Times of Pancho Villa*, p. 506.

764. *The New York Times*, September 8, 1915, "Lansing's Mexico Service." The article quotes a piece in *El Mexicano* alleging Lansing's legal services for Huerta.

765. See, for example, NA RG 60 Department of Justice, File 9-16-12-5305, Sommerfeld to Boy-Ed November 11, 1914, Boy-Ed to Count Bernstorff, December 18, 1914, Sommerfeld to Boy-Ed, April 28, 1915, Sommerfeld to Boy-Ed, May 4, 1915.

766. NA RG 242 Captured German Documents, Roll 377, document 735, Dernburg to von Holtzendorff, May 10, 1915.

767. The response from Foreign Secretary von Jagow is referred to in Katz, *Secret War in Mexico*, p. 334.

768. NA RG 65 FBI Case Files, M1085, File 8000-174, Agent Offley to Chief Bielaski, June 28, 1915.

769. Willis tried everything in his power to get Sommerfeld released in 1918, such as getting General Hugh Lenox Scott to write a letter on his friend's behalf, as well as, writing himself to the Justice Department.

770. Ibid.

771. *The New York Sun*, May 26, 1915, "Even British Ships Broke Own Blockade."

772. *The New York Times*, May 3, 1917, "Rintelen's Agent Warned Tumulty."

773. Ibid.

774. NA RG 65 FBI Case Files, M1085, File 8000-174, Agent Offley to Chief Bielaski, September 29, 1915.

775. Ibid.

776. Doerries, *Introduction to Rintelen's The Dark Invader*, p. xxii.

777. NA RG 65 FBI Case Files, M1085, File 8000-3089, Captured document from Stallforth's office, report entry for August 13, 1915.

778. NA RG 59 Department of State, File 341.112 M49/35, Count Bernstorff to Secretary Lansing, December 15, 1915. Also Ibid., 341.112M49/60 Robert Lansing to Woodrow Wilson, May 23, 1918.

779. *The Federal Reporter*, Volume 274, West Publishing Company, St. Paul,

Minnesota, 1921, p. 172. Also NA Southeast Region, Index to Atlanta Federal Penitentiary, Inmate Case Files, 1902-1921, File 5780, "Conspiracy and Delivery of Bomb Onboard Ship."

780.   NA RG 65 Albert Papers, Box 23, Koenig to Albert, undated memorandum.

781.   Ibid.

782.   As quoted in *American Revolution to World War II*, Chapter 3, Central Intelligence Reader, www.fas.org, viewed January 24, 2013.

783.   NA RG 65 Albert Papers, Box 23, Memorandum on lost briefcase, unknown author and date.

784.   *The New York World*, August 15, 1915, "How Germany Worked in U.S. to Shape Opinion, Block the Allies, and Get Munitions for Herself, Told in Secret Agent's Letters."

785.   *The New York Times*, August 17, 1915, "May Involve Embassy Men."

786.   Ibid.

787.   *Ibid.*, August 15, 1915, "May Prosecute Agents." The article covers the reporting of the *Providence Journal*.

788.   *Ibid.*, August 17, 1915, "May Involve Embassy Men."

789.   Ibid.

790.   Ibid.

791.   Ibid.

792.   NA RG 65 Albert Papers, Box 23, Letter to Ida, January 17, 1916.

793.   *The New York World*, August 15, 16, 17, 18, 1915.

794.   Papers of Woodrow Wilson, "Americanism and the Foreign Born," May 10, 1915.

795.   Bauer, Hermann, *Als Führer der U-Boote im Weltkriege: Der Eintritt der U-Boot-Waffe in die Seekriegsführung*, p. 342.

796.   Ibid., 340.

797.   *The New York Times*, August 30, 1915, "German Navy Man in Fire Bomb Case." Six men had been arrested earlier that week for suspicion of smuggling pencil bombs only on ships. The New York Bomb Squad had shadowed the men since the end of July. See also Tunney, *Throttled*.

798.   See, for example, *The Washington Times*, September 2, 1915, "U.S. Starts Probe." Also, The New York Tribune, September 3, 1915, "Held in Britain as Kaiser's Spy."

799.   *The New York Times*, June 30, 1915, "Seize Ship with Arms."

800.   NA RG 65 Albert Papers, Box 33, Tauscher to von Papen, July 30, 1915.

801.   *The New York Tribune*, July 2, 1915, "Rifles for Java Seized on Dock by U.S. Agents."

802.   *The Ogden Standard*, December 10, 1915; Also Marine Crew Chronik MIM620/ CREW, Marineschule Mürwik, Flensburg, Deutschland, p. 46. Both sources mistakenly cite the *HMS Baralong* as the British ship. See www.uboat.net for more details on the Q-ship fleet.

803.   *The New York Times*, February 9, 1916, "Consul of Germany and his Aid Indicted."

804.   Lansing, *War Memoirs of Robert Lansing*, p. 77.

805.   Link, Arthur S., *Woodrow Wilson and the Progressive Era, 1910 - 1917*, Harper and Brothers Publishers, New York, NY, 1954, p. 200. See also NA RG 65 FBI Case Files, M1085, File 8000-174, Agent Cantrell to Department, interview with Mr. Hammond, July 23, 1915.

806.   Link, *Woodrow Wilson and the Progressive Era*, p. 200.

807.   NA RG 59 State Department, File 341.112 M49/46, Assistant Attorney General Warren to Secretary Lansing, September 15, 1915.

808.   NA RG 65 FBI Case Files, M1085, File 8000-174, William Offley to Chief Bielaski, October 7, 1915. The memo contains the full transaction record of Rintelen's two accounts with the Transatlantic Trust Company.

809.   Doenecke, Justus D., *Nothing Less Than War: A New History of America's Entry into World War I*, The University Press of Kentucky, Lexington, KY, 2011, p. 146.

810.   Lansing, *War Memoirs of Robert Lansing*, p. 84.

811.   *The New York Times*, August 2, 1915, "Shanklin here from Mexico." The *Times* quotes the *Army and Navy Journal* referring to Wilson Administration policy towards Mexico.

812.   NA RG 76 Mixed Claims Commission, Box 5, William W. Flynn (son of the former Secret Service Chief) to William Kiler, June 5, 1931.

813.   See the actual phone transcripts in NA RG 131 Alien Property Custodian, Box 165.

814.   *The New York Times*, November 27, 1915, "Try to Bar Evidence of Quesada's Cruise." Also, *The New York Times*, November 28, 1915, "Boy-Ed Not to Testify."

815.   *The New York Times*, September 16, 1918, "Karl Buenz Dies in Atlanta Prison."

816.   NA RG 65 FBI Case Files M1085, Roll 264, file 156.

817.   Ibid., File 8000-174, Agent Offley to Department, March 9, 1916. Stallforth steadfastly refused to testify in 1915, was finally slapped with contempt of court and arrested on February 24, 1916. See *The New York Herald*, February 26, 1916, "German Banker Gives Bond." After stringent interviews he finally caved and spilled all he knew.

818.   *The New York Times*, October 2, 1915, "Trace Meloy in Mexico."

819. Scott, Hugh Lenox, *Some Memories of a Soldier*, The Century Company, New York, NY, 1928, p. 514.

820. See von Feilitzsch, *In Plain Sight*, Chapter 2, "Boyish Mistakes."

821. NA RG 65 Albert Papers, Box 1, Boy-Ed to Hossenfelder, October 28, 1915.

822. Ibid., Hossenfelder to Boy-Ed, October 28, 1915.

823. NA RG 60 Department of Justice, File 9-16-12-5305, Statement of F. A. Sommerfeld, June 22, 1918. See, also, von Feilitzsch, *In Plain Sight*, pp. 12-13.

824. NA RG 65 FBI Case Files, M1085, Roll 865, file 232-931, Memo E. B. Stone to Bielaski October 25, 1916.

825. *The New York Evening News*, December 3, 1915, "Boy-Ed Said Persona Non Grata."

826. Lansing, *War Memoirs of Robert Lansing*, pp. 72-75. The Secretary of State maintained that Boy-Ed was the man behind the navy supply operation, and that he was somehow involved in the passport fraud scheme. He does not mention the Rintelen funding as a reason.

827. NA RG 76 Mixed Claims Commission, Box 14, Memorandum , June 7, 1932, discussing von Papen.

828. *The New York Times*, September 6, 1915, "Dumba Admits Plot to Cripple Munitions Plants."

829. *The Washington Herald*, September 26, 1915, "Von Papen Explains 'Those Idiotic Yankees'."

830. Rintelen, *The Dark Invader*.

831. Rintelen, *The Return of the Dark Invader*.

832. See, for example, *The Milwaukee Journal*, November 5, 1943, "A True Story of First World War Spies That Outdoes Most Imaginative Fiction." Also, *Delaware County Daily Times*, July 30. 1966, "50 Years Ago U.S. Felt Part of War." "In January 1940, von Rintelen declared he conceived the idea of the Black Tom explosion and while he was not in the United States at the time, he was certain it was carried out by his aides. 'I wanted to destroy the source of supply, but I issued orders that it be done without killing anyone,' Von Rintelen said. 'My idea was that I could get the watchmen drunk and the rest would be easy.'" See, also, NA RG 65 FBI Case Files, M1085, File 8000-174, Statement of J.C. Hammond, July 16, 1915.

833. See, for example, NA RG 65 FBI Case Files, M1085, File 8000-174, Agent Garbering to Chief Bielaski, September 27, 1916.

834. Ibid., Statement of J.C. Hammond, July 16, 1915. Also Ibid., Agent Offley to Chief Bielaski, October 15, 1915.

835. Ibid., Statement of Paul Hilken.

836. Bundesarchiv für Militärgeschichte, Freiburg, RM 3, File 7934, Rintelen to von Tirpitz, November 9, 1914.

837. NA RG 65 FBI Case Files, M1085, File 8000-174, Statement of J. C. Hammond, July 16, 1915.

838. NA RG 87 U.S. Secret Service, A1, entry 65, "Synopsis of Franz von Rintelen mission."

839. NA RG 65 FBI Case Files, M1085, File 8000-174, Statement of George Plochmann, undated (October 1915).

840. Stallforth Papers, Private collection, Correspondence 1915, Proposal of Stallforth Inc. as a successor of Stallforth Brothers. Records indicate that Stallforth had defaulted on a $50,000 loan for his family company in March 1915. Indeed, he did get Heinrich Albert to invest $50,000 in the new company Stallforth Inc. in April 1916.

841. NA RG 165 Military Intelligence Division, File 9140-878, Document 129, Memorandum on Stallforth and Company.

842. NA RG 65 FBI Case Files, M1085, File 8000-3089, Statement of Frederico Stallforth, April 22, 1917.

843. Stallforth Papers, Private Collection, Letter from Oren Sanborn to Frederico Stallforth, November 4, 1915.

844. See, for example, Stallforth papers, Private Collection, Letter from Hugo Schmidt to Stallforth March 7, 1916, whereby the Deutsche Bank grants a stay for his outstanding debt.

845. NA RG 65 FBI Case Files, M1085, File 8000-3089, Statement of Melville S. Forrester, April 19, 1917. This recruit came to the attention of the U.S. Secret Service in 1917, after he decided to snitch on his handlers.

846. NA RG 65 FBI Case Files, M1085, File 8000-3089, Statement of Frederico Stallforth, April 22, 1917.

847. Ibid.

848. Ibid.

849. Stallforth Papers, Private collection, William H. Wherry, Jr. to Frederick [sic] Stallforth, June 14, 1916.

850.

851. NA RG 65 FBI Case Files, M1085, File 8000-3089, Bielaski to Warren, August 29, 1917.

852. NA RG 76 Mixed Claims Commission, Box 7, Hilken Diary, Entry for August 16, 1915.

853. NA RG 65 FBI Case Files, M1085, File 8000-3089, Stallforth to Albert, Captured document from Stallforth's office, entry for August 14, 1915.

854.   Ibid., entry for August 13, 1915.

855.   NA RG 65 FBI Case Files, File 8000-3069, Interview between A. Bruce Bielaski and Frederico Stallforth, undated (likely April 1917).

856.   John Singleton, "Britain's Military Use of Horses 1914-1918," *Past and Present*, Oxford University Press, No. 139 (May 1993), p. 178.

857.   NA RG 59 Department of State, Emergency Passport Applications, Argentina through Venezuela, 1906-1925, A1 544, Box 4776, Record 176.

858.   NA RG 85 Immigration and Naturalization, T 715, Roll, 2435, page 131.

859.   "A New Era of Biological Warfare," by Annelie Wendeberg, www.scilogs.com, August 2013.

860.   Ibid.

861.   NA RG 76 Mixed Claims Commission, Box 14, Memorandum, Re: References in sabotage record to Stallforth, February 17, 1931. Also Ibid., Box 3, Timeline of Anton Dilger in the United States. The lawyers of the American team mistakenly claimed that Dilger arrived in April and had meetings with Stallforth, Hinsch, and Hilken in August and September 1915. Hilken's diary recounts meetings with "Dr," probably referring to Dr. Scheele, not Dilger. His INovember diary entry for meetings with Dr. Dilger show "Dr. D."

862.   NA RG 76 Mixed Claims Commission, Box 6, Deposition of Friedrich Hinsch, Berlin, August 1930.

863.   Ibid.

864.   Ibid.

865.   NA RG 76 Mixed Claims Commission, Box 7, Hilken Diary 1915.

866.   NA RG 76 Mixed Claims Commission, Box 6, Deposition of Friedrich Hinsch, Berlin, August 1930.

867.   NA RG 76 Mixed Claims Commission, Box 6, Statement of Frederick L. Herrmann, October 21, 1931.

868.   NA RG 76 Mixed Claims Commission, Box 13, Memorandum August 3, 1938, Re Testimony of six principal German witnesses.

869.   NA RG 76 Mixed Claims Commission, Box 6, Deposition of Friedrich Hinsch, Berlin, August 1930..

870.   NA RG 76 Mixed Claims Commission, Box 14, Memorandum, Re: Denials by German Officials of Sabotage Activities During the Period of Neutrality, February 27, 1934.

871.   NA RG 65 FBI Case Files, M1085, File 8000-174, Statement of George Plochmann. Plochmann testified that $40,000 remained in the Transatlantic Trust Company. NA RG 165 Military Intelligence Division, File 9140-646, Van Deman to Chief Bielaski, April

12, 1918. Rintelen told MID agents that he had $75,000 in funds in the United States. NA RG 65 FBI M1085 Case Files, file 8000-3089, Statement of Frederico Stallforth, April 22, 1917. Stallforth testified that he retained an additional $12,000 and $25,000 in two other bank accounts of Rintelen's. Stallforth's role in the explosion of Black Tom Island in 1916 will be covered in later chapters. Also, NA RG 59 Department of State, File 341.112 M49/39, Walter Hines Page to Robert Lansing, March 22, 1916, "He stated that he had some $75,000 to his credit at the bank in question."

872.   NA RG 76 Mixed Claims Commission, Box 14, Paul Hilken testimony, June 7, 1933.

873.   Stallforth Papers, Private Collection, Indenture, dated September 4, 1915 by Anita and Frederico Stallforth.

874.   NA RG 76 Mixed Claims Commission, Box 8, Deposition of Friedrich Hinsch, August 1930.

875.   Ibid., Testimony of Edward Felton, April 11, 1930.

876.   Ibid., Deposition of Friedrich Hinsch, August 1930.

877.   Ibid., Diary of Paul L. Hilken for 1915.

878.   Ibid.

879.   Ibid.

880.   Ibid.

881.   Ibid., Entry for August 29, "Capt. H. at 5:12 with Dr. & Hispe... " Also, entry for August 31, "11:54 to N.Y. Capt. B." September 1, "meet B[ode] and ST[allforth]"

882.   Ibid., see entries in June, July, August, September all referring to "K."

883.   The New York Times, December 18, 1915, "Virginia Barge with Horses for French Government Sinks."

884.   The New York Times, August 26, 1915, "Say German Agents Stampeded Horses."

885.   The New York Times, August 19, 1915, "Fake Passport May Solve Sea Mystery."

886.   Koenig, The Fourth Horseman, p. 313.

887.   www.pbs.org/wgbh/americanexperience, viewed 12-2013.

888.   See National Army Museum, London. www.nam.ac.uk viewed 12-2013.

889.   Statistics of the Military Effort of the British Empire During the Great War, 1914-1920 WO 3/22.

890.   NA RG 76 Mixed Claims Commission, Box 8, Diary of Paul Hilken, entry for August 31, 1915.

891.   NA RG 65 Albert Papers, Box 24, Letter to Ida, September 13, 1915.

892.   See earlier notation in Hilken's diary on September 21, "Get 500 fr. St. [from

Stallforth] after much trouble."

893. NA RG 65 FBI Case Files, M1085, File 8000-925.

894. *The New York Times*, April 15, 1916, "Bomb Plot Men, Deserted in Jail, May Name Chiefs."

895. NA RG 65 FBI Case Files, M1085, File 8000-925. The debriefing went on for months, filling entire filing cabinets with Scheele's information.

896. *The New York Times*, October 16, 1920, "Wall Street Explosion Laid to Gelatin."

897. Ibid.

898. NA RG 87 U.S. Secret Service, A1, Entry 65, "Synopsis of Franz von Rintelen Mission."

899. *The New York Times*, January 6, 1916. Also *The New York Times*, May 1, 1916.

900. The losses are an aggregate of the reported damages in newspapers. Excluding the $12 Million losses of the Salem, Massachusetts fire in June 1914, the total comes to $10,235,000

901. Ibid.

902. *The Philadelphia Evening Public Ledger*, July 21, 1915, "Two More U.S. Warships Attacked by Fire Epidemic" and "Nine Compartments Damaged By Flames On Great Warship."

903. Tunney mentioned these three ships as bombed in January and February 1915. The *Hennington Court* he quoted actually was the *SS Hanmington Court*, which was firebombed in February 1916. The other two ships could not be verified at all.

904. NA RG 65 FBI Case Files, File 8000-925, Debriefing of Scheele in 1918.

905. NA RG 65 FBI Case Files, M1085, File 8000-3089, Report captured in Frederico Stallforth's office in 1917, entry for August 13, 1915.

906. *The New York Times*, May 18, 1915, "Sailings for War Zone." The article mentions that surety bonds for cargo were up by 100% for transatlantic transport.

907. NA RG 76 Mixed Claims Commission Box 14, Exhibit 128, Interview with Friedrich Hinsch, August 21, 1930.

BIBLIOGRAPHY:
SECONDARY LITERATURE

Ackermann, Carl W., *Mexico's Dilemma*, George H. Doran Company, New York, 1918.

Albertini, Luigi, *The Origins of the War of 1914*, vols. 1-3, Enigma Books, New York, 2005.

Baecker, Thomas, *Die deutsche Mexikopolitik 1913/14*, Colloquium Verlag, Berlin 1971.

Bailey, Thomas A., Ryan, Paul B., *The Lusitania Disaster: The Real Answers behind the World's most controversial Sea Tragedy*, The Free Press, New York, NY, 1975.

Baker, Ray Stannard, *Woodrow Wilson, Life and Letters*, seven volumes, Doubleday, Doran and Company, New York, 1938.

Bernstein, Herman, *Celebrities of our time: Interviews*, Joseph Lawren, New York, 1924.

Bihl, Wolf Dieter, ed., *Deutsche Quellen zur Geschichte des Ersten Weltkrieges*, Wissenschaftliche Buchgesellschaft, Darmstadt, 1991.

Bisher, Jamie, *World War I Intelligence in Latin America*, unpublished manuscript, 2008.

Bonsor, N. R. P., *North Atlantic Seaway: An Illustrated History of the Passenger Services Linking the Old World with the New*, four volumes, Brookside Publications, Wheat Ridge, Colorado, 1978.

Calvert, Peter, *The Mexican Revolution 1910-1914: The Diplomacy of Anglo-American Conflict*, Cambridge University Press, New York, 1968.

Carlisle, Rodney P., *World War I,* Facts on File Inc., New York, 2007.

Carosso, Vincent P., Carosso, Rose C., *The Morgans: Private International Bankers, 1854-1913*, Harvard Studies in Business History, Harvard University Press, Cambridge, MA, 1987.

Cartarius, Ulrich ed., *Deutschland im Ersten Weltkrieg: Texte und Dokumente*, DTV, München, 1982.

Cecil, Lamar, *Albert Ballin: Wirtschaft und Politik im Deutschen Kaiserreich*, Hoffmann und Campe, Hamburg, 1969.

Chalkley, John F., *Zach Lamar Cobb: El Paso Collector of Customs and Intelligence During the Mexican Revolution, 1913-1918*, Southwestern Studies, No. 103, University of Texas Press, El Paso, TX, 1998.

Clendenen, Clarence, *The United States and Pancho Villa: A study in unconventional diplomacy*, Cornell University Press, Ithaca, New York, 1961.

Colby, Frank Moore, Williams, Talcott, eds., *The New International Encyclopedia*, Volume 24, Dodd, Mead, and Company, New York, 1918.

Collier, Peter and Horowitz, David, *The Rockefellers, An American Dynasty*, Summit Books, New York, NY, 1989.

Cooper, John Milton Jr., *Woodrow Wilson: A Biography*, Alfred A. Knopf, New York, 2009.

Cumberland, Charles C., *Mexican Revolution: The Constitutionalist Years*, University of Texas Press, Austin, TX, 1974.

Daniels, Josephus, *The Life of Woodrow Wilson*, John C. Winston Company, Chicago, Philadelphia, 1924.

De Bekker, Leander Jan, *The Plot Against Mexico*, Alfred A. Knopf Publishers, New York, NY, 1919.

Dehn, Paul, Dernburg, Bernhard, Hale, William Bayard, Hall, Thomas C. and various editors, *The Truth About Germany: Facts about the War*, The Trow Press, New York, NY, 1914.

Doenecke, Justus D., *Nothing Less Than War: A New History of America's Entry into World War I*, The University Press of Kentucky, Lexington, KY, 2011.

Doerries, Reinhard R., *Imperial Challenge: Ambassador Count Bernstorff and German-American Relations, 1908-1917*, University of North Carolina Press, Chapel Hill, NC, 1989.

Doerries, Reinhard R., Editor, *Diplomaten und Agenten: Nachrichtendienste in der Geschichte der deutsch-amerikanischen Beziehungen*, Universitätsverlag C. Winter, Heidelberg, Germany, 2001.

Doerries, Reinhard R., *Prelude to the Easter Rising: Sir Roger Casement in Imperial Germany*, Frank Cass Publishers, Portland, OR, 2000.

Ecke, Heinz, *Four Spies Speak*, John Hamilton Limited, London, Great Britain, 1933.

Eisenhower, John S. D., *Intervention! The United States and the Mexican Revolution, 1913-1917*, W.W. Norton and Company Inc., New York, 1993.

Fabela, Isidro, *Historia diplomática de la Revolución Mexicana*, vol. I. (1912-1917), México Ciudad, Fondo de Cultura Económica, 1958.

Feldman, Gerald D., *Army, Industry, and Labor in Germany, 1914-1918*, Berg Publishers Inc., Providence, RI, 1992.

Fischer, Fritz, *Griff nach der Weltmacht: Die Kriegszielpolitik des kaiserlichen Deutschland 1914/18*, Droste Verlag, Düsseldorf, 1961.

French, David, *British Economic and Strategic Planning 1905 to 1915*,

Routledge Library Editions, Abingdon, Great Britain, 2006.

Fuehr, Karl Alexander, *The Neutrality of Belgium: A Study of the Belgian Case under its Aspects in Political History and International Law*, Funk and Wagnalls Company, New York, 1915.

Gabrielan, Randall, *Rumson: Shaping a Superlative Suburb*, Arcadia Publishing, Charleston, SC, 2003.

Geiss, Immanuel, Ed., *July 1914: The Outbreak of the First World War: Selected Documents*, Charles Scribner's and Sons, New York, 1967.

Geissler, Erhard, *Biologische Waffen – Nicht in Hitlers Arsenalen: Biologische and Toxin-Kampfmittel von 1915 bis 1945*, LIT Verlag, Münster, Germany, 1999.

Gerhardt, Johannes, *Albert Ballin*, Hamburg University Press, Hamburg, 2010.

Hadley, Michael L., Sarty, Roger Flynn, *Tin-Pots and Pirate Ships: Canadian Naval Forces and German Sea Raiders 1880 – 1918*, McGill-Queens University Press, 1991.

Hale, William Bayard, *Germany's Just Cause*, The Fatherland Press, 1914.

Hale, William Bayard, *The Case Against Armed Merchantmen*, timely reprints from the New York Press, "The Real Issue in Washington," pp. 6-9, unknown publisher, undated (1915).

Haley, Edward P., *Revolution and Intervention: The Diplomacy of Taft and Wilson with Mexico, 1910-1917*, The MIT Press, Cambridge, MA, 1970.

Hamilton, Douglas T., *Shrapnel Shell Manufacture*, The New Industrial Press, New York, NY, 1915.

Hardach, Gerd, *The First World War, 1914-1918*, University of California Press, Berkeley and Los Angeles, 1977.

Harris, Charles H., III and Sadler, Louis R., *The Secret War in El Paso: Mexican Revolutionary Intrigue, 1906-1920*, University of New Mexico Press, Albuquerque, NM, 2009.

Harris, Charles H., III and Sadler, Louis R., *The Texas Rangers and the Mexican Revolution: The Bloodiest Decade, 1910-1920*, University of New Mexico Press, Albuquerque, NM, 2004.

Hau, George William, *War Echoes or Germany and Austria in the Crisis*, Morton M. Malone, Chicago, 1915.

Hirst, David Wayne, *German Propaganda in the United States, 1914-1917*, Northwestern University PhD. Dissertation, Evanston, IL, 1962.

Hopkins, J. Castell, editor, *The Canadian annual review of public affairs, 1915*, The Annual Review Publishing Company, Toronto, 1916.

Huertner, Johannes, editor, *Paul von Hintze: Marineoffizier, Diplomat, Staatssekretär, Dokumente einer Karriere zwischen Militär und Politik, 1903-1918*, Harald Boldt Verlag, München, Germany, 1998.

Huldermann, Bernhard, *Albert Ballin*, Cassell and Company Ltd., New York, NY, 1922.

Jeffreys, Diarmuid, *Aspirin: The Remarkable Story of a Wonder Drug*, Bloomsbury Publishing, New York, NY, 2005.

Jeffreys-Jones, Rhodri, *Cloak and Dollar: A History of American Secret Intelligence*, Yale University Press, New Haven, CT, 2002.

Jensen, Joan M., *The Price of Vigilance*, Rand McNally and Company, Chicago, IL, New York, NY, 1968.

Jones, John Price, *The German Spy in America: The Secret Plotting of German Spies in the United States and the Inside Story of the Sinking of the Lusitania*, Hutchinson and Co., London, Great Britain, 1917.

Jones, John Price, Hollister, Paul Merrick, *The German Secret Service in America, 1914-1918*, Small, Maynard and Company, Boston, MA 1918.

Katz, Friedrich, *The Secret War in Mexico: Europe, the United States, and the Mexican Revolution*, The University of Chicago Press, Chicago, IL, 1981.

Katz, Friedrich, *The Life and Times of Pancho Villa*, Stanford University Press, Stanford, CA, 1998.

Keegan, John, *The First World War*, Alfred A. Knopf, Inc., New York, NY 1999.

Kelly, Patrick J., *Tirpitz and the Imperial German Navy*, Indiana University Press, Bloomington, IN, 2011.

Kessler, Graf Harry, *Walther Rathenau: His Life and Work*, Harcourt, Brace and Company, New York, NY, 1930.

Knight, Alan, *The Mexican Revolution: Volume 2: Counter-revolution and Reconstruction*, Cambridge University Press, Cambridge, MA, 1986.

Koenig, Louis W., *Bryan: A Political Biography of William Jennings Bryan*, G.P. Putnam's Sons, New York, NY, 1971.

Koenig, Robert L., *The Fourth Horseman: One Man's Mission to Wage the Great War in America*, Public Affairs, New York, NY, 2006.

Koerver, Joachim, ed., *German Submarine Warfare 1914-1918 in the Eyes of British Intelligence: Selected Sources from the British National Archives, Kew*, Schaltungsdienst Lange, Berlin, Germany, 2010.

Landau, Henry, *The Enemy Within: The Inside Story of German Sabotage in America*, G.P. Putnam's Sons, New York, NY, 1937.

Leibson, Art, *Sam Dreben, the Fighting Jew*, Westernlore Press, Tucson, AZ, 1996.

Lemke, William, *Crimes Against Mexico*, Great West Publishing

Company, Minneapolis, MN, 1915.

Lill, Thomas Russell, *National Debt of Mexico: History and Present Status*, Searle, Nicholson and Lill C.P.A.'s, New York, NY, 1919.

Link, Arthur S., editor, *Woodrow Wilson and a revolutionary world, 1913-1921*, New York, NY, 1982.

Link, Arthur S., *Wilson and the Progressive Era 1910 to 1917*, Harper and Brothers, New York, NY, 1954.

Link, Arthur S., *The Papers of Woodrow Wilson*, vols. 23-26, Princeton University Press, Princeton, NJ, 1966.

Löwer, Thomas, *American Jews in World War I - German Propaganda Courting the American Jewry*, München, GRIN Publishing GmbH, 2004.

Love, Alaina and Cugnon, Marc , *The Purpose Linked Organization: How passionate leaders inspire winning teams and great results*, McGraw Hill, New York, NY, 2009.

Ludwig, Emil, *Wilhelm Hohenzollern: The Last of the Kaisers*, G. P. Putnam's Sons, New York, 1927.

Luebke, Frederick C., *Bonds of Loyalty: German-Americans and World War I*, Northern Illinois University Press, DeKalb, IL, 1974.

Luff, Jennifer, *Commonsense Anticommunism: Labor and Civil Liberties between the World Wars*, University of North Carolina Press, Raleigh, NC, 2012.

Machado, Manuel A. Jr., *Centaur of the North: Francisco Villa, the Mexican Revolution, and Northern Mexico*, Eakin Press, Austin, TX, 1988.

Mauch, Christoff, *The Shadow War Against Hitler: The Covert Operations of America's Wartime Secret Intelligence Service*, Columbia University Press, New York, NY, 1999.

McKenna, Marthe, *My Master Spy: A Narrative of the Secret Service*, Jarrolds Publishers Ltd., London, Great Britain, 1936.

McLynn, Frank, *Villa and Zapata: A History of the Mexican Revolution*, Basic Books, New York, NY, 2000.

McMaster, John Bach, *The United States in the World War*, D. Appleton and Company, New York, NY, 1918.

Meed, Douglas V., *Soldier of Fortune*, Halcyon Press, Ltd., Houston, TX, 2003.

Meyer, Michael C, *Mexican Rebel: Pascual Orozco and the Mexican Revolution, 1910-1915*, University of Nebraska Press, Lincoln, NE, 1967.

Millman, Chad, *The Detonators: The Secret Plot to Destroy America and an Epic Hunt for Justice*, Little, Brown and Company, New York, 2006.

Muensterberg, Hugo, *The War and America*, D. Appleton and Co., New York, NY, 1914.

Nasaw, David, *The Chief: The Life of William Randolph Hearst*, Houghton Mifflin Company, New York, NY, 2000.

Newman, Bernard, *Secrets of German Espionage*, The Right Book Club, London, Great Britain, 1940.

Peterson, Horace Cornelius, *Propaganda for War: The Campaign against American Neutrality, 1914-1917*, University of Oklahoma Press, Norman, OK, 1939.

Preston, Diana, *Lusitania: An Epic Tragedy*, Walker and Company, New York, NY, 2002.

Quirk, Robert E. *The Mexican Revolution, 1914-1915: The Convention of Aguascalientes*, University of Indiana Press, Bloomington, IN, 1960.

Raat, W. Dirk and Beezley, William H., editors, *Twentieth Century Mexico*, University of Nebraska Press, Lincoln, NE, 1986.

Rafalko, Frank J., Ed., *A Counterintelligence Reader*, volume I, Chapter 3 "Post Civil War to World War I," www.fas.org/irp/ops/ci/docs/ci1, viewed 9-22-2011.

Reiling, Johannes, *Deutschland: Safe for Democracy?* Franz Steiner Verlag, Stuttgart, Germany, 1997.

Ritter, Gerhard, *Der Schlieffenplan: Kritik eines Mythos*, Verlag R. Oldenbourg, München, Germany, 1956.

Ritter, Gerhard, *Staatskunst und Kriegshandwerk*, Verlag R. Oldenbourg, München, Germany, 1954.

Rößler, Eberhard, *Die Unterseeboote der Kaiserlichen Marine*, Bernard und Graefe Verlag, Bonn, Germany, 1997.

Scheina, Robert L., *Villa, Soldier of the Mexican Revolution*, Potomac Books, Washington D.C., 2004.

Schieffel, Werner, *Bernhard Dernburg 1865 - 1937: Kolonialpolitiker und Bankier im wilhelminischen Deutschland*, Atlantis Verlag, Zürich, Switzerland, 1974.

Schröder, Joachim, *Die U-Boote des Kaisers: Die Geschichte des deutschen U-Boot-Krieges gegen Großbritannien im Ersten Weltkrieg*, Bernard und Gräfe, Lauf a. d. Pegnitz, 2003.

Scott, James Brown, editor, *The Declaration of London: A Collection of Official Papers and Documents relating to the International Naval Conference held in London December, 1908 to February, 1909*, Oxford University Press, New York, NY, 1919.

Shrapnel and other War Material: A Reprint of Important Articles Presented in the American Machinist from January to June 1915, McGraw-Hill Book Company, New York, NY, 1915.

Skaggs, William H., *German Conspiracies in America*, T. Fisher Unwin Ltd., London, Great Britain, 1916 (estimated).

Small, Michael, *The Forgotten Peace: Mediation at Niagara Falls, 1914*, University of Ottawa Press, Canada, 2009.

Smith, Arthur D. Howden, *Mr. House of Texas*, Funk and Wagnalls Company, New York, NY, 1940.

Smith, Arthur D. Howden, *The Real Mr. House*, George H. Doran Company, New York, NY, 1918.

Smith, Leonard V., Audoin-Rousseau, Stephanie, Becker, Annette, *France and the Great War, 1914-1918*, Cambridge University Press, Cambridge, Great Britain, 2003.

Sperry, Earl Evelyn, Willis Mason West, *German Plots and Intrigues in the United Stated during the Period of our Neutrality*, Committee on Public Information, Washington D.C., July 1918.

Starke, Holger, *Vom Brauereihandwerk zur Brauindustrie, Die Geschichte der Bierbrauerei in Dresden und Sachsen, 1800-1914*, Böhlan Verlag, Köln, Germany, 2005.

Strother, French, *Fighting Germany's Spies*, Doubleday Page and Company, Garden City, NY, 1918.

Stubmann, Peter Franz, *Ballin: Leben und Werk eines deutschen Reeders*, Hermann Klemm AG., Berlin, Germany, 1926.

Synon, Mary, *McAdoo: The Man and his Times, A Panorama in Democracy*, The Bobbs-Merrill Company, Indianapolis, IN, 1924.

Teitelbaum, Louis M., *Woodrow Wilson and the Mexican Revolution, 1913-1916*, Exposition Press, New York, NY, 1967.

Thomas, William H. Jr., *Unsafe for Democracy: World War I and the*

U.S. Justice Department's Covert Campaign to Suppress Dissent, The University of Wisconsin Press, Madison, WI, 2008.

Tuchman, Barbara, *The Zimmermann Telegram*, Macmillan Company, New York, NY, 1958.

Turner, John Kenneth, *Hands off Mexico*, Rand School of Social Science, New York, NY, 1920.

Volkman, Ernest, *Espionage: The Greatest Spy Operations of the 20th Century*, John Wiley and Sons Inc., New York, NY, 1995.

Volkman, Ernest and Baggett, Blaine, *Secret Intelligence: The Inside Story of America's Espionage Empire*, Doubleday, New York, NY, 1989.

Von Mach, Edmund, *What Germany Wants*, Little, Brown and Company, Boston, MA, 1914.

Welsome, Eileen, *The General and the Jaguar: Pershing's Hunt for Pancho Villa*, University of Nebraska Press, Lincoln, NE 2006.

West, Nigel, *Historical Dictionary of Sexspionage*, Scarecrow Press Inc., Plymouth, Great Britain, 2009.

Wile, Frederic William, *Men around the Kaiser: The Makers of Modern Germany*, The MacLean Publishing Company, Toronto, Canada, 1913.

Wilkins, Mira, *The History of Foreign Investment in the United States, 1914-1945*, Harvard University Press, Cambridge, MA, 2004.

Witcover Jules, *Sabotage at Black Tom*, Algonquin Books of Chapel Hill, Chapel Hill, NC, 1989.

Wittke, Carl, *The German-Language Press in America*, University of Kentucky Press, Louisville, KY, 1957.

Womack, John, Jr., *Zapata and the Mexican Revolution*, Alfred A. Knopf Inc., New York, NY, 1968.

Young, William, *German Diplomatic Relations, 1871-1945*, iUniverse, Inc., New York, NY, 2006.

Zuber, Terence, *Inventing the Schlieffen Plan: German War Planning 1871-1914*, Oxford University Press, New York, NY, 2002.

BIBLIOGRAPHY:

NEWSPAPERS, BULLETINS, DIRECTORIES, AND MAGAZINES

The Americas, Vol. 30, No. 1 (Jul., 1973), "The Arms of the Ypiranga: The German Side," by Thomas Baecker, pp. 1-17.

The Americas, Vol. 32, No. 1 (Jul., 1975), "The Muddied Waters of Columbus, New Mexico," by E. Bruce While and Francisco Villa.

The Americas, Vol. 39, No. 1 (July, 1982), "The Underside of the Mexican Revolution: El Paso, 1912," by Charles H. Harris, III and Louis R. Sadler.

The American Historical Review, Vol. 83, No. 1 (Feb., 1978), "Pancho Villa and the Attack on Columbus, New Mexico," by Friedrich Katz.

American Machinist, Volume 29, 1906.

Arizona and the West, Volume 21, No. 2 (Summer, 1979), pp. 157-186, "The Battle of Naco, Factionalism and Conflict in Sonora: 1914-1915," by Stephen P. Mumme.

The Bankers Magazine, Volume 77 (July to December 1908), Bankers Publishing Company, New York, NY, 1908.

Centre for Constitutional Studies, University of Alberta, "German Internment During the First and Second World Wars," by Alexandra Bailey, http://www.law.ualberta.ca/centres/ccs/issues/germaninternment.php, viewed 12-2011.

www.ColorantsHistory.Org, "Spies and Dies," by Robert J. Baptista, updated March 4, 2010.

The Day Book, Chicago, IL, 1914.

The El Paso Herald, El Paso, TX, 1910-1920.

Film History, Volume 4, No. 2 (1990), pp. 123-129, "Shooting the Great War: Albert Dawson and the American Correspondent Film Company, 1914-1918," by Ron van Dopperen.

German Studies Review, Volume 8, German Studies Association, "The Hindu Conspiracy in California, 1913-1918," by Karl Hoover, pp. 245-261.

Harper's Magazine, September, October, November 1917, "Diplomatic Days in Mexico, First, Second, Third Papers," by Edith O'Shaughnessy.

Harper's Magazine, November 1942, "The wind that swept Mexico: Part I, II, and III, by Anita Brenner.

History Review, December 2002: "The unpredictable dynamo: Germany's Economy, 1870-1918," by F.G. Stapleton.

Huachuca Illustrated, Volume 1, 1993, by James P. Finley, Fort Huachuca, AZ.

Journal of Intelligence History, Volume 4, Number 1, Summer 2004, Reinhard R. Doerries.

Journal of Latin American Studies, Vol. 35, No. 1 (Feb. 2003), "Railroad, Oil and Other Foreign Interests in the Mexican Revolution, 1911 to 1914," by John Skirius, Cambridge University Press.

Journal of Military and Strategic Studies, Fall 2005, Vol. 8, Issue 1, "Karl Respa and German Espionage in Canada during World War One," by Grant W. Grams.

The Journal of Interdisciplinary History, Vol. 2, No. 1, Summer, 1971, "George Sylvester Viereck: The Psychology of a German-American Militant" by Phyllis Keller.

Law Notes, Volume 7, April 1903 to March 1904, Edward Thompson Company, Northport, Long Island, NY, 1904.

Lewiston Evening Journal, 1915.

The Massey-Gilbert Blue Book of Mexico for 1903: A Directory in English of the City of Mexico, The Massey-Qilbert Company, Sucs., Mexico D.F., Mexico, 1903.

Metal Industry Magazine, Volume 13, January to December 1915, The Metal Industry Publishing Company, New York, NY, 1916.

The Mexican Yearbook 1912, McCorqudale and Company Limited, London, Great Britain, 1912.

Mexican Studies, Vol. 17, No.1 (Winter, 2001), "Exiliados de la Revolución mexicana: El caso de los villistas (1915-1921)," by Victoria Lerner.

The Nation, volume 109, July 1, 1919 to December 31, 1919, The Nation Press, NY 1919.

The Northern Mariner/Le marin du nord, XVII, No. 3 (July, 2007), "The Attacks on U.S. Shipping that Precipitated American Entry into World War I," by Rodney Carlisle, pp. 41-66.

Oakland Tribune, Oakland, CA, April 18th, 1915.

The Pacific Historical Review, Vol. 17, No. 3, "The Hindu Conspiracy, 1914-1917," by Giles Brown, pp. 299-310.

The Pacific Historical Review, volume 40, "The Hindu Conspiracy in Anglo-American Relations during World War I," by Don Dignan, pp. 57-76.

Sabazius, "The Invisible Basilica: Dr. Arnoldo Krumm-Heller (1876 -1949 e.v.)," Ordo Templi Orientis, United States, 1997.

Southwestern Studies, Monograph number 47, "Luther T. Ellsworth: U.S. Consul on the Border During the Mexican Revolution," by Dorothy Pierson Kerig, Texas Western Press, El Paso, TX 1975.

The Historian, Volume 59, Issue 1, pages 89–112, "K. A. Jahnke and the German Sabotage Campaign in the United States and Mexico, 1914-1918," by Richard B. Spence, September 1996.

The Day, New London, CT, 1914-1916.

The Evening Herald, Albuquerque, NM, 1914-1916

The Fatherland, Volumes I and II, The Fatherland Cooperation, New York, NY, 1914 to 1917.

The Financier, Volume 114, New York, August 1, 1919.

The Fort Wayne News, Fort Wayne, TX, 1914 to 1918.

The Milwaukee Journal, Milwaukee, WI, 1942.

The Metal Industry, Vol. 13, January to December 1915, The Metal Industry Publishing Company, New York, NY, 1916.

The Morning Call, "Forging America: The Story of Bethlehem Steel," November 1, 2010.

The New York Times, New York, NY, Archives 1896-1942.

The New York Times Current History: The European War, Volume 1, The New York Times Company, New York, NY, 1915.

The New York Tribune, New York, NY, 1910-1918.

The Times-Picayune, New Orleans, LA, July 1 to July 6, 1914.

The San Francisco Call and Post, San Francisco, CA, 1908-1917.

St. John Daily Sun, St. John, Newfoundland, Canada, 1899.

"The United Kingdom during World War I: Business as usual?" June 2003, by Stephen Broadberry and Peter Howlett, www2.warwick.ac.uk/fac/soc/economics /staff/.../wp/wwipap4.pdf, viewed 12-2012.

The Washington Post, Washington, D.C., 1911-1922.

The Washington Herald, Washington, D.C., 1910-1922

The Washington Times, Washington D.C., 1910-1914

The World's Work, Volume 28, May to October 1914, Doubleday, Page and Co., New York, NY, 1914.

The World's Work, Volume 30, May to October 1918, Doubleday, Page and Co., New York, NY, 1915.

The World's Work, Volume 36, May to October 1918, Doubleday, Page and Co., New York, NY, 1918.

www.rootsweb.ancestry.com/~ww1can/cef14_15.htm, "A Brief History of the Canadian Expeditionary Force," by Brian Lee Massey, 1997-2007.

www.HistoryLink.org, "U.S. Customs at Grays Harbor seizes the schooner Annie Larsen loaded with arms and ammunition on June 29, 1915," by David Wilma, May 18, 2006.

University of Calgary, "The Peopling of Canada: 1891-1921," The Applied Research Group, 1997.

The Trow: Copartnership and Corporation Directory of the Boroughs of Manhattan and the Bronx, Association of American Directory Publishers, New York, NY, March 1908.

The New York Times Current History: The European War, Volume 17, October, November, December 1918, New York Times Company, New York, NY, 1919

BIBLIOGRAPHY:

ORIGINAL, ARCHIVAL, AND GOVERNMENT SOURCES

National Intelligence Center, *American Revolution to World War II*, Chapter 3, Central Intelligence Reader, www.fas.org.

Department of Commerce, Bureau of Foreign and Domestic Commerce, Miscellaneous Series, No. 57, *German Foreign Trade Organization*, Government Printing Office, 1917.

Ministry of National Defense, Commonwealth of Canada, *The Official History of the Canadian Army: The Canadian Expeditionary Force, 1914-1919*, by Colonel G. W. L. Nicholson, C.D., Army Historical Section, Roger Duhamel, F.R.S.C. Queen's Printer and Controller of Stationary, Ottawa, 1962.

Holmdahl Papers, University of California at Berkley, Bancroft Library, C-B-921.

German Diplomatic Papers, University of California at Berkley, Bancroft Library, M-B 12.

Horne, Charles F., editor, *Source Records of the Great War*, Volumes I to VII, National Alumni, New York, 1923.

Körver, Joachim, ed., *German Submarine Warfare 1914-1918 in the Eyes of British Intelligence: Selected Sources from the British National Archives, Kew*, Schaltungsdienst Lange, Berlin, Germany, 2010.

Silvestre Terrazas Papers, University of California at Berkley, Bancroft Library, M-B-18.

Carey McWilliams Papers, University of California at Los Angeles, 277.

Lázaro De La Garza Collection, University of Texas, Benson Library, Austin, TX.

Papers of Hugh Lenox Scott, Library of Congress, Washington, D.C.

Library and Archives Canada, Department of Militia and Defence, Record Group 13.

The National Archives of the UK, Board of Trade, Commercial and Statistical Department and successors, Inwards Passenger Lists, Kew, Surrey, England, BT26.

National Archives, Washington DC

Record Group 36	Records of the U.S. Customs Service, Vessels arriving in New York 1820-1897 and 1897-1957
Record Group 38	Office of Naval Intelligence 1913 to 1924
Record Group 45	Naval Records Collection, Caribbean File 1911 to 1927
Record Group 59	Department of State 1908 to 1927, specifically Papers of Robert Lansing, Volume I and II, Papers relating to the foreign relations of the United States 1914, 1915, 1916 (Latin America), File 812.00 (Mexico).
Record Group 60	Records of the Dept. of Justice, Straight Numerical File, 157013, Boxes 1230 to 1236; Specifically file 9-16-12-5305, Statement of F. A. Sommerfeld, June 21 to June 24, 1918.
Record Group 65	Bureau of Investigation Case Files 1908-1922, Bureau of Investigation Miscellaneous Case Files 1908-1922, Papers of Dr. Heinrich F. Albert, Numbered Correspondence 1914 to 1917, Old German Files, Old Mexican Files.
Record Group 76	Mixed Claims Commission, 1922 to 1941.
Record Group 80	General Records of the Navy 1916 to 1926.

Record Group 85	Records of the Immigration and Naturalization Service.
Record Group 87	Records of the U.S. Secret Service, Daily Reports 1875 to 1936.
Record Group 129	Bureau of Prisons, Inmate Case Files, 1902 to 1922.
Record Group 131	Records of the Alien Property Custodian, Records seized by the APC.
Record Group 165	Records of the War Department, MID Specifically file 9140-1754 (Felix A. Sommerfeld), file 9140-878 (Frederico Stallforth), file 9140-646 (Franz Rintelen).
Record Group 242	German Captured Documents, Foreign Office, Mexiko Band 1 bis 10, "Old German Files."
Record Group 395	Records of the Army Overseas Operations, Mexican Punitive Expedition.

United States Senate, *Investigation of Mexican Affairs, Hearing before a Subcommittee of the Committee of Foreign Relations*, Government Printing Office, Washington, DC, 1920.

Unites States Senate, *Brewing and Liquor Interests and German Propaganda, Subcommittee of the Committee of the Judiciary*, Volume 2, Government Printing Office, Washington D.C., 1919.

United States Senate, *Revolutions in Mexico, Hearing before a Subcommittee of the Committee of Foreign Relations*, Government Printing Office, Washington, DC, 1912.

United Nations, Reports of International Arbitral Awards: Lehigh Valley Railroad Company, Agency of Canadian Car and Foundry Company, Limited, and Various Underwriters (United States) v. Germany (Sabotage Cases), June 15, 1939, Volume VIII, pp. 225-460, New York, NY, 2006.

YIVO Institute for Jewish Research, New York, Record Group 713, Papers of Herman Bernstein (1876-1935).

Die Österreichisch-Ungarischen Dokumente zum Kriegsausbruch, hrsg. vom Staatsamt für Äußeres in Wien, National-Verlag, Berlin, 1923.

G.P. Gooch, D. Litt, and Harold Temperley, editors, *British Documents on the Origins of the War, 1898-1914, Vol. XI: The Outbreak of War: Foreign Office Documents, June 28th-August 4th, 1914*, His Majesty's Stationery Office, 1926.

Staatsarchiv Hamburg, Hamburger Passagierlisten, 1850-1934.

Auswärtiges Amt, Politisches Archiv Berlin, Mexiko, Volumes I to X.

Staatsarchiv Berlin, Deutsche Dienststelle (WASt), Deutsche Verlustlisten 1914 bis 1917, Berlin, Deutschland.

Marine Crew Chronik MIM620/CREW, Marineschule Mürwik, Flensburg, Deutschland.

Marineschule Mürwik, Verlustlisten 1914-1915, MIM381, KAI17 040 (Band 3).

Bundesarchiv für Militärgeschichte, Freiburg; Record Groups RM 2, RM 3, RM 5.

National Archives of the United Kingdom, BT26, Board of Trade: Commercial and Statistical Department and successors: Inwards Passenger Lists, Kew, Surrey.

Rangliste der Königlich Preußischen Armee und des XIII (Königlich Württembergischen) Armeekorps für 1907, Ernst Siegfried Mittler und Sohn, Berlin, Germany, 1907.

Rangliste der Deutschen Marine für das Jahr 1914, Ernst Siegfried Mittler und Sohn, Berlin, Germany, 1914.

Stallforth Papers, Prevo Collection.

United Nations, *Reports of International Arbitral Awards*, "S. S. 'Edna.'

Disposal of pecuniary claims arising out of the recent war (1914-1918), United States, Great Britain, Volume III, December, 1934, pp. 1585-1606.

United States Census, *Cotton Production and Distribution,* Government Printing Office, Washington D.C., 1915.

United States Department of Agriculture, *Monthly Crop Reporter, May 10, 1915,* Government Printing Office, Washington, D.C., 1915.

United States Department of Commerce, *Commerce Reports, Part 3, July, August, September, 1918,* Government Printing Office, Washington, D.C., 1918.

United States Senate, *Revolutions in Mexico,* Hearing before the Subcommittee of the Committee on Foreign Relations, Government Printing Office, Washington DC 1912.

United States Senate, *Brewing and Liquor interests and German and Bolshevik Propaganda,* Report and Hearings of the Subcommittee on the Judiciary of the United States Senate, Government Printing Office, Washington D. C., 1919.

The United States Senate, *Hearing before a Subcommittee of the Committee on Foreign Relations, Revolutions in Mexico,* Government Printing Office, Washington D. C., 1913.

United States Senate, Committee of the Judiciary, *Alleged Dye Monopoly,* Senate Resolution 77, Government Printing Office, Washington D.C., 1922.

United States War Department, *Annual Reports 1915,* Government Printing Office, Washington D.C.

The Southern Division of the United States District Court for the Northern District of California, First Division, United States of America vs. Franz Bopp, et al., April 23, 1918.

Immigrant Ancestors: A List of 2,500 Immigrants to America before

1750, Frederick Virkus, editor; Genealogical Publishing Co., Baltimore, Maryland, 1964.

Scott, James Brown, editor, *Diplomatic Correspondence Between the United States and Germany, August 1, 1914 - April 6, 1917*, Oxford University Press, New York, NY, 1918.

Secretaría de Comunicaciones y Obras Públicas, Estadística de ferrocarriles de jurisdicción federal año de 1918. México, Talleres Gráficos de la Nación, 1924.

BIBLIOGRAPHY:
ONLINE DATABASES AND SEARCH ENGINES

www.Ancestry.de   This search engine is a tool, with which many archival documents, especially those related to immigration, birth and death records have been found. The references in the end notes of the book relate to the actual depository of the archival record such as "NA RG 85," although they often were found in through this search engine.

www.fold3.com   This database belongs to the National Archives of the United States. Many court records as well as FBI files are displayed digitally here. Most of the cited records did not come from this source. However, keyword searches helped identify where to look.

http://chroniclingamerica.loc.gov
The Library of Congress digitized hundreds of historical US newspapers. The search engine allows searching by keyword, publication, and date. Many of the newspaper articles quoted in the book have been located using this tool.

www.lib.byu.edu/ Brigham Young University Library
offers a complete collection of archival documents related to WWI.

www.uboat.net   An accurate list of losses of commercial shipping through German submarines by month.

BIBLIOGRAPHY:
AUTOBIOGRAPHICAL WORKS

Albert, Heinrich F., *Aufzeichnungen*, Büxenstein, Germany, 1956.

Dr. Atl, *The Mexican Revolution and the Nationalization of the Land: The Foreign Interests and Reaction*, Whitehall Building, Room 334, New York, NY, 1915.

Bauer, Hermann, *Als Führer der U-Boote im Weltkriege: Der Eintritt der U-Boot-Waffe in die Seekriegsführung*, Köhler und Amelang, Leipzig, 1941.

Boy-Ed, Karl, *Verschwörer?* Verlag August Scherl GmbH, Berlin, Germany, 1920.

Charles, Heinrich, *The Electro-Individualistic Manifesto: The Anti-Thesis of the Communistic Manifesto by Karl Marx and Friedrich Engels, and the Synthesis of Social-Individualism*, published by the author, New York, NY, 1913.

Churchill, Winston S., *The World Crisis, 1911 to 1918*, Odhams Press Limited, London, Great Britain, 1939.

Count von Bernstorff, Johann Heinrich, *My Three Years in America*, Skeffington and Son, London, Great Britain, unknown date (approximately 1940).

Count von Bernstorff, Johann Heinrich, *Memoirs of Count Bernstorff*, Random House, New York, NY, 1936.

Delbrück, Hans, *Delbrück's Modern Military History*, translated by Arden Bucholz, University of Nebraska Press, Lincoln, NE, 1997.

Dernburg, Bernhard, *Search-Lights on the War*, The Fatherland Corporation, New York, NY, 1915.

The Truth about Germany: Facts about the War, unknown authors, unknown publisher (likely the "Fatherland" press, unknown place (likely New York), September 20, 1914.

Garibaldi, Guiseppe, *A Toast To Rebellion*, The Bobbs-Merrill Company, New York, NY, 1935.

Gerard, James W., *My first eighty-three years in America: Memoirs of James W. Gerard*, Doubleday and Company, Inc, Garden City, NY, 1951.

Gerard, James W., *Face to Face with Kaiserism*, George H. Doran Company, New York, NY, 1918.

Guzman, Martin Luis, *Memoirs of Pancho Villa*, translated by Virginia H. Taylor, University of Texas Press, Austin, TX, 1975

Hale, William Bayard, *The Story of a Style*, B. W. Hübsch, New York, NY, 1920.

Krumm-Heller, Arnold, *Für Freiheit und Recht: Meine Erlebnisse aus dem mexikanischen Bürgerkriege*, Otto Thiele Verlag, Halle, Germany, 1916.

Lansing, Robert, *War Memoirs of Robert Lansing, Secretary of State*, The Bobbs-Merrill Company, New York, NY, 1935.

McClure, Samuel S., *My Autobiography*, Frederick A. Stokes Company, New York, NY, 1914.

Mencken, H. L., *My Life as Author and Editor*, Alfred A. Knopf Inc., New York, 1993.

Nicolai, Walter, *The German Secret Service*, translated with an *additional chapter by George Renwick*, Stanley Paul and Co., London, Great Britain, 1924.

Von Papen, Franz, *Memoirs*, E. P. Dutton and Company Inc., New York, NY, 1953.

Rintelen von Kleist, Franz, *The Dark Invader: Wartime Reminiscences of a German Naval Intelligence Officer*, Lovat Dickson Limited, London, Great Britain, 1933.

Rintelen von Kleist, Franz, *The Return of the Dark Invader*, Peter Davies Limited, London, Great Britain, 1935.

Rintelen von Kleist, Franz, *The Dark Invader: Wartime Reminiscences of a German Naval Intelligence Officer*, with an introduction by Reinhard R. Doerries, Frank Cass Publishers, London, 1997.

Rumely, Edward A., *The Gravest 366 Days, Editorials Reprinted from the Evening Mail of New York City*, The New York Evening Mail, New York, NY, 1916.

Scheer, Reinhard, *Germany's High Sea Fleet in the World War*, Cassell and Company, London, Great Britain, 1920.

Scott, Hugh Lenox, *Some Memories of a Soldier*, The Century Company, New York, NY, 1928.

Steffens, Lincoln, *The Autobiography of Lincoln Steffens*, Harcourt, Brace and Company, New York, NY, 1931.

Tunney, Thomas J., *Throttled: The Detection of the German and Anarchist Bomb Plotters in the United States*, Small Maynard and Company, Boston, MA, 1919.

Viereck, George Sylvester, *Spreading Germs of Hate*, Duckworth, London, Great Britain, 1931.

Von Bethmann Hollweg, *Reflections on the World War*, Part 1, Thornton

Butterworth, Ltd., 62 St. Martin's Lane, London, Great Britain, 1920.

Von der Goltz, Horst, *My Adventures as a German Secret Agent*, Robert M. McBride and Company, New York, NY, 1917.

Von der Goltz, Horst, *Sworn Statement*, Presented to both Houses of Parliament by Command of His Majesty, April 1916.

Von Schlieffen, Count Alfred, *Cannae*, The Command and General Staff School Press, Fort Leavenworth, KS, 1931.

Von Tirpitz, Alfred, *Erinnerungen*, K. F. Koehler Verlag, Berlin, Germany, 1927.

Voska, Emanuel Victor and Irwin, Will, *Spy and Counter-Spy*, George G. Harrap and Co Ltd., London, 1941.

Wilson, Henry Lane, *Diplomatic Episodes in Mexico, Belgium and Chile*, Kinnikat Press, Port Washington, NY, 1971, reprint of original 1927.

Wilson, Henry Lane, "Errors with Reference to Mexico and Events that have occurred there," *International Relations of the United States: The Annals*, Vol. LIV, July 1914.

Wilson, Woodrow and Hale, William Bayard, *The New Freedom*, Doubleday, Page and Co., New York, NY, 1913.

INDEX

E

F

O

P

S

T

Z